Old Ironsides

Old Ironsides

Eagle of the Sea—The Story of the USS *Constitution*

Colonel David Fitz-Enz

TAYLOR TRADE PUBLISHING
Lanham • New York • Boulder • Toronto • Plymouth, UK

Published by Taylor Trade Publishing
An imprint of The Rowman & Littlefield Publishing Group, Inc.
4501 Forbes Boulevard, Suite 200
Lanham, Maryland 20706

Distributed by National Book Network

The hardback edition of this book was cataloged by the Library of Congress as follows:

Fitz-Enz, David G., 1940–
    Old Ironsides : eagle of the sea : the story of the USS Constitution / David Fitz-Enz.— 1st Taylor Trade Pub. ed.
        p. cm.
    Includes bibliographical references and index.
    ISBN 1-58979-160-6 (hardcover : alk. paper)
    1. Constitution (Frigate) I. Title.
    VA65.C7F573 2004
    623.822'5'0973—dc22
                                    2004005889

ISBN 978-1-58979-427-6 (pbk. : alk. paper) — ISBN 978-1-58979-428-3 (electronic)

♾™ The paper used in this publication meets the minimum requirements of American National Standard for Information Sciences—Permanence of Paper for Printed Library Materials, ANSI/NISO Z39.48–1992.
Manufactured in the United States of America.

To Valerie and her son Teddy,
who stood by me
throughout the research and writing.

The Contrast Meant Conflict

Between England and the United States of America a spirit of animosity, caused chiefly by the impressment of British seamen, or of seamen asserted to be such, from on board of American merchant vessels, had unhappily subsisted for a long time prior to the war [of 1812]. It is we believe an acknowledged maxim of public law, that no nation but one he belongs to can release a subject from his natural allegiance. Every nation has a right to enforce the services of her subjects wherever they may be found.

—William M. James, expressing the view "born British, always British"

The view professed by Great Britain in 1812 respecting the rights of belligerents and neutrals was dramatically opposite to that held by the United States.

—Theodore Roosevelt, age 24

Contents

America * American Privateering, or Just Plain Pirates? *
A Chilling Account of American Activity

~

Foreword: Sailing On 200 Years Later

In May of 1996, I was made aware of an idea being circulated within the Navy to refit USS *Constitution* to operate under sail. Like all New England schoolchildren, I had visited the ship many times while growing up near Boston. I started my naval architecture career at Boston Naval Shipyard, and one of my first jobs involved renovation work on the ship. That was my first chance to see the ship belowdecks, beyond the standard visitor's tour. In 1986, I had been involved in the investigation of the loss of S/V *Pride of Baltimore* and had the opportunity to research and write about sailing-vessel stability. Now, I was the director of the Hydrodynamics Division and former director of the Stability Division of the Naval Sea Systems Command. Needless to say, I had a strong personal and professional interest in any plans to sail USS *Constitution*. The command's program manager for the ship accepted my offer to help with the planning, and I began the adventure of a lifetime.

The first thing you notice when you look at USS *Constitution* is the enormous size of the masts and yards. The ship carried thirty-one sails (twenty square, eleven fore-and-aft) with a total of nearly 43,000 square feet. At the time of construction, naval and commercial ships seldom placed more than three sails on the mast—the courses, topsails, and topgallants. USS *Constitution* carried four and was instantly recognizable to other ships. Even today, she remains the tallest of the tall ships, by about eleven feet. If you are a stability analyst, worried about keeping the ship upright, that can be a little worrisome.

The next worrisome feature of the ship is the total lack of watertight bulkheads to limit flooding. The open space was necessary for handling the guns and for moving shot and powder around the gun deck. Gun and air ports pierce the hull very close to the waterline. Although they have closures, none could be called watertight.

Finally, the ship would not have any of the shot, powder, and stores located low in the hold that provided stability during her sailing years. The simple solution of adding ballast was complicated by the fact that the keel is original and has three scarf joints in line just below the mainmast. The keel had already been flexed fourteen inches over the years and that deflection had been removed during overhaul. Placing additional weight in the hold, which would add stress to the keel structure, was not considered desirable.

The ship does not meet any of the conventional stability criteria applied to large sailing vessels today. The anomaly is that the ship was operationally successful, surviving storms, collisions, groundings, and battle damage. USS *Constitution* holds a special place in United States and U.S. Navy history and holds a very special place in the hearts of the people of New England. No doubt if we harmed this ship, those people would hunt us down.

In 1996, the ship had just completed an extensive overhaul and was approaching her two hundredth anniversary. Commander Michael Beck, U.S. Navy, Sixty-fourth in Command of USS *Constitution*, was enthusiastic about sailing her on that anniversary, *if* it could be done safely. Protection and preservation of the ship were top priorities. It would not be easy. The people who knew how to tension the rigging and handle a 44-gun frigate under sail were all dead and gone, and they left few notes behind. Modern technology and historical research would have to join hands.

Fortunately, a National Oceanic and Atmospheric Administration data buoy had been stationed in the proposed sailing area for many years and the records from that buoy told us what we might expect for wind speed and wave characteristics. Computer analysis of the effect of wind acting on the sails, masts, and rigging was compared to rules of thumb from eighteenth- and early nineteenth-century textbooks. The results were encouraging but not sufficient to justify operations under sail.

The only way to evaluate the combined effects of wind and sea under sail was to build a model of the ship and test it in a ship-model towing-tank facility. Such tests are time consuming and expensive, and no funds had been programmed for the sail event, let alone preliminary exploration of its feasibility. But USS *Constitution* generates excitement and enthusiasm, and the U.S. Naval Academy administrators agreed to build and test a model in their 380-foot towing-tank facility. The Academy's Technical Support Shop built the model, the Hydromechanics Laboratory staff devised a system to measure the model's motions in wind and waves, and my wife made the lightweight nylon sails for the model. We were in business.

The Hydro Lab staff gave up Christmas and New Year's holidays to run the tests. We established wind limits that would ensure the safety of the ship. We also learned that the waves we might experience would cause the ship to pitch more than expected during the tow to and from the sailing area. That proved to be important information and caused the towing arrangement to be changed to avoid damage to either USS *Constitution* or the tugboats.

The results of these tests were presented to the chief of naval operations staff and were key in obtaining permission for the sail. With that permission granted, the pace picked up. The ship's crew began daily practice in handling sails and "learning the ropes" at the pier. Plans were made for the crew to obtain sail-handling experience on USCGC *Eagle* and the sailing vessel HMS *Bounty*. Navy structural engineers crawled through the ship evaluating wooden beams and mast supports and placing dozens of "telltale" markers on the structure to detect any unexpected movement while under sail. The U.S. Coast Guard (USCG) offered two sets of motion instrumentation, which permitted us to monitor the ship's response to wind and waves. This would allow us to cease operations if the ship's motions were not as predicted by the calculations and model tests.

In the 1800s sailors feared fire and flooding at sea. They still do in the twenty-first century. Consideration was given to evacuation of dignitaries in case of extreme emergency. USS *Constitution* was designed with restricted access to deter boarders. There is one access port through the bulwarks, port and starboard. The access will admit one person at a time. The engineering staff was on board observing one turnaround cruise that was extended to provide for towing drills with the tugboats. The invited guests for the turnaround were on board longer than they expected, and the portable toilets were inadequate for the mission. This was a crowd with incentive to get off the ship and find the shore facilities! Even with this incentive, the time to disembark 450 persons was fifteen minutes—at the pier, with no vessel motion.

Emphasis was therefore placed on protection in place. Water seepage from planking seams that could be submerged under sail was estimated to be in the range of 200–300 gallons per minute (gpm). Of more concern was the possibility of springing one of the 10- to 14-inch-wide bottom planks, which could cause flooding at rates of up to 1,000 gpm. Electrical generators and pumps were placed on board to supply 2,660 gpm of pump capacity. Navy reservists, specialists in shipboard damage control, volunteered their services for the sail. Smoke detectors and TV monitors were backed up by a roving patrol of U.S. Marines. A tugboat with fire pumps remained nearby, ready to come alongside and supply fire hoses located on the ship. A team of Navy salvage divers stood by on board a tugboat with their equipment in case they needed to go over the side to plug any leak or sprung plank. Drills were held to polish the skills of the emergency response teams.

The international scene during the summer of 1997 was fairly peaceful. Nevertheless, there were concerns about safeguarding both the ship and the high-ranking visitors against those who might wish them harm. There was also high expectation that the president of the United States would be on board for the sail event. Prior to departure, access to the ship was controlled by a detachment of marines. Navy and police divers made daily inspections of the underwater body. A dog trained in explosives detection searched the inside of the ship before the arrival of dignitaries. Once under way, the ship was screened by a destroyer, a frigate, eight Naval Academy patrol craft, the two escorting tugs, one hundred USCG, USCG Auxiliary, and state and local police boats . . . and three helicopters. It would be fair to say that all those on board considered themselves well protected.

The sail event was a great success. It received national television coverage by all of the major networks and days of newspaper coverage leading up to the sail. The coastal areas around Boston were jammed with people anxious to catch a glimpse of the ship. Rain held off until the ship was headed back to her pier in Boston. In spite of the rain, the shores of Boston Harbor were filled with people cheering the ship, and a fleet of well-wishers followed the ship in both private and charter boats of every description.

A person unfamiliar with USS *Constitution* and her history might well be baffled by the attention and enthusiasm the ship generates, and by the dedication of all those committed to her preservation and care. Why does USS *Constitution* capture such imagination, dedication, and enthusiasm? The answer to that is contained within this book, so ably researched and written by Colonel David Fitz-Enz. No doubt, if you read it from cover to cover, you too will join those who greatly appreciate the significance of this remarkable historical treasure.

Howard Chatterton
Naval Architect

Preface

I was very fortunate, some would say lucky, during my research. While signing books at the International Napoleonic Fair in London, I was introduced to an English architect who had worked on the restoration of a Royal Navy frigate designed during the War of 1812. It had just been opened to the public in Hartlepool, a seafaring town far up along the northeast coast. He arranged for me to meet with the leader of the effort on board over a wet and windy spring weekend. It was the start of this book.

The two-year trail led to American private collections, a classified British Admiralty library, and a royal dockyard where a nest of knowledgeable veterans directed a journey that was not only enlightening but a delight to travel.

Before I visited USS Constitution, which I had not seen since I was a boy, I wanted to be rehearsed in the lore of sailing ships so I could appreciate what I was going to experience. Acquiring that knowledge was a mind bender for a soldier, but my luck held. Through the efforts of folks I had met along the way, my wife and I were invited by the captain to be aboard USS Constitution on her three-hour turnaround voyage that took us out to Boston's Castle Island fort.

In this day and age, to be able to stand on the deck while the great warship paraded for the people of Boston who love her made the toil of book writing a joy, one that I wish to share with you.

Acknowledgments

Some may think that the "U.S. Army" after my name disqualifies me from writing about something so personal to the U.S. Navy as USS *Constitution*, "Old Ironsides." Additionally, I am not an academic historian but a military officer who served for thirty years with a passion for the people and technology that have been sent to war. My second book was about the heroic lieutenant Thomas Macdonough on Lake Champlain. I was enamored by his little flotilla's victory and the impact he had on national affairs. *Old Ironsides* is not a textbook on naval warfare or an academic exercise in obscure nautical facts but the story of a national treasure. The story is of men and machines against the odds. It chronicles two hundred years of threat and conflict that can be found nowhere else.

Nonfiction cannot be written alone. I am indebted to Professor Donald Hickey, Ph.D., who is the national authority on the War of 1812. Equally supportive was Jim Cheevers, curator of the United States Naval Academy Museum, who was so helpful with *The Final Invasion*, and who came through once again, volunteering the 1933 scrapbook held in his collection. Bob Sumrall, assistant director and curator of ship models at the Naval Academy, provided guidance and information that could be found nowhere else. During the three-hour meeting of his model club, which ended six hours later, reference books were seized by eager hands to prove a point. The level of knowledge I gained on passage through the little rooms in the basement of the Naval Academy Museum was unrivaled. Experts deferred to each other as the diverse subjects and intricacies of the age of sail were exposed among the tables crammed with models. Grant Walker, a former army officer and member of the faculty, stood behind the team I depended upon at the academy. Howard Chatterton, naval architect, long associated with the Naval Academy, went the extra mile and searched the records for me. His foreword, based on the preparation and voyage on the two hundredth anniversary of the *Constitution*, is riveting. Sigrid Trumpy, curator of the Beverley R. Robinson collection at the Naval Academy, the best and most complete selection of sailing ship prints, opened my eyes to the vast accumulation of images honoring the *Constitution*'s achievements.

Captain Kenneth Johnson, U.S. Navy, retired, of the Naval Historical Center in Washington was my rock. His intricate knowledge of the period ships of all navies is unchallenged. He dispelled the myths, keeping the narrative free from conflict.

The National Archives's Sam Anthony gave me an introduction that opened the doors to the collections. Rebecca (Becky) Livingston, archivist and reference librarian and specialist in naval history, and her assistant Kim McKeithan provided insight into the vast collection and eliminated blind alleys. Becky used her detailed knowledge to root out correspondence from the twentieth century, which illuminated the true feelings of the people who saved the ship.

Captain Liam Murphy, an experienced seafaring man, vetted my attempts to explain navigation before the days of satellite positioning. He also made it possible to connect with the U.S. Marine Corps' great artist Colonel Charles Waterhouse, ably assisted by gunny Ed Sere, who provided prints for the book. He introduced me to Major Bert Prol, New Jersey State Militia and curator at Ringwood Manor, who surprised me one evening at the West Point investiture of the Sovereign Military Order of the Temple of Jerusalem when he asked if I had seen the *Constitution* cannon in his collection. It led to a little-known story about the preservation of the ship. In turn, I crossed the street to the antiquities collection at the Military Academy where Allen Aimone, senior special collections librarian, located a handwritten note from 1880 that confirmed the record at Ringwood Manor.

Eugene Urban, a surveyor and amateur astronomer from Onchiota, New York, probed the clear northern sky for me, pointing out the navigators' way of the stars. Former midshipman John T. "Tom" Ward, Coast Guard Academy alumnus and top man on the royal gallant of USS *Eagle*, told me in detail what it was like in all weather to be at the highest point of a sailing ship and survive. Today he is an attorney and noted breeder of champion West Highland terriers.

The commanding officer of USS *Constitution*, Commander Lewin C. Wright, U.S. Navy, and crew provided a great day spent on board during her three-hour turnaround voyage. Naval lieutenant William Marks took particular time out of his duties to ensure that I found her hidden story deep within the timbers, decks, and rigging. It was a rare experience while under way on a ship more than 206 years old. The USS Constitution Museum and, in particular, librarian Kate Lennon Walker expanded the experience. Though small, the museum is one of the finest in the world.

I very much wanted to write the story from the perspective of the British since much of the early turmoil involved them. History is often written solely by the victor, which skews the reader to one side. Captain Eric Fraser, Royal Navy, opened the doors of the Admiralty Library in London's Whitehall. There the obscure became available with the help of Director Jenny Wraight and Ian MacKenzie. Not only did they send me on with introductions to the Public Records Office, the London Library, and the British Museum, but they also acquainted me with the British Library Newspaper Library, where I found out what Englishmen were saying about war with America while in the grip of the Napoleonic campaigns. At Chatham Royal Dockyard, south of London, Peter Dawson, president of the dockyard historical society, invited me into their library and introduced me to the Marine Mirror, Society of Nautical Research. With the help of Jim Young and Peter Padfield, volunteers, he scraped the shelves clean of records unique to the dockyard that date back to Henry VIII and include the building of HMS *Victory* and the supplier of material used by the Royal Navy in North America during the campaigns of the War of 1812. The Naval Maritime Museum in Greenwich, England, was at its best after the renovation of the reference library. The ladies brought out rare books that they knew would be of assistance, in addition to demonstrating their new computer system and illustration collection, which was amazing. They acquainted me with the "Guide to British Naval Papers in North America," a total record.

At the Naval & Military Club in London, Mr. Allen Gilham, restoration architect, led me to my greatest find, HMS *Trincomalee*, which lies at Hartlepool, England. There the site supervisor took Carol and me through a detailed tour of the ship, on hands and knees. It was an unforgettable tour served up with great hospitality. Captain Adrian Caruana is remembered from earlier research at Woolwich Arsenal. He and its noted director, Brigadier K. A. Timbers, were of immense importance when it came to understanding naval cannons and the horrific damage they could do.

Books become family affairs. So it is that I must mention the support of our son Timothy, who provided unending patience and expertise when on numerous occasions he saved the text captured inside my computer, which fought me every step of the way. Our son Jonathan and our daughter-in-law Stephanie put us up and put up with us on sudden stays in their home in Frederick, Maryland, near Washington and Annapolis. Thanks to my wife, Carol, who spent untold hours in dusty archives in two countries, pencil-copied nearly invisible records, and edited the text the first time through.

While an individual can write a book, it takes a talented team to publish that book successfully. The head of our team was Lynn Weber, the editor. We struck a deal: she did not tell me how to fight wars, and I did not tell her how to publish books. Thanks, Lynn.

I hope this book does justice to all of you who have given me so much.

Chronology

July 1812	Great Chase, HMS *Shannon*, HMS *Belvidera*, HMS *Guerriere*, HMS *Acolus*, HMS *Africa*
August 1812	Capture of HMS *Guerriere*
September 1812	William Bainbridge becomes captain
October 1812	USS *President* captures HMS *Macedonian*
December 1812	Capture of HMS *Java*
June 1813	USS *Chesapeake* captured by HMS *Shannon*
July 1813	Charles Stewart becomes captain
March 1814	Napoleon defeated in Paris
April 1814	HMS *Junon* and *Tenedos* chase USS *Constitution* into Marblehead
August 1814	Washington, D.C., is burned by the British
September 1814	Battle of Plattsburgh and Lake Champlain
September 1814	Baltimore attacked by Royal Navy fleet at Fort McHenry
December 1814	Treaty of Ghent
January 1815	Battle of New Orleans fought by General Andrew Jackson
February 1815	Capture of HMS *Cyane* and *Levant*
January 1816	Ordinary at the Boston Navy Yard
April 1821	Jacob Jones becomes captain; USS *Constitution* refurbished and becomes flagship of the Mediterranean fleet
May 1824	Thomas Macdonough becomes captain
October 1825	Daniel Patterson becomes captain
January 1826	George Campbell Read becomes captain
February 1826	Daniel T. Patterson becomes captain
July 4, 1827	Fires gun salute echoed by other nations' men-of-war in Smyrna
January 1828	Ordinary in Boston
1833–1834	Overhauled in new dry dock in Boston
March 1835	Jesse Elliott becomes captain; flagship of the Mediterranean fleet
March 1839	Daniel Turner becomes captain; flagship of the Pacific fleet
July 1842	Foxall A. Parker Sr. becomes captain; flagship of the Home fleet
April 1844	John Percival becomes captain; round-the-world cruise
December 1848	John Gwinn becomes captain; pope visits
December 1852	John Rudd becomes captain; last capture, slave ship
June 1855	Decommissioned at Portsmouth, New Hampshire, by Isaac Mayo
1858	Converted to a training ship
August 1860	Arrives at the United States Naval Academy, Annapolis
May 1861	Safe at Newport, Rhode Island, as training ship for relocated Naval Academy
August 1865	Returns to United States Naval Academy, Annapolis
October 1871	Ordinary at Philadelphia Navy Yard
Summer 1874	Restored for centennial of the United States of America
1878	Paris Exhibition; transports the show material

1881	Portsmouth, New Hampshire, apprentice training; cruises the east coast
1896	John F. Fitzgerald and John Long save ship to be brought to Boston
1900	Congress authorizes private funds for restoration
1907	Somewhat restored and put on display in Boston
1925	Funding for deep restoration undertaken
1926	Christmastime motion picture *Old Ironsides* shown
1927	Work begins on restoration
1929	Depression slows progress
July 1931	Commissioned, and visits begin by the public as she sails once more
1932–1934	Transits Panama Canal and visits western seaboard
1954	Public law passed to protect the USS *Constitution*; restored and installed at Boston
1992–1995	Restored at Boston
1997	Sails on her two hundredth birthday

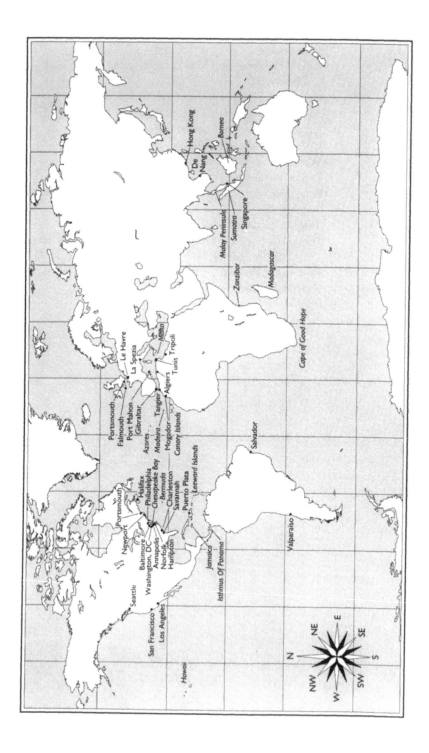

CHAPTER ONE

~

Days of Sail

This war should be studied with diligence; the pride of two people to whose naval affairs are so generally familiar has cleared all the details and laid bare all the episodes, and at every step can be seen that great truth, that there is only success for those who know how to prepare for it.

—Admiral Julian de La Graviere

You may not believe me, but there was a time when 12 miles per hour was blinding speed. All societies moved at 2½ miles per hour, unless on horseback, then double that. No one spoke with clipped words but in flowery phrases, for there was plenty of time. Then, speech was not cluttered with acronyms and abbreviations, patience was a virtue, and to hurry was considered to be the epitome of bad behavior. There was no road rage over someone impeding your pace, no airline-passenger rage at a delayed takeoff, and never a thought given to the time wasted at a red traffic light.

There was such a time in the world before minutes were measured by the hum of a quartz watch attached to the pulsating left wrist. It was not really long ago. The chronometer was so rare and expensive that only sea captains had one, kept in a brass-fitted mahogany box. Those officers were regarded with awe. They were the astronauts of 1797. Boys dreamed of becoming one and followed them down the cobblestone streets, matching them step for giant step. This time was well within the short history of the United States of America. People marveled at the sleek lines of a sailing ship, gossamer, with her score of billowing white sails straining to the wind. Lloyds of London bet on 'round-the-world races, not on who would be first but on who would finish at all. In those not-so-long-ago days, the superhighways were not autobahns, thruways, or intercontinental air routes. No, those invisible high-altitude jet streams were there all right, but they were the trade winds that reached clear down to the surface of the oceans and drove the world's commerce. Passengers then too cursed, as do those today, standing exasperated in tiresome lines at Chicago's airfield or stacked up in Newark's dark, cluttered skies. Two hundred years ago, passengers were soaked to the skin, pacing the sodden planks of corvettes, barks, brigs, sloops, and men-of-war, impatient thirty days into a voyage that should have taken only a fortnight. They watched leaden eighteenth-century heavens and tested the wind with wetted fingers, waiting for the wind to change so they could, at last, see land once again. An hour or two of airsickness would have been a treat compared to the mal de mer that gnawed endlessly at stomachs crushed in whalebone corsets.

Did you know that often ships with vital missions, emergency cargoes, and foot-stomping messengers put to sea with hope and, indeed, anticipation of reaching a sought-after destination that was months away? Yet thirty days later, in the grip of a gale, they were still within sight of the cliffs of Dover, their port of embarkation. A long-awaited vacation to take the family to see relations in Ireland would be planned to take the entire summer. A large sailing ship, thirty feet wide and a hundred-and-fifty feet long, made of saltwater-soaked creaking wood, whose swaying deck was just yards above the churning sea, was the most sophisticated, technologically advanced vehicle in the world.

Old Ironsides, USS *Constitution*, was one of those marvelous machines—and still is. She is the oldest commissioned warship still afloat. Laid down in Boston, in 1797, she was one of the United States Navy's very first men-of-war.

Ships were made almost entirely of wood, powered by the wind and crewed by exceptional men. The ability to go to a destination by sea, over the horizon, was the mark of modern man. Seafaring ranks with the highest accomplishments of human beings. The mastering of that skill took an untold number of lives. As late as the reign of Henry VIII, in 1545, the naval architects thought they had cracked it. Yet the king was watching from the shore when his pride and joy, the warship *Mary Rose*, only a few teetering miles from her moorings, rolled over and was lost. The intrepid oceangoing nations of Europe continued to refine, experiment, and learn from their mistakes, which were frequent and costly. The oceans of the world, which they attempted to tame, did not have to be filled with hideous sea monsters, like those that adorn the sides of their inaccurate charts, to be dangerous. The storm-tossed seas in their natural state were quite enough to sink ships without a trace or break them upon the rocks for all to see.

The venture capitalists of the day speculated that new design would carry more cargo cheaper, faster, and safer. They were similar to today's venture capitalists who invest in information technology. In particular, exotic items from the Far East reached the West over circuitous land routes, which were long and hazardous. Often, only small quantities got through. It was just enough to whet the appetite of consumers, who clamored for more. The Portuguese, Dutch, Spanish, and English sailors made it their business to conquer the oceans and bring home the riches from the outer world. Just as it does today, it took money to make money. The royal governments, opulent sponsors, and avaricious outfitters lured men to risk their lives by promising rewards of power, position, and property.

Wooden Walls against the Sea

To protect that investment, navies were established. The building of the warships of 1797, the first United States Navy warships constructed, was watched by amazed onlookers. The last Continental navy frigate, *Alliance*, had been sold off a dozen years before. The citizens of the United States no longer believed that they had a need for a navy, according to their government. Warships were the most complex objects people had ever seen. Citizens admired the multi-decked, gun-laden leviathans with wonder, the way we marvel at the space shuttle. Though they belong to different times, both the warships and the space shuttle were intended to make voyages for the purpose of exploration, scientific research, military defense, and commercial enrichment. Those multipurpose vehicles required the best of materials, were put together by the most skilled craftsmen of their day, and cost far more than any other single moving object.

The wisdom of the age of sailing ships was devoted to ship design. Naval architects in the United States, in particular Pennsylvanian Joshua Humphreys, had freedom of action not known under the rigid rules of the Admiralty dockyards of England.[1] When performance proved the superiority of radical changes in design, all navies were encouraged to borrow from the best formulas. In the early 1700s the Dutch and Spanish ships were favored. By the mid-1700s, navies turned to French designs. The French ships were not only faster than the English, but they were also better at taking the wind. With the wind from anywhere except directly aft, a sailing ship is blown both forward and to some degree sideways: the closer the ship attempts to point toward the direction of the wind, the greater the element of crabbing sideways, which is called "leeway." But design factors also affect the amount of leeway a ship will make: shallow draft increases it (which is why modern sailing dinghies have centerboards), as do high topsides, which catch the wind. A ship that makes relatively little leeway is said to be "weatherly," the opposite being "leewardly." This is highly significant because a square-rigged ship like a frigate could not point within 68 degrees of the direction of the wind, and it made progress to windward in a series of zig-zags called tacks. Leeway made each leg of the tack longer, so it took more time to cover the same distance forward. Therefore, it was quite possible in chase situations for a leewardly ship that could go faster through the water to be overtaken by one that, although slower, was more weatherly.[2]

The British improved on the French innovation. The cross-braced hull design of Englishman Sir Robert Steppings was incorporated into the concept of the new American frigates, according to William James, the English naval historian. Steppings's diagonals were more effective in regulating depression than tension. That meant that the ship would resist hogging more than twisting, although it also resisted twisting.[3]

While longitudinal stiffening was seen in English frigates, it appears that Joshua Humphreys took it considerably further in his proposal to Congress. Humphreys must have been a man of great vision, a genius. His analysis of the world's navies was nothing short of remarkable. In 1794 he wrote to Congress in support of a design of American warships that could make them unique.

From the present appearance of affairs, I believe it is time this country was possessed of a navy; but as that is yet to be raised, I have ventured a few remarks on the subject.

Ships that compose the European navies are generally distinguished by their rates; but as the situation and depth of water of our coasts and harbors are different in some degrees from those in Europe, and as our navy for a considerable time will be inferior in numbers, we are to consider what size ships will be most formidable, and be an overmatch for those of an enemy; such frigates as in blowing weather would be an overmatch for double-deck ships, and in the light winds to evade coming to action; or double-deck ships that would be an overmatch for common double-deck ships and blowing weather superior to ships of three decks, or in calm weather or light winds to outsail them. Ships built on these principles will render those of an enemy in a degree useless, or require a greater number before they dare attack our ships. Frigates, I suppose, will be the first object, and none ought to be built less than 150 feet keel, to carry twenty-eight 32 pounders or thirty 24-pounders on the gun deck, and 12-pounders on the quarter-deck. These ships should have scantlings equal to 74's, and I believe may be built of red cedar and live oak for about twenty-four pounds per ton, carpenters' tonnage, including carpenters, smiths' bill, including anchor, joiners, block makers, mast makers, riggers and rigging, sail markers and sail cloths, suits and chandlers' bill. As such ships will cost a large sum of money, they should be built of the best materials that could possibly be procured. The beams for their decks should be of the best Carolina pine, and the lower futtocks and knees, if possible, of live oak.

The greatest care should be taken in the construction of such ships, and particularly all her timbers should be framed and bolted together before they are raised. Frigates built to carry 12 and 18-pounders, in my opinion, will not answer the expectation contemplated from them; for if we should be obliged to take a part in the present European war, or at a future day we should be dragged into a war with any powers of the Old Continent, especially Great Britain, they having such a number of ships of that size, that it would be an equal chance by equal combat that we lose our ships, and more particularly from the Algerians, who have ships, and some of much greater force. Several questions will arise, whether one large or two small frigates contribute most to the protection of our trade, or which will cost the least sum of money, or whether two small ones are as able to engage a double-deck ship as one large one. For my part I am decidedly of opinion the large ones will answer best.

In a second letter he wrote,

All the maritime powers of Europe being possessed of a great number of ships of the first size contemplated, and the Algerians having several, and considering the small number of ships directed to be built, the great necessity of constructing those ships in such a way as to render them less liable to be captured and more capable of rendering great services to the United States according to their number, the construction and sizes of frigates of the European nations were resorted to and their usefulness carefully considered. It was determined of importance to this country to take the lead in a class of ships not in use in Europe, which would be the only means of making our little navy of any importance. It would oblige other Powers to follow us in tact, instead of our following them, considering at the same time it is not impossible we should be brought into a war with some of the European nations, and if we should be so engaged, and had ships of equal size with their, for want of experience and discipline, which cannot immediately be expected in an engagement we should not have an equal chance, and probably lose our ships. Ships of the present construction have everything in their favor, their great length gives them the advantage of sailing, which is an object of the first magnitude. They are superior to any European frigate, and if others should be in company, our frigates can always lead ahead and never be obliged to go into action, but on their own terms, except in a calm; in blowing weather our ships are capable of engaging to advantage double-deck ships. Those reasons weighed down all objections.[4]

From 1794 through the laying of the *Constitution*'s keel at Hartt's Naval Dockyard in Boston before Christmas of 1795, the Congress dithered over creation of the United States Navy. A treaty had been signed with the dey of Algiers, which paid him off once again. Not only was he given nearly one million dollars, but the United States promised to provide a frigate and stores to go with the ship. This could have ended the effort to build the United States Navy. President Washington did not believe that paying off tyrants was a good long-term approach to sovereignty. He saved the day by putting the importance of a navy in perspective. He said, "It is our own experience that the most sincere neutrality is not sufficient guard against the depredation of nations at war. To secure respect to a neutral flag requires a naval force organized and ready to protect it from insult or aggression." Here he was referring to a French privateer that had recently raided Charleston, South Carolina. In spite of the delay, Washington ensured that a navy would be founded. In the shipyard, there was a great deal to do before the *Constitution* could begin to take shape. Before the Industrial Revolution, the dockyard was the largest manufacturing site in the world. Twenty-six trades were employed to produce the largest moving structure in the world.

A small coaster arrived in Boston Harbor with cut wood of compass oak, red cedar, and several kinds of pine from as far south as Georgia, while barges from the canals and rivers brought wood from the western and northern forests. Logs began to stack up, the ends scribed with chalked directions.

Plans, Drawings, Measurements, and Mishaps

From the design grew the draft, or construction plan, of the master shipwright. Meticulously the draftsman labored to picture the extreme detail of each of the thousands of parts it took to build a great ship. Since few workers among the hundreds in the dockyard could read the English language, or any language for that matter, the multiple sheets contained detailed measurements to accompany the drawings. In early America the skills in the shipyard came from many nationalities, and variation in language could cause terrific problems. Additionally, many of the nautical terms were confusing to the landsmen employed in the Boston shipyard. Several of the words were derived from the languages of the old seafaring countries. There were Nordic, Dutch, Portuguese, Spanish, and French terms all mixed together. A passage from John Harland's *Seamanship in the Age of Sail* is the best illustration.

> The most surprising example, of course, is the discrepancy between French "mat de misaine," which means foremast, and English "mizzenmast," Dutch "besaansmast," Italian "albevo di mezzana," etc., which all mean "mizzen mast." However, we also have French "foc," Italian "fiocco," Spanish "fogue," meaning "jib," in parallel with Dutch "fok," and similar words in Swedish, etc., which mean "fore course." The latter sail is "misaine" in French, but "trinchetta," "trinquete," in Italian and Spanish.

Dimensions

Numbers were ubiquitous and universally understood. The transfer of accurate measurements to the burgeoning ship was the key to success. Plans were to scale:

1 inch equals 4 feet (¼ inch equals 1 foot) was the rule in England. Humphreys's scale was first thought to be ⅛ inch equals 1 foot. But when repairs were done later, the underwater divers measured the ship to be 10 feet 10 inches longer than suggested by the plan, which set her length at 147 feet.[5] This leads historians to believe that the scale was ⁹⁄₃₂ inches to a foot, which seems very awkward. The displacement in water, a universal measurement used to compare the size of one vessel to another, was 2,250 tons (see appendix 1 for the formula).

There would be multiple pages to the overall plan. One page was devoted to the ornate stern, with the filigreed cabin windows prominent. The bow, with the distinctive beakhead, might show the proposed full figurehead mounted. A full view of the hull from the side was amplified by other views in perspective. The rudder was of particular interest since it was the only piece of the hull that was articulated. There was a cross section of the completed hull. Other pages concentrated on sections of the ribs and provided information to position the decking, wales, and railing. The most interesting of the drawings was the sheer draft, defining the waterline, the spacing between the ribs, and the shape of the hull under the water. From this drawing the streamlining of the hull could be judged. Top views of the quarterdeck, forecastle, gun deck, crew (berth) deck, and orlop would show such detail as hatches, capstan, and bulkheads. Naturally, a good number of copies would be required. Rather than beginning from scratch, apprentice draftsmen copied the original plan by pushing pins through key points to ensure accuracy on the paper below. Then it was just a matter of connecting the holes.

The plan began with a line representing the keel, which was the lowest and principal timber of the ship. It extended the entire length of the vessel and acted as its backbone. Attached were the stempost, ribs, and sternpost.[6] The drawing resembled the skeleton of an animal lying on its back. The stempost, which formed the basis of the bow of the ship, was a curve, often the arc of a circle, and was tangential to the line of the keel.[7] This gave the front of the ship the severely upturned nose so familiar to sailing ships of the time. The ribs began at intervals on the keel and curved outward and upward to form the body of the ship. The tumble home, the amount by which the two sides of a ship are brought in toward the centerline after reaching their maximum beam, was just under one yard in frigates and larger ships.[8] This feature of wooden warships provided a wider lower deck for larger guns and an offset, which made it more difficult for boarding parties to jump on board. The sternpost was nearly vertical at the very end of the keel and would support the hinged rudder.

All boats leak; the warship was no exception. The practical solution was to warp the hull and all the decks upward on both ends. This forced seepage, rainwater, or the water that was dumped upon the exposed decks in heavy seas to find its way to the keel and collect in the center, the lowest point of the vessel.

There it could be pumped out into the ocean. That upward curve was known as the "sheer."

The wales were the principal difference between a man-of-war and a merchantman. The main-wales on a man-of-war were an extra thickness of wood bolted to the sides above the waterline the entire length of both sides of the ship. Just above were the gun ports, which had thick channel-wales added between the openings. Lastly were the chain-wales, large blocks of wood that terminated the standing rigging for the masts. The gunwales were the extra reinforcement above the gun ports that formed a portion of the rail that ran along both sides. A drawing of the midship showed the widest section of the hull but was not necessarily in the exact center of the vessel. From there in both directions, the decks became more narrow and also took up the sheer, or curve upward, from the waist.

The added sections of the ship were all linked to the midship in ever-more-complex convex curves. This was done through mathematical formulas, which were applied to the drawings. The naval architect was critically concerned with the underwater shape, which, if too broad, would make the ship slow. If it were too narrow, the vessel would be unable to displace the weight of the guns. This shape also contributed markedly to the crank of the ship. A sailing ship is "crank" when it heels (tilts) over too far in the wind or when it cannot carry the needed sail without the danger of capsizing. Ships that are built excessively deep in relation to their breadth are notoriously crank.[9] Of critical importance was the shape of the bottom of the hull at the stern, or buttock. If it were too round, it would not permit the water to pass by the rudder with sufficient resistance to make the ship respond to command.

Shipwrights and Wood

The shipwright broke the plans down into pieces at the mold plant. Under cover of a roof, to prevent rainwater from swelling the wood, a full-size three-dimensional pine pattern was made of each piece of the hull's skeleton. A chalk outline of the curved rib was traced on the wooden floor. The mold maker, using thin softwood, would cut an exact likeness as an overlay. The measurement of the thickness would be chalked on the replica. The shipwright would meticulously check the measurement before releasing it to the carpenters and joiners. In the wood yard, the pattern would be matched precisely to a piece of seasoned compass oak. Compass oak twisted naturally as it grew, usually for more than eighty years. It was not found in planted oak forests, where the trees tended to grow straight. That oak was used for planks. The oaks that grew in hedgerows or singly tended to spread out their branches in great displays of strength and dominance. Found within those gnarled, twisted trunks and branches were the curves and radical angles that made up the inner structure of a great sailing ship.

The limiting factor in eighteenth-century ship construction was the natural shape and lengths of timber. Oak, a hard wood, was preferred for the futtock and knee portions of the frame because it could be cut in one continuous piece. Care was taken to cut with the grain where possible, since cutting across the grain could significantly weaken the piece. A futtock is "a separate piece of timber, which forms a rib in a wooden ship. There are normally four or five pieces in each futtock in a moderately sized ship. The one nearest to the keel is the naval futtock and the succeeding ones are upper futtocks."[10] The knee is a support fashioned at a right angle that supports the decks. There are many varieties of knees—hanging, lodging, bosom, and carling. These names refer to the position and purpose of the support. Knees secured decks and beams from below and above. Wooden knees were cut from oaks' natural curves as well. In later times they were replaced during construction or repair with metal knees. The problem was not the strength of the wood but the availability of natural shapes, which were becoming rare as oaks were consumed by the shipbuilding industry around the world. Timber merchants searched the forests for twisted oaks and paid premium prices for contorted old oaks. There was only a limited quantity, and the process of cutting and transporting the special timber was costly. Once cut, it was aged in the timber yard, becoming stable as it dried. This oak, as well as elm, which was used in the keel, was cut and pieced together with joints that were so tight that the seam was barely noticeable. In 1797, American forests appeared endless and were filled with all varieties of trees. It was one of the treasures of North America that the Old World envied. It would be a very long time before metal replaced wood for ships.

> Straight oak planks were warped into shape for the strakes, line of planking on the hull, by steaming. The wood yard had metal ovens that look like black refrigerators, containing boilers. A slot in a steam filled chamber was opened on opposing sides, large enough to pass an eight inch plank. Very slowly the wood was pushed in and pulled out until it became supple. This could take a considerable amount of time. Young boys, early in their apprenticeship were supervised in the task. When the plank became pliable, it was given to the strakers for attachment to the ribs of the hull. The hull form therefore consists of rows of strakes from the keel up to the top edge of the vessel's hull.[11]

It took great skill to bend the planks tightly together. While spikes and copper bolts were used as fasteners, they were not used to attach the skin to the hull. Treenails, pronounced "trunnals," were the choice. Round pegs an inch and a half in diameter, they were made of oak and thoroughly dried. Pounded into predrilled holes made with a brace and bit, they were forced into place and expected to swell when wet. Thousands of treenails were required, and they were made by older or disabled carpenters who were semiretired.

The thick strake had a mind of its own. It was not unknown for one to pop out by morning or to snap out at a carpenter just after he thought it was in place. Working with heavy hunks of wood was an invitation for accidents. The sudden springing out of the end of an installed strake would launch an unwary joiner off the scaffold with surprising speed.

The timber was transported down the rivers of the frontier towns of Pennsylvania and Ohio. From the forests of New England and Georgia it came by coasters. Specially constructed craft were configured to haul long, straight, thick fir-tree trunks for masts, which stuck out over the prow like lances. Fir trees were not only straight and tall, but they were also full of pine oil, which made them limber enough to bend with the wind while supporting tons of wet canvas sails. Masts were cured in saltwater mast ponds. The process allowed the sap to die back without drying out the timber resins.

Yards, round wooden spars that were hung with sails, were fashioned of the shorter, thinner white and yellow pines. Much of the timber arrived at the shipyard unfinished, with the bark still on to protect it during shipment. Each shipyard had a "timbermaster" who inspected the load before it was accepted. He was responsible for storage, aging, cutting, finishing, and warping. The most arduous and boring task was the saw pit. Long logs, which had to be sliced lengthwise into strakes, were placed over a pit, similar to the pit in an auto garage. A top man stood on the log and a bottom man in the pit. They pulled and pushed a single 10-foot crosscut saw along, making boards the hard way, lengthwise. The top man, there by virtue of seniority, was paid more. The bottom man just ate sawdust and hoped to take the place of the top man. Twenty years of that, seems worse to me, than assembly-line labor today.

Skilled Workmen

The most prestigious trade was that of the shipwright. He was the master carpenter who learned his craft by working as an apprentice in a recognized and registered guild. Apprenticeships consumed seven years as a rule. They were sought after since the trade guaranteed a living wage for life and a respected place in the community. Once a shipwright was certified, his skill traveled well. Not only could he work in any yard, but there was plenty of work all along the American coastline in 1797. Or he could choose to go to sea as a ship's carpenter and see the world. Like most guilds, shipbuilding guilds tended to take on family members, and generations would be found working together. The apprenticeship program favored teenagers and younger boys.

Caulkers and Painters

Regardless of the skill the shipwrights brought to the task, they could not hope to make the hull watertight. Caulkers were further down the skill ladder but vital to the health of the ship. The caulkers used oakum. "Oakum was tarred hemp made from condemned ropes which have been un-picked. It was rammed down between the seams with a caulking iron and heavy hammer, and then held in position with hot pitch poured along the seams. In England the un-picking of oakum for naval use was the principal labor of the workhouses to which the old and infirm were condemned when they were no longer able to support themselves by their labor. It was also an old naval punishment, every man condemned to cells on board ship having to un-pick a pound of oakum daily." It was a monotonous and slow process and very hard on fingers and thumbs.[12] Oscar Wilde, the author, poet, and playwright, while imprisoned wrote about the pain and tedium of picking oakum. On deck, quarter-inch gaps were left for the caulkers. Like treenails, the dried fibers of the old rope would swell when wet and form a tight seal against the saltwater. The process was unending, like all maintenance on ships, and was a prime part of refitting as well as initial construction. Caulkers were never short of work.

Painters, again further down the skill ladder, had to protect the outer surface of the entire ship, above and below the waterline. Underwater, the hull was vulnerable to shipworms, which attacked the wooden hull and in a short time ate their way through, destroying the integrity of the vessel. The painters coated the bottom with a mixture of tar and animal hair. The hull was then sheathed in thin copper plate. Barnacles, crustaceans that attach themselves to the hull, ruined the hard work done on streamlining the bottom. Their rough shapes encrusting the keel caused drag. There are only two ways to get rid of them. One is to heel over the ship, expose the bottom, and scrape them off; this is slow, hard work that no one wants to tackle. The other option is to maneuver the ship into freshwater, where the barnacles cannot survive. In modern times, that is a secondary use of the Panama Canal. Ships transiting the Isthmus of Panama often linger long enough on the inland lakes to clean their bottoms.

Above the waterline, the outer hull was payed, or daubed, with a mixture of tar and thin oil. This protected the wood like a varnish and gave a golden color to the surface. The remainder of an English ship was painted with a variety of colors, including dark blue, light green, or red. In the American navy, the interior colors were straw, light green, or white.

Smiths

There were many shops and trades that contributed in addition to the carpenters. Blacksmiths were in high demand across all sectors of industry, but shipbuilding had a particular need for them. The life of a smith who worked with horses could be routine. Smiths at the forge in a shipyard were called upon to make miracles and were primary partners in the assembly of ships. They were expected to create custom fittings, which called for little standardization. Iron bands, grommets, chains, hinges, spikes, nails, pins, plates, and pulleys were only a few of the metal parts that had to be made to specifications. The quality of their work was tested to the limit when they made the metal brackets to clamp the trunnions of the heavy cannon. The trunnions were the metal cylinders that stuck out of the side of a cannon barrel, just forward of the balance point, for attachment to the wooden gun carriage. While the carpenters made the thick squat wooden carriage, the smiths added the hardware for restraining ropes, which had to withstand the force of the recoil of the 2,500-pound gun as it shot backward across the deck. Each shipyard contained a large fire hearth, and the fire was not allowed to go out. Young apprentices tended the fire around the clock, even when it was not in use. It was difficult to maintain the very high temperatures required with the fuel that was available.

Anchors

USS *Constitution* would become known widely as "Old Ironsides," but in her first engagement during the War of 1812, it was not her sides but her anchors that enabled her to fight another day. While it is true that the anchor is just a hunk of weight on a long rope that is dragged on the bottom, it is very important since it secures the ship in port from drifting into danger or damage. A great deal of effort has been put into anchor design because of the anchor's numerous uses. To make an anchor that was strong enough to hold back a multiton warship was a challenge.

There are several kinds of anchors, from very large to small, which are carried for particular situations. The main bower anchor, which was hung near the beakhead from the cat, along with a spare on the opposite side, was used to secure the position of the ship in deep water or in a harbor. The wooden stock, the crosspiece at the top of the metal stem, was made from two pieces of oak banded together with iron straps. The sheet anchor, also forward near the bow, was an added security to reinforce the bower anchor. The stream anchor was smaller and was dropped upstream against the current to hold a vessel in a flowing river. The kedge anchor was the smallest and was carried out under a small boat and dropped. The ship would then take in the rope or spring, pulling the ship up to the point of the anchor. It was used to maneuver or rotate a ship in the confines of a harbor or move it a short distance. The shank, or long metal center member of the anchor, was made up of a number of long iron bars. They would be heated over the hearth of the smithery and, when red hot, hammered together to form one homogeneous piece. A very high and sustained temperature had to be maintained before the hammer could bang them together. It was not possible in the winter to make a large anchor. Conversely, it was not possible in the summer either, because the smiths could not stand the heat. Therefore, kedge and stream anchors tended to be made in spring and summer. The Naval Historical Center has a letter complaining that the yard in Washington hired blacks over whites in 1810, a charge of discrimination. The hiring was justified by the navy, which claimed that the black smiths could stand the heat in the summer but the white smiths could not.[13]

Rope Makers

Some of the most skilled labor was found among the rope makers. While a watertight hull is essential and metal fittings are key, rope is the third and equally important element to shipbuilding. High-quality coarse natural flax fibers were not native to the United States. The best fiber was hemp imported from the Baltic and was from the same family as *Cannabis sativa*. Lower-quality material could be found in South America and Africa. Even though hemp is strong, it cannot stand up to sea spray and rots. The rope was coated with tar to increase its longevity. Today, many prefer man-made modern fiber, such as polypropylene and nylon, as a replacement for hemp, but these can snap without warning. A natural-fiber rope will make a great deal of noise and part one strand at a time when it fails, giving some warning. At the time of USS *Constitution*'s birth, the five-foot-long fibers of hemp were the primary material available. Later, fibers from the Philippines, taken from coconut plants, would add Manila rope to ship rigging. Rope has been found in the tombs of the pharaohs, made three thousand years before the birth of Jesus Christ.

Metal chain was not in wide use on ships before 1800, so cordage in many sizes was employed. Typically, a frigate would require twenty miles of rope, since even the anchors were secured with hawsers. A hawser is a heavy rope with a circumference of five inches or more.[14]

A complex factory, known as the ropery, manufactured rope. One of the buildings had to be over 1,000 yards in length, ten football fields, to accommodate the making of the rope. The longest rope was 120 fathoms, or 720 feet. That was the length required to anchor a ship in 40 fathoms, 240 feet (73 meters) of water. This meant that the yarns and strands had to be much longer since the twisting reduced their length.[15]

Rope Making

It all began with one-ton bales, which had to be cool and dry. This was a challenge to the shipper in leaky wooden ships, where everything was moist under the best of conditions. A bundle of sixty-seven pounds of fiber had whale oil poured over it to make it supple. Then men called "parters" would draw the bundle of fiber through foot-long iron spikes set in rows on a board. This combing straightened and cleaned the fibers for spinning. The spinners tucked the fibers under one arm and slowly fed them with both hands into yarn on a giant spinning wheel. The spinner would walk backward the length of the hall until he had made a piece of yarn of even thickness that was 1,020 feet long (311 meters). This was very skilled work. Fibers were spun into yarn, yarn was twisted into strands, and usually three strands were twisted into rope. Each was twisted in the opposite direction, which stopped the rope from unraveling. A goke is the strand that is laid down the middle while other strands are twisted around it—this core is not attached to the other strands. Three strands are called a hawser; four strands are called a cable.

The yarn was drawn through a kettle of hot molten tar, which coated the fibers to preserve it from decay. To make a three-inch rope, twenty-four yarns were twisted into three strands. Rope makers showed their skill by placing each of the yarns under the same amount of tension so that no strand carried more of the load than any other.[16]

Decks for the Crew, Supplies, and Guns

If you asked a navy sailor of 1797 what kind of ship he wanted to crew, the answer would be predictable: "a frigate." The frigate had it all. He would tell you that she was sleek, nimble, and fast. Soldiers who watched her said she was the light cavalry of the ocean. Like all experienced military men, the first thing he would have mentioned, though, was "creature comfort." A frigate boasted a berth deck. Yes, it was low, and any crewman of nearly six feet walked with a permanent stoop, but it was dry. "Physical size, said the forensic people, is interesting because recent research has suggested that the stature of our great great grandfathers may not have been as short as we're often told when we visit, for example, the cramped quarters between decks of the USS Constitution. The Smithsonian has checked (the remains of) 28 soldiers of the War of 1812 and found their average height to be almost the same as that of today's GI's."[17]

On the berth deck there were no leaky gun ports or hatches spraying water at each pitch and roll. Stuck between the orlop, supply deck, and the wet gun deck, the berth deck provided the crew with accommodations that were unlike those of other vessels. In other major navies, the crew appeared to be ancillary to the guns. On ships of the line, with three gun decks and an orlop, there was no space devoted entirely to the crew. Men were clustered around a massive, impersonal iron cannon, their station. There they hung their hammocks, ate their meals, cleaned the equipment, and said their last prayers before going into action. A dozen or more crewmen lived, ate, and slept in a space that was not big enough to swing a cat in and had a massive immovable gun as its centerpiece. That was the sailor's home, and a mean home it was.

On a frigate, which was the largest ship in the small American navy, the crew, officers, and men lived on what they called the mess deck (which was the same as a berth or crew deck). At the forward end, the enlisted crew was divided into messes of a dozen or so. The frigate mess table was made of wood two inches thick and hung from twisted and knotted ropes just above the knees of a seated man. It swung with the movement of the ship. The knots on the support cords were splayed out in thick tassels and used to wipe greasy hands. Sailors sat on long benches and kegs when not on shift and had space for a small personal chest. Their hammocks were hung twenty-two inches apart, from hooks on the supports for the gun deck overhead. In good weather, some of the men might sleep on the gun deck above. The marine contingent occupied the middle of the crew deck, separating the sailors from the officers. On either side, aft of the steering wheel, tiny low cabins lined the berth deck. They accommodated the midshipmen and officers. Quarter galleries, toilets for the officers, were hung aft. The crews' toilets were open seats forward of the beakhead next to the bowsprit. They gave a grand view in all weather. The center space between the cabins was reserved for the wardroom, an open space where the officer's mess was served. There the surgeon held sick call. Because of the close quarters for months at a time, any malaise that was at all contagious ran through the crew like wildfire. However, sailors believed that a ship at sea was more healthful than any land shop or factory. At the time, when disease was unchecked by modern medicine, the sailor was probably correct. Some sailors wore metal earrings, believed to ward off illness. On the *Constitution*, mullions and pilasters framed the stern windows of the berth deck and the windows of the captain's cabin directly above, adding a touch of ornamentation to the black ship with a white stripe along the side.

The capstan, or man-powered winch, was installed just aft of the mainmast and was double headed. That is, it had a single axle and positions on both the gun and berth deck. It was primarily used to recover the bow anchor as the ship got under way. If need be, and the need did arise during USS *Constitution*'s first combat contact in the War of 1812, two hundred men could apply muscle and pull the ship up to the kedge anchor dropped hundreds of feet forward. It was an unconventional method for moving the ship without the use of the sails. The hand-driven pumps, used to suck water from the bilge, were nearby, in the centerline of the ship, one before and one aft of the mainmast. They could also be employed as firefighting equipment.

The orlop deck was the supply storage area below the berth deck and just above the hold. Reached through hatches in the berth deck, and through the waist, it was divided into compartments for bread, fish, and spirits. Platforms set at various levels provided access to the magazines forward and aft. These self-contained, specialized rooms were more like big boxes lined with copper sheets that seemed suspended above the keel. Copper, a soft metal, was resistant to sparking, which could set off the unstable charges by accident. Since the open flame of a lamp was equally dangerous, the room was dark. On one wall there was a glass window to an adjacent light chamber where a lamp was kept. The glow of the lamp provided illumination for the powder monkeys when retrieving cartridges for the guns up on deck. The lamp sat beneath an exhaust vent to the open deck above to dissipate the heat from its flame. Racks held cartridges of bagged gunpowder shaped to fit into the mouth of the guns. Under the racks were small kegs of extra gunpowder waiting to be loaded into paper or flannel packages. The magazines not only kept the gunpowder inert, but they also kept it dry. Damp powder was of no use and could not be recovered. The shot locker near the mainmast was stocked with cannon balls, which, due to their weight, were considered ballast for the ship.

Much of the food, along with the drinking water, was sealed in barrels of various sizes. They were laid on their sides in rows according to their expected use. Between the barrels were bags of charcoal and sticks of wood for the cook. As the barrels and kegs were used, the carpenter would take them apart and store them for reassembly or give them to the cook for the fire. The barrels lay on a bed of gravel, which was placed over the ballast of pig-iron slabs at the very bottom of the ship.

The Business End—Gun Deck

Above the berth deck was the gun deck. If the keel was 157 feet 10 inches long, the gun deck overhung it by another 20 feet. USS *Constitution* was a big frigate. The weight of the guns was significant. A third-rate 74-gun ship of the line, which had nearly the same hull as the 44-gun Old Ironsides, could not catch the big frigate because of the added weight of the guns.

The deck rails were designed so that the futtocks and gunwales could withstand the recoil of the cannons. At Chatham Dock Yard in southeast England, the late captain Adrian Caruana, Royal Artillery, retired, the foremost expert on smooth-bore guns and author of *The Pocket Artillerist, or The Art of Coarse Gun Firing*, demonstrated for me the action of a naval 32-pounder with a live-fire exercise. The cannon was mounted on the standard elm-wood carriage and rolled into position by ten men. The old gun sat majestically on a concrete sidewalk, only the captain in attendance. The cannonball was replaced by a bag of wet sand, which he claimed would have the same effect on the charge. Free of the retaining ropes that would have been attached on board ship, the gun was loaded with the standard charge of black powder. Gunner Caruana reached out from the left side with a lighted smoldering match twisted around a three-foot pole and touched off the goose-quill primer filled with black powder. The pop of the igniter was lost in the explosion of the main charge. The roar was deafening, but the massive gun did not jump as I expected, due to its enormous weight. It careened backward at a high rate of speed. The soccer field to the front, which was clear of players, disappeared in the blast of fire and white smoke. The thick white cloud rolled across the green field like a thunderstorm, completely obscuring the view. It came to me that on a relatively calm day at sea, scores of firing guns would have enveloped the combatants in a man-made shroud. But my interest was in the recoil. Captain Caruana stood alone to take his bow; the gun was gone, thirty-six feet to his rear. It was an equal and opposite reaction. If it had been unrestrained on board a ship, it would have crashed through the rail on the opposite side.

The 24-pounders on the *Constitution* were made in England, according to William James, the noted Royal Navy historian. "The standard production method for cast iron guns was that they were cast vertically, breech down, with a dead head or feed head at the muzzle of a sufficient size to feed the casting as it shrank while cooling, to compress the metal at the breech end, and to provide a reservoir into which any dross or impurities could rise clear of the body of the finished piece."[18] The casting was then bored out, according to Captain Caruana's book. However, someone once said that history is an unending argument. American records show a bill paid to Furnace Hope in Providence, Rhode Island, for 24-pounders.[19] Yet others at the Naval Historical Center point out that the guns changed often, but in 1809 the English "Congreve" 24-pounders were on the ship, as they are today in Boston.

The 24-pounder cannon barrel was ten feet long, with a six-inch bore and a weight of 2,500 pounds. Its effective range was about a mile and a half, but it had no sighting device, as modern guns do. A gunner's experience was his best friend. The velocity was such that the recipient might have been able to see the cannonball coming. The gun was rolled and levered about by the muscle of a dozen men, if they were available. It was a brute of a machine. While gun drill was practiced, combat conditions quickly trimmed the crew. The primary aim of the attack was to subdue the crew, not sink the ship. The gun crew was reduced by calls to maneuver the ship, put out fires, and repel boarders. The wounded were taken below, and decks were cleared of fallen rigging, all of which reduced the serviceability of the gun batteries. As a result, little aiming was done as the battle lengthened and the enemy closed in. Often the gun was double shotted.

That meant that the powder charge remained the same, six pounds of black powder, but two 24-pound iron cannonballs were shoved down the muzzle before discharge. That added to the already-extreme pressure exerted against the gunwales, where the recoil rope was anchored, when all guns were firing. All the guns on one side of the ship were never fired at one moment. They were discharged in a ripple to reduce the stress on the ship.

Many a captain reconfigured the armament on his ship over the years. Captains never asked for less until the added strain damaged the side of the ship. At the ordnance yard, the captain would "anoint the guns" desired. The gold coin placed on the touchhole of the unauthorized weapon encouraged the master parker to look the other way. Captain Hull found it prudent to remove the 42-pound carronades put on board by a previous commander, opting for 32s. The weight of the projectile was only limited by the ability of the crew to pick it up and push it down the barrel. Land-based guns often fired heavier cannonballs since they could be loaded with the assistance of a winch.

Smashers

The carronade was invented by a major in the British Army in 1774 and produced by the Carron Foundry in Falkirk, Scotland. It was lighter in weight and cheaper to manufacture, required a much smaller crew, and fired a larger ball. All this was traded off for range. The mile-plus range of the cannon was shortened to the carronade's effective range of less than five hundred yards. The crews called it the "smasher." Rather than penetrating the enemy ship and punching a neat six-inch hole in the side, it broke through the side of the ship and showered the crew with splinters. The other advantage was that it sat on a carriage that did not recoil out of position. Mainly confined to the upper decks, it was most effective in close combat.

The carronade was a trade-off. The *Constitution's* main gun battery consisted of thirty long 24s during the War of 1812. This was augmented by 32-pound carronades. There were sixteen on the quarterdeck and six more on the spar deck. One 18-pound cannon and two more 24-pound cannons were used as bow chasers[20] (the Naval Historical Center believes that the extra pair of 24s was taken off prior to sailing).[21] That brought the total to fifty-five gun tubes. Is that why they called her a 44-gun frigate? The counting of guns, though the watchword when it came to characterizing a man-of-war, particularly in the press, had little to do with what was actually available to the commander in battle. The Royal Navy did not count anything but cannons when rating a ship. The American navy stuck to the number attached upon commissioning, which was not a true count either. Armaments varied according to many factors as the years of service passed for a sailing ship. Yet, to the end, the ships were known as 44s, 60s, or 74s.

Split Deck

The single gun deck of the frigate was the highest continuous deck. Above and forward was the forecastle (pronounced "fo'c'sle"), which covered less than a third of the length of the gun deck and provided a platform for six carronades. It also provided protection for the cooking range in the galley below, which was central on the gun deck. Aft, just beyond the mainmast, was the quarterdeck, which provided cover for the remainder of the cannons on the gun deck. Reserved for officers, it was also the deck where the captain could be found as he paced the starboard side. Additionally, the navigator took his readings from the quarterdeck. Between the forecastle and quarterdeck was the open waist of the ship, where access to the hold and orlop was provided down the main hatch. More than any other feature, the split in the "spare deck" identified the ship as a frigate. The spare deck is the quarterdeck or forecastle deck of a deep-waisted ship, possibly because in the days of sailing ships, spare spars could be lashed to these rather than at the waist of the ship.

Limits of the Dockyards

There were no U.S. Navy dockyards when the *Constitution* and her sisters were constructed. Private yards in the major cities were chosen to spread the federal money around. It was a way of subsidizing the economy. There was no single yard that could handle more than one major warship at a time. The amount of space needed to accumulate the materials was considerable.

There were several constraints on how large a ship of the age could be. Factors such as the length of the natural growth of trees and the strength of the keel material affected size. Also, the depth of the stream at the dockyard and the size of its lifting gear were of primary concern to the naval architect when designing the ship. Hartt's Naval Dockyard was one of the largest in the country. Today, the U.S. Coast Guard occupies the same location in Charlestown, Massachusetts. The first dry dock would not be constructed until 1830, and *Constitution* would be its first customer.

A great deal of lifting was called for, though there were no steam-powered cranes in existence in 1796. Before the invention of the steam engine, heavy lifting was done by gangs of men experienced in the use of ropes, pulleys, levers, scaffolding, and derricks.

Around the edge of the construction site, a lattice of wooden masts was erected. Sheers, or king poles, were lashed together to form derricks and equipped with pulley-filled blocks and ropes to lift heavy timbers into place. They were positioned at the top and bottom end of the slip. Ropes were strung between the two derricks, and a system similar to an overhead crane was established. This could handle a preformed rib of futtocks and top timbers as the construction continued to form the outer layer or skeleton of the ship.[22]

A thin false keel was put down first to be loosely attached by staples to protect the keel if the ship ran aground. It also gave some protection against shipworms. The keel was notched on each side, or rabbeted, which allowed for the attachment of the ribs. Then the "deadwood," which protected the topside of the keel and assisted in the installation of the ribs, was attached. Foot-long copper bolts, threaded at both ends, clamped the pieces together. Copper was used because it did not rust. However, copper was expensive. It was not unknown for a shipbuilder to cut the center out of the bolts and just stick the threaded portion in the hole from both sides. He then sold the center shafts.

The framing became more complicated as the bow and stern of the ship were assembled. The pieced ribs of the ship, which were known as timbers, extended upward to form the frame. The timbers were notched, like the corners of a log cabin, over the deadwood of the keel. As the bow and stern began to rise at an ever-steeper angle, the framing methods changed. Now the complicated "cant" framing called for pieces in both the vertical and horizontal plans to the floor. Here the skill of the joiner was tested.

> To maintain the shape of the hull during construction and take the load that the water would supply, three types of supports were used, ribbands, harpins and shores. Ribbands along the sides, harpins on the stem and stern and shores as props under the hull to keep it upright and keep it from torqueing and becoming misshapen. Internally, cross spalls did the same job. It was recommended that a ship should stand for a year to season once all the supports were fitted. Lastly, long planks of elm were used below the water line and short pieces of oak were used above. In battle, damage could be more easily repaired if only short planks had to be replaced. The hull was planked inside and outside, double thick. It added a great deal of strength to the hull and the whole structure. In the bow, where the planks were too thick for warping, short pieces were used and carved instead.[23]

In June of 1797, with the completion of the hull, decks, and rails, USS Constitution sat high and dry on Boston's waterfront.

CHAPTER TWO

~

Early Days of the United States Navy

As you from this day start the world as a man, I trust that your future conduct in life will prove you both as an officer and a gentleman. Recollect that you must be a seaman to be an officer, and also that you cannot be a good officer without being a gentleman.

—Admiral Lord Nelson, Royal Navy

The secretary of war, James McHenry, notified the congressional committee wrestling with the finance for the new navy that before the summer was over, they could expect the *Constitution* to join the *United States* and the *Constellation* on patrol against the French. But she was not a pretty sight out of the water, more like a beached whale than a great lady going to sea. A lady should never be viewed so openly when she is preparing to go out in public. Set on props, surrounded by heaps of timber and stacks of molded metal fittings, the warship badly needed her masts to provide stature and grace. Those Bostonians who watched her progress each day took her to their hearts; she would forever be a member of the community. Could they have guessed what great deeds she would perform, or how she would become the emblem of the greatest navy on earth? Whatever her fate, USS *Constitution* would be their own.

Masts

The lower portions of her three-part main-, fore-, and mizzenmast were fitted before launch in September of 1797. They had been resting in saltwater ponds so that the sap would die back but the timber's resin would not dry out. That allowed the mast to be supple and bend but resist breaking in the strong, steady sea winds. Stripped of bark, the mast portions looked like giant toothpicks as the riggers snatched them up. Each would be pieced together by the addition of two more sections once the ship was afloat. The composite mainmast would reach 220 feet, higher than a fifteen-story building. The combination would be strong yet flexible. This was accomplished by tapering the pieces so that they were thick at the bottom and thinner at the top.

Each mast was swung over the centerline, inserted into the guide hole in the decks, and plunked down on the wooden step fixed to the keel on the button, a square protrusion that kept the mast from twisting. This would not be the last time new masts would be furnished. No part of the ship was more replaceable than the masts.

When the *Constitution* was readied for sea during preparations for the voyage on her two hundredth birthday, 165 coins were found set deep into the keelson by the weight of the masts above. When new masts were set, or stepped, on the keel, coins were placed there beforehand to bring the ship good luck. If the ship sank, the coins were to pay the ferryman to carry the sailors' souls across the fabled river Styx to a peaceful eternal rest.[1]

The masts were, in essence, the superstructures on which the engines, or sails, were hung. Other than the integrity of the hull to keep out the water, there was nothing more vital than the frigate's three fir masts. As the mast's sections were cobbled together into a tall tower, many hands worked on each section, augering holes and attaching fittings. The fat lower section passed through the gun deck and was held fast by the partners, which were a framework of short planks secured to the deck around the hole containing the mast. This lower section protruded eighty feet above the gun deck. The beam, or width, of the ship determined the height of the masts. Therefore, the mainmast, positioned just forward of the center of the keel step, was the tallest since the ship was widest at that point. Partners provided support for the deck against the strain of the mast's pressure when the ship was under sail. The mast was cut square where the first and second sections were strapped together with iron bands, and the hounds, or cheeks, gripped the masts and provided support for the trestle-tree. The platform secured to the trestle-tree was repeated on each mast at the junction with the next section and provided a place to attach lines, sustain lookout posts, and allow marines to snipe at the officers on enemy ships.

Literally, dozens of accoutrements were attached to the masts to anchor yards, accommodate fids, and latch on lines. A fid is "a square bar of wood with a wider shoulder at one end, which takes the weight of a topmast when stepped on a lower mast. The topmast is hoisted up through a guide hole in the cap of the lower mast until a square hole in its heel is in line with a similar hole in the head of the lower mast. Then the fid is driven through both and hoisting tackles slacked away until the fid is bearing the weight."[2] The two masts were then generally secured firmly together with a parrel[3] lashing. This operation was done routinely in the shipyard. When a static facility was not available, the masts of another ship, close at hand, could be rigged to do the lifting. The replacement of masts, heavy work indeed, was done routinely during the life of a sailing ship, in some of the worst possible conditions. It took great ingenuity to replace a dodgy mast. Often the ship's carpenter had to employ all his tricks to provide temporary repairs until the ship was once again in port.

The bowsprit, which stuck out of the prow of the ship like a spear, along with its extension, the jibboom, was in place before the launch. It supported the foremast with forestays, standing rigging lines. Since masts were extremely tall and were expected to support several heavy yards hung with sails that were being driven away from the masts by the wind, the masts needed more support to the hull than the step on the keel and partners on the decks. Standing rigging, the fixed and permanent lines, were attached as soon as the masts were in place. They prevented the masts from falling forward or backward. Those lines were called stays, and they could be adjusted when they became slack due to change in temperature or age. They were coated with pitch to add longevity to the hemp. For lateral support, the shrouds, in pairs, were attached to the hounds on the mast and the tops of the futtocks as they reached the rail. Crossed every two feet with ratlines, they looked like a spider's web as they reached to the top of the masts in ever-decreasing numbers. One could adjust them by pulling on the entwined deadeye pulleys near the rail. In addition to providing stability to the masts, they provided rope ladders for the crew to go aloft and tend the sails. The tarlike coating made the lines tacky in warm weather and slippery in the wet and cold winds.

Launch Days

In the midst of the rigging process, the dignitaries assembled with great ceremony around the ship's prow. The anonymous ship, begun in December of 1795, was now, twenty-one months later, ready to be christened USS *Constitution* just before leaving dry land and sliding into the waiting waters of the Charles River, in Boston, her home port. The local people, interested for so long in her fabrication, were excluded from the list of dignitaries clustered around the prow. President John Adams, of Quincy, Massachusetts, who had a personal interest in the new warship, was in attendance, and the politicians were thick on the ground inside the confines of Hartt's shipyard. Many citizens took the day off work and sat in small boats on the river, bobbing on the noon high tide. These observers were out of earshot of the speech makers, who droned on up to the moment when the *Constitution* would be free of the confines of the slip. The talk was that the twentieth of September would be the first day of a long and glorious life to come. There was still no U.S. Navy. Congress was hoping that the problems with France would soon be calmed and that the pirates of the Mediterranean would just go away. Even at this late date, funds were not appropriated to outfit and send the ship to sea, and she sat unfinished on her props that ceremonial morning. The superintendent of naval construction, Colonel George Claghorn, the government official charged with oversight, gave the order at the appropriate moment in the ceremony to knock out the props and send her down the slip into the service of the nation.

The USS *Constitution* disobeyed. She did not tremble but remained upright and static, to the horror of the entire crowd. The colonel quickly gathered men with jacks to lift her and screws to push her off. The frantic effort only succeeded in a slide of twenty-seven feet, a mere nudge. The dignitaries muttered and shifted from one foot to the other, desperately seeking a scapegoat for the newspaper people, who now had quite a different story to post than the one they had already written prior to the event. The yardmen discovered that the ways had sunk during construction. "A similar mishap had occurred prior to the launch of her sister. The USS *United States*, earlier that spring, had begun her way into the water prematurely, causing some damage," writes Alexander Magoun, the noted historian.[4]

Two days later, with the crowd of well-dressed luminaries absent, little progress was accomplished when the ship was moved only four feet further than twenty-seven feet, her last recorded attempt. There was nothing for it but to jack her up and rebuild a steeper ramp since the ground under the ways had sunk:

> The part of the ways on which her stern rested had settled. There was no remedy but to rebuild them with increased declivity and more rugged support. In the meantime the excessive pressure on the keel, amidships, gave the vessel a permanent hog, which has never yet been completely removed. Indeed, before the present reconstruction this hog was determined by divers to be fourteen inches, a deflection which we hoped will be entirely corrected before the old ship puts to sea again.[5]

Other historians dismiss this explanation for the hogging, or droop, in the end of the ship.

At the next high tide, on October 21, 1797, a very different group witnessed the launch of the *Constitution*. While her first captain, Samuel Nicholson, stood confidently on her deck, Captain James Sever broke a bottle of wine on her bowsprit. A shore gun fired as she moved into the river to the applause of the future king of France, Louis Philippe, and Napoleon's famous intriguer, Prince de Talleyrand.

Make Ready to Sail

The USS *Constitution*, though in the water, was just a hull and masts as she was towed to a dock for outfitting. She smelled of new wood. By December the nonperishables, charcoal for the cook fire, shot, powder, canisters, small arms, a surgeon's medical kit, hammocks, carpenter's tools, cordage, and a collection of small things for a crew that was not yet in existence were stowed. To arrange the stowage for ballast and balance, Captain Nicholson was allowed to hire his officers and warrant officers. It would not be until the spring of 1798 that the XYZ Affair would spur the reluctant Congress to provide the funding to crew the ship and establish the Department of the Navy.

Even though the first eight months of the *Constitution*'s life had passed, she had not lain idle. Over the past year, Ephraim Thayer's firm had been making her sails. The sails, which appeared to be nothing more than big bed sheets from a distance, were serious business. Several hundred years had gone into their design. While merchantmen's sails had been developed to take advantage of the trade winds, warship sails had to perform in all seas, in all weather, and in all directions.

Trade Winds, Highway on the Sea

The square-rigged merchantmen were built to take advantage of the direction of the steady trade winds. They were intended, for the most part, to be driven by the prevailing winds from abeam (the direction at a right angle to the fore and aft line of a ship) and aft, according to the seasons of the year. The square sails took maximum advantage of predictable winds. At sea, the winds are much stronger and more consistent than on land. In crossing both the Atlantic and the Pacific oceans, I was always surprised by the power of the wind in my face that never seemed to slacken by day and fell off little by night. The large sailing vessels were rigged to be most efficient in those steady winds. A square-rigger made little headway when having to continually tack across the wind. Additionally, frequent tacking required larger and more experienced crews, which drove up operating costs. The big cargo ships were like the massive eighteen-wheeler tractor-trailer trucks on the express roads of today, which are of little use until they are free to roll at high speed on highways built to take advantage of their design.

Passat

The Germans called them passat, or trade winds, which are steady regular winds that blow in a belt between 30 degrees north and 30 degrees south of the equator. They are caused by the action of the sun on and near the equator in heating the atmosphere and making it rise; the heavier air to the north and south then moves in to fill the resultant vacuum. If the earth did not revolve, the wind would come directly from the poles. But since the speed of the earth's rotation is greater at the equator, these winds are diverted toward the west.[6] They assisted sailing ships because of their predictability. Christopher Columbus used those hot winds coming off the desert of North Africa to blow his fleet to the west and India. Fortunately for us, he landed in the northern Caribbean on the same parallel as his intended destination. In the Northern Hemisphere of the Atlantic, trade winds had a profound effect on the development of western Europe and the eastern shore of the Americas.

Therefore, the wide oceans, though trackless in the water, were regulated by the trade winds. Sea-lanes refer to the broad paths followed in response to trade. At first, just after Columbus, the Spanish and Portuguese filled the passage with treasure ships and exotic commodities. Later, after the native populations were devastated with Western disease, the route became the sorrowful direction of the slave industry. Ships from England voyaged to North Africa, captured people, and sold them to the new planters in the Caribbean and southern United States. There they picked up sugar, cocoa, herbs, flax, and cotton as the trade winds pushed them up the eastern seaboard of North America and out across the North Atlantic to England. In England the sugar was consumed and the cotton was processed and sold to Europe along with the other riches of the New World. The ships then began the circle once again. In the Pacific the trade winds performed as well in a similar fashion, bringing the spices of the Orient to Europe.

Ocean Currents

Current is the flowing of the sea in one direction. Currents may be periodic in relation to the tides, seasonal in relation to the prevailing wind, which blows only at certain times of the year, or permanent in relation to the main rotational or trade winds. While the ocean looks like it has no particular direction other than that of the surface wind on a particular day, it is very deceiving. An experienced sailor in the days of sail knew these currents as well as the trade winds. He could "read" the ocean. Testing the temperature of the water, the navigator could tell when he had entered a particular current. Even without the use of a longitude chronometer he could guess where he was on the chart through dead reckoning and a feel for the current. A sudden increase in speed could indicate the gaining of a current. Not only did the wind push the square-rigged ship along, but the flow of the current, an unseen channel in the waves, dragged the heavy merchant ship in the direction predicted. Along the Atlantic coast from Cuba up to Norfolk, Boston, Halifax, Greenland, Iceland, and on to the British Isles, the combination of trade winds and the Gulf Stream current brought ships and moderating weather to Edinburgh and London.

In the Doldrums

There is a great deal of ocean that is not blessed with trade winds and favorable currents. The central Atlantic was nearly devoid of shipping, as were the southern oceans. Ships went where there was money to be made. Other than the voyages of discovery, there was little reason to risk lives and ships on vast tracks of open water. Fishing was always confined to relatively shallow water where the fish thrived in great numbers. The deep ocean is not a profitable place to cast nets. The one exception was the large whaling industry. Before the use of petroleum and its by-products, whale oil was in high demand. Chasing whale herds could bring the hunters into uncharted waters. In particular, the water off the coast of South America near 30 degrees, as well as similar latitudes in the Atlantic, was avoided. These were the "doldrums," a belt of low pressure at the earth's surface near the equator. With minimal pressure gradient, wind speeds are light and directions are variable. There are often hot, sultry days with overcast skies and frequent showers, according to *The New Practical Navigator* by Nathaniel Bowditch, written in 1802.

Light, variable winds hundreds of miles from shore are not conducive to profitable sailing. What the definition does not say is that a crew could be becalmed for weeks in the doldrums, watching their supplies dwindle and their fresh water consumed in the heat. The other thing it does not mention is that a ship was often very much alone and could not expect assistance. All that the crew could do was to wait it out and remember not to go near the area again, once they were free.

Yards, Yardarms, and Their Sails

Recently, a woman accompanied by her children was touring on board the USS *Constellation*, moored in Baltimore harbor. She was overheard to expand on the explanation of the ship's yardarms to her girls: "They are just like curtain rods, except much higher." Well, she hit it on the head. Yards are thick poles of pine that are tapered at both ends. These spars crossed the masts of a ship horizontally or diagonally, and a sail is set from them. Yards were supported from the mastheads (the top of each mast section) by rope slings and blocks, which were used to lift them into place. The yard was tied to the mast by rope parrels, which allowed the yards to be braced or swung around to take advantage of the wind. Yards serve one purpose, like the curtain rods: they support the sail. Yardarms are extensions of the yards. Smaller, lighter spars were attached on either side of the yard in order to increase the sail area. Like outriggers, they spread more canvas outward to both sides of the sail to catch light winds. In the days to come, this arrangement of canvas would be more important to the ship than her battery of guns.

Sail Making

Sails are as old as boats. Why paddle when the wind would push the boat along? Considerable currents of air constantly sweep the open landscape of unrestricted water. There have been as many designs of sails as there have been shapes of boats. The principal merchant fleets that routinely operated at sea, rather than along coastlines, were outfitted with square-rigged sails. The warships that protected them were similarly set up. However, the warship often operated in all waters and indeed had to cross trade winds to accomplish its mission. The man-of-war chased, cut off, crisscrossed, pursued in toward shore, and ran before the wind when engaged in combat. The ship was expected to be unrestricted and therefore carried a variety of sails, which were rigged to take advantage of any wind in order to fight and win.

Square Sails

When a three-masted vessel, that is, one that has fore-, main-, and mizzenmasts, has a minimum of three yards with square sails on each mast, it is said to be "ship rigged." A large square-rigged warship could carry as much as four thousand square feet of sail. Not all sail was flown at the same time. Only when winds were light were all the sails put on. Additionally, heavier sail material was used in storms and high winds. The lighter sails were "kites," and the heavier ones were simply known as canvas. There was also a supply of replacement sail in the sail locker, in the hold. This might seem like overkill, but remember that the only source of propulsion was sailcloth.

Sails were custom made for each ship according to a formula based on the height of the masts and placement of the standing rigging.[7] To assemble sails, Ephraim Thayer provided a loft, which was a large, dry open space under a roof, free of posts and pillars. The sailcloth came in two-foot widths, which were sewn together in double flat seams with 108 to 116 stitches per yard. At that time, sewing was done by hand, which explains why it took a year to make the *Constitution*'s complement of sails. The edge of the sail was turned over and sewn down to form a kind of hem, known as tabling. Around all the edges of the sail a boltrope was sewn. At the corners of the sail loops were left to attach lines.

As there is for everything on a ship, there is a name for each piece and part of a sail. The four sides of a square sail are the head, foot, and leeches, weather and lee. The two top corners are the earring cringles. At the bottom corners there are clews, or clues, which differ by weather and lee sides. The center portion of a square sail is cut with a full belly to catch the wind and is called the bunt. The sails are named, in ascending order, mainsail, or course, and topsail, topgallant, and royal. If you add the mast name to the sail in question, you get main topgallant for the third sail up the mainmast. The slang phrase "all nine yards" comes to mind, which means the ship is flying all sails and moving out smartly. A sail is sent or hauled aloft by the deck gang with the sail secured in a bundle to the yard by a series of short tie lines, or gaskets. The top men, as a gang, crawl out on the yard, high above the deck, and loose the gaskets. The sail is allowed to unfurl and take the wind. If the intensity of the wind is too great and could damage the sail, its area of exposure to the wind can be reduced, or reefed. This is true of only the two lower sails, the main and top. In a square-rigged ship, a reef is the amount of sail taken in by securing one set of reef points. It is the means of shortening sail to the amount appropriate to an increase in the strength of wind. Main- and topsails normally carried two rows of reef points, enabling two reefs to be taken in; sails set above them usually had no reef points as they would normally be furled or sent down in a wind strong enough to require the sails to be reefed.[8] Headsails were those set on the foremast, and aftersails were the ones on the main- and mizzenmast.

Staysails

In addition to the square sail, there were sails that were fore-and-aft rigged. These were called staysails. They were triangular in shape and had rings sewn into their edges called brail cringles, which were loops that rode on the standing rigging that supported the masts from falling forward or aft. They were not attached to yards but pulled up the standing rigging like curtains on a rod, just like the woman said on USS *Constellation*. The staysails were primarily used when the wind was coming across the bow, nearly straight into the desired direction of the ship. Since the square-rigged vessel could not move forward within 34 degrees on either side of a headwind and had to tack, the staysails could operate more efficiently in those conditions. In heavy weather, staysails were the primary means of movement, providing some steering or control as well. The steering was dependent on a volume of water passing by the rudder at speed. The more speed, the quicker the rudder would cause the ship to respond to command. The heavy canvas storm sails were bent to the stays under these conditions.[9]

Large merchant ships were not generally equipped with a full complement of staysails since they traveled preplanned routes that counted on the wind to be abeam or aft. Smaller craft such as schooners, sloops, and cutters were exclusively rigged with staysails. They could hug the rocky shoreline, which called for better maneuverability.

Running Rigging

The halyard, which may come from *haul-yard*, was the light lines attached to yards to control their position and therefore the attitude of the sails. Toiling without end, sailors hauled on ropes all the days of their sea lives. Their palms became thick with muscle and their fingers profoundly callused from coarse tarred rope. To provide leverage, a purchase was rigged. A purchase is a rope rove through one or more blocks by which the pull exerted on the hauling part of the rope is increased according to the number of sheaves in the blocks over which it passes. It is best described to landsmen as a double block and tackle. The sail, rolled in a bundle and lying on the deck, was attached by the head to the yard. Then the heavy assemblage was hoisted up the mast with the aid of a jeer. A jeer is a very heavy tackle with double or treble blocks used for hoisting the lower yards in an operation known as swaying up the yards.[10] The loose end of the jeer tackle was wound around the capstan, and manpower took the yard up the mast to be secured to the parrel. Slung below the yard were footropes the men stood on, bending over the yard at the hips, while they loosened the sail and let it fall.

The running rigging not only hoisted things aloft, but it was also used to brace or swing the sails around. Some of the running rigging was connected to the ends of the yards and lower corners of the sails. The crew hauled in or let out the lines according to the shouted directions from the quarterdeck, which were relayed throughout the ship. The action turned the sail into or away from the wind. This operation was known as bracing the sails.

Bracing is the most important operation done by the crew to take advantage of the wind. It requires constant attention by the watch officer in order for the ship to stay on course and get the most out of the wind. If it is done correctly, at the direction of the captain, the angle of the sail will provide the power in just the correct amount. The ship will go as fast as it can without damaging the masts. The sail acts both as an accelerator and a break. With a change of sail attitude, the ship can go in reverse. To brace is to swing around the yards in order to present a more efficient sail surface to the wind. By bracing the yards at different angles through the use of fore-and-aft lines, the captain can take the best advantage of any wind that may be blowing. Thus the yards are braced "aback" to bring the winds on the forward side of the sails to take the way (forward speed) off her and are braced "about" to bring the ship on the opposite tack when going about (changing tack).

Once the sails were positioned, the lines were secured to belaying points on wooden pins. To "belay that" means to tie it off or simply to stop operations.

The Crew

Normally, a ship's crew would rig her. But with the foot dragging over the political state of affairs and therefore the indecision over the creation of a navy, Captain Nicholson's temper, which was none too even to begin with, was strained to the limit throughout the spring of 1798. At least his officers were in place to supervise and keep track of the outfitting of the ship. Securing all the items he had signed for must have been a constant worry, since there was no loyal crew to watch the busy traffic of landsmen who came and went each day. Of course there was no "navy yard," so the ship lay at anchor where the people of Boston could admire the fine work they had done.

Nicholson was authorized to recruit a crew of 253 midshipmen and sailors. "The 44 gun frigates were planned to have 80 officers and petty officers, 180 able seamen, ordinary seamen 145, marines 65 and 5 boys."[11] That would have given the big American frigates an authorization of 475 total crew, which seems very large for a ship of the *Constitution's* size. By July the ship was moved from the shipyard dock out into King's Roads, some say to prevent desertion.

In late May, President Adams ordered the U.S. Navy to sea against armed vessels of France. The 24-pounders of the main battery were in place, but the minor guns for the quarterdeck and forecastle were not. Panic set in for both the secretary of the navy and Captain Nicholson. The captain arranged to borrow sixteen 18-pound cannons from the local coastal artillery stores. USS *Constellation* was on station in June, and the *United States* followed at the start of July, which made Captain Nicholson all the more anxious to get under way. Boston's Castle Island fortification provided the powder for the magazine, while food was stowed below in anticipation of going to sea.

Congress called for a review of the construction of warships. The cost had escalated during the four years it took to build the first frigates. Secretary of War McHenry told Congress that it had gone about the program by the most expensive method possible. It took too long and did not have a system to access in order to contract, procure, invoice, transport, store, and pay for what was the most complex vehicle the government had ever tried to construct. There were no standards and no designated facility to gather, piece, fabricate, and construct ships for the government. He could have added that foreign governments, who had been building and equipping navies for generations, did so very deliberately within the strict confines of regulations and oversight. Although merchant ships looked similar to warships, they were not. It was one thing to convert a merchantman to war and another to build a capital combatant that could stay the course and match the might of England and France. A navy was not to be played at but pursued seriously in its construction, crewing, training, and sustenance. There was no navy in the world that had been whipped up like this one. It was doubtful that France or any other nation would take it seriously.

Under Way at Long Last into the Quasi War with France

With the tide running in Boston Harbor on the evening of July 22, 1798, USS *Constitution* went to sea and began the saga. Her orders were to slide up and down the eastern seaboard from New Hampshire to New York, seeking out armed French ships, and engage them in combat. She was also to free any American ship that had been captured by the French. The captain would receive amendments to his instructions from the station at Newport, Rhode Island. The fifty-five-year-old skipper, Samuel Nicholson, was at home on his quarterdeck, renewing the rhythmic pacing that passed the time. He had learned that exercise was essential to maintaining a quick mind in the confines of a ship. As commander of the Continental navy frigate *Deane*, he had gained his reputation as a no-nonsense commander, which he enjoyed both on land and at sea.

The hull appeared sound, although more water washed in than expected. Many passing merchant ships saw the big frigate for the first time as they sailed to berths in the safe harbors of the northeastern ports. By August, her orders took her south, where she cruised from the mouth of the Chesapeake Bay to Savanna, Georgia. Although the captain's instructions spoke of the coast, they did not mean that his command should hug the land and entrances to the harbors. The *Constitution* ranged well out into the Gulf Stream, two hundred miles from land. There, free from the snags of the outer banks, the shipping lanes were well traveled, and sails on the horizon were checked out as the frigate swept along in the trade winds. Her crew was more a pickup bunch of untested amateurs than a professional bunch of "swabs," as we might think. In the month of July 1798, the navy could not have been younger; there were no standards. Even the officers were untried; some said before they left Boston that they had taken on a third-rate batch. As far as Nicholson was concerned, he had picked them and he would make them into a competent and cohesive crew. That is what captains did. Before the month was over, he would have three men flogged for breach of discipline.

The following entry by the ship's clerk, James Pity, in his personal journal of August 1, is most revealing.

First part, this 24 hours clear and pleasant weather. People employ'd washing decks. Birth'd the people anew—8 P.M. wore ship to the north & west. Middle part clear W. all hands employ'd at different jobbs, on examing the compasses I found they did not agree with any two in the ship by reason of so much iron work round the binnacle, had the binacles taken to pieces and took out of each 3½ in. nails and put them together again with copper nails since which they agree with latter part, clear weather inclinable to calm.

Latitude observed 40.13.[12]

The duties of the captain's clerk, according to the record in the National Archives, were

To make a plain copy of and transcribe all letters written by the captain.
To file away all letters and documents, any matter of whatever kind received, and preserve them.

To file away and preserve all reports.

To keep an account of all weekly and quarterly expenditures rendered by the Yeoman of the ship.

To keep a record of punishments in a book provided for the purpose.

To read to prisoners sentences of Summary Courts Marshal, and to read to the crew, once a month, the "Articles of War."

And to perform such minor duties as may be necessary, or the Captain may direct.

While altering the binnacle does not fall within these guidelines, I am certain he must have kept track of the position of the ship for the logs and must have noticed the deviation.

The Atlantic coast was cluttered with American naval frigates and sloops of war, linked together with customs cutters, all searching for French blood. The politicians in Congress who had worked so diligently to create the U.S. Navy now urged the first secretary, Benjamin Stoddert, to show the colors and attack the French ships. For several years, American envoys had toiled endlessly to get the French to swallow their hurt pride at the American overtures to Great Britain. But dealing with the volatile French revolutionary councils was more complex and far less rewarding than talking to a sovereign's throne. To the French, there was no room for neutrality when it came to Great Britain.

The First Frenchman

It is believed that Captain Nicholson was after a substantial prize when he began to chase the sail on the horizon on the morning of September 8, 1798, off the coast of Charleston, South Carolina. He was not getting any younger. He was not a rich man. Others say that he wanted to be the first U.S. naval officer to bring his ship into combat. Whatever the motivation, Nicholson chased the sail with a single-minded pursuit that brought the target up short. It showed the friendly color of England when challenged. That was not good enough, and the *Constitution* closed in on the foreigner. The *Niger*, much smaller, showing twenty-four light guns, heaved to under the threat of the big frigate's battery as she came close enough to destroy her with one broadside. Pity writes,

Obliged the chace to hoist out 2 boats upon examining her papers had reason to suspect her being a French cruizer. Sent Mr. Beale, 3rd Lieut. on board and took possession of her. She was call'd the *Niger* and mounted 24 guns and carried 70 men at 2 P.M. removed the officers & crew on bd. the frigate and confind the crew.

Middle part fair prize in company. At 2 A.M. hove too & order'd the prize to hoist out her boat & send her on board the frigate with the commanding officer upon examining Martin de Rose seaman on board the frigate Constitution he made affadavit that the boatswain of L'Niger had taken him in the *Masy* of Portsmouth N.H. plundered him of every thing and carried him into Guadaloupe.[13]

The French-speaking captain claimed that his ship was under "letters of marque" from Great Britain and bound for Philadelphia. Captain Nicholson believed she had many flags in her locker and did not accept the claim. He took her as a prize and followed her into Norfolk, Virginia, to be evaluated and paid out. At first the secretary of the navy accepted the assurances of the American captain. His assessment declared that the *Niger*'s crew members were French privateers in disguise. But as Benjamin Stoddert probed the waters, he began to alter his opinion and leaned toward Nicholson's critics. The secretary, who had overlooked the captain's strident demeanor, soon found that the navy was embroiled in a very difficult diplomatic situation. His Majesty's representative backed the word of the captured French-speaking captain, who was a royalist. This was not the action contemplated by the Congress when it authorized the interruption at sea of foreign ships.

Upon return to his ship at Hampton Roads, the chastened American captain found fever on board. Within a day of his return his son, sixteen-year-old midshipman Samuel Nicholson Jr., was dead. Pity's account reads,

9 A.M., Mr. Samuel Nicholson, midshipman on board the Frigate *Constitution* & oldest son of Sam Nicholson Esq. (com. of Said Ship) departed this life aged 16 years, of the prevailing epedemic fever after an illness of 4 days. The colors of the frigate cutter *Virginia* & *Niger* were hoisted half mast. Got a Coffin made & prepared to bury him at 10 Capt. Bright of the cutter *Virginia* came on board to attend the funeral. Made Signal for a boat at ½ past 11 a schooner came along side and docked on board the corps of Nicholson which was carried to Hampton attended by several officers & men. At ½ past 7 the boat returned from Hampton having buried Mr. Nicholson in the church yard by the side of Commodore Mowat. 8 sent doctor read on shore being ill of the same fever.[14]

It was not unusual for a captain to have young relatives among his crew. There was no naval academy, yet the profession was highly desirable. Relations and friends who had eligible sons besieged men in important positions for appointments to the profession. Sea captains were of particular interest since the only way to become a naval officer was to serve an apprenticeship.

The *Constitution* was sent south as escort to a merchant convoy while the secretary of state, Timothy Pickering, the former secretary of war, agreed with the British assertions that the *Niger* was under English protection. The American government paid eleven thousand dollars in damages and released the *Niger*'s French crew.

Captain Nicholson, unaware of the settlement, was consumed with other problems. On the voyage south, rain squalls repeatedly interrupted the flow of the convoy and the *Constitution* damaged her bowsprit so seriously that the carpenters attempted to fish the boom. But it was not holding, and the captain abandoned the convoy, turning north for a safe harbor. The storms did not abate, and two men were lost, one into the sea and the other when he fell to the deck from aloft. The heavy bowsprit shifted, in spite of the lashing, and damaged the beakhead in the process as they labored north under reduced sail. By the second week of November the *Constitution* was at home in Boston undergoing repairs.

In Pity's personal journal there is a disturbing entry:

[November 1798] Masters mate was confined in irons for speaking seditious words tending to stir up the minds of people, also Mr. Connell Boatswain for abusing Mr. Cordis 2nd Lieut. for inspecting the store room. I was also arrested & confined to my cabin by order of Capt. Nickolson without any reason being given (except unofficer like conduct) and was kept under arrest till the 1st of December, followed when I received written order from Capt. N. to go on shore at the same time declaring that I was dismissed from any further service on board the frigate agreeable to his orders. I went on shore nothing of consequence took place till the 22n. Instant when I read his orders to repair on board the frigate as I was reinstated in my former office and orders in writing to the commands officer to receive me as such. I did not return to the ship till the 27th Instance to the Justice of the business I shall not say much but every one who knows the circumstances must suppose that I was not arrested for anything very criminal or I should not have been reinstated.

Memo: Mention was made in the day book when I left the ship but not when I return'd on board, which I think is wrong.

There was no love lost between the crew and the captain during the repair. The officers were even more hostile. It was apparent that the captain was intent upon his reputation and fortune, giving little consideration to the ship, her crew, and their families. With early winter storms all around, however, the *Constitution* was at sea by the end of November, attended by a number of new officers and with sailing master Nathaniel Haraden's steady hand at her controls. He had his hands full getting to know her during the next thirty days of unrelenting storms as they drove off the coast of New England. Lieutenant Isaac Hull—a name to remember—moved up from fourth lieutenant to second. Nicholson was not supposed to remain so far north, close to Boston. Finally, just after Christmas, the captain succumbed to orders and moved south.

By mid-January of 1799, the *Constitution* was crossing the equator, and splinter nets, tied by the crew from the spools of cording stowed in the hold, were rigged. Awnings were sewn by the sailmaker to provide some protection from the searing sun. It appeared that the northern storms of the previous month had sprung the first section of the foremast. A most serious injury; the carpenter fished and then added coils of thick rope around the crack until it looked as if a constrictor snake of nearby South America had attacked. The rope was wetted to shrink and conform to the mast.

Nicholson's Foolish Notion

With the loss of his first prize, Captain Nicholson was determined to regain the respect of the navy and, more importantly, his crew, who would have "shared out" on *Niger*. Off the Leeward Islands of the Caribbean he gave chase for a day and a night until he brought up what he believed was a 36-gun French frigate. However, he was mistaken. She was the *Spencer*, an English merchantman that had been captured by the French warship *L'Insurgente*. On board was a French crew, which he exchanged for a handful of Americans from his crew with the intent of sending the prize to port. Before separating, however, Nicholson changed his mind. Afraid that he may have exceeded his orders to capture French ships and those American ships that had been taken by the French, he dithered.

Here is a firsthand account written by Pity, who was not a great fan of the captain, in his personal journal:

16 January 1799 . . . saw two sail, gave chace at 4 and discovered one to be a ship of war. Made the private signals as American & English which she could not answer upon which the crowded sail took in studding sails & hauld our wind & cleared ship for action At 7 squally with rain, at 8 the chace bore N.N.W. 5 or 6 miles distance housed in the lee guns &down ports kept sight of the chace between the squalls until ½ past 11 when we lost her . . . At 20 minutes past 12 saw the sail bearing N.W. Supposed to be the vessell we had been in chase of. Bore up and fired 2 guns at her. He then wore round & Make sail gave her two more guns to the South and boarded her. She prov'd to be the ship *Spencer* from Shields England bound to Barbadoes prize at the time we boarded to the *Insurgente* French frigate of 36 guns. Took the prize master & crew out & sent an officer & 9 men to take charge of her.

Pity's journal of the following day, January 17, 1799, reads,

at 9 A.M. bro't too and took out of the ship *Spencer* the officers & men we sent on board her. Captain Nicholson not thinking himself authorized from the instructions he has rec. from the President of the United States to recapture any English Merchantmen notwithstanding she was captured by an Armed vessell of the French Republick, and the act of congress not giving him power to keep her it was tho't prudent by him to release her.

The orders said nothing about the status of allied British ships taken by the enemy, the French. The captain ordered the French prize crew restored and withdrew his men, who were intent on taking her in for compensation.

The next day he was to rendezvous with USS *United States*, according to his instructions. Commodore John Barry, commander of the *United States*, established a patrol route for him to the north and along the Atlantic coast of Dominica, a French possession. A hurricane-like storm, very early in the season, ripped its way across the tops of the *Constitution*'s masts, endangering the ship and limiting her usefulness to Barry. Soon the *Constitution* was alone since Barry took his flotilla away in convoy with American merchantmen. The deep draft of the big frigate restricted her ability to chase vessels, which eluded her by driving inshore along the island chain.

A Bright Day for the Crew

On the first day of March 1799, a frigate was sighted off Deseada Island. The chase was soon over when HMS *Santa Margaretta*, 36 guns, a convert from a Spanish frigate now in the service of His Majesty, heaved to. The captains agreed to sail in concert. On the following day, the American showed her speed, and the Anglo-Spaniard, in spite of adding some studding sails, could not keep up. As Joshua Humphreys had predicted, the *Constitution*'s speed and size were turning out to be a formidable combination. Nothing could contain the spirits of the crew when the "Brit" fell well astern and then out of sight. Morale had been suffering from the continuing accidents that had claimed the lives of a number of sailors, which had been topped off with the accidental shooting of boatswain Hancock while "beating to quarters." But the episode with the *Santa Margaretta* proved to the crew that even though the captain was a bit of a bungler, he was nonetheless a good sailor and could get the most out of USS *Constitution* when he put his mind to it.

It Is Possible to Go Downhill at Sea

It was plain to everyone in the navy that restricting the big frigate to a squadron was a misuse of her power. Yet the missteps of Captain Nicholson lost him the one thing a commander at sea must have. He must be the embodiment of his government's intentions and possess the demonstrated judgment to keep the confidence of his "betters" while out of touch. In an instant, the raw power of his command could be used for the enhancement or to the detriment of his nation. There have been numerous examples of such abuse by a naval captain in our own time, and it is never pretty. The accidental sinking of a Japanese merchant vessel off the coast of Hawaii in 1999 by an American submarine, which broached the surface without due care, caused much grief and needless suffering. The shooting down of an Iranian commercial airliner by an American guided missile cruiser in 1987 appeared to the world to be a misjudgment of enormous proportions. In essence, Captain Nicholson had lost the respect and confidence of his boss and was now the subject of a communiqué to the entire navy that held him up to ridicule. The message from the secretary of the navy to the fleet read, "A Misconstruction of his authority by Captain Nickolson in relation to a Vessel of friendly Nation, captured by the French renders it necessary that I should make some explanatory observation on the Subject."[15]

Nicholson, on station in the Caribbean, continued to hunt and within days captured two small prizes, which was more important to his future than he could have imagined. The money would come in handy. On the same day, Secretary Stoddert signed an order for the *Constitution* to return to Boston. Captain Nicholson was to be beached.

All Commanders Are "Captains" but Only Some Commanders Are Captains

I would like to attempt to explain the rank system in the navy. The commanding officer of a vessel is titled "the captain." The naval rank of captain, and therefore the pay grade, is equivalent to colonel in the other military services. To try to eliminate the confusion for the reader, captains and colonels are one grade lower than the flag rank of admiral or general. (Admirals and generals have personal flags with their stars in white.) Therefore, the commanding officer in 1798 of a vessel smaller than a frigate, while addressed on board as "captain," wore the rank of lieutenant and was paid as a lieutenant. To try once more to remove the confusion, think of the word "captain" as both a position and a pay grade. On a frigate, a ship, the man in command was both the captain and wore the grade of captain on his uniform. Now, "commodore" was merely a temporary designation given to any commanding officer in the navy who was charged with command of his own vessel and those assigned to his command. As a rule, this changed frequently and was governed by the mission at hand. If the threat warranted a flotilla, a group of navy vessels, to accomplish the mission, it was formed, and the senior officer in command was named the commodore for as long as that group was together and a more senior officer did not join. As an example, on Lake Champlain on September 11, 1814, Commodore Thomas Macdonough, the master commandant of the lake, and lieutenant in the U.S. Navy, was senior officer, at age 30, and therefore in command of the flotilla. "Commodore" was a sought-after designation and jealously guarded.

Because of the nature of ships at sea, men confined in a small space, out of touch with society and its rules and safeguards, will function best when discipline is maintained. The commander/captain must ensure that the safety of the vessel is not compromised by division and derision. Therefore, in that unique isolation at sea, which is a very dangerous place, one man is put in charge and is responsible for the safety of the ship, accomplishment of the mission, and health and welfare of the crew. He is held accountable by law for everything that happens or fails to happen while he is in command. Since he is so charged, he is given the authority in law to rule according to his own judgment. Standing behind his authority is the Department of the Navy and the United States government. Today that authority and conduct is spelled out in the Uniform Code of Military Justice. In 1798 it was a part of English common law, which was the basis for the laws of the sea subscribed to by the American government.

Living Conditions

Punishment for aspiring officers, midshipmen and above, did not include flogging, They were not protected, however, from the health hazards of communal living. Young Samuel Nicholson was not the only man to suffer a terminal illness among his peers in the naval service. Even though he was favored with a billet, his life could still be very perilous and even brutal, in spite of the family relationship. Young Samuel would have served under the warrant officers. Expected to learn the skills of an officer, midshipmen would study navigation and assist in the taking of readings. They also worked high above the deck in the tops with the sailors. Put in charge of small working groups, midshipmen led gun crews. As a future officer, Samuel would have captained a small boat on replenishment. The young midshipmen lived together as a group in conditions little better than the seamen's, aft of the mainmast on the crew deck. As cadet future officers, they expected to serve for three or more years, depending on the state of the navy, and then be elevated to the ranks of the officers as junior lieutenants. As the new service was sure to expand in those uncertain times, a career appeared to be possible.

Crewmen

The first crewmen of the USS *Constitution*, these sailors, these men of the sea, had no idea that they were witnessing or, indeed, making history. These weary men, half starved by our standards, who were never completely dry, even in their hammocks, toiled by day and by night to make that leviathan of the age plow about the most dangerous two-thirds of the earth with little hope of family, long life, and love. They learned to never look further than the season or the sea they plied. They would be amazed that we take the time to write and read about them. They never thought of themselves as participants in a glorious war once the quay was out of sight. When they could no longer see the smudge of their native land just above the horizon, they were overtaken by events. They were at the mercy of the ever-changing seascape, which could be calm one hour and so violent the next as to destroy their wooden world and cast them down to Davy Jones's locker.

Unlike the English sailor, though, they were indeed recruited by friendly persuasion. There were the positive incentives of pay, rather good food on a regular basis, comradeship, travel, service to the nation, and adventure. Going to sea meant leaving the plow behind and escaping, perhaps from an unrequited love, an abusive family, poverty, disease, or a name wanted in several states. In exchange, though, there could be harsh discipline, plenty of hard physical work, the danger of drowning, and the specter of the rest of one's life spent as an invalid. The navy was too young to promise health care, pensions, education, and early retirement.

A Day in the Life of a Sailor at Sea

Routine was the watchword. The watch defined every move. Repetitive action dominated the training program. Each man had a job, in fact several jobs, depending on the attitude of the ship at that moment. The ship's crew was divided into two groups, those who could stand watch and those who did not. The latter were known as the idlers, or specialists. The former, and the bulk of the crew, were either able seamen or ordinary seamen. An able-bodied seaman had two years of experience behind him and was qualified to steer. Next came the ordinary seaman, who aspired to promotion and looked down on landsmen who were recruited as adults, new to the ship and the sea. These three classes of sailors tended the ship and sprang to orders that sailed the ship. In short, their labor made it go. They were divided equally between the starboard and port watch. Since a ship never stops to rest at night, each watch was worked half of the twenty-four-hour day.

A glimpse of service aboard the Constitution, under the trying and dangerous conditions of heavy weather, has been preserved for us by a member of the crew.

A ludicrous affair occurred in the midst of the storm, which was my fortune to witness. Mr. Reed ordered one of the men who stood by to pull upon a certain rope. Just then a flash of lightning had dazzled his eyes, rendering it still more difficult to discern the nearest object. The sailor reaching for the rope, grasped the Lieutenant, though [by] mistake, by the nose! Discovering his error, he stuttered forth in confusion—

"I—I beg pardon, sir; it's so dark, nobody on earth can see."

"Granted my lad," said Reed, laughing, for the accident was too ludicrous to be resented.

"Here's the rope," he added, handing it himself, "Here! Here!" He shouted, as the sailor plunged at him again. "Here it is; I've got hold of it. There, pull away,"

And at it they both went.

A hundred men or more waited the Lieutenant's bidding. The gale was at it's height. All at once was hea[r]d a cry—"House top-gallant masts."

"Ay, ay, sir," echoed all around.

Amidst the pitchy darkness, the men sprang to the shrouds. Quick as thought they were at their stations, far up in the blast. But you could not see them there. Now and then, a stream of lightning darted along the sky, bringing out all the rigging and spars in bold relief against the clouds. Then might be discerned the forms of those sea-boys, as they bent to their work, fearless and firm. Helpless indeed would men be in such a moment, without the stout heart of the sailor, to risk all for duty.[16]

The watches began at 8 P.M. with the most senior officer standing the watch, which continued until midnight. Of course, the problem was that if they alternated every four hours, that is, six watches, the same watch would be on each night. To solve the dilemma they staggered the watches by splitting the watch between 4 P.M. and 8 P.M. into two two-hour watches. Therefore, five watches were of four hours and two were of two hours in duration. It simplified the meal in the evening, which suited the cook. It is confusing to those not familiar with the sea. Included is the eyewitness account of Midshipman Philip C. Johnson, a teenager:

There is always one watch on deck—half of the crew not quite half either for there are about 40 who don't keep watch—called Idleres—such as the stewards, cooks, cabin, ward room & steerage boys.

When 6 bells is reported by the orderly in the morning the Officer of the deck will say "call all hands and pipe the hammocks up Gentlemen." [The orderly is a marine or sentry stationed by the timepiece to report the time to the quartermaster every half hour so that the bell can be struck. He is watching the sand in an hourglass.] The Midshipmen will call a messenger boy and tell him the same. The messenger boy will go forward on the forecastle and tell him the same. The Boatswain then goes on to the main deck—by the main hatch—that being the most central part of the ship—and gives a long shrill whistle on his call [a silver whistle called a boatswain's call]. Immediately you will hear half a dozen similar sounds in different parts of the ship—wherever the Boatswain's mates may be. They assemble around the boatswain in a few moments when they are all there—He gives another similar whistle which is repeated by his mates then they all cry out at the top of their voices "All HANDS." He then gives another call which is repeated the same as before—and he calls out "UP ALL HAMMOCKS" which is repeated by the mates as before.

Then the Mates go about the deck crying out in their coarse, base voices—"Come Heave out—Heave out there, Break out there, Tumble out—Take your hammocks on deck." In a few minutes the men will come pouring up the hatches with their hammocks under their arms to be stowed in the nettings. In half an hour after 7 bells one can hear these calls all over the ship piping the sweepers—the pipe for sweepers is just the same tune. . . . The sweepers clear up the decks for breakfast. Another half-hour and eight bells are reported. The Officer of the deck says "Pipe to breakfast, Gentlemen." The Midshipman goes himself or sends a messenger boy—as he choses—and tells the Boatswain to pipe to breakfast. The Boatswain goes to the main hatch as before and repeats the exercise. . . . At 1 Bell (first bell of the next watch) the sweepers are piped again. At 2 Bells the hands are "turned too" the same as in the morning. The watch on deck is employed in various ways doing anything and everything. When not employed in working ship, they are making [illegible] or mending cloths or anything they wish to do.

The watch below are doing about the same thing. At 7 bells (half past eleven) the sweepers are piped—the Masters and Midshipmen are called to take the sun and work out the Latitude & Longitude.

When it is 12 o'clock (by the sun) the master says to the officer of the deck "It is 12 o'clock-Sir" Latitude (so-an-so) as reported by the reading taken. The officer of the deck verifies the reading. The Captain then replys "Make it so" (12 o'clock is always reported to the captain as well as 8 o'clock in port) The officer of the deck gives the order—"Strike eight bells—and pipe to dinner—and call the relief," which is done the same as in the morning. Grog is served at breakfast and dinner. (whiskey and water)

There is a line stretched across the deck by the main mast. A grog tub on each side of the deck is placed aloft this time—the men standing forward. One of the officers who attends to the serving of the grog gives the order "roll the grog." The drummer then beats a roll on the drum—to let the men know that all is ready for serving. The Purser's steward and asst. steward call off their names—the starboard watch on the starboard side and the port on the port side. As their names are called they step up to the tub and get their "tot of grog" (half a gill—a gill each day) and leave [a gill is about two-thirds of a modern-day cup, plus the addition of water].

At 7 bells (half past three) the decks are cleared up for supper. At 8 bells we pipe to supper. At 3 bells (half past 5) Beat to Quarters to inspect the crew—and see they have jackets for the night watches. As soon as all the divisions are reported to the 1st Lieut., recreation begins. Then "Call the watch to stand by their hammocks."

Tonight the starboard watch will have the first and morning watch—eight hours watch—which is called eight hours out. The port watch will have the Mid watch or 4 hours watch and eight hours sleep—which is called eight hours in—to-morrow the port watch will have eight hours out and the starboard eight hours in. The watch that has eight hours in, will have their hammocks. They turn into each others hammocks.

At 8 bells (8 o'clock) "the watch is set"—that is the watch that has the first watch—it is set by the boatswain and his mates—the same as all hands are called.

Watch Makeup

Within the watches, the group was divided into a starboard and port section. Each man was given a station or position on the deck or in the rigging, within his watch. Therefore, there were two men aboard trained for each position. As the watches changed, a counterpart from the oncoming watch would take each man's place. It was always the same man, and the person who was leaving helped pass on information from the previous watch. When general quarters were called for, that is, all hands regardless of watch were called to the deck for work, each station was double manned. In the case of enemy action, extra hands were needed at the guns, to repel boarders, to fetch powder, to clear battle damage, to respond to sail changes, or to evacuate and then replace wounded.

On a daily basis the transfer of duty was routine.

> When the watch came on deck, the practice was to have them "answer their station." This constant repetition meant that in the event, they knew "in their sleep," as it was, exactly what their job would be in any evolution or exercise. The first lieutenant would assign a specific evolution, in the Night Order Book. "First watch, answer to 'Furl Sails,' Middle watch answer to 'Shifting Topmasts,' Morning Watch answer to 'Reef topsails in Stays.'" The mate of the watch called out the evolution, and each man responded with his station in that circumstance—"Reeve fore top-tackle fall," "Weather reef-tackle, fore tack, and bowline," or whatever.[17]

Additionally, the sections were further subdivided into eight parts to service the deck and sails. They were the foretopmen, maintopmen, mizzentopmen, forecastle men, quarterdeck men, gunners, afterguard, and waisters. The topmen on each of the three masts were highest paid among the seamen. Their job was to set, reef, and retrieve the sails on their mast in all conditions. In battle fewer sails were flown. The higher a sailor worked on the mast, the lighter the sail. The best and fastest men went to the very top, which was certainly dangerous; but then again, they had less sail to handle.[18] Lower down, the courses and topsails could be shortened or reefed. It was a great deal of work to hang over the yard and pull up the sail, a handful at a time, to the first or second gaskets and tie it off, reducing the sail area. The men who worked the topgallants and royals would furl them completely when the command to shorten sail was shouted.

The forecastle men had the heavy task of anchor watch, in addition to operating the jeer and other heavy-lifting tackle. Weighing anchor from the bottom was a vital, difficult, and complex effort. The bower, or main anchor, was in excess of a ton, in addition to the heft of its wet eight-inch hawser. A messenger rope was wrapped around the capstan, which was a vertical windlass, and played out in a long loop to the bower anchor port. A dozen nippermen knotted the anchor hawser to the messenger line. Twelve-foot-long capstan bars, or sweeps, were stuck into the square pigeonholes that lined the top edge of the capstan drumhead. More than a hundred sailors, shoulder to shoulder on the bars, would walk the messenger around the winch. Slowly the soaked hawser would be pulled in and passed down into the hold for stowage. As the messenger reached the capstan, the nippermen would untie their grip on the hawser and walk back to the bower hole to get another grip. At last the anchor would break the surface of the water and be pulled up to the cathead, a wooden arm that stuck out from the side of the bow and held the anchor high above the water until it was needed again. The water drained from the hundreds of yards of sodden anchor hawser and seeped into the hold of the ship, where it had to be pumped out by hand. It would not be until the 1830s that metal chain was used to secure the anchor.

The brawny forecastle men also had to attend to the bowsprit and jibboom, which protruded from the beakhead at the prow. There, some of the most vital adjustments were made to the lower foremast stays and preventer stays that supported the foremast. They had to deploy the flying jib, the jib, the foretopmast staysail, the sprit topsail, and the spritsail. Found on either side of the bowsprit boom was the head, or toilet. I have never found who was responsible for cleaning the toilets, other than the sea spray generated by the bucking of the bow. I suppose it was the forecastle men—what an image.

The quarterdeck men were divided between the gunners and the afterguard. The gunners worked the lines in support of all the yards on the mainmast. They bent and braced around the main course and main topsail, along with tending the staysail if it was deployed. They picked up around the forward quarterdeck while the afterguard assisted at the mizzenmast duties and tidied the quarterdeck where the officers presided and paced. These sailors were hand picked since they worked with the officers and were expected to present a good appearance at their high-visibility watch station. As cleaners of the officers' quarters, they were often in close contact with them. Lastly, the mizzentopmen worked the sails on the mizzenmast and boom. They tended the after section of the quarterdeck, including the taffrail, which was the curved wooden top of the stern.

The most humble of the sections was the group of men who worked the waist, or the waisters. They were the least skilled and worst paid. Often the landsmen filled these jobs. They were lifters and carriers of bulk goods into and out of the hold. Theirs was the only portion of the ship that was unarmed, and it was the place where enemy boarding parties loved to leap onto the ship. These men got all the bad jobs. They emptied the garbage for the cook, pumped water from the hold, and shifted cargo and ballast to trim the ship. In company with the marines, they rotated the capstan. Detailed to do the donkey work for the warrant officers, they broke down barrels, fixed rope, cleaned everything, moved hammocks, and were the general dogsbody of the crew. The job possessed an inherent incentive to move up to ordinary seaman, where the pay was better and the air fresher.

Making Sail

With so many individuals running and climbing to their stations, order of movement was a priority. Each man had a slot to fill as the order was given to "make sail." The men proceeded from the crew deck in sequence. The first were the light top yard men, then the top yard men, who were sent aloft several minutes ahead of the deck men. If there was a strong wind, all the men climbed up on the weather side. The wind held them against the ratlines. Therefore, it took longer to mount the yards than in calm conditions. The Royal Navy surgeons reported, across the fleet, that the men who climbed the highest yards suffered from heart problems.[19] Aloft, they waited on the platforms between the sections of the masts, the tops, for the yards with the sails bent to them. On command, the deck men left the crew deck and bent the sail to the yards in preparation for others to hoist them aloft. The yards were secured to the parrels so that they could be braced around. Once on the yard, the men shunned the footropes unless the weather demanded it. They undid the gaskets and let the sails fall to flood with air. The deck men then took hold of the bracing lines and pulled in and let off according to instructions shouted from the quarterdeck. When the yards were positioned, the lines were tied off at belaying points on the rail. All extra rope was "neatened up" and the men stood by at all stations for further instructions.

Perhaps the carpenter and his assistant were the hardest workers on the ship. While not on watch, it is hard to believe that they had a minute's rest. A wooden ship, subjected to the smashing and corrosive power of the sea, must have presented a never-ending battle. Each watch reported cracked this, broken that, or splitting and sprung yards. Even though the shipyard caulkers had done a great job of providing a watertight hull, within days at sea the USS *Constitution*'s logs noted that a great deal of "shipping water" was to be pumped out.

The sailmaker on the crew repaired torn canvas, made special sails, and repaired hammocks and netting. While the colors, signal flags, and captain's pennant were made by sail-loft workers along with the sails, at sea the salt air and slapping winds tore flags to ribbons and shredded colors. The sailmaker on board was capable of remaking the colors. He was also known to make the national colors of England, France, and Spain. It was common practice to go in under false colors. When entering an enemy port, passing under substantial coastal artillery secure deep inside stone fortifications, only a fool would fly his true colors. Once the attack began, the Stars and Stripes would snap open at the head of the mast for all to see. The way out, therefore, was often most unfriendly. The sailmaker was known to supplement his income by sewing up officers' uniforms and making repairs to clothing just before reaching port. He made the sea anchor in a storm.

The cooper, or barrel maker, was a busy man. It seemed that everything came in a barrel of one size or another. When the cook finished with a cask, the cooper took it apart, providing the stays as kindling for the cooking fire. He could also stow them away for the day when they were filled again at a replenishment port. He would often double as a blacksmith for ironwork. The cooper as smith was hampered in the range of work he could do since there was no safe place to conduct a fire hot enough to soften metal. Wooden ships and hot fires don't mix. In the French navy they operated "shot furnaces" to heat cannonballs before firing them at enemy ships. The purpose, of course, was to set the enemy on fire or at least distract the crew long enough to board and take the ship. This proved costly, however, since the operation often got out of control and set the Frenchmen on fire instead. It was not popular with the gun crews either. Handling red-hot 24-pound cannonballs and shoving them down the bore was a demanding operation on the rolling deck of a warship. Additionally, there was a danger that the intense heat would set off the charge prematurely.

On the way home to Boston, the figurehead of Hercules, carved at Skillens Wharf, was looking the worse for wear and would have to be spruced up before USS *Constitution* carried the colors to sea again.

CHAPTER THREE

~

The Elements of Sea Power

The Flag covers the Goods.

—Captain Alfred T. Mahan, U.S. Navy, 1889

To appreciate the contribution of the USS *Constitution*, one must first know what those who paid to have her commissioned expected of her, her crew, and her leaders. Sea power does not come easily or cheap. There are some nations that will never become powerful, earth-swaying countries. Captain Alfred T. Mahan, U.S. Navy, completed the first serious study of sea power in modern times. He lists six conditions that contribute significantly to a state becoming an influential player in world commerce. They are geographical position, physical conformation, extent of territory, number of population, character of the people, and character of the government.[1]

Captain Mahan was an instructor in naval warfare at the United States Naval War College. Born in 1840, he produced his great work, *The Influence of Sea Power upon History, 1660–1783*, in 1890. He examines numerous battles chronicled in the period to illustrate his theory. Ocasionally he reaches back into ancient times or forward into the 1800s to support his ideas. His writing is compelling and his arguments sound. Published at the height of the Industrial Revolution, his vision of what was to come was seized upon by leaders around the world.

Perhaps the first to grasp the importance of Mahan's work was Teddy Roosevelt. He was attuned to things nautical from his younger days as a political appointee to the Navy Department. Later, as president, he built the Great White

Fleet and sent it around the world. As the ships plied the seven seas, the good-will voyage was a demonstration to the Old World that the United States of America, isolated in North America, was to be reckoned with around the globe. Even though the fleet did not call at German ports, Teddy made sure that Kaiser Wilhelm knew that he was a player. The kaiser knew Mahan's volume cover to cover. His English grandmother, Queen Victoria, claimed to "rule the waves." Envious of the Royal Navy, Wilhelm shoved Germany into a naval arms race. He was determined to match and defeat if the chance came his way, and his shipyards in the north began turning out superior men-of-war on the drawing boards. Meeting his cousin, Czar Nicholas of Russia, on the Baltic, aboard re-spective yachts, he entertained. At the meeting, which did not include any gov-ernment advisers, he added new nautical titles to their already thoroughly en-crusted crowns. Like schoolboys, they called themselves the Admiral of the East and Admiral of the West, dividing the oceans between them. In a way, of course, he was correct; if he and Nikki could pull it off, two such dominant great fleets could take over the world, for control of the trade routes was a very at-tractive prize.

Britain had already learned the importance of sea power, having vanquished several of the most renowned national armadas, beginning in the 1600s, by the time of the printing of Mahan's great work. England's insight into the wealth potential of the maritime industry had produced the boast, "The sun never sets on the British Empire." England knew that it all was hinged on a strong, skilled, and ubiquitous fleet of men-of-war that protected an efficient merchant marine. They had confirmed over three centuries that a mix of armed platforms, some slow yet impregnable, and others light and quick, allowed for tailoring to fit the tasks called for in faraway places with strange-sounding names. Therefore, it is no surprise that the principles laid out by the American captain were, in a way, easily illustrated within the story of Englishmen and their ships.

The Application of Mahan's Principles

Geographical Position and Physical Conformation

A continuous seacoast that does not restrict or canalize the movement and con-solidation of naval elements is of great advantage. While France has a long sea-coast, it pivots on the Strait of Gibraltar, which is controlled by France's age-old rival, England. Taken by the Royal Navy from Spain in 1704, the garrison has remained a thorn in the side of other countries' maritime activity in the Mediterranean Sea. Simply because they are there, the Royal Navy station and land-based weapons systems must be dealt with in war and peace. It gives the English a control envied around the world. If it were for sale, customers would be lined up, national treasuries poised. Such choke points have enormous value.

In the Pacific, the long coastline of China would lead to the assumption that she would dominate the far Pacific. American admiral George Dewey defeated the Spanish in Manila Bay during the Spanish-American War and established a naval station at the keystone of the Pacific Rim. When the Spanish-American War is looked at from the perspective of Mahan, it becomes clear how significant that "lovely little war" would become to America during its expansion abroad in the twentieth century. But by seizing the Philippine Islands, half a world away, the New World democracy appeared to overreach itself as it took its first baby steps from isolationism to world power. Those foreign entanglements, which would ring in the newsprint a few years later, had a hollow sound in light of the gains in the Spanish-American War. The United States was already entangled in foreign lands.

Manila Bay was not just a military exercise to pick off strategic ground on the edge of a far-off ocean. It was not just a grab to be exhausted in the time of war. Its primary purpose was to support and secure unrestricted trade. The navy was there to protect the maritime industry. Ships, American and those of foreign countries, that work in conjunction with requirements of the home market are the justification for the navy.

Within the confines of a nation that sports a seacoast, there is a specific requirement that must be met if there is going to be a bid for sea power. A variety of natural seaports that are fed by commercial rivers are paramount. The Philippine Islands have untold miles of seacoast but are not blessed with numerous natural deep estuaries fed by rivers that host large consuming populations or viable industries. They do contain great forests, but it is difficult to export the timber. The Philippines would not fit Mahan's 1890s model of a potential sea power.

While France had a half-dozen deep-water ports, England had sixty. During the days of sail, the few French channel ports could be easily blocked. When the wind was from the east, the English could maintain ships on station, easily obstructing the exit. When the winds shifted fresh from the west, the French could not get out since the flow was in their face, and the Royal Navy could take refuge in nearby Plymouth and Portsmouth, hastened by a following wind. The limitation imposed by the meager number of channel ports, combined with the British naval station at Gibraltar, limited France's naval prominence.

The United States' eastern and Gulf coasts are blessed with some of the best-protected harbors in the world. Boston, New York, Philadelphia, and ports around the Chesapeake Bay, to say nothing of the Carolinas, Alabama, and Louisiana, are made to order, even in the days of sail. Not only did that promote safe passage for traders and ease of movement of large quantities of goods to the interior, but it also established a shipbuilding industry and a population to build, service, and sail ships. In a way, the maritime industry consumes much of its own cargo. Like the "Red Ball Express," the system of truck convoys that replenished Patton's dash across France, it consumed half of what it delivered. Much of the merchant fleet haulage was occupied in procuring parts and supplies for ships.

Those nations that supplied or consumed timber, hemp, and flax for canvas were at the top of the list of nations who needed to maintain sea power. In evaluating "geographic position," more than the homeland must be considered. Foreign positions incorporated into the English, French, and Spanish empires were important. The acquisition of committed supporting outside lands to enhance a powerful country became essential in the expansion of trade.

Ships didn't operate in a vacuum. They required intensive tending. Made of ever-deteriorating wood, rotting rope, and torn canvas, they were not permanent structures like stone buildings. Their very movement worked against them. The wind was ever threatening to break a vessel above the deck, while the water was always seeking flaws and seeping in or bursting over. The health of the ship was constantly monitored and maintained by the crew. However skilled and resourceful, shortly they would be exhausted by the sheer size of the task and needed to seek support. The mere nature of sailing put the home port and dockyard out of reach much of the time. Bases around the world had to be established in numbers that matched the military and civil fleets. Without foreign stations equipped and funded, only home coastal fleets could thrive. It therefore is not surprising that Great Britain established the largest number of foreign naval stations. Bermuda and Halifax stations would greatly hinder American naval operations at the start of the War of 1812 and close down America's blue-water navy by the end. In a way, England had a leg up to begin with by her very position in the Atlantic right from the start of the conflict.

England is protected by the English Channel, whose very name tells of its ownership from the earliest times. By far, the English side was a haven in the days of sail and provided easily accessed home ports in the event of ever-deteriorating weather. Numerous bays and protected estuaries provided a boon the French did not boast. The British Isles sit like a cork at the entrance to the Baltic and North seas. Additionally, Great Britain anchors the European end of the Gulf Stream. It sucks up the warmer temperatures and trade winds from the New World. The Vikings found it to be a strategic rock during their early conquests. A few centuries later, it acted as a watchtower obstructing the Dutch. The home fleet was well served from its Scappa Flow and east-coast bases when bottling up the German navy in two world wars. During the Cold War, the geography of the British Isles prevented the USSR's active navy from having free passage into the Atlantic. Furthermore, England is only a hop, skip, and jump from the Atlantic coast of Portugal and Spain, as well as that of Africa and the Canary Islands. No other nation has such a natural sea link at its fingertips. Yet she exhausted her oak forests by the time of the Napoleonic Wars and required connections to the Nordic and Canadian forests to maintain the fleets. This dependence on the empire and friendly trading partners made England vulnerable, and the country required a large navy to protect its world interests. Napoleon recognized England's need of hemp and flax that must be imported and sent privateers to disrupt the flow to the nation of "shopkeepers." In an attempt to deny England access to the Baltic raw materials, he risked everything in the 1812 attack on Russia.

England realized the danger of Napoleon's "Continental System," designed to deny markets and commodities. It also forced Britain to provide finance to buoy up the governments of Napoleon's enemies. Great Britain had become so wealthy from trade with her own colonies and friendly countries that she financed the wars against French forces by the Austrians, Prussians, Spanish, Portuguese, Dutch, and Russians. It was the maritime efforts backed by the colonies and the Royal Navy that made it all possible. It was sea power that made her a superpower.

It should not be surprising that England wanted to normalize relations with the new United States as soon as possible after the Treaty of Paris in 1783 that ended the colonial time. While Canada had remained loyal, she did not possess a climate that allowed year-round commerce. The new United States was a prime trading partner. It was an alternative source of timber, which rode so easily on northerly trade winds of the Gulf Stream.

Even though the world changed after the days of sail, the British Isles still occupy a geographic position of importance in modern times. During World War II, and later during the lingering Cold War, she was described as a moored Allied aircraft carrier. Of reduced circumstances after the loss of her empire, she menaced the USSR, frozen in place to the far north.

Extent of Territory: The Confederate States of America and Sea Power

The extent of territory is the third principle that contributes to the sea power of a nation. Captain Mahan cites the Confederate States of America during the Civil War, which was very much a part of his recent experience. He points out that even though the breakaway states had an enormous coastline, they were effectively blockaded by the Union navy, which, while good, should not have been able to bottle up the Confederacy. Even though there was a considerable landmass and population, it was not oriented toward the sea. Defending its interior border became more important than breaking out into the Atlantic in order to gain support from Europe. While the need for overseas markets for its agrarian products was essential, the will to produce an effective maritime and navy presence was never the priority it had to be. The attention of the government was consumed by the pressure from the army of the North. If the South was to sustain itself, it required an alternative source of income to the one that was lost with the closure of markets in the North. Commercial shipping and outside intervention was its only hope to save the land. Even though its geographic size was large, the new Confederacy could not support both a land and naval war. The money necessary to fulfill the naval plans written the year before the conflict was used for the army and railroad construction. The longer the war lasted without outside trade, the more moribund the Confederacy became.

The population was not made up of sailors to the same extent as that of the traditional New England states, where the sea is a family affair. Although it is a highly dangerous occupation, it is simply what they do and can be expected to do well. The men of the Northern states, most of which bordered the sea or had great inlets that led to the sea, were mariners. The Southern states indeed had a fishing industry, but it was not nearly the same size. The deep-water merchantmen were primarily from the North, often servicing Southern and Gulf ports. While a long coastline can be a blessing, it can also be a vulnerability unless it is backed by a population that embraces going to sea. Additionally, the South failed to realize the importance of the inland waterways. In particular, it neglected the Mississippi, which should have been a source of great strength and turned into another front, according to Mahan. A highway and natural barrier could have nourished the Southern farmers but became internal lines for the North. For much of its great length, the Mississippi River was secured on both banks by the Confederacy. It was defended valiantly but not well, and its loss was the undoing of the Confederacy's western frontier. Like a dagger, once breached by the North, it pointed at the heart of the Southern states.

Modern China

In the twentieth century, China provides some similarity. Although it developed a great seagoing enterprise in the fifteenth century, it turned its back on long international voyages, even though its great mercantile fleets were unmatched for the next three hundred years. A change of emperors reduced the giant culture to landlubbers who opened China's ports to European adventurers. They set up shop and made as much on the shipping costs as they did on the sale of exotic Chinese goods. Even though China had an enormous population and an extent of land to match, there was no seafaring tradition. After World War II, China could have reversed the trend and built a navy and fleets of ships under the centrally controlled government of the Chinese Communists. Their leader preferred isolationism, perhaps fearing that he could not control a portion of his subjects who moved freely among capitalist countries. The Chinese maritime and naval industry has never been proportional to China's size or capability. The country relies instead on a very large army for defense, which dominates military thinking. The American Seventh Fleet in essence has blockaded the vast Chinese coast to prevent it from invading Taiwan. The little island Formosa, a haven for the defeated nationalists after the Chinese Civil War of the late 1940s, should have been taken by the Chinese Communist government troops, but they simply could not get there. No real navy and a lack of seagoing transport has limited what could have been a superpower. Even with a billion people, an extensive coastline, natural ports, and a strategic position, the will of the government has denied China sea power and a position of supremacy in the world. Today she produces a tremendous amount of commercial goods, which are in demand throughout the world. Yet others carry the goods, making a fortune that could be China's if she were a seafaring people.

Sailors within the Population

Mahan considered the ratio of traditional seamen to the size of the population as key to sea power. In the days of sail, the vessels were very labor intensive. They demanded a considerable crew who worked twelve hours a day, every day of the voyage. Skilled sailors were the product of an apprentice program that took years to complete. Living conditions were not just communal but also cramped, highly intense, and lonely. The discipline was extreme, far beyond that on land. Being confined for months to years with four hundred men on a ship that was generally 150 feet long was not the most desirable way to make a living. Yet the men of some countries thrived in such a profession. Here Mahan considers France after the Revolution, when it went to war with the English. Even though the population of France was much larger than that of Great Britain, proportionally there was no contest when it came to manning a fighting fleet. Frenchmen were landsmen for the most part. Drawn to farms and market towns, they were content working within the vast breadbasket of central Europe where life was good and stable.

At war, the navy ship consumed far more labor than a merchantman. Crews were four times larger. More ships were required. Ship losses and crew deaths demanded replacement. The navy, like the army, was seriously expanded during conflicts. It was faster and simpler to train a soldier in 1800 than a sailor. Captain Mahan speaks of reserve, or the depth of skilled men, which could be found in the interior of the British Isles, where the economy pointed to the sea. The canal system ran like veins, touching every extremity. Rather than leading to the heartland, the canals ended at the sixty ports that dotted the coast every few miles. Crowded to the point of gridlock at inland market centers and seaports, they provided the large coastal fleet with a never-ending supply of cargoes. Not empty on the return trip, they carried finished goods from the ports inland to the markets, feeding the appetites of landsmen a hundred miles inland. The rural road system was incapable of carrying heavy traffic, and horsepower would never replace canal boats for cheap transport. The horse teams along the towpaths could deliver many tons on a barge, but they could not hope to pull this much on rutted roads. The canals thrived in the wet climate of England, while the roads melted. This reserve of watermen added to the potential sailors available in wartime to man not only men-of-war but also the merchant fleet that carried supplies, horses, and men to battlefields throughout the empire. While France could build the finest ships of the day, it could not find the number of skilled sailors necessary to crew them.

A ship requires more than just sail handlers and deckhands. Learned men, in considerable numbers, schooled in navigation and ship handling, leaders who had honed their skill at sea over many years, were in supply in England. The Royal Navy had a policy of laying off such officers when peacetime reduced the fighting and support fleet. They were retained on "half pay," which, though not a substantial amount of money, could sustain a bachelor who required little more than a rented room and a few coins for food and drink. They worked at tutoring positions, introducing older male children to sea lore and preparing them to become midshipmen or cabin boys. Middle-class families often sent sons to sea in such capacities, which were considered an apprenticeship to a career in the navy or merchant marine. Out-of-work officers could find jobs in sea-related firms during the downtime to make ends meet until they could "get a ship." There was a considerable number of these men scattered about, many from well-to-do or landed families. The profession was considered most honorable and given great respect. Officers wore their naval titles for life and were always referred to by rank, although years may have passed since they were on active service. When the time came, when they were needed, they were there. It was a tradition among professional officers to maintain their skill when it was out of fashion; they knew that it would be required once again in those troubled times. Even Admiral Lord Horatio Nelson was put on half pay during his career. It was a time of patronage, and whom you knew was as important as what you knew about sailing a ship. That deep pool of potential officers was not to be found in France. In fact, since the French navy's officer corps was composed almost entirely of aristocrats, it found itself out of favor during the Revolution. As the new republic took shape, it cleansed itself of the nobility who commanded the ships of the line. While there was once a considerable reserve of officers eager to man the fleet, the government in Paris dismissed them. When Napoleon and his government attempted to reestablish the fleet, it turned out badly.

The idlers, though maligned by the sailors, were essential. Maintenance was the watchword. Carpenters, riggers, medics, coopers, even cooks who could excel at sea were in terrific demand. Ships at sea were battered by weather, and although wood floats, ships with holes in them do not. While a carpenter is a carpenter, a ship requires added skill. Most ships' carpenters came from dockyards, where they learned their trade making hulls watertight. The dockyards were a big part of the reserve Captain Mahan counted on in his analysis of sea power. Not only must dockyards be operational, but they must also be agile enough to switch to meet demands. While building was primary, most yards were required to divide their time between constructing and repairing the naval fleet. Men-of-war often required refitting once or twice a year. Shipbuilding and maintenance was a primary industry along the estuaries of England, Scotland, and Ireland. Timber, in abundance in 1660 when England took to the oceans, was now carefully allocated according to Admiralty rules.

Not only did ships require constant attention, but the crews did as well. While it is said that the days of sail were known as days of wooden ships and iron men, it was a gross overstatement. The lifestyle was so hard that desertion was a constant problem. The primary purpose of the Royal Marines afloat was to maintain discipline and prevent sailors from leaving the ships. Even a good and loyal crewman needs to be replaced now and then. Injury by accident or act of war demanded a program to supply men just as it did to replenish stores. Surprisingly, the Royal Navy found a ready-made reserve of sailors in the most astonishing profession. One of the largest industries in the country was mining. Miners were men used to danger and hard work, and they were strong, with tenacious spirits, which made them ideal for naval service. It must have been culture shock for men who spent generations in the dark on their hands and knees to be thrust into the great outdoors. Of course, they were used to being wet in those cold, dark, damp, dripping pits. Perhaps it was not such a chore to get men to leave that life for the open ocean. However, the traditional family life of the mining community was strong. The lonely plight of a sailor may not have been their mug of tea.

A country's capability for raising a reserve over time is the true test of sea power. Not only must it have a pool of population to fight, build, and devote itself to the effort, but it also must have control over a merchant fleet where the reserves lie. In the time of war, the Royal Navy had the authority to commandeer crewmen, who were impressed into service for the duration of war. In the long protracted wars that filled the 1700s and early 1800s, a population that had sufficient depth to yield armed forces year after year could sustain power and influence. The combined naval fleets of Spain and France were unable to recover their maritime might after the single defeat at Trafalgar. Earlier, the disaster suffered by the Spanish Armada in the English Channel had so crippled Spain's navy in a single battle that the navy never recovered. The catastrophic loss drained away the country's sea power. She was no longer able to defend the merchant fleet that brought the wealth of the New World to the Old, and her treasure ships were looted by the British.

Character of the People or Natural Charter
Mahan is quite outspoken when it comes to the national will concerning a maritime industry and its protection. He believed that "if sea power be really based

upon a peaceful and extensive commerce, aptitude for commercial pursuits must be a distinguishing feature of the nations that have at one time or another been great upon the sea. . . . All men seek gain, and more or less love money, but the way in which gain is sought will have a marked effect upon commercial fortunes and the history of the people inhabiting the country."[2]

His interest in "commercial" pursuits brings up a peculiar illustration in history. There is more to a powerful nation than great coffers of gold and silver. Spain and Portugal invested in the New World and in the ships that brought them wealth. They were perhaps the first modern long-distance trading nations to strike it rich on a huge scale. They had nearly free rein for the first hundred years after the discovery of Central and South America and plundered the precious metal mines. There was no effort to change Mexico, Brazil, or any other state into a modern European society. The two outrageously rich kingdoms spent the money rather than investing it in their own homelands. They could have used the wealth to become traders, merchants, manufacturers, and investors while building an infrastructure financed by the wealth brought by the conquistadores. There was no will to step out of the agrarian role and change the culture. Rather, they paid England and Holland, both of whom have been called "nations of shopkeepers," to transport and supply them with desirable finished goods. Not interested in building merchant ships capable of carrying more than coin and bars of gold, they had to rely on the large Dutch cargo carriers to fetch things to adorn their villas. In the end, the mines ran out and the once-humming economies on the Iberian Peninsula declined back into isolated backwaters. Spain even gave up Gibraltar to Englishman Sir George Rooke, who took it in 1704 just because he could. It may be the most strategic bit of land on any coastline.

The opposite seems to be true of Holland in Mahan's day. Devoid of a large amount of arable land, confined in population, and possessing scant natural resources other than fish and a great deal of water, the Netherlands should not have strolled onto the world stage and remained there even to today. Captain Mahan recognized that the national character of the Netherlands brought her wealth, power, and influence far beyond her due. Her willingness to risk life and limb in creaky wooden trading vessels and deliver on demand made her popular and profitable. The Dutch people seem to have a wanderlust matched by no other. Willing to risk what little they had, Dutch merchants could be found in numbers from the Spice Islands of the South Pacific to the great harbor of New York, which they settled as New Amsterdam. Their merchantmen were well armed and ready to defend themselves. The Dutch were perhaps the most nautical people, man per man, in the West; their sailors could be found as ships' officers in fleets of many countries, and their skilled seamen were willing to tackle everything from Arctic seas to whaling. They were known to be parsimonious; no fleet of traders got more out of less and sold it at a better profit than the

Dutch. They established trading companies, reinvesting the wealth in more and bigger ships and establishing far-flung possessions and colonies. It was all linked together by sea power. It could be said that the wealth of the nation was afloat—highly liquid—at all times. Their insurance exchange netted as much profit as did their fishing industry.

Here Mahan chooses to bash the French for timidity and caution. He tells of a conversation with a Frenchman concerning the Panama Canal, which was a French venture of the time. The Frenchman said, "I have two shares in it. In France we don't do as you do, where a few people take a great deal of shares each. With us a large number of people take one share or a few. When these were in the market my wife said to me, 'You take two shares, one for you and one for me.'"[3] Mahan believed that venture on a small scale as a national characteristic was a definite impediment. The unwillingness of a people to take risk would hinder economic development and slow maritime investment.

A country's attitude toward money is important. Within some cultures, money and its pursuit are not supported. The people respected wealth in Holland. Those who could make it were championed. Holland was a freewheeling state, not bound by stifling religion; those with ideas that spun money were praised and emulated. One could say that the Dutch worshipped wealth wherever they could find it. To them, the free floating of capital for investment and enterprise would provide employment. They boasted a very high standard of living envied by larger and more naturally endowed nations. An example of the Dutchmen's enterprise comes from the copying of Chinese tableware. Most households could not afford fine glazed plates for the dinner table and used wood or metal. Only the rich owned china. Made in the same popular blue and white with Chinese motifs, delftware looked like the genuine article but was marketed at a fraction of the price. Soon all of Europe could afford a dinner set of pretty, functional "china."

The willingness of the people to colonize distant and dangerous lands was essential to any country that wished to extend her sea links. Not only must products be procured for shipment to market in the homeland, but friendly replenishment stations also must function in support of the fleet. If the scheme were to survive, families must be willing to go abroad and establish a community of national charter; they must "keep the faith," or, in other, more modern terms, "not go native." There was a great deal of effort, risk of life, and money invested in colonial operations. There must be Western efficiency built in if the home investors were to see continued profits. In hostile locations the cost of maintaining a defense force could bankrupt the operation. In America this became a problem that led to the Revolution. The cost of the British Army in the colonies to maintain order, fighting off the French and Indians, was so high that the mother country was losing money. As a fix, Parliament began to levy taxes. This taxation without representation was a prime cause of the loss of the colony.

Shortly after the Treaty of Paris was signed in 1783, England and the new United States rushed back to full and friendly maritime operations for their mutual benefit. Since the people of the new country were for the most part English and Dutch, the colonists' inbred culture saved the enterprise after the exhausting conflict. They went back to business as usual.

When it came to colonizers, though, the English and French were the large leaders as they followed the Dutch into the deep Pacific. Setting up communities meant to last with more than just a few trading stations, the English went a step further. Australia began as a penal colony, but the people sent there, deemed "not fit to live in the homeland," proved themselves through their character to be a great loss to Great Britain. Their unrecognized talent and drive could have been of great benefit if they had been allowed to remain in the British Isles. Yet, surprisingly, they remained loyal, promoting unrestricted trade with those who had expelled them. If one were writing fiction telling of a penal colony that within a few generations would come to the defense of the motherland in a great European war and shed its blood more than generously on the beaches of Gallipoli and in the trenches of France, the plot would be dismissed by the editor as preposterous. Yet the British Islanders did not forget their roots and fought side by side with England once again during World War II. Loyalty was essential to successful colonization.

Examined more closely, on an individual basis, the case could be made for the people of the British Isles that it is in the DNA. The building blocks that shape the national charter are stacked up in a very impressive order. Great Britain could lay claim to being a melting pot of cultures before that moniker was put on the United States. Early the Picts, Gauls, and Romans intermixed with ancient Britons. They were followed by Vikings, Saxons, Angles, and Normans. All of these influences shared one trait: they were adventurers who used the sea to extend their culture. As the years passed, Hudson, Raleigh, Drake, Cooke, and Nelson led thousands of Englishmen abroad in search of wealth, power, conquest, and investment. Collectively, this willingness to reach out must sustain itself over long periods when the going gets sticky. It takes generations to become a powerful nation, and the path is never smooth. Many setbacks must be weathered and many a life lost. The resolve by the national character to continue on in spite of overwhelming odds is difficult to find. When the Germans were pounding on the door, could it be said that "this was their finest hour"?

Character of the Government

An individual, group, company, or organization cannot hope to invest its labor and capital in an enterprise unless the government is in accord. It should follow that an energetic people is reflected in the government and its institutions. In the mid-1600s, the government in Holland, though a monarchy, was known for its free thinking, which was not constrained by the noble class, known to be protective and cautious when it came to new and risky investment. A simple example of government support of the maritime industry occurred in England, not under a king but during the government of Oliver Cromwell, lord protector of England from 1653 to 1658. Captain Mahan discusses the Navigation Act, which required that "all imports to England or her colonies must be conveyed exclusively in vessels belonging to England or her colonies."[4] That kind of government support, backed with a navy to enforce it, was crucial to the development of a national merchant marine.

In 1661, under Louis XIV, Minister Colbert defined a program of government participation in the French maritime industry. The cooperation between the merchant trader, the navy, and the colonies, supported by the attentive intervention of the central government, became institutionalized.[5] Backed by government guarantees established by the ministry, trading companies were formed and stock was sold publicly. Customs regulations were changed to favor the importer/exporter. Bonding and warehousing in French ports was established similar to the Dutch system. Following the British model, France and her colonies were closed to foreign shipping. Colbert's own words best describe his intent:

> To organize producers and merchants as a powerful army, subject to an active and intelligent guidance, so as to secure an industrial victory for France by order and unity of efforts, and to obtain the best products by imposing on all workmen the processes recognized as best by competent men. . . . To organize seamen and distant commerce in large bodies like the manufacturers and internal commerce, and to give as a support to the commercial power of France a navy established on a firm basis and of dimensions hitherto unknown.[6]

These militant words set the stage for wars of commerce, which, based on sea power, picked up steam in the 1660s and on for two hundred years. These wars were unlike wars during the Middle Ages, which were set in place by rulers intent on stretching their personal holdings, or wars concerned about men's souls; there was indeed a "sea change" occurring that would take in the entire world. In the twenty years after Colbert began his program, the French navy increased four times over in power and size. Louis was an absolute ruler. Colbert lost influence as the long reign, which lasted fifty-five years, wearied. The Sun King lost interest and no longer shone on the program. The navy was left intact but was no longer the darling of the court and decayed, as did the other elements contained in the sea power of France. England, allied with Holland, helped the process along, to her great benefit. A despotic head of state can make or break sea power with the speed of lightning. The government attitude did not change when Louis left the earth, so that by 1756 there were only forty-five men-of-war able to put to sea. The state-backed system, which linked colony, merchant, and navy—superior to England's in size and responsiveness—efficiently together, evaporated through neglect.

In 1760 the people of France demanded that the government restore the maritime industry and championed the navy. A golden age began, and the government was dragged along behind the people. But the French Revolution did not favor the navy since it was top-heavy with nobles, and it became a prime target for the various governments that marched from 1789 through the Napoleonic age.

In addition to the obvious warship-building program and naval crew recruitment/training, government must establish a system of reliable stabilized foreign stations that welcome both merchant and naval vessels. While colonies were preferred, they were not always practicable or possible. Procuring long-term special arrangements within other states that allow entry of both merchant and naval vessels can easily be seen as an attempt to meddle with their sovereignty. It can also upset the balance of power in an area, which can lead to war. In more modern times, the Cuban Missile Crisis of 1962 did not happen overnight. The United States had been threatened by the presence of Soviet soldiers and sailors (military advisers) in Havana for years. The stationing and replenishment of Soviet navy vessels ninety miles off the Florida coast called for watchfulness. The Soviet decision to increase the threat by introducing long-range offensive nuclear missiles made the positioning of hostile troops on that station untenable. Indeed, it nearly led to the most potentially catastrophic war in history. Inexplicably, the United States has continued to operate a considerable naval station at Guantánamo Bay, Cuba, throughout the reign of the Communist government. In spite of the crisis, the presence of American marines and sailors on the navy base was never threatened, and today the arrangement continues unabated. It is certainly the most bizarre stationing agreement in naval history.

Stationing arrangements come in all varieties. In the United States, they are a matter for the State Department on behalf of the Department of Commerce, in conjunction with the navy. Delicate in nature, they can lead to new alliances while bolstering old ones. Qatar, set on the coast of the Persian Gulf, was established during the Cold War and was key to operations in the Indian Ocean. It was a lonely outpost for many years for the crew of the American ship *LaSalle*, which was tied to the dock most of the year. When the Gulf War erupted unexpectedly, the outpost took on a significance never before envisioned. Within ten years, it became invaluable to the expansion that accommodated the headquarters for the joint American force conducting the war against Iraq. Though these events were never imagined by the men who so wisely established it, the American presence there was of great strategic value to naval operations.

Stationing arrangements also strengthen old alliances that go on year after year. American naval bases in Wales and Scotland were vital in the nuclear age after World War II. Providing support for surface and submarine vessels and platforms for surveillance of Soviet ship movements was key during the Cold War. The American naval headquarters in the heart of London, which began in 1942, has been continuously in use ever since. Though it was expected to close at the end of the Cold War for lack of purpose, it hums on from crisis to crisis as if nothing had changed in the last sixty years. The original rent was a dollar a year, yet the rental of the ground-floor shop and tourist office that faced the street provided a moneymaker for the Defense Department. Terrorism, though, boarded up the enterprises in recent years and replaced them with concrete barriers and walking armed bobbies. Without such stations, the constant worldwide fleet operations would be in jeopardy. Replenishment would have to be conducted at sea, which was difficult to predict and undependable at best in the days of sail. But even today, with modern nuclear-powered ships, the need for naval stations and friendly ports for sea power is still of paramount importance to national goals. Without stations, major repairs can be accomplished only in home ports. Such constraints severely limit all merchant and naval operations, diminishing sea power.

Sea Power in Defense

The remaining element of sea power that the government is responsible for is the degree of defense it will provide the merchant fleet, colony, and home ports. It is charged with identifying the enemy naval threat and attacking it before it can interdict civilian interests. At the time of the French Revolution, England demonstrated an active defense by blocking English Channel ports in France. By preventing the French warships from venturing out of channel estuaries, England protected its own merchant ships and other neutral traffic. Therefore, France was not threatened with invasion or destruction of any land facilities but was merely restricted from operations. Of course, this did provoke the French to take extraordinary measures to exercise sovereignty over their own territory. Due to the configuration of the French channel ports, England found blocking the ports to be a cost-effective way of defending its commercial interest when threatened by its neighbor during time of war.

Security can be purely defensive as well. The government can choose to establish land forts and mine navigable approaches. It can patrol the entrances to harbors and escort merchant fleets as they go about their business. Here the nations wait to be attacked and then swing into an offensive mode until the threat is destroyed. This defensive approach was best illustrated by the yellow flag of the American Revolutionary War, which showed the American rattlesnake in a defensive posture coiled to strike and the words, "Don't Tread On Me."

The Nation Must Be Committed

Lastly, the government cannot be lukewarm over sea power. It must show a long-term commitment. There is great expense involved in the enterprise. After Louis XIV lost interest in the project, the wealth spent on colonies, ships, and the navy withered away. The small amount spent on such a complex operation could not sustain it and, indeed, would reduce the efficiency of scale to a point where the money was simply wasted, for the return might be nonexistent. If not supported at a high level, the profit margin plunged and that portion of the economy ceased to exist. Sea power was a national commitment that took a large percentage of the national wealth and was labor intensive. Ships of the days of sail were the single most expensive system. Unlike buildings, they had a short life, even though they were constantly being refurbished. Much of the cost of sea power was spent by the public purse. In turn, the profits found their way back to the government in many forms connected with trade and taxes, and the system paid for itself. A nation-state that was constantly reevaluating the decisions as to whether such support was to be continued was bound to be diminished.

Those six principles did not change because the nature of man did not change, according to Captain Mahan. Mahan laid out a strategy for sea operations that parallels the essential study for land operations, General Carl von Clausewitz's *On War*.

The United States of America and Sea Power in 1812

The "geographic position and physical conformation" of the United States in 1812 included the same eastern seaboard as when it was a colony of Great Britain, forty years before. The western expansion had swelled the states from thirteen original colonies to twenty-one states, but the national colors still reflected a count of fifteen stars and fifteen stripes. Congress had not settled on a format that would honor the thirteen original colonies in stripes and admit each new state with an added star. A casual glance at the map in 1800 would lead to the conclusion that the New World nation was going to be dependent on commerce with her former ruler, Europe, the Mediterranean rim, and the slave states of West Africa. The United States had become a major player in the maritime trading circle. Slave ships brought their human cargo from Africa for the plantation industry of the South and returned with cotton, timber, and finished goods to Europe. The isolationists who attempted to dominate American political life for the next two hundred years had not made themselves known prior to the Industrial Revolution. The survival of the experiment in democracy hinged on one thing, in light of the geographic position, and that was sea trade.

The physical conformation of the newly formed United States, now entering the world stage on its own, would indicate that it was going to depend on sea power for its well-being. It sported a coastline dotted with some of the most favorable natural deep-water harbors in the world. Combined with a long coastline favored by the trade winds of the Caribbean, this made the new nation a natural for seafaring activities. The climate, too, encouraged waterborne industry. Astride the Temperate Zone, the fertile land provided a long growing season, which blossomed with a bumper harvest every few years. As the country expanded inevitably westward, it became clear that it would surpass Europe in the production of foodstuffs and fibers. Blessed by navigable river services, industry flourished. Where needed, a few canals to bring the harvest to port were possible. The natural cover provided by the Chesapeake Bay, combined with the protection of the Outer Banks along the Carolinas, enlarged the investment in shipping. Coastal maritime industry was made easy and flourished, linking communities and enhancing trade.

The opportunity to move bulky and heavy goods in large quantities along the Atlantic coastal highways was seized on, too, as a water road to fortune. The internal road network was surprisingly advanced for its time, mostly as a result of the Revolutionary War. The numerous formations followed by endless supply trains allowed Washington's army to move. Soldiers turned civilians were acquainted with parts of the country that otherwise they would not have seen. It furthered the wanderlust so necessary to an expanding and emerging nation. It should not be surprising that the citizens of the Revolution were more widely traveled and knew of the opportunities afforded across the country. War not only united the new nation, but it also broadened the culture. A man born and raised in the North could have fought at Yorktown, Virginia. He may have walked the whole way and returned by coastal schooner. The road network supplemented the rivers, providing access to the port cities, which were growing in response to the commercial demands of the country's former ruler, Great Britain.

The infamous Benedict Arnold had been apprenticed to a relative in Connecticut as an apothecary. Later he sailed to the Caribbean in his own vessels, buying the makings for medicine. By 1775 he was an experienced sea captain. After his service in Canada; Lake Champlain; Rome, New York; and Saratoga, he applied to the Continental Congress for a commission in the navy. Like many, he was more at home at sea than on the land. Arnold would have been a good one to ask about the geographic position of the United States. While the weather along the coast of New England could be disturbing, it did not compare with the storms and high winds of the Caribbean islands during the hurricane season. Weather there affected the sailing season as it did in the Mediterranean and the English Channel. A few months of the year, sea travel was restricted. During ships' long trek north, however, along the seaboard, the vicious storms lessened. Arnold's little fleet continued north after discharging medicinal herbs at his shop in Connecticut. They carried cocoa and other exotic tropical items north to Canada. He could have lent testimony to the misfortune of ice-choked harbors and fierce North Atlantic gales that slowed the progress of Canadian sea power in the days of sail.

The "extent of the territory" with regard to access by the sea was both a good and bad thing. Those obvious strengths could be deceiving. If a nation boasted a long seacoast, replete with convenient harbors and an anchorage, marauding pirates and strong navies found it equally attractive. Vulnerable to attack by small parties, the affluent coastal communities invited looting and worse by their very ease of access. On a larger scale, great fleets, always looking for stations to replenish themselves, scoured the world for such rich pickings. The extended coastline from Maine to Louisiana put a heavy and expensive burden on the Congress of the United States. In the earliest days, the colonies in America relied on England and the Royal Navy to protect their holdings and ships around the world. Congress scrapped the Continental navy; the last surviving warship of the era was sold in 1785. A very few coastal defenses were maintained in name only by a tiny army. This did not go unnoticed by others, and the long coast became vulnerable to adventurers. Harbor entrances in some cases were invested with defenses. Fort McHenry, protecting Baltimore, was garrisoned with soldiers who were going to earn their keep in the coming conflict. Therefore the U.S. Army was able to maintain a few hundred soldiers on active service during the period after the Revolutionary War while the Continental Navy was disbanded. The result was that the army has a unbroken line of service from 1775, making it the senior service.

While the narrow entrances, or choke points, that guarded the superb natural harbors of the eastern seaboard aided in their defense, they also invited the blockade. A favorite tactic of the Royal Navy, a blockade was far easier to maintain than expected. In the days of slow sailing ships that depended totally on the direction and force of the wind, the geographic orientation of the harbor entrance could in itself diminish usage. If there was also a narrow-necked channel, a prowling warship or two on station could seal it off so that nothing could get under way. The idea of a blockade suggests a massive commitment, sails bristling on the horizon day and night for months on end. That may not be accurate. With one or two major men-of-war, 60-guns and above, and a small number of quick lesser frigates and sloops, Boston, New York, and Philadelphia could be invested for long periods of time. It was essential that the United States have a considerable navy if it were going to prevent the blockading of its most vital interests at home.

Population

The "number of population" was looked upon as an asset to the United States in 1812. The people were coming in greater numbers now that the Revolutionary War was over. The news had spread about the great gamble. The experiment in government of, by, and for the people was established and thriving. Like a lighthouse's bright beacon across the water from crowded Europe, oppressed by feudal laws and restrictions, the beam shone in their eyes, and they could not look away. The New World of North America was finally open to man instead of conquerors. Merchantmen of all countries found an expanded demand for passenger travel for whole families at a time. These ships were no longer solely goods-carrying vessels; space was made for immigration. Immigrants were most welcome since they packed their trades along with their baggage, filling the sea-coast towns with skilled labor. The movement of goods at sea required a large functioning effort focused on trade. It called for numbers as well as talent. Space and opportunity were abundant in America, accommodating mass migration. More ships were required, and they could be built all along the eastern seaboard, turning more and more trade to profit.

Sea power was driven by many factors, but in the United States one stands out. The "character of the people" was most crucial. While England was a melting pot that took more than a thousand years to boil, the United States was in a hurry if it were to reach the promise of prosperity. England's infusion of diverse peoples began before the Roman invasion and was not completed until the Norman-French invasion in 1066. The same process would only take a couple of hundred years in the turbulent mixing bowl of North America.

Those who responded then were steeped in the sea. Agriculture was the only calling that matched the maritime industry. Yet the two went hand in hand. Prosperity grew from overproduction on the land. When a farmer could produce more than his family and near neighbors could consume, the marketplace was rewarded with abundance. As demand and production interacted, transportation became key. Whenever practicable, waterborne movement was cheaper than land haulage. However, the water proposed a greater challenge than a network of good roads. Dozens of highly skilled trades were demanded that required great skill and ingenuity. Those skills were already well developed in the Old World. They were often controlled by guilds, which limited the number of applicants and fed on nepotism. Stories from America spread the word that it was a land of limitless horizons. The natural harbors and great forests cried out for shipbuilders. Carpenters, coopers, riggers, woodsmen, watermen, stevedores, draftsmen, sailmakers, whalers, fishermen, naval architects, clerks, lawyers, surgeons, expediters, spirits providers, tailors, packers, pursers, provisioners, bankers, sea cooks, deckhands, top men, mates, and masters streamed across the Atlantic, accompanied by their families, and began a new life of freedom. These polyglots can best be described as risk takers. They were just what the unformed country needed. Willing to take a chance, they had been given the freedom to fail, but they saw it more as an opportunity to succeed. These gamblers soon got the reputation in the Old World as brash, undisciplined, unruly, uncouth, and under no one's control. In short, they were "Yankee Doodles" and proud of it. Rule break-ers, they challenged the status quo wherever they found it. In their fine new ships, they could be found in any port in the world. Always willing to take a chance, they often brought enmity down upon their heads from their competi-tors. They were the new generation imitating their forefathers from Europe.

While the lure of the frontier was irresistible to many, the wealth offered by sea was far easier and simpler to exploit. This turning east, toward the ocean, should not be surprising. Though they had broken away from England, the ma-jority of Americans were tied to the British Isles and nearby lands. Their tradi-tions, extended families, religion, and culture drew them back to the Old World. It is believed that once they abandoned their roots, they never returned. That is untrue. Many traveled again and again over their lifetime back home, like pilgrims to a shrine. They sent gifts, sent children to school, visited on fam-ily occasions, established trading partners, sought brides, and buried loved ones. Such behavior only added to the demand for ships.

The villages, towns, and cities were named for familiar communities from the homeland. To reduce confusion, the prefix "new" was common. Their children inherited the traits of self-determination and open society, encouraging upward movement. "Sink or swim" was a motto that would become the basis of capital-ism, which stood behind the country. Moving on after failure was easy in Amer-ica, in the land of plenty. The investment of venture capital was drawn out of Europe in an effort to bring some of the new promise and wealth back to the Old World.

If ever there was a new model that was made to support sea power, it was the United States of America. The "charter of the government," wrapped around free enterprise, was well suited to pull America up onto the world stage. In 1812, however, the last thing the nation needed was a war with Great Britain, soon to become the world's superpower.

Government's Role

There were many tasks government had to perform to ensure the success of the nation in conducting a profitable merchant marine. But when one is declaring war, the first thought must be on military matters. President Thomas Jefferson started the whole thing with his trade restrictions designed to penalize England. At the urging of Jefferson and the war hawks who saw a chance to grab Canada, President James Madison asked Congress for a declaration of war. It was not the first time the new nation had contemplated war. If it were not for the "Quasi War" with France, there would be no navy to call upon. However, there was no comparison between the U.S. Navy and the navies of England, Spain, or France. A naval military force consists of men, materiel, bases, and, above all, warships. With a handful of men-of-war, all on a small scale, and a loose arrangement of support facilities outside the homeland, Congress had no business entering a war. It was an act of military madness.

The U.S. Navy had been successful in its first efforts in the Mediterranean against the Barbary pirates of North Africa who supported and encouraged the raiding of American merchantmen. Between the Quasi War and the limited actions against pirates, the sailors and officers of the new navy had gained some very valuable experience and had only begun to form the traditions so necessary to the profession.

Bases had been established with working agreements, and they now had to be expanded to other theaters in support of the strategy to disrupt, deny, and disorganize the Royal Navy and England's merchant fleet. The shipping industry in America, which required ever-increasing armed escort support, lobbied Congress heavily over the increase in the U.S. Navy. But to confront the Royal Navy at sea as France and Spain had done in 1805 at Trafalgar was unthinkable.

The government went one important step further in its new war with England. It issued "letters of marque" that encouraged privateers to attack commercial shipping on the high seas. This not only brought in rich cargoes for sale in American ports and fine craft to be sold at auction, but it also diverted Royal Navy assets away from blocking American ports and seizing American ships. The expense of creating defenses now that war was declared fell to the people. The restrictions placed on trade, which were intended to penalize England for her conduct on the high seas, were curtailing the very profits from seaborne trade that were needed to fight the war. The New England merchants in particular chafed at and in large part ignored, out of necessity, Mr. Madison's war.

It is clear that the United States of America fit the model Captain Alfred Mahan proposed. He had the advantage of looking back at the first hundred years of history and put the puzzle together for us. All the elements were clear to him. In his day, he was opposed by isolationists who believed that Europe was an evil place ruled by those whom many citizens had worked so hard to rid themselves of. America had just emerged from a devastating civil war, the horrors of which we cannot imagine. It was not unreasonable to want to build a wall around such a potentially prosperous country, which appeared to have all it needed, and go it alone. Yet if the captain's study had been ignored and America had remained aloof during the European wars to come, what would the United States look like today?

Mahan, who wrote in 1889 from his position at the Naval War College in Newport, Rhode Island, thought globally when no one else in the United States was thinking in those terms. His view of history was that of the days of sail and the beginning of steam-powered ships. He concentrated on large fleets confronting each other or threatening to confront each other for all the marbles. He saw Trafalgars, decisive battles, as the inevitable engagements that shaped history. The modern submarine, which appeared during the 1914–1918 war, went a long way in breaking up clustered fleets, which banged away at each other in line, Lord Nelson style. The defeat of the Russian navy in the Sea of Japan in 1905 was the closest thing to Trafalgar once steam ruled the waves. The battle of Jutland between England's home fleet and the Kaiser's armada, which was at first said to be indecisive, sent the great German fleet into home port, never to be seen again. In our time, Mahan's "sea power" is still relevant at the Naval Academy and the Naval War College as a point of departure. For the academics, it raises as many questions as it answers. Therein lies its value today.

~

CHAPTER FOUR

Caribbean Capers
and the Barbary Pirates

Only a seaman realizes to what extent an entire ship reflects the personality and ability of one individual, her commanding officer. To a landsman this is not understandable, and sometimes it is even difficult for us to understand—but it is so.

—Joseph Conrad

In mid-May 1799, USS *Constitution*, ship of war, awaited her second commander. Forty-eight-year-old Silas Talbot, from Dighton, Massachusetts, began his military service in the great year of 1776 as a soldier. Captain Talbot became known for running a fire ship into a 50-gun English man-of-war on the Hudson. Still suffering from burns, he was promoted to major and sent to Fort Mifflin to recover. There he fought to defend the fort and was wounded once again. Severely disabled and unable to march due to a wounded hip, he was put back on board Continental navy craft, where he captured thirteen enemy combatants. Transferred permanently to naval status, he was elevated to captain in the fall of 1789. Promoted beyond the availability of a ship, he took command of a privateer, was captured by the British, and finished the War of Independence as a prisoner. He remained in good health in spite of his thirteen wounds and a considerable amount of lead that he carried within his body the rest of his life. Well connected, Silas Talbot served as a congressman from New York through 1798.

Absent from military service for ten years, Captain Talbot assumed command on June 4, 1799. USS *Constitution* was taken apart for repair and her crew paid off. The U.S. Marines and warrant officers were still in attendance. All the running rigging, spars, and sails were ashore for repair and renewal. The empty barrels for water were sent for filling and provisions were on the way. The officers were on shore, busy recruiting a new crew. In this new navy, employment was determined one voyage at a time. The officers who retained their commission from the Navy Department were obliged to cajole the favored members of the previous year to stay on. Recruiting was accomplished in and around Boston. The ship must be back on station as soon as possible and there was no time to be too picky.

Captain Nicholson did not complain at the loss of his command. He was content after two nasty diplomatic incidents at sea to oversee the construction of the largest ship in the new navy. A 74-gun ship of the line, the first in the American inventory, was his responsibility. He saw his new post as vindication, but the secretary of the navy regarded it as an opportunity to relieve him of command and still save face. Besides, the former commander was better at making ships than commanding them. He ramroded replenishment activities supporting the navy fleet in Boston Harbor and began the establishment of what would become the navy yard.

The most serious repair to the *Constitution* was to the sprung foremast, which was replaced by late June. In anticipation of the problems of split yards and masts, in light of the approaching hurricane season, extra spars were lashed to the open waist of the upper deck. The entire ship, with the exception of the light ocher strip at the gun-port level, was painted black. While the new rigging was tarred, whitewash was splashed on the inside of the lower decks to improve visibility in the dark spaces below. The captain had his choice of three colors. The other two were straw and light green.[1] The crew must have been quite a sight between the pitch, tar, lampblack, and whitewash slopped from buckets, which must have coated the crew as well as the wood. The hard labor was not what some of the nearly four hundred members of the crew had signed up for, and before sailing, nearly two dozen jumped ship.

At Sea on Station

On July 23, 1799, just sixty-five days after her return to Boston and her first voyage, the *Constitution* was refurbished and turned around with a new captain and crew. This departure was a far cry from the troubles she had at birth. Ordered to Hampton Roads, Virginia, across from Norfolk, she beat against the strong trade winds that swung up the eastern seaboard every summer. In order to make it into the narrow entrance to the Chesapeake Bay, Talbot found it imperative to pass it at first, tacking south to Cape Hatteras and then coming back north with the wind. His waiting orders were no surprise. The *Constitution* was to take over operations in the Caribbean off the island of Guadeloupe and block the passage of French privateers as they preyed upon American merchantmen.

Unlike his predecessor, Talbot did not hesitate when confronting a merchant ship out of Hamburg that had a French crew on board. He knew she had been captured, so he took her as a prize, to the glee of the crew. Swinging off the South American coast, he sought rendezvous with U.S. frigate *General Green* and brig *Norfolk*. Now Commodore Talbot met with his captains for dinner on his flagship. He found that the *General Green* was well past her prime, and he was concerned about her welfare. Captain Christopher Perry and Master Commandant William Bainbridge briefed the new boss, and Bainbridge got a look at the ship that one day would make him famous. But there wasn't any enemy activity to make anyone famous that fall in the Caribbean. Yellow fever, stomach disorder, consumption, and accidents were the causes of death to members of the crew, while others were flogged in an effort to maintain a tight ship in the boring world of a warship without much of a war.

The islands of the Caribbean were not quite as they looked. The French and British, when not fighting each other over their possessions, were intimidating the Spanish and free communities. Internal factions kept everything in a hover, and the American naval agents, responsible for providing the interface with local suppliers of food and water, warned the commodore to keep a low profile. That was hard to do in a warship the size of the *Constitution*. Small resupply vessels were chartered to bring the goodies of citrus and fresh vegetables over the horizon, along with clean water, to sustain her on station. The crew became more disgruntled, deprived of onshore liberty. The schooner *Elizabeth* was sent out to assist with replenishment. She was taken in tow behind the big frigate while ship's boats transferred enough supplies to keep the crew operational. It was an early example of underway replenishment.

Even though the enemy had not appeared, the sea's naturally destructive power was doing its work. The masts and spars began to break down under the strong winds. Most serious was the bowsprit once again. It was vital to operations because the sails that it supported were involved in every maneuver. Sprung, it had to be gammoned, which was a very tricky task. Overwrapping the boom and securing it to the two stout timbers of the knighthead on either side of the bowsprit in the beakhead called for great skill if it was to be of benefit. It was difficult to get it tight enough to prevent the bowsprit from swinging with the action of the waves. A fat hawser was fished around the mainmast when it was discovered damaged.

There was no action over the holidays as the cruising flotilla maintained contact in calm conditions and watched the New Year come and go. The American presence became dominant in the Caribbean as more vessels were added. After the navy furnished her with more light craft to work the inshore areas, the frigate stood out and waited for something to be flushed her way. Hostile French activity all but ceased on the Leeward Islands, and it can be said that the American navy accomplished its mission to protect interests by its very presence. But it was slow work as spring emerged in the tropics.

"Light breezes from the Northwest and clear weather," read the log.

PM at 3 in staysails a moderate breeze ½ past 4 Beat to quarters and examined Great Guns and Small arms.

At 6 In Top Gallant Sails the Monte S E ½ S Brought too main topsails to the Mast, ½ past 7 filled the Main Topsails light sirs, at 11 wore ship to the Northward, Am at 6 the Monte bore S By W ½ W 15 miles. Saw a strange sail bearing S E and Another to the Westward let the Reefs out of the Topsails bore up and Gave chase to the Sail bearing S E, at ½ past 10 came up with the chase and boarded her she prov'd to be the ship Nancy, Captain Joy from Boston who informed us that he had been attacked by a French privateer from Guadaloupe Mounting Sixteen Guns Six and Nine pounders, and after her coming along side three times he had beat her off although she made use of every possible means to board him.

Captain Joy's ship was very much damaged and her sparrs and rigging was much cutt to pieces.

At 12 fresh breezes made all sail to the Westward the Tender and ship Nancy in company.

Latitude observed 20 degrees 18' North.[2]

April of 1800: A Little Action, at Long Last

On the windward side of the Caribbean, Captain Talbot began to probe the port cities for French privateer hideouts. A chance action by Lieutenant Collins led him to Puerto Plata and a privateer's lair. Manning an innocent-appearing captured sloop, *Sally*, with a boarding party of sailors and marines, First Lieutenant Isaac Hull, another name to remember, and crew slid into the harbor. Hull successfully took the French privateer, which turned out to be a former British packet. The marines were ferocious in their attack, giving no quarter, building the traditions of the service with every step. While the actions were plucky, it turned out that since the privateer came from a neutral Spanish port it could not be sold as a prize, and it was returned with diplomatic language of "affly sorry." The event was similar to the Nicholson incident but so convoluted that there were no repercussions.

This action, however, is significant. The Continental marines had nearly disappeared onto revenue cutters after the Revolutionary War. With the coming of the Barbary pirates again in 1797, along with the Quasi War action, Congressman Samuel Sewall proposed that the marines should be formalized into a corps. As an integral part of the new navy, they would furnish a trained, equipped, and disciplined body of naval infantry to protect the ship and augment the sailors in offensive actions at sea and on land. On July, 11, 1797, the

Marine Corps was formed. In one of their earliest actions, they served Lieutenant Hull with distinction on board the *Sally*.[3]

As the summer began, Captain Talbot sent messages via the naval agents in the Caribbean that extensive repairs were necessary upon his return to Boston. By December, the French and Americans had tired of the Quasi War, peace was on its way, and the secretary of the navy began to slow proceedings and added further restrictions to the rules of engagement in order to prevent an ugly incident. With President Adams's days in office waning, the Peace Establishment Act was ratified by Congress on March 3, 1801. Word was sent to all ships at sea by courier vessels to return to port. The world moved at ten knots, which saw the USS *Constitution* home in the second week of June 1801. The big frigate was as tired as her crew and went into refitting.

Nine months before, on August 27, 1800, a most telling document had been forwarded from the *Constitution* to the secretary of the navy, Benjamin Stoddert:

> Returns of the Names & Stations of those on board the Constitution that propose to resign their appointments in the Navy of the United States.
>
> Lieutenants, Samuel Pools
> Midshipmen, John Shore
>   Samuel Prestcott
>   John Folsom
>   James Nazro
> Acting Midshipman, William Peare
> Surgeon's Mate Jonas Fay
> Acting Chaplain, William Austin, who is absent, and it is expected he will decline the Service.[4]

The captain would have expected to lose a number of the higher ranks at the end of a long voyage. It is surprising that they made their desires known nine months before docking in Boston. The lack of prizes, boring days and nights, bad weather, and strict discipline not only affected the crew, but it took a toll on the leadership as well.

Millions for Defense, Not One Cent for Tribute

A new President, Thomas Jefferson, meant that a new broom would sweep through the navy now that the Quasi War with France was concluded. A quiet time of reorganization, led by Secretary Robert Smith, sent all but six frigates, which were being refitted, into ordinary or to the auction block. By July, Captain Talbot had resigned, and USS *Constitution* was placed in ordinary near where she was built in Boston.

Just when Thomas Jefferson thought that the world was a safe place to launch American free enterprise once again, up popped the devil. This time it was not the old curmudgeons of France and England with whom he was so familiar. The unruly state of Tripoli, a mere enclave of vandals, once again was terrorizing American merchant ships. How history does repeat itself. With the Cold War over, the USSR defeated and dismembered, world economic trade no longer needed military might to ensure safe operation. Then a small insignificant crew of fanatics, numbering in the hundreds, sent the mightiest nations in the world into a spin. So it was in 1801, two hundred years earlier.

The bey of Tripoli, Yusuf, had picked the wrong president to intimidate when he cut down the flagpole in front of the American mission. Though a man of peace who was opposed to raising a standing army and navy, which he saw as expensive, threatening, and a throwback to European ways, Jefferson came out swinging. The previous administrations, against the advice of former president Washington, had paid off—rather, bribed—the North African states of Algiers, Tunis, and Tripoli to leave American merchant ships alone, and that was not to Jefferson's liking. Those states had taken the money but had continued to snipe at American merchantmen during the past year, demanding ever more tribute, the transfer of vessels, and the use of American warships in the Mediterranean Sea.

Angered by outrageous demands on behalf of Tripoli and Algiers from American envoys in the capitals of those Muslim states, Jefferson dispatched a navy fleet. Under Commodore Richard Dale, the frigates President, 44 guns; Philadelphia, 38; and Essex, 32, along with Enterprise, a 12-gun sloop of war, were ordered to proceed to the Mediterranean and observe the conduct of the Barbary States. The orders read, "Defend yourself and any American vessel that was attacked." Commodore Dale entered the Mediterranean and paused at Gibraltar. He left Captain Bainbridge behind on the Philadelphia to ensure that the Barbary pirates did not interfere with American ships transiting the straits.

The undeclared blockade of Tripoli concluded as the heavy winter weather closed down the bulk of sea traffic in the Mediterranean. Only the Philadelphia and the Essex remained there in winter quarters. The next sailing season of 1802 was similar; the names changed, but the U.S. Navy continued to intimidate and blockade the marauding pirates.

Out of Ordinary with a New Skipper

Captain Edward Preble served as a young man in the Continental navy and was captured by the British. Exchanged a short time later, he finished the war on the Massachusetts 12-gun sloop the Winthrop. Continuing to gain valuable skill in the maritime profession, he returned to naval service in November of 1798 as commander of the U.S. brig Pickering, 14. Within a few months, his prize list brought not only fortune but promotion to captain. By the new year of 1800 he was preparing his ship for the first voyage of an American warship to the East Indies to show the flag and protect American shipping interests there. It was said by members of the crew on that voyage that his infamous irritability sprang from stomach ulcers. The medical condition became so acute that he remained on land in 1801 and 1802.

Somewhat recovered in June of 1803, Edward Preble took command of the *Constitution*, which was anchored at Boston in ordinary. He inspected the ship with the help of the skeleton crew headed by Sailing Master Nathaniel Haraden. The years spent wallowing in the channel had not been kind. As expected, numerous planks, masts, and spars had to be replaced, along with rigging. Seams needed caulking and gun carriages needed to be renewed. The guns, in storage at Castle Island, several miles east of the shipyard, were restored to operation. The massive stone fortress, which had been commanded by Paul Revere during the Revolutionary War, remained in service as guardian of Boston Harbor.

The most serious damage was the deterioration of the hull's copper sheeting, which had been Revere's 1795 contribution. No task could be more arduous than the replacement of the sheeting. Sliding carefully into a wharf, the big frigate was going to have her bottom exposed for all of Boston to see. In order to list her over and raise the keel just above the waterline, the ballast had to be shifted. Here the fifty-two guns, weighing over a ton each, found a new use. They were all coaxed to the port side. This was not enough, so the pig-iron blocks below the orlop deck were transferred as well. Still it was not nearly enough, and a web of lines was passed around the masts and heaved until she lay on her left side like a condemned whale.

Water damage meant that the old sheets had to be pried loose, which exposed the strakes, long sodden black planks eight inches thick. Some were replaced and others were scraped and caulked. Then a new gleaming pattern of rectangles in perfect rows once more covered her unveiled buttock. The thin copper sheets, about four feet long and a foot high, were tacked down, giving her a shiny bottom.

The other repairs had been suspended and now added time to the process that was unwanted but necessary. To add to Preble's bad temper, he was informed that as commodore of the Mediterranean fleet, he could expect to be gone a long time. Begun in May, the repairs were finished to his satisfaction in early August of 1803. The officers had been desperate, looking for sailors as far afield as New York City while the craftsmen of Boston made the ship look like new. By August 14, the new crew was watching their home port fade away until only the gray-white stone of the ramparts at Castle Island were visible, and then nothing but the unending sea surrounded them.

At Gibraltar, a British colony on the southern tip of Spain, Preble met the ships and captains of the Mediterranean fleet, taking their briefings and addressing the aggression of Tangier, Morocco. The American brig *Hannah* was bottled up several hundred miles south at the Moroccan port of Mogador and was being held until the American commander released two Moroccan privateers, *Mirboba* and *Meshuda*, which had been attacking American merchantmen. Negotiations, which had been going on for a month, were finally concluded when Preble brought the bulk of his command, three frigates and a sloop of war, into Tangier harbor and moored them within gun range of the city. The problem was solved with an exchange of captured vessels.

On October 24, at Algiers, Preble was told by a passing British ship that the American navy frigate *Philadelphia* had been captured in Tripoli harbor. Captain William Bainbridge had been chasing a Tripolitan xebec and had run aground on a shoal. The attitude of the ship caused her to list. She was defenseless since her guns could not be brought to bear, so Bainbridge instructed his carpenters to scuttle the ship by breaking through the hull and letting the seawater flood in. A large number of Barbary pirate gunboats were at her almost immediately. The *Philadelphia* surrendered and the crew was taken to prison. Two days later, a storm surge lifted the stricken frigate off, and her new owners, the pirates, patched the hull. She was taken into the broad harbor, a present to Bey Yusuf.

Commodore Preble could not permit the enemy to spot the *Philadelphia*, a big American frigate, under the flag of the Barbary pirates. By December he had moved his supply base from Gibraltar, after a dispute with the Royal Navy, to Syracuse on Sicily, closer to the action to come with Tripoli. The week before Christmas 1803, Preble pressed outside the harbor to get a look at the status of his former frigate. The *Enterprise* was sent after a Tripolitan ketch as it attempted to slip past the Americans. The *Mastico* was carrying bits and pieces of the *Philadelphia* among her possessions. Bad weather drove Captain Preble's squadron off, but he was back a week later. The Mediterranean sailing season was closing.

Enter . . . Stephen Decatur

At Malta the prize vessel was renamed the *Intrepid* under United States colors, and Lieutenant Stephen Decatur was given command. Specially equipped for return to the enemy harbor, the commodore led the American fleet back to the entrance to Tripoli harbor and waited in deep water. Meanwhile, the *Intrepid* and her crew of volunteers—one of which was Midshipman Thomas Macdonough, whom we will meet again later—slipped in under her old colors. Her familiar silhouette was well known by the defenders to be friendly. "The *Philadelphia* was moored in the inner harbor . . . and within easy range . . . of the batteries of the harbor. She mounted 40 guns . . . a full complement of men was on board to serve them."[5] Lieutenant Decatur's report to Commodore Preble reads,

Stealthily she [the *Intrepid*] slunk along in the gloom with all but a few of her crew concealed. . . . Unchallenged by guard boat or sentry she crept by the forts and had drawn quite close to the Philadelphia when the [enemy's] frigate hailed her . . . the Intrepid's pilot replied that the ship was a trader from Malta, that she had lost her anchors in the recent storm and that they desired permission to make fast to the frigate during the night. It was then about half past nine o'clock. Mean while a boat's crew from the Intrepid attached a line to the Philadelphia's fore chain. . . . Hauling on these lines the crew, still concealed, had brought their vessels almost alongside when the Turks were aroused; the cry "Americanos" rang through the ship.[6]

Decatur led the boarding party onto the dark decks of the unfortunate *Philadelphia* and was immediately engaged in hand-to-hand combat with the pirates. At a critical moment, Boatswain's Mate Ruben James stepped between a sword-swinging pirate and his leader, taking the blow and saving Decatur's life. James recovered and spent the next thirty-two years in naval service.[7] Thomas Macdonough led ten crewmen below and set fire to the berth deck and forward storeroom. In less than half an hour, Decatur had accomplished his mission to destroy the American frigate and had escaped with only one casualty. Decatur's action caught the eye of the great English naval hero Lord Nelson, who said that it was "the most bold and daring act of the age."[8]

Sad was the fate of the *Philadelphia*'s captive crew, whose only bright spot was the "prison school" conducted by David Porter, which figures high in American naval history.[9]

The Summer of Discontent in Tripoli, 1804

After the *Philadelphia* incident, Preble's blood was up and he scurried around the ports of the Mediterranean, from Tunis to Malta. From the two Sicilys, which were a British interest, he sought slight draft military vessels to send ahead of his flotilla to take the harbor and force the bey to give up the pirating of American merchant shipping. With the great assistance of the Royal Navy, he assembled a slew of slow-moving gunboats and bomb ketches. They bristled with guns of all sizes and types of mortars. The crews were Italian for the most part. Heavily burdened with the great weight of cast-iron cannonballs, the vessels wallowed slowly south toward Tripoli, much of the time under tow.

His plan was twofold for the large assemblage, both offensive and defensive. He would strengthen the blockade, isolating the bey, and insert an active force into the inner harbor to destroy, disrupt, disorient, and disarm the Barbary pirates. At morning light of July 25, 1804, Yusuf Karamanli, bey of Tripoli, found that he was about to be invested by the largest enemy fleet ever to set foot on his doorstep. Through his glass he could identify the American frigate *Constitution*, which for the occasion had far more than her rating of 44 guns. In her company were the *Siren*, 16 guns; the *Argus*, 16; the *Scourge*, 14; the *Vixen*, 12; the *Nautilus*, 12; and the *Enterprise*, 12. Intermingled were six gunboats and two bomb ketches.[10] It was a classic deployment of sea power, intended to demonstrate that the payment of tribute was a thing of the past. But the weather was not in Preble's favor, and although the sailing season was at its zenith, he was forced to take his formation back out and wait for the first week of August before reappearing.

On the third of August, American sails cluttered the approaches to the harbor. Lieutenant Decatur led half of the gunboats, with the sloops of war close in, protecting the bomb ketches as they shelled the bey's palace. He took aim at the most vulnerable group of pirate combatants. The winds were light and the billows of dense white gun smoke hugged the churning green water and drifted into enemy lines. The clouds of smoke stung the eye and obscured both the enemy and friendly craft. In the confusion of battle, American engaged American. But Decatur held to his course and took two gunboats in tow after receiving a wound from a close encounter with a pirate. Unfortunately, his brother, James, was killed during the same action in another American gunboat close by. Preble's tactics of short-, medium-, and long-range fires were effective. When the front line of pirate craft were in need of reinforcement from waiting reserve, they were engaged at long range by the *Constitution*'s long guns. When the wind turned against maintaining station, the Americans were able to disengage without casualty. Even the land-based fortified batteries were kept off line by Preble's gunnery. A count after the battle found that the Americans had a six-to-one ratio of casualties in their favor.

Unlike armies in the field, ships cannot hold positions at night in a sea battle. After replenishment outside the harbor, the fleet took to the sea, orbiting the port until the following day, when the attack could be renewed. A message was sent to the bey via a French vessel allowed to enter the harbor predicting annihilation of the port if the Tripolitans continued to resist. The bey sent the Frenchman out with only his adamant refusal to cooperate. Preble increased his strength by two gunboats with the reconfiguration of the ones captured by Decatur. A council of war with his officers produced a plan to bombard the palace and force the pirates to come out to fight. Using the wind direction, it would be possible to cut them off from their protective harbor and prevent their return, therefore ensuring their capture or destruction.

Preble Presses On

Just after midday the American attack was renewed. As Prussian general Carl von Clausewitz, the great theorist of war, once noted, no plan survives intact in the presence of the enemy. So it was that the Tripolitans had erected gun batteries along the shoreline, very near the proposed positions of the American gunboats. The gunboats were engaged as they reached their station, and time was lost while the land-based guns were pacified. Then too, the cutoff of the enemy gunboats went awry when the sloops tipped their hand, which nearly cost a bomb ketch its safety. Fortunately, the "Eagle of the Sea," the *Constitution*, swooped down and drove the attack off before it was sent home.

The end of the second attack was marred by the arrival of the *John Adams*, which brought more than supplies. It carried a communiqué from Secretary of the Navy Smith commending Preble but also informing him of reinforcements. While such news would often be welcomed by field commanders, this news was not. Two of the additional ships were captained by officers who were more senior in rank; therefore he would be compelled, by the system, to relinquish his title of commodore and the responsibility for the conduct of the war.

From the beginning, the American commander had insisted on the release of the crew from his lost frigate, the *Philadelphia*. He had made an offer of $50,000. The bey had been playing this game with not only the Americans but also most of the crowned heads of Europe for many years, if not generations. He wanted six times that amount. Preble expected that the reinforcements would provide added leverage to the negotiations and would quickly end the conflict in his favor. Anxious to settle the affair for the sake of the American prisoners from the *Philadelphia*, Commodore Preble upped his offer to $90,000, which only reopened the bargaining. The bey countered with $150,000, which was half of the original ransom. Preble's increase to $120,000 did not receive an answer.[11]

The Fleet Takes a Breather

Still on station two weeks after the original investment, the commodore needed supplies. The *Enterprise* was given up to go to Malta. The third week ended with little progress due to winds and currents that were not advantageous to the rowed gunboats and ketches. On August 27 a small action took place with little effect. On the twenty-eighth, the enemy seemed tired of the whole affair, and a dozen gunboats came out of the inner harbor with something in mind. Commodore Preble, too, was distressed, with the enemy on one side of him and his relief just over the horizon. He signaled all vessels in his fleet to back off as the big frigate flew to the attack. Courses up and sails full, she caught the wind and pounced on the enemy. Roaring broadsides, one after another, blasted from her shining black sides. The menacing pirate galleys stopped in their wake, turned, and attempted to flee. Several went to the bottom, smashed, while the others scattered, their only defense. The *Constitution* was something to see when her master was angry.

It was coming to an end now. When the pirates came out once again on the morning of September 2, 1804, the wind was in their favor. The *Constitution*'s escorts towed her gunboats into a new position and prepared to attack. It was like watching men running in molasses; intolerably slow progress resulted from the American efforts. At the other end of the line, the bomb ketches hit their targets in the city and the pirate fortification returned fire. Supporting the ketches, the *Constitution*, violent now, using all her guns on the "English" fort that sat proudly above, swept the shoreline, sending clouds of blackish debris in all directions that enshrouded the ramparts and hovered over the city like doom. But as had happened so often before, the wind did not cooperate, and the American battle squadron could not maintain direction and fell away. The geographic position of the harbor of Tripoli, with respect to the prevailing winds, continued to favor its inhabitants. The wind had lured the *Philadelphia* to her grounding and capture; Preble was not going to get hung up and be a victim like Captain Bainbridge. He would no longer risk his command. No one could say he was timid, nor could they accuse him of being foolhardy. That was how he would have to leave it.

Commodore Preble's Last Trick

Near dark on the third of September, the American commander decided to return the *Mastico*, no longer the *Intrepid*, to the bey and the citizens of Tripoli. Taking off her American crew, he replaced them with tons of explosives. Master Commandant Richard Somers volunteered for the mission, along with a dozen more. They were just enough to manage her on a test run two nights before, which brought home just how tricky it would be in the dark to slip her through the narrow western entrance. His objective was the inner harbor, crammed with dozens of small craft manned day and night with full crews. Once on the inside, Somers would set course, tie down her wheel, ignite the fuse, and send her home once again. If it were done just right, the devastation would be colossal. Preble considered it to be the last chance to ransom the lost American crew and weaken the Barbary pirates to the point of surrender. Later the *London Times* said it was "a very plucky act." It also reported that it failed. The American commodore witnessed the blinding explosion and subsequent fireworks, but it came too soon. While it succeeded in exploding, it failed to change anything. In the gray morning autumn light, the wreckage littered the rocks at the mouth of the harbor. The *Mastico* had claimed the lives of her last crew. Somers was not known to be a lucky officer.

Relief and Relieved

By September 13, 1804, Captain Samuel Barron, on the *President*, had assumed the broad pennant of the commodore of the fleet, and Captain Preble sailed USS *Constitution* to Malta for repairs prior to his leaving on the *John Adams* for the voyage home and his account to Congress. Back home, his efforts had been widely reported, and he was received as a hero and given the thanks of his nation in the tangible form of a gold medal.

In Malta the Hercules figurehead, which had been nearly destroyed by the heavy pounding of the sea, was replaced with a carved billethead scroll picked out in white, a decorative touch. It complemented the ocher gun-level streak that banded the length of the black hull. The promised carronades, eight 32-pounders, were mounted on the quarterdeck. Though short range, the "smashers" were extremely valuable inside five hundred yards. Lieutenant Stephen Decatur took care of the *Constitution*, waiting for the new captain, who gave up command of the frigate *Congress*, which had come over with Barron's reinforcements.

Captain John Rodgers Assumes Command

Born two years before Concord Bridge, the new commanding officer had not been old enough to fight in the Revolutionary War. Raised by the water in Maryland, the thirty-year-old had commanded three of the new navy's ships prior to the *Constitution*. Before his feet were firmly planted on the deck of his new command, fate took the young man by the neck and thrust the broad pennant of commodore into his hands. It was not the way Secretary Smith had planned the matter, but by November Samuel Barron was seriously ill with "internal organ dysfunction" and beached himself for the betterment of all concerned. Though the change of command was a temporary arrangement, it would become permanent.

Time Out, while the Marine Corps Steps Up

Remember Yusuf Karamanli, who was the bey of Tripoli? He seized power in Tripoli by overthrowing his brother and exiling him to Egypt. In May of 1801, knowing that the Americans could be cowed into paying for protection, he attempted to extort money by cutting down the flagpole at the American consul residence and demanding tribute or war.

In 1804, Mr. William Eaton, naval agent to the Barbary States, came up with a "cunning plan" to depose the bey. On board Commodore Samuel Barron's flagship, he asked Captain Isaac Hull, captain of the *Argus*, who had been the officer in charge of the *Sally* during the action in the Caribbean, to provide a marine escort. Lieutenant Presely N. O'Bannon, along with his sergeant and six marines, was augmented by a platoon made up of itinerant Europeans that accompanied Eaton to Alexandria, Egypt. There Eaton persuaded Yusuf's brother Hamet, along with a contingent of several hundred Arab supporters gathered up along the way, to depose the bey and take over Tripoli. The six-hundred-mile march was punctuated with squabbles, hardship, and division. When they reached the Tripolitan town of Derna, Captain Hull sent three of his smaller combatant vessels inshore to provide naval gun support for the attack. The land attack came from two sides. The *Hornet*, 10 guns; the *Nautilus*, 12; and the *Argus*, 18, concentrated their fire on the fortress within the walls. The successful assault took the fort, which accounted for the loss of two marines and the wounding of a third. Lieutenant O'Bannon was granted a scimitar for his bravery by the contingent of Mameluks who fought their way across the town to the palace. The distinctive thin-bladed, curved weapon with a white ivory hilt became the pattern for the Marine Corps' officer's swords. That handful of marines are remembered today in the words of the Marine Corps hymn, "to the shores of Tripoli."[12]

In the meantime, other diplomatic elements were working on behalf of the American prisoners. In June of 1805, the bey of Tripoli accepted a ransom in the neighborhood of $60,000, contingent upon the return of his subjects in enemy hands. The bey's acceptance of the original amount offered by Preble must have been influenced by the potential of another naval investment, the loss of Derna, and the threat of his brother's wrath. Commodore Rodgers welcomed Captain Bainbridge and the three hundred American sailors back aboard the fleet after their long captivity. Captain Samuel Barron, returning to America for medical treatment, took the former prisoners home on the *President*, which was commanded by James Barron.

Rodgers's Independent Action

The Barbary States of Morocco, Algiers, and Tunis were watching the proceedings closely. They had been encouraged by the lack of military success at Tripoli and were becoming more aggressive. The treaty took them by surprise. Then Commodore Rodgers took the pasha of Tunis by surprise. On the first day of July 1805, the potentate was host to an estuary filled with American sails. Looking through his telescope he saw the *Constitution*, 44; the *Constellation*, 36; the *Congress*, 36; the *Essex*, 32; the *John Adams*, 28; the *Siren*, 12; the *Nautilus*, 12; the *Hornet*, 10; the *Enterprise*, 8; and the *Franklin*, 6.[13] Interspersed were eight new seventy-foot-long gunboats, each with a long gun in the prow and a carronade amidships, that had arrived recently from the United States. They were small but lethal, and their boarding parties could get in close, right up to the docks if necessary. It was a display of projected raw power, a long way from home. Rodgers showed, with oak and iron, a commitment by the president of the United States not to take it anymore. The reign of mischief and mayhem that had terrorized American shipping, cast crews and passengers into slavery, and demanded tribute was moribund. Rodgers's fleet's presence constituted a blockade sealing the harbor and threatening invasion and annihilation. Within forty-eight hours, good feelings blossomed and the fleet stood down.

Rodgers enjoyed the last part of 1805 and the first few months of 1806 touring the coastal ports of the Mediterranean, observing the French and British naval activity in support of the Napoleonic Wars. Over those months he had gradually sent home his fleet; only the *Constitution*, the *Hornet*, and the *Enterprise* were left to show the American navy's ensign. At Gibraltar in May, Commodore Rodgers once again became Captain Rodgers as he relinquished command of the squadron to Captain Hugh G. Campbell of South Carolina. Campbell had come out with Barron and Rodgers in 1804 and commanded smaller frigates in the Mediterranean. Barron's influence in Washington with the secretary of the navy must have been pivotal to Campbell's appointment in this new peacetime role.

The *Leopard* Prevents the Eagle of the Sea from Returning

Commodore Campbell received orders to return the *Constitution* to Boston in the spring of 1807. He prepared to go home, calling at Leghorn, Italy, to load the marble carving and blocks purchased by the grieving members of the fleet's officer corps who had survived the attacks on Tripoli (today, the memorial stands next to the Naval Museum at the U.S. Naval Academy). The relief did not materialize. Captain James Barron was about to start another war. Appointed commander of USS *Chesapeake*, he refused to allow a Royal Navy man-of-war, HMS *Leopard*, to search and remove British sailors from his crew near the port of Norfolk, Virginia. At close range the *Leopard* fired on the defenseless American, who had not had time to run out her guns. Suffering casualties and significant damage from the unprovoked assault, the *Chesapeake* was unable to carry out its mission to replace the *Constitution*.

The spin-off of history was that the crew, expecting to return home, considered themselves sentenced to an unending tour of duty, some beyond their enlistment. According to an eyewitness, "the nature of the crew was to villainy and roguish behavior." The marines remained armed and on guard. The officers saw mutiny behind the eyes of every sailor. Tension grew and led to desertion as endless sailings took the great ship from port to port for replenishment.

James Durand was an able seaman from Milford, Connecticut. He went aboard the *Constitution* from the *John Adams*, which was at Tripoli under command of John Rodgers. His personal account of the discontent on board the ship during the period is riveting.

> By coming to the US this Mr. Blake [a Lieutenant cashiered out of the Royal Navy] initiated himself into the American service by throwing around a little money and a few high sounding high words. He thought to cut as many capers and exercise as much power as his tyrannical disposition could suggest to him.
>
> The old rat, however, was soon caught in his own tricks. His treatment of the crew was so ill that with great delicacy I attempt to detail a few of his outrages.

When [a man] was ordered lashed for not going to his proper station in the tops, Blake took the whip away from the boatswain because he did not hit hard enough and continued the punishment himself. When this practice continued Durand and the rest of that watch went to the captain and refused to serve under Blake.

Blake transferred at Gibraltar when Rodgers left the ship.

Malta

On Sunday, all hands were called to go into the water to wash. One of the men swam as far as the ships buoy. A Lt. called him to return but the noise of the water prevented the sailor hearing the command, the Lt. then ordered someone to swim out and tell him to come aboard, which he did immediately he heard the order.

The Captain was ashore and the Lt. ordered the man flogged. The boatswain mate refused and was backed by the men. The officers armed themselves and the marines were called out. Eventually the men were sent to their hammocks. The Captain was put in the middle—no man shall be punished unless he deserves it said the Captain.

Unrest continued the remainder of the voyage.[14]

Once in New York, Durand quit the ship after another flogging that was unjust. Durand's final remarks on discipline in the Navy follow.

I must here ask the reader the propriety of making small boys, 10 to 12 years of age, officers [he means midshipmen] and giving them full authority to flog and abuse men when they are as yet unacquainted with the actual duty belonging to a ship. I have know them to give orders which, were unexecuted according to their commands, but which proved wrong, when reviewed by an older officer. Then I have heard the midshipmen deny having given the order in question and the men who obeyed them faithfully were flogged for it.[15]

In 1807, because of the attack in American waters on the *Chesapeake* and other denials of sovereignty, war was imminent with Great Britain, and the *Constitution* was ordered to abandon the Mediterranean and return home.

Navigation

Navigation is defined as the art of conducting a vessel from one place on the earth's surface to another by sea safely, expeditiously, and efficiently. Man would not fulfill that definition until after the USS *Constitution* had made her reputation as a fighting ship. Movement on land is simpler and presents fewer problems than the same operation at sea. On land, the general directions of the four points of the compass or the casual use of the sun can be easily mastered. With the simple addition of a map or general directions, which include permanent, prominent terrain features and landmarks, most journeys can be successfully accomplished. The stability of the land, the known positions of lakes and rivers, the memory of past journeys, the trail of man-made marks, and dead reckoning all team up to allow anyone to navigate successfully. At sea, out of sight of land, a person in a boat can be very easily lost. Those who made the earliest attempts to voyage beyond the horizon used the sun and stars for general direction, which, while effective, could run them up on the rocks or cause them to miss an important landfall altogether.

While there is much evidence of early navigation, as recounted by Thor Heyerdahl, Tim Severin, Carl Sauer, Frederick Pohl, and others, much of what came before the great Christopher Columbus was island-hopping, rather than the transoceanic navigation that was as much Columbus's great contribution as was his discovery of America (although the Admiral of the Ocean Sea always insisted it was the Indies that he had discovered an alternative route to, out of respect for which the aboriginal inhabitants became known as "Indians" to Europeans). When you read Saint Brendan's *Navagatio*, you are reading a text intended to teach a religious message, not provide sailing directions. And while the Icelandic sagas are more useful as directions, they also lack sufficient precision to settle the argument as to the exact location of Leif Eriksson's Vinland the Good.

Often hearsay or "sea stories" of the later generations of seafarers, which could be notoriously exaggerated, were relied upon, with sometimes disastrous results. Water is always in motion, changing by the minute and moving the ship with it. There are no landmarks; maps (charts, their proper name) are blank for the most part, with the exception of islands, hazards, and shorelines. The wind, which is of little consequence on land, becomes a major factor, driving vessels off course. Ships don't stop when it gets dark; they operate virtually in the blind one-third of the time. An overcast night on the ocean is as dark as dark can be. Storms on land, while converting good road to bad, are merely annoying. At sea, storms, gales, hurricanes, and typhoons can destroy even the most meticulously laid down navigational plan and turn it into a shambles in minutes. The picture is not all that bleak though; dead reckoning or the memory of past journeys can contribute to good navigation when the sea conditions are right.

Early History of Navigation

Navigation is much older than we think. After all, when the Americas were discovered by Columbus (and, unlike previous "discoveries" by the Irish, the Vikings, etc., stayed discovered), there were already people there who we believe migrated from Eurasia, or even Africa. Whether they found their way by land or sea, they must have navigated on their journey.

Speed, Distance, and Measurement

Once out of sight of land, the early sailors strained to find their way, knowing that there was a pot of gold at the end of that beautiful rainbow that stretched along the horizon. Distance was a function of time and movement. They knew time by the hourglass and a count of oar strokes. How far they had gone could be surmised. The speed of the vessel was simpler. A line with a floating object attached was tossed overboard at the bow of the ship and timed by an hourglass until it reached the stern. This was known as the "log." The speed was recorded in the logbook. To determine both speed and distance, a slightly more complex system was developed. A flotation device was tied to a light line on a reel that had knots tied in it at intervals. The sailor would throw the "log" into the water and recite a line of verse of a known length of time, or a small hourglass would time the event. When the time was up, the knots that had played out from the reel were counted and the speed was recorded in "knots per hour." In addition to the hourglass (or half-hour glass) to mark the time or watch, there were two sizes of sandglass, of twenty-eight and of fourteen seconds in duration. The log line was 48 feet long. Once the ship *Constellation* reported the wrong speed in her logs because the line was too short. This was unknown until the end of voyage when someone measured the line, which turned out to be 3 feet short, at 45 feet.[16]

We could have a discussion on the length of the land mile and nautical mile, but it would not resolve anything. It suffices to say that an international dispute raged for many years, resulting in a standard. The American statute mile consists of 5,280 feet, and the international nautical mile is a hair over, at 6,000 feet (6,076.1 feet, but in gunnery and in maneuvering, taken as being 2,000 yards). Further, a degree of longitude and latitude, therefore, is equal to 60 nautical miles at the equator, but that is another story. Many of the old bits of measurement were based on local customs. A "span" is the width between the tip of the little finger and the tip of the thumb when the hand is spread wide. That piece of knowledge is of little use in bridge construction. A cubit is the distance from the tip of the middle finger to the elbow. Of more meaningful use is the fathom, which is 6 feet. It comes from the length of a man's body. A cable is 600 feet in the Royal Navy and 720 feet in the American navy. There are still differences internationally in measurement today. Many of the measurements go back to the Romans and the construction of their road network and harbor facilities.

Direction

Mariners knew the positions of the stars, sun, and moon and used them as rough guides. Those in the Northern Hemisphere must have relied on the polestar, Polaris (also known as the North Star), which appears to remain motionless. The Big Dipper, an asterism of constellation Ursa (bear) Major, and the lazy W, or Cassiopeia, appear to move about Polaris and were used as pointers to the North Star. The first real technical breakthrough came from the Chinese. They played a game in the imperial court in which a spoon made of lodestone was spun. When it came to rest, it always pointed in the same direction, north. When a thin piece of magnetized metal was balanced on a needle in a wooden box, and it became the compass, useful on land and sea. However, the origin of the compass is widely in dispute.

At sea, the direction of travel must contend with the direction of the wind. Since the wind provided the propulsion at sea, a role it did not play in land travel, the wind was the determining factor in sea voyages. The destination must be compatible with the direction of the wind, or there was little use in attempting the journey. William Richards, an impressed British sailor, recounts an excursion on HMS *Caesar* in the fall of 1808. The intent of the captain was to sail from an English Channel port to the northern coast of Spain, a very straightforward voyage. They sailed in late October, expecting to join the fleet within a fortnight. They were attached to a convoy off of Ushant in the English Channel and turned south. But strong gale winds were blowing in their faces, and on November 15 they put into Torbay on the English "Riviera" to replenish and wait out the storms. "On the 27th the wind having come to the north-east, we got under way with the fleet and got off Ushant again, but next day it shifted to the westward, blew a storm, and drove us back to Torbay again." He continues,

> on the 8th of December the wind got to the north-east again, got under way and got off Ushant, but the wind increasing and continuing for several days drove the fleet a long way to the westward [well off course]. On the 22nd our signal was made to proceed to Rochefort and relieve the [HMS] *Gibraltar*. It blew so hard that we bore away and scudded under our foresail [to scud in a sailing ship is to run before a gale with reduced canvas, or under bare poles in the case of a gale so strong that no sails could be left spread].[17] Next day, in setting the close-reefed maintopsail, it still blowing hard, rain and hail, it blew to pieces; sounded frequently in eighty fathoms [480 feet of water].[18]

On December 25 they reached the northern coast of Spain. It took fifty-seven days to go about five hundred miles.

Soon after the employment of the compass, a set of directions on a card was placed under the needle. Now the track at sea was identified in terminology that was identical with the direction of the wind. The arrows on the card and associated terms represented the orientation of the ship. The notations standardized language across the maritime community.

Compass Reading

The compass card is divided into 360 degrees, increasing clockwise from north through east, south, and west. . . . In addition there is a notation of 32 points added to the degree graduations. The four cardinal points are north, east, south and west. Midway between these are four intercardinal points at northeast, southeast, southwest and northwest. These eight points are the only ones appearing on the cards of compasses used today. The eight points between cardinal and intercardinal points are named for the directions between which they lie, the cardinal name being given first, as north northeast, east northeast, east southeast, etc. The remaining 16 points are named for the nearest cardinal or intercardinal point "by" the next cardinal point in direction of measurement, as north by east, northeast by north, etc. Smaller graduations are provided by dividing each point into four "quarter points," thus producing 128 graduations altogether.[19]

It was widely known that there was a slight difference between true north, the direction to the geographic pole, and magnetic north. Additionally, the metal in the vessel itself caused a deviation in the needle. In 1801, Captain Matthew Flinders, Royal Navy, of HMS *Investigator*, came up with a fix. He placed a vertical bar of soft metal opposite the side of the compass from the affected pole.[20]

Maps and Charts

More than three hundred years before the birth of Christ, the Greek Eratosthenes observed that the bottom of a well was lit by the sun on the summer solstice. Later, on the same day of the year in Alexandria, 500 miles away, he observed that the sun cast a shadow. He correctly reasoned that the earth must be spherical. In fact, he calculated the circumference of the earth as 24,000 miles, short by only 500. One hundred and fifty years closer to the time of Christ, the philosopher Posidonius published a study that underestimated the earth's circumference by 6,000 miles. In 1409, Ptolemy, another Greek, produced a global map covered by a grid of both longitude and latitude markings that showed the curvature of the earth but was mistakenly based on the latter calculations. Columbus relied on Ptolemy's estimates and thus believed that the land he found was India. Ptolemy's conic projection, if nothing else, set a standard of placing north at the top of all future charts.

Such charts, though highly inaccurate, came into common use along with the compass in the Middle Ages. The land masses that surrounded the Mediterranean and touched the oceans were known to be exaggerated. The flat maps distorted the curve of the earth. It was not until 1569 that the Flemish mapmaker Gerardus Mercator published his projection, which portrayed both land and sea in proper perspective.

Soon a market developed for books containing sailing directions. The accumulation of nautical knowledge from extended voyages was popularly published first in Spain and later all around the maritime nations. Such books read like guidebooks today and contained useful descriptions of hazards, encounters, replenishment, and whimsy. Here is an example:

> Libya begins beyond the Canopic mouth of the Nile. . . . The first people in Libya are the Adrymachidae. From Thonis the voyage to Pharos, a desert island (good

harbourage but no drinking water), is 150 stadia. In Pharos are many harbors. But ships water at the Mariau Mere, for it is drinkable. . . . The mouth of the bay at Plinthine to Leuce Acts (the white beach) is a day and night's sail; but sailing round by the head of the bay of Plinthine is twice as long.[21]

Navigation: The Art of Going Where You Want to Go without Endangering the Ship

The first step in navigation is leaving the harbor. Here the pilot's service is often required. It may be one of the oldest naval specialties. Found in the Bible, pilots were provided to King Solomon's fleet. They are an aid to safe operations when entering and leaving harbors, for the first obligation of a captain is to the welfare of his ship. In addition to the human guides to safe navigation, there were static guides as well. When approaching land, sailing ships were most vulnerable to rushing currents and shallow water. The one item known by every mariner is the depth of water required to float the vessel. Often marked clearly on the prow, it is essential to safe operation. Sunken obstacles, shoals, sandbars, rocks, and reefs were never far from the mind of the captain. Lookouts strained their eyes for white water, the mark of breaking waves above hidden hazards. Often mariners depended on nautical notes and notations on charts to warn them of danger. By the time the *Constitution* and her sisters were sailing, an industry had grown up to mark the hazards with buoys and lights. In England, Trinity House was established. Funded by a tax put on every vessel, it built and manned lighthouses and serviced markers around the British Isles. In America in 1789, Congress legislated a system of day and night warnings along the Atlantic coastline and in the Chesapeake Bay, which added to the already-established assemblage of private markers.

Navigators' Means and Methods

"Plane sailing was based upon the assumption that the surface of the earth is a plane, or flat, this method was used by navigators for many centuries. The navigator solved problems by laying down his course relative to his meridian, and stepping off the distance run to the new position."[22] The problem was that wind and weather altered the course at will, which caused the navigator to estimate the effect on the ship and assume things, which was always dangerous, sometimes fatal.

Celestial observation was known and used by the Babylonians and Chinese several thousand years before the time of Jesus Christ. They had accurate calendars based on the movement of the stars. A list of famous names—Galileo, Tycho Brahe, Johannes Kepler, Sir Isaac Newton, and Frenchmen Lagrange and Laplace—provided the progression of mathematics that would enable the American Nathaniel Bowditch to produce theorems and tables that were usable by the mariner to compute his position by the time of the *Constitution*.

What Does Mathematics Have to Do with Being Lost at Sea?

To move from one place to another on the ocean, it is essential to know the starting point before you can plot a course to another place. There are two pieces of information on the sphere called earth that must be confirmed. What is the vessel's location relative to a line drawn around the ball in the middle (equator, or east-west latitude), and what is its location relative to a line drawn from the top of the ball to the bottom (pole to pole, or north-south longitude)? Once that is established, "X" then marks the spot on the nautical chart and a straight-line course can be established to the destination. Latitude is a line of position extending generally in an east-west direction. Longitude is a line of position extending in a generally north-south direction. "The latitude lines, the parallels, really do stay parallel to each other as they girdle the globe from the Equator to the poles in a series of shrinking concentric rings. The meridians of longitude go the other way. They loop from the North Pole to the South and back again in great circles of the same size, so they all converge at the ends of the Earth."[23]

To find the latitude, or where the ship was to the north or south of the equator, it was necessary to master a quadrant or sexton. To find the longitude, or where the ship was to the east or west of the prime meridian at Greenwich, England, required the assistance of a chronometer and specialized charts. The quadrant, which was succeeded by the sextant, was a handheld wood or brass instrument that measured the angle from the point of observation (the ship), taken from the horizon to the sun (or known celestial body). Referring that angle to a table, produced by mathematicians, would provide the coordinates of the ship along the east-west axis of the earth. That information was then transferred to the chart.

Determining latitude by celestial observation has been known since early biblical times. The height of the sun over a period of the six months from its high point on the longest day of the summer to its low point on the horizon on the shortest day in the winter, as recorded by the angle to the person taking the observation, was the key. That is a difference of 47 degrees and never varies from year to year. From that, tables were constructed.

Still, it was not easy to get an accurate measurement on the deck of a pitching and rolling ship at noon on a particular day. If it was heavily overcast or storming, the reading could not be taken. The tables had adjustments for the height of the deck above the sea, which could affect the delicate reading. Often several officers would take the readings or assist others in the task, only to come up with conflicting results.

While the latitude, the attitude north or south, of a ship could be calculated to within a few miles, longitude, the position to the east or west, was a mystery. As late as the mid-1700s the primary method was a combination of dead reckoning (guesstimating from past experience or possibly the gut feeling of the first mate) and parallel sailing. Navigation was more an art than a science. The navigator would sail eastward or westward once the correct latitude had been gained, and the search pattern would be continually expanded until the destination was stumbled over. Such a method could add days, if not weeks, to the voyage.

Longitude: The Story of an Englishman and an American
The problem is succinctly described in Dava Sobel's book *Longitude*.

> To learn one's longitude at sea, one needs to know what time it is aboard ship and the time at the prime meridian. The two clock times enable the navigator to convert the time difference into geographic separation. Since the earth takes twenty-four hours to complete one revolution of 360 degrees, one hour makes one twenty-fourth of a spin, or fifteen degrees. And so each hour's time difference between the ship and the prime meridian marks a progress of fifteen degrees of longitude to the east or west. Every day at sea, the navigator resets his ship's clock to local noon, when the sun reaches its highest point in the sky, and consults the prime meridian clock, and every hour's discrepancy between translates into fifteen degrees of longitude.[24]

But since the lines of longitude (meridian) are not parallel, as are the lines of latitude, the above is only true at the equator, where 15 degrees is equal to 1,000 nautical miles. One degree is equal to 60 nautical miles (68 statute miles) at the equator. The closer a ship moves to the poles, the degree equivalent shrinks until at the pole there is no value in distance since the meridians converge, even though 1 degree of longitude is equal to four minutes' time no matter where it is found.

The Lunar Distance Method.   The position of earth's visible moon, as it careened across the sky each night and halved the days of months, was the focus of study for hundreds of years. The problem was that the positions of the stars and planets were not very well known in conjunction with the moon. With the invention of the telescope, Galileo tracked the moons of Jupiter, which enabled cartographers to successfully establish longitude on land. But observation through a telescope of such minute distant objects from the rolling deck at sea was not practical. However, after 1650 the maps of the land were accurately surveyed by this method. It encouraged astronomers to continue to follow that course of research; they felt that they were sure to find the answer for longitude at sea in the stars.

Not only did ships have difficulty finding safe harbor without the ability to know their longitude, but in October of 1707 an entire English flotilla of warships ran aground in fog off the Isles of Scilly, and two thousand sailors were lost. Bishop's Rocks were added to the charts, thus immortalizing the name of the admiral commanding. An outcry of the people to solve the problem of longitude spurred Parliament to establishment the Board of Longitude in 1714. It would rely on early work started by King Charles II with Sir Christopher Wren's construction of the

National Observatory at Greenwich in 1675. The board offered a prize of £10,000 for the discovery of longitude at sea, within 1 degree at the end of a voyage. If the method determined the position within 40 minutes, the prize increased to £15,000, and within 30 minutes, the fortune of £20,000 would be rendered. Assured by mathematicians that the answer lay in the heavenly bodies, the board clearly favored the astronomical-observation approach. Its first act was to establish the prime meridian at the Greenwich Observatory on the banks of the Thames River, twenty miles downstream from the city of London. The marking of a starting point (prime meridian) was not new. But in the past, the starting point could be as informal as the last port of call. Since England was the most visible presence on the oceans, its effort to solve the problem was appreciated and most welcomed.

The contestants accepted the establishment of Greenwich Mean Time (GMT) as the standard. Scientists like Sir Isaac Newton and others came up with complex formulas based on lunar observation that approximated the correct longitude. None was within reach of the prize. Many seafaring families, after generations at sea, were convinced that the problem was unsolvable. Taking observations on land did not approximate the trials of instability at sea. At that time, all of the proposed methods were beyond the practical use of deck officers.

There Must Be Another Way.   Others followed a different tack. In 1530 the Dutch maritime community was looking for a timepiece that could be set when a ship left port and referred to along the voyage to establish longitude. The land clocks were not very accurate, just good enough for daily activities. Their internal works were far too delicate to travel. At sea, the problems were multiplied by the rocking of the ship, corrosion, and change in temperature. The use of a mechanical timepiece (a watch) was out of the question.

The Dutchman Christian Huygens modified the idea of the pendulum clock in 1664 and took it to sea with some success. But the machine could not stand up to operations at sea. At the start of the Board of Longitude, Sir Isaac Newton remarked that one of the possibilities was a watch but that since gravity varied across the earth, a watch would never work (he was credited with the discovery of the force of gravity). The only enduring contribution at that time was the term "chronometer," which was coined by the writer Jeremy Thacker.[25] His watch, which was mounted on gimbals for stability and enclosed in a vacuum housing, was a failure.

Enter the English Carpenter.   John Harrison was a carpenter, born in Yorkshire, England, in 1693 of humble origins. His first clock, made of wood, dates from 1713 and is on exhibition in the Guildhall in London. It was not until June of 1737 that Harrison successfully demonstrated his all-metal sea clock on a return voyage from Lisbon, Portugal. The Longitude Board met in session for the first time in its twenty-three-year history to consider the success of that voyage. Before Harrison, there had never been a proposal that warranted a session. At his own request, the board gave him more time and the financial assistance to continue with an improved model. H-2, as the new clock was known, still was a mammoth eighty-five pounds and did not satisfy the inventor, although it passed harsh environmental tests on land.

In the meantime, the astronomers and mathematicians had not been idle. John Hadley had come up with a hand-held quadrant (soon to be perfected into the sextant) that was having some success when combined with ever-improving star charts. Yet it took seven sittings along with complex calculations to establish longitude. The problem was the eighteen-year cycle of the elliptical orbit of the moon that caused variations. The board was not convinced that the celestial method would meet the criteria for the prize. But by 1757 the moon trackers were showing progress.

H-3 weighed in at only sixty-five pounds and looked like drawings of the Ark of the Covenant. In 1759 John Harrison had topped it with H-4, which resembled a giant pocket watch. At three pounds, the chronometer was only five inches across. It was said that the difference between H-3 and H-4 would be the same as taking a bicycle and altering it to fly across the English Channel. Even though H-4 passed every condition of the test for the £20,000 prize, the petty jealousy of the astronomical community, whose members were competing for the prize, delayed the award until 1774. It is worth noting that on Captain Cook's second voyage of discovery in the 1770s he carried four chronometers to record accurately his longitude and make charts. It is believed that the first time the *Constitution* carried a chronometer was in 1812. Because they were not mass produced, the cost of the handmade precision chronometers was very high. They were found, in pairs, in the captain's cabin, safe inside hardwood boxes.

The American Navigator. While most warships were furnished with time-pieces, they were very expensive; therefore, they were not in common use in the merchant fleet. Harrison had been a landsman and clock maker, while the American Nathaniel Bowditch was born to the sea only a few years after Harrison invented the chronometer. He was the son of a sea captain who died young, delaying Nathaniel's first voyage until he was twenty-one, in 1794. Young Nathaniel by age ten was working for a chandler, which supplied all things nautical. His quick mind for figures gained him support from businessmen in Salem, Massachusetts. He found a calculation error in Sir Isaac Newton's *Principia*. A natural scholar, he gained a reputation as the brightest boy in the county. He worked as a surveyor during his teenage years. Once at sea, the young ship's clerk and record keeper used the calculations found in *The Practical Navigator*, by John Hamilton Moore.

His ship's owners could not afford a chronometer, so the captain relied on dead reckoning and parallel sailing. A time-consuming exercise, it not only took time, but it also cost money. When the crew's rations of food and water were cut as the ship wandered around aimlessly, it led to discontent and loss of confidence in the leadership of the captain. For many years, officers had relied upon *The Practical Navigator*'s tables and calculations to bring them safely into port. Between 1799 and 1800, Bowditch reported over eight thousand errors to the publisher in Salem. Soon he was asked to make the corrections. It is a wonder that any ship ever found home port using that reference. In 1802 it was agreed that a *New Practical Navigator* should be published with Nathaniel Bowditch as the author. His formulas simplified the process and allowed far less educated men to become successful navigators.

In addition to the improved method of determining longitude, Bowditch's book gave the ship's officer information on winds, currents, and tides; directions for surveying; statistics on marine insurance; a glossary of sea terms; instruction in mathematics; and numerous tables of navigational data. He simplified methods so that they could be easily grasped by intelligent seamen willing to learn. Captain Bowditch was a successful sea captain as well as a navigator. He retired at thirty to become a significant figure in the marine insurance business in Boston. His intentions were to provide a compendium of navigational material understandable to the mariner. Nathaniel Bowditch paved the way for "Yankee" supremacy of the seas during the clipper ship era.[26]

According to Commander William A. Murphy, USN, ret.,

American leadership in navigation would continue as Bowditch was followed by Commander Matthew Fontaine Maury, the "Pathfinder of the Seas," who would begin practices of recording and reporting water conditions which continue in the US Navy to this day. [Maury would later serve as a commodore (flag officer) of the Confederate States navy, and then as a professor at the Virginia Military Institute.] *Bowditch* and *Maury* became virtual holy writ among navigators. The essential elements of information regarding navigation were summarized (if you can call a book of over nine hundred pages a summary) by Commander Benjamin Dutton in 1926 for Midshipmen at the US Naval Academy. *Dutton's Navigation and Piloting*, published by the Naval Institute Press in Annapolis Maryland, is the standard text for all line officers of the US Navy; it is under constant review and revision, to keep up with the latest developments in navigation, without neglecting the skills and methods of the sailing masters of 1812, including those of the *USS Constitution*.[27]

~

CHAPTER FIVE

Intolerable Grievances Lead to War in 1812

What men will fight for is worth looking into.

—H. L. Mencken

The Troubles in Europe

It is easy to confuse the American Revolution with the War of 1812. Both were a long time ago and both occurred before the American Civil War. The customs and dress were quite similar and, indeed, people who fought in the first could and did fight in the second. There, the similarity ends. From the end of the Revolution in 1783 to the beginning of the first war the United States would declare in 1812, nearly thirty years had passed. The United States of America was a sovereign nation by 1812 and proud to stand on her own as long as it did not cost too much. The Federalists in Congress were having difficulty funding standing military forces, which were opposed by the Republicans.

The successful revolt of the American colonists against a sitting English colonial government was expected to fracture the relationship with England and turn the new nation of the United States toward the French. After all, it was France who pulled the flagging Continental army's irons out of the fire at Yorktown. That action forced the British to see "reason," ending the conflict by 1783. But the world did not stand still for the next thirty years.

France had provided vital support to the Continental Congress as a part of her unending struggle against Great Britain for control of trade and territory in the Americas. Defeated on the Plains of Abraham in 1760 at Quebec, she was still smarting over the loss of French Canada. In the Caribbean the British and French were engaged in a race to eliminate the Spanish and Portuguese, who had had their way since discovery in the previous century. King Louis XVI of France put the wealth of the nation in the hands of the army and navy in order to dominate the Western world and diminish English enterprise wherever possible. His reckless abandonment of the home economy and the welfare of the French people finally overwhelmed the constituted government and upset the throne he was seated upon.

The French Revolution of 1789 was not only a blow to the Bourbons, but it was also another warning to crowned heads that nothing was secure. It was a common opinion among educated men that, like it or not, monarchy was the only way to govern. Many in the Continental Congress had deep reservations about whether people could rule themselves successfully over the long haul. While the United States Congress struggled mightily, sometimes on a short-term basis, to stay afloat, the Revolution in France suffered in terror and turmoil, ripping itself apart. When "all the king's horses and all the king's men" were removed by the people, anarchy took their place. The Revolution in France bore little resemblance, other than in name, to that of America. Reactionary elements careened about, destroying rather than building. Pandemonium, murder, chaos, and blood ruled the streets of the capital city of Paris and strangled every institution. The army, one of the finest in Europe, was gutted. It, however, would rise again, like a phoenix, from the fire of the barricades. The excellent navy, run on aristocratic lines, would be a prime target for the powerful Parisian zealots. The heart was ripped out of the leadership and it stumbled along into the next century unaided.

At first, the Parliament in London saw great opportunity in the civil upheaval of France. Now England could get on with economic domination while the French were sidelined. The early years of the 1790s could not have been better, as England gathered strength in the absence of organized French maritime and navy involvement. Soon King George III, who had considerable interests in Hanover, could see that revolutionary behavior could present significant danger to himself and his holdings. He had tasted revolution firsthand in colonial America. While it had to be tolerated there, it could not be condoned close to home. He feared exportation across the land borders of Europe and infestation at home. Additionally, if it were proved that people could rule themselves without the heavy hands of monarchs, the Christian right of kings could become a historical memory. Like many royals before him, he could be conducted through "Traitor's Gate" at the Tower of London, the last in the long line of English sovereigns.

George was not alone in this vision. The fear of the phrase "off with their heads" echoed under the crowns throughout Europe. England's army united with other royal forces to surround France and attack before the revolutionary government in Paris could muster a credible defensive army. But by 1795, England was in the fields of northern Europe pressing down while Austria and Prussia pushed in on the side. To their horror, the new French army, composed of men defending freedom, won victories that stunned their opponents. It appeared that the attacks of outside, intended to restore the Bourbons, only succeeded in solidifying Parisian discord and bringing forth a new France, lethal and determined to spread "liberty, equality, and fraternity."

They Called Him the Ogre

Now, at the worst possible moment for the enemies of France, September 1793, at Toulon, a man on a white horse was seen commanding the artillery. Napoleon Bonaparte began his struggle to escape the grasp of divisive politicians, seized power, and never looked back. By March of 1796 he was in command of the army of Italy. A reborn France strolled forward out of the smoke of chaos and upheaval, healthy and hungry. Europe was going to see just how powerful an idea could be. Every soldier carried not only a "marshal's baton" in his pack but also the mission to help others to see that bright light. Rule by the people, under a code of civil law based on the rights of every man, equal and protected by the state, was going to rattle crowns and cause change.

The king of England and the Parliament realized that a strong central power in Europe could alter the center of gravity away from Great Britain. No single state was the focus of control; instead, political and economic influence had been spread out over a number of relatively moderate states loosely controlled by the moribund Holy Roman Empire, elected aristocrats, high churchmen, feudal houses, Eastern rights, and assorted dukes on thrones. England had intrigued on the Continent for generations in her own national interests, maintaining a solid trading base and extending a "helping" hand when needed. She could not afford to be excluded from that lucrative market. Britain depended on selling finished goods and buying items of raw materials from the Baltic States. Its merchant fleet provided oceangoing transport for many European interests.

After the turn of the century, the unexpected and unwelcome leadership provided by Napoleon included contributions to the law, education, industry, and commerce sectors of the republic. Fortified by his talent on the battlefield, he forced England to take him very seriously and mount an army and navy much larger and more costly than ever before. Additionally, Great Britain was driven to seek assistance from the European kingdoms in an alliance to fight and stop the "Ogre." Her allies were willing but short of funds on the scale needed to contend with the onslaught of France's Grand Army. Britain provided serious funds for the next twenty years to provision and arm Russia, Prussia, Austria, southern Italy, Holland, Spain, and Portugal. As each of these was gobbled up by Napoleon, England suffered. Large blocks of central Europe were wiped off of Great Britain's trading map.

By November 21, 1806, Napoleon had inaugurated his "Continental System." It was a free trading arrangement between the new provinces of conquered states, which excluded England. The war, which began with the fall of the royal French government, came and went with succeeding campaigns waged by Bonaparte and his ever-victorious armies. The British Army supported Portugal against incursions from the French forces occupying Spain. In January of 1809, with Napoleon in personal command of the French army, Sir John Moore's British army was routed and driven into the sea. Not until Lieutenant General Arthur Wellesley, soon to be the Duke of Wellington, prevailed in Portugal and later Spain, was home rule restored and England enjoyed her prerevolutionary position. Short intervals of peace did intervene between 1793 and 1815, but France's victories left her more powerful and pervasive with each campaign on the continent of Europe.

A Close-Run Thing

England was not always on the offensive. In the last month of 1796, French general Hoche's attempted invasion of Ireland, in support of an insurrection, was an unexpected concern that could have had significant complications. "The Directory of France embarked 25,000 soldiers from Brittany intent on landing and swelling the ranks of the four million Roman Catholics. If successful it might shake the English power and divert troops intended for the West Indies."[1] December was not known for good sailing weather, and France's attempt failed in the stormy waters of the English Channel and Irish Sea. A few months later, in the fall of 1797, Bonaparte kept the pressure on. He gave the British Islanders a scare they would never forget. It was so audacious that Hitler repeated it in 1940, with the same result. Napoleon mounted an invasion force along the English Channel. "More than a hundred and fifty thousand [veteran soldiers] were spread out from Brittany to the Pas-de-Calais . . . as the new general [Napoleon] inspected every point."[2] In order to ferry the transports across the thirty-odd miles from the Pas-de-Calais to the white cliffs of Dover, and the 120 miles from Brittany, Napoleon must have freedom of action in relatively calm seas for at least thirty-six hours. The Spanish were pledged to join the French navy in the naval blockade of the English Channel. Napoleon believed that England did not have trained ground troops in the numbers needed to repel his landing. He was correct.

The one bright spot for King George III in the midst of the threat was the Royal Navy. At Cape St. Vincent, off the coast of Spain, Admiral Jervis's squadrons caught and destroyed the Spanish fleet. The loss of the allied ships denied France a safe crossing. Napoleon decided to abandon the strike. In his memoirs written in exile on the Island of Saint Helena, he wrote, "Mysterious journeys [referring to his inspections] increased the anxiety that was felt in London, and contributed to mask the preparations making in the south."[3] The comment was framed many years later; Napoleon managed to save face by calling the plan of invasion a ruse. The Frenchman's "preparations" in the south referred to the mounting of the Egyptian expedition to cut London's line of trade to the east.

The Royal Navy was the single most expensive sector of the economy, but it proved to be cheap when it saved the nation from the fate of occupation. The royal fleet never let the king of England down. But just because Bonaparte abandoned one adventure did not mean he had turned his back on plans to isolate Great Britain. Instead he whirled around and struck England's vital trade link to the Orient by invading Egypt. Though his land campaign was a success, it was spoiled once again by the Royal Navy. While the French army landed at Alexandria Bay and moved inland, the Royal Navy found the French fleet at anchor, and Admiral Lord Nelson destroyed it in place, stranding Napoleon's army on the south side of the Mediterranean Sea. It was not the only decisive victory for the Royal Navy. At Trafalgar, off of Cádiz, in 1805, it cost the admiral his life, but he struck a blow that removed the French and Spanish fleets from the seas. Now it was Napoleon who was isolated on the continent of Europe, denied vital trade by sea power.

America's Quasi War with Revolutionary France

The Jay Treaty (Treaty of Amity, Commerce, and Navigation) of 1794 between England and the United States made peace with England and ensured the right for our ships to trade as a neutral nation, which meant they could conduct business with France without Royal Navy interference. Paris considered it to be a breach of faith in a relationship that was formed during the American Revolution. The French navy and privateers attacked American commerce at will. The pressure from the business community, which relied on merchant shipping, drove Congress to create the United States Navy in 1797. During the Quasi War with France, America acquitted itself with distinction, bringing to American ports prize enough in French shipping to nearly offset the losses to the American maritime industry. John Adams was able to work closely and tirelessly with the French to mediate the grievances and establish stability in the Convention of 1800. In addition to normalizing relations with a very good friend from the past, the convention also established the early traditions of the United States Navy. The agreement put American business on a solid footing, and profits began to rise at an unprecedented rate, building a substantial federal treasury.

President Jefferson's Blind Spot

But Jefferson saw the Jay Treaty simply as the cause of the Quasi War with France. Thomas Jefferson, the third president of the United States, wanted to take advantage of England's preoccupation with the emperor Napoleon. Changes were coming during the Jefferson presidency because he was of a different persuasion. Taking office in 1801, a most critical moment in Western affairs, he harbored different views of the Old World.

President Jefferson, a young man at the center of the colonial revolution, was later ambassador to France and had witnessed the French Revolution firsthand. While he was away, the Federalists favored pro-British foreign policy and promoted preparedness at home with the beginnings of an American army and navy.

> The cornerstone of this policy was the Jay Treaty of 1794, an Anglo-American agreement that regulated commerce and defined belligerent and neutral rights in time of war. The Republicans denounced this treaty—one newspaper called it the "death warrant to our neutral rights"—but there is no denying that it achieved two important ends. It ensured peace with the one nation whose naval power could menace the United States, and it ushered in an era of Anglo-American accord that allowed American commerce—and hence the American economy—to flourish.[4]

The legacy of the previous party left an army that had grown from 840 in 1789 to 5,400 by 1801. The American navy had thirteen frigates in commission and a budding construction program. Professor Donald Hickey, the foremost scholar on the period, points out that Jefferson soon reduced the army to 3,400. Jefferson had no love for expensive navy ships either.

The President's well-known dislike for anything English carried over to the Jay Treaty. Jefferson was a farmer and saw the future of the nation in those terms. He was not in favor of increasing support to the merchants and industrialists up in New England or their big-business attitude toward investment and finance.

Expensive and Dangerous

Believing that standing military organizations were dangerous European establishments that cost far too much money, Jefferson cut defense spending to the bone and beyond. When threats loomed, Jefferson reluctantly made modest adjustments to the military strength but supported the commissioning of Republican Party members to fill the officer ranks. Party hacks and office seekers with no military background took over, to the detriment of the force. The plans to construct several major ships of the line were scrapped, and half of the existing fleet of frigates became unserviceable through neglect. The Republican Party favored state militias, which were formed by the British and grew into the Continental army. They were cheaper to maintain, easy to control, and were a place to play at soldiers for "the boys." Many were drinking clubs that allowed men to get together out of the sight of their wives. Badly trained and poorly equipped, they could not be relied upon to fulfill the mission of a national army. But the old myth remained that the minutemen of Massachusetts and militia formations of the Revolutionary War had beaten the regular army of Britain and her mercenaries from Germany. The intervention of the French army and navy at the critical moment was not considered to be the determining factor in the great victory.

Operations of the American navy could be expected to combine with the American privateers who had been so effective against the French during the brief Quasi War. A fleet of private fighting vessels was sure to rise up again, spontaneously if needed, since they had made so much money in the prize market. But privateers were offensive weapons and could not be expected to protect American harbors or keep open the sea-lanes against much more capable British ships of the line. There were no maintenance costs to privateering for the federal government, while the costs of operating navy vessels were unending.

The heat was off England in 1801 as Jefferson assumed his duties, when the Peace of Amiens was concluded, ending the Anglo-French war. On March 23, 1801, seventeen American navy war vessels were sold off. However, Jefferson was persuaded to maintain the frigates *Untied States, President, Constitution, Philadelphia, New York, Constellation, Congress, Essex, Boston, Adams, General Green,* and *John Adams.* When the crews were paid off, the American marines were retained on board for protection.[5] The authorities in Boston were becoming concerned that the guns loaned to USS *Constitution* had disappeared into the navy inventory and wrote in very kindly terms, "No remuneration has been paid for the loan of the guns and if not that the same guns be returned or whither it would be preferable to return new guns."[6]

Royal Navy at War Meant Impressment

The European peace did not hold, and war between England and Napoleon resumed once again in 1804. James Monroe, minister in London, reported, "The truth is that our commerce never enjoyed in any war, the freedom, and indeed the favor of this government, as it now does."[7] As the Royal Navy found itself short of crews to man an ever-expanding fleet against the French and Spanish, the party was over, and impressing seamen became the issue that haunted Jefferson.

Service on American merchant ships was attractive to British subjects because of higher pay, better food, and superior treatment. England considered anyone born in the British Isles a subject for life, even if he had attained American citizenship. The loss of able-bodied seamen at time of war was intolerable to the English, and they boarded American craft and other neutral ships regularly to search for their nationals. It is believed that as many as twenty thousand of the men serving on American ships were from the British Isles. Identification was difficult, but when in doubt the Royal Navy pressed the man into its service by force. Even if the sailor produced identification, it was known that forgeries were common, and it was therefore disregarded.

National sovereignty had a number of tests. One of the most important was respect of territorial limits. Not only was the land an element, but so was the air above and the sea that surrounded it. In 1800, the coastal water for three miles was internationally agreed upon to be within the confines of a nation. With war under way once again between England and France, the Royal Navy ignored the convention and stopped American ships as they left port, without regard. While searching for their errant sailors, the boarding parties would also seize cargo that they considered helpful to the French. Even containers of food were regarded as contraband. The British considered anything intended for her enemy or a shipment owned by the French as fair game for seizure. Boarding parties examined the vessel manifest to identify such items and took them. American ship owners complained that if the item did not have a clear war use, it was American property while on their neutral ship until it was delivered, regardless of the intended purchaser. But in 1805, on the high seas, "might made right." When you were stopped at sea by a powerful warship whose clear intention it was to do you harm if you did not comply with its wishes, there was no contest.

Jefferson had angered the British in 1803 when he had allowed the commercial agreements contained in the Jay Treaty, established by the rival political party, to lapse. Additionally, Thomas Jefferson's personal dislike for the English, a carryover from his earlier days, never left him. He was not alone; many American voters carried the grudge. They were willing to trade with and make money from trade with the English, but they were proud to be "former" colonists and were intent on not becoming a client state of Great Britain. In his defiant actions, the president had broad support. The belligerent attitude of the American president did irreparable harm to diplomatic affairs when he refused to acknowledge efforts on the part of the British to negotiate a new treaty. Jefferson believed he had the English just where he wanted them. The British lion was decisively engaged with Napoleon, up to his ears in financial commitment, and spread out very thin on the ground, and on the oceans for that matter. What Jefferson had miscalculated was his own country's inability to protect itself. His neglect of national military and naval forces and formations while he tweaked the nose of the English lion shows a myopia that is hard to explain for a man so experienced in war and peace. As a result, affairs of state were about to spiral out of control.

HMS *Leopard* versus USS *Chesapeake*

On June 22, 1807, USS *Chesapeake*, a 36-gun frigate, was under way leaving Norfolk, Virginia. HMS *Leopard*, a 50-gun frigate, hailed her to stop, claiming to have a dispatch for Captain Barron. Both ships were well within American waters. A search was demanded instead by the British boarding party. Barron refused to allow the search and sent the boarding party packing. When the party repaired to the *Leopard* empty-handed, the *Chesapeake* was attacked at close range. The ship was unprepared to defend herself so close to port, and Captain Barron found himself victimized. Within minutes, several volleys of English cannon fire destroyed the *Chesapeake*'s ability to defend herself. Three American sailors were killed and nearly twenty wounded. The British captain ordered the *Chesapeake* to stop, and a boarding party was sent to search for English sailors. The following letter to Vice Admiral Berkely, chief of Halifax Station, from the Right Honorable Lord James Towshend, dated August 15, 1807, reveals the British version of the incident.

Sir.—I beg leave to represent to you, that the five men named in the margin belonging to HM Sloop Halifax, under my command, who sent a petty officer in a jolly boat, in Hampton roads, on the 7th of March last, to weigh a kedge anchor, which had previously been dropped for the purpose of swinging the ship by, taking advantage of the dusk of the evening, mutinied upon the petty officer, some of them threatening to murder him; but the rest interfering they desisted. However, taking the boat under their own command, they succeeded in deserting, by landing at Sewoll's Point. The whole of the above mentioned deserters I have since been informed entered on board the US frigate Chesapeake and were seen by me and several of my officers parading the streets of Norfolk in triumph, under the American flag. A few days after their desertion, I accosted one of these men, Henry Sounders, asking the reason of his desertion, and received for answer, that he did not intend anything of the kind, but was compelled by the rest to assert, and would embrace the first opportunity of returning. At that moment Jenkin Radford, one of the said deserters, coming up, took the arm of the said Henry Sounders, declaring with an oath, that neither he, nor any of the rest of the deserters, should return to this ship, and with a contemptuous gesture told me that he was in the land of liberty, and instantly dragged the said Henry Sounders away.

Finding that my expostulating any longer would not only be useless in obtaining the deserters, but in all, ultimately have collected a mob of Americans, who no doubt would have proceeded to steps of violance I instantly repaired to the house of Colonel Hamilton, the British Counsel there, and related everything circumstance which occurred, and applied to him, as also to Lieut. Sinclair, of the rendezvous of the US service, went to recover the said deserters, but without effect.

> Being since informed that Jenkin Radford has been recovered in action on board the US frigate Chesapeake with HBM [His Britannic Majesty] ship Leopard, and is now a prisoner on board HMS Bellona, I have to request that you will be pleased to direct a court martial may be assembled for the purpose of trying the said Jenkin Radford, for the within-mentioned charges of mutiny, desertion and contempt"
>
> I Have the Honor to be
>
> Signed
>
> Captain James Towshend, RN[8]

Jenkin Radford was found hiding in the coalhole of the Chesapeake by the purser of the Leopard and recognized as the deserter from the Halifax. He said he was hiding to prevent the Americans from forcing him to fight against his own country and that Lieutenant Sinclair of the U.S. Navy had persuaded him to join the U.S. Navy. He was hung on August 31, 1807, by the yardarm of HMS Halifax.

Jenkin Radford and Henry Sounders were two of the four men taken from USS Chesapeake. American accounts differ, reporting that three of the four were Americans; the British disagree, believing that all were long-standing members of the crew of HM sloop Halifax. However, Vice Admiral Berkely was transferred, and the British government offered an apology. What made the incident so noteworthy was the proximity to Hampton Roads, clearly inside the borders of the United States. There were other similar occurrences in which the Royal Navy boarded American merchant ships, but they were out of sight and received much less publicity. There were hidey-holes in between decks on merchant ships that were used by the best sailors as they came into English ports so the Royal Navy could not take them out of service.

Jefferson and the nation considered the USS Chesapeake incident an act of war.

Mr. Jefferson's Solution

Angered, the president decided to use a national power other than force to cow and humiliate Great Britain. She would have to admit that the United States of America was a sovereign nation that had the power to withhold trade as a result of England's outrageous behavior. With the support of Congress, he placed a trade embargo on England. On December 22, 1807, the embargo was in force. The scope was far too broad, prohibiting commerce with everything English, including the United States' northern neighbor, Canada. Ship owners were required to post bonds worth double the value of craft and cargo, guaranteeing embarkation at U.S. ports. Foreign ships were prohibited from carrying away American cargo.[9] In New England and along the Canadian border, it amounted to an economic disaster since England and Canada were the primary markets. American ships were supplying the British Army in Portugal. Smuggling became a major industry. American navy and treasury revenue cutters were given a mission impossible, outlined in the following letter.

Lieutenant Samuel Elbert
  Saint Mary's Georgia   2 May, 1808
  You will hereby review a copy of the embargo laws . . . and enforce the law. . . . Seize the boats and vessels of American Citizens that may be found violating or attempting to violate the embargo . . . seize the boats and vessels belonging to Citizens or subjects of any other nation that may be found violating or attempting to violate, within the waters of the United States. Carefully avoid any collisions with the subjects.
                                                          Secretary of the Navy Smith[10]

The enforcement along several thousand miles of the coast and inland waterways of the United States by such a small force was ludicrous. Yet the embargo caused a great deal of financial hardship among Americans. It was modified several times, making a nuisance of itself.

Napoleon's Unsettling Strategy

In the Berlin Decree of December 21, 1806, Napoleon formalized his economic strategy and changed from attacking the British Isles to instigating mercantile high jinks. His "Continental System," a more severe restriction on trading outside the continent of Europe than the present-day European Union's, demanded that countries under his control would not trade with Great Britain.[11] With the great French fleet a memory after the battle of Trafalgar in 1805, his strategy was to empty the shops of that nation of "shopkeepers," as he referred to the English. Rather than crossing the channel with armies, he sent French privateers out to disrupt and destroy British merchant ships and divest the British of their all-too-precious watery trading lines. He believed that England could not survive as a power without her empire and foreign imports of raw material. It was the empire that made Great Britain great. With French privateer marauders in the West and East Indies, the Royal Navy was forced to fan out. To accomplish that, they had to be both effective and efficient. Considerable numbers of new first-, second-, and third-class men-of-war were not affordable. But the forth- and fifth-rate frigates were ideal for merchant fleet protection and service around the edges of the trading world.

While the French forbade trade with England, the Royal Navy blockaded French ports. In a way, this can best be described by a newspaper headline that appeared in the mid-1900s when a particularly dense fog filled the English Channel. It read, "Continent Isolated." While it is true that the French declared that they would do the same to the British, they were not capable of such a military presence and so were content with privateers taking prizes wherever possible. A considerable portion of the French navy remained bottled up. A blockade of that magnitude calls for an examination of the map of the waters of the Baltic, English Channel, and Mediterranean. Applying Captain Mahan's principles of sea power, it becomes apparent that the burden placed on the Royal Navy became untenable. An all-consuming program of ship construction and prize conversion to navy service created a demand for experienced crews. There were no training schools for sailors; it was all OJT—on-the-job training. Rated seamen would have to be dragooned into service on the men-of-war. Impressment, that dreaded word that caused so much misery for mariners and their kin, put a "black spot" on the Royal Navy.

French Privateers

While American trade was of keen interest to the British, the French privateers harassed and menaced the sea-lanes around the British Isles, interdicting cargoes often within sight of land. French privateers in small, swift, shallow draft craft were an ever-increasing challenge to the Royal Navy as the wars continued.

With the dismemberment of the French navy during the Revolution, merchants took a page from hundreds of years of Barbary pirates, and privateering began on a large scale. Chaos in government, coupled with the war with Britain and her neighbors, destroyed the French economy and drove her armed merchant marine into attacking British commerce in the English Channel and its approaches. Such activity was sanctioned by the revolutionary government, which was longing for a return to vibrant markets and provided written permission and encouraged the sacking of enemy ships. Not only were the attacks a payback for war, but the vessels were to be sold, along with their cargoes, in French ports. Disguising raiders became an art form—everyone was doing it. French privateers looked like Dutch traders, harmless slow movers with few crew, lumbering along. Men-of-war of all nations flew false foreign flags, which enabled them to creep up before declaring themselves. Then, with a great flourish, the true national ensign was unfurled, along with a broadside of cannon fire. The most valuable tool for identifying an approaching vessel was the memory of experienced mariners who recognized ships by their silhouettes.[12] During a more modern era, silhouette training for identification of enemy and friendly ships and aircraft was widespread in both World War I and II. The submarine service was indebted to outlines on the horizon during those wars. In 1800, navy ships of combatant nations were able to alter their outlines with clever camouflage. Odd bits and pieces were added to the bow or stern to obfuscate or misidentify both merchants and combatants, enabling them to slip by a coastal defense or run a blockade.

Privateering in France and other countries was seen as an alternative to honest trade and an adjunct to the navy. A merchant would invest in the outfitting of a ship built for speed and arm it with cannon. He could own it outright or be a shareholder. The captain would provide the crew and was given a share for himself and his crew in proportion to their duties. They regarded any merchantman not flying the flag of France as fair game. Sinking the target was not the goal; therefore, weapons were intended to disable the crew and secure surrender with the least possible losses to the attacker. They would attempt to kill or capture the crew and take the vessel into port for sale, along with the goods.

Dunkirk and Saint-Malo, on the English Channel coast, were the prime centers for the action, the former looking to the northern approaches and the latter to the southern traffic from the Mediterranean and Bay of Biscay. Governments found that privateering was cheap and tended to occupy and confound the navy of their opponents. Commercial raiders were capable of capturing sloops of war and navy cutters, the lower rates of fighting craft. These prizes were most welcome: not only did they remove a threat, but the vessel could be renamed and flagged for commercial or naval use. It was a cheap source of warships that took little time to convert in the shipyard, while making a significant contribution to the fleet capability.

Napoleon used privateers to screen French aggression in the Mediterranean on his expedition to Egypt, disrupting the Royal Navy intelligence and delaying their attack. At sea his privateers were a constant menace off the northeastern coast of North America and intertwined among the rich islands of the Caribbean. They took American merchant ships as well as British, thus posing the first war the new nation would have to fight. The Quasi War with France, a name given after the fact, was important since it goaded Congress into the formation of a regular navy. Congress had divested the country of the Continental navy, expecting the navies of friendly nations to protect American merchantmen because they were bound for their ports.

Privateers or Just Plain Pirates?

It seems that the only difference between pirates and commercial raiders (privateers) was the latter's tie to a legitimate government that recognized their activity with written permission. Letters of marque were issued, condoning the marauding of the seas. They were a license to kill, steal, and destroy. Government permission was not new, having been common since the days of Elizabeth I and Sir Walter Raleigh. Nor was it exclusive to England.

Privateering was a gamble on the part of the investor and the crew. If they encountered a man-of-war of any size, their defense was speed. It cannot be overlooked that the turbulence of the sea itself was a significant danger since many of these ships were in poor condition and good for little else. When England and France were joined by their allies in war, prowling privateers sent the insurance rates soaring, only adding to the expense of sea trade. Commercial raiding was a risky business, but the rewards were great. A legitimate shopkeeper of some size could provide the privateer with foodstuffs for the voyage in return for a share in the payout at the end of the adventure. He risked little, only time. He paid no wages and hoped for the best, while the crews backed the gamble with their lives. Such labor drew seamen who were more proficient at cutting throats than splicing lines.

Merchant trade investment in the Americas required ships of one hundred tons or so, but the East Orient trade, because of the long voyages, required a higher return and demanded ships four times that size. The vessels from the East Indies, therefore, were prime targets as they ran the west coast of Africa and crossed the Bay of Biscay. In comparison, a British naval frigate was nearly four hundred tons and the same dimensions as an East Indiaman. Built of teakwood in shipyards in India and Ceylon, East Indian merchant ships were as expensive as ships built in Europe. England had to pay particular attention to protecting this long trade route, which took a considerable amount of the Royal Navy to defend.

While protecting the sea-lanes, the Royal Navy devoted a number of squadrons to blockading the French ports. Lyon was a center for silk and weaving, while Marseilles produced soap and finished goods. France suffered from a lack of natural harbors, having only a half-dozen all-weather moorings. This was a handicap to the privateers, who could be excluded, kept at sea, or forced into neutral harbors to cash in their prizes. In addition to bottling up the French navy, the Royal Navy prevented the privateer from landing his cargo in the most lucrative ports. Deep-water ports of Bayonne, Marseilles, Bordeaux, and Nantes were prime targets for Royal Navy blockaders. The small raiders slipped into Saint-Jean-de-Luz and Le Havre, which became a haven for privateers. Shallow-draft French coasters, hugging the rocks, plied between those locations safe from the warships of the English.

America Was Making a Killing, as Long as the Politicians Stayed Out of Commerce

While gold and silver treasure ships from the New World come to mind when one thinks of theft on the high seas, they were no longer plentiful in the early 1800s. Prior to the coming of the Industrial Revolution, commodity transfer on a large scale dominated global trade, particularly in the Western Hemisphere. Markets sought stabilization, moving quantities of American wood, minerals, cotton, tobacco, and flour. Elsewhere, Russian hemp, Canadian timber, Nordic pitch, and

Caribbean sugar, indigo, and coffee were in demand. Due to conflicts that came and went between England and France, port blockades had to be minimized.

By 1806–1807, England gripped French seaports and demanded that American vessels be restricted from French ports. All neutral ships, often American, landed goods in neutral ports such as Hamburg and Amsterdam for transshipment by inland waterways to the mills of central France. Thus, the English blockade was eased. Trade restriction became a plaything of kings, emperors, and heads of state. The emerging merchant class was not amused and subverted the rules at every opportunity. Between 1793 and 1814, England lost eleven thousand merchant ships to privateers, which was only 2.5 percent of all English shipping.[13] The statistic demonstrates two important facts of the age: first, how widespread the losses were and, second, what a tremendous amount of super sea power Great Britain possessed.

Commercial raiding was becoming a substantial and permanent industry that threatened the entire trade system. There were exceptions when it came to all-out banditry, and coalers were rarely taken as they moved along coastlines because they were just too much to handle for too little profit. Additionally, whalers were left alone because the crews were capable of putting up a creditable fight against a boarding attempt.

A class of businessmen known as the "managing owners" established commerce raiders. These were the brains behind the enterprise. In France, they were known as "the armateurs." They procured the vessel, settled the captain and crew, financed the provisions by selling shares, procured the letters of marque, sold the captured ship and cargo, distributed the profit, avoided taxes, and charged commissions wherever they could get away with it. If there was a fortune to be made, and there could be, these were the great shipping magnates who built the great estates, while never going to sea.

What to Do with the Prisoners

Captured by the Royal Navy, the privateers were given two choices. They could become members of the Royal Navy and join the fight against their native country, or they would be forgotten deep within the bowels of the English prison system. The conditions aboard the prison hulks, out-of-service warships tethered in some stinking backwater bay, were well known. Later Charles Dickens featured them in *Great Expectations*. Hulls of large warships had their masts and rigging removed, the fittings taken out, and bars installed over the hatches. One ship moored on the Thames lost 150 of the first 600 imprisoned due to the filth on board. They were known to be extremely unhealthy. Prisons, no more than medieval tombs of stone and damp deprivation, were no better. In England,

John Howard was responsible for prisons established for combatants in the Napoleonic Wars, who were initially confined with common criminals. At first the hulks, moored near shore in estuaries, provided the prisoners with work on river-improvement projects. Later the prison ships supplemented the prisons since there was not sufficient space to accommodate the influx as the wars continued. They became crammed full and then some. Overcrowding was the obvious problem, but to the good luck of the prisoners, a prison reform movement had been established. It moved very slowly. The men rotted along with the wooden hulls of these cold, damp floating dungeons.

In 1806 Thomas Tyrwhitt, Lord Warden of Stanneries, broke ground for a new prison at Dartmoor. There were five major two-story buildings housing 1,500 prisoners. Double tiers of hammocks hung from cast-iron pillars. There was a hospital on the fifteen-acre site, which was surrounded by a twenty-foot wall of stone.[14] The American government paid for the cost of feeding and clothing its captured sailors through an agent in England. That agent was also responsible for inspecting the prison and checking on conditions. Food became the main concern since it was too easy for the contractor to substitute poor quality and pay the guards to look the other way. In the boredom, tedium, and hopelessness of prison, the men turned to gambling. They sold their clothes to get money, only to lose it and live in the attic near naked. Prison clothes were dyed yellow to prevent them being sold outside the confines of the gates by the guards. Many men turned to making items for sale outside the prison. They carved bones and made shoes, baskets, ladies' bonnets, and straw figures. Forgery of banknotes was popular. Sick prisoners received a special diet including tea, sugar, milk, bread, and broth. Dartmoor had an outbreak of smallpox in June 1815 and seventy Americans died. This occurred six months after the War of 1812 was over. Most died from respiratory infections and diarrhea, which swept through the hulks and prisons. The few cases of smallpox in England as compared to the Continent was a result of inoculation, which was common. A pin or needle was used to prick a smallpox blister of an infected victim, and then it would be inserted into the skin of a healthy person. The transfer of live disease in that form would provide protection as the body would then make antibodies that provided immunity. Crude but effective, it worked.

Not all died young. The record shows, "Nicolas Lucas, former cook of the *Revanche* privateer, died 1811, age 67 of old age and confusion."[15] Some went crazy. Their death was shown as "hectic fever." A thirty-two-year-old seaman died of rabies in 1808. Former slaves captured on privateers could not stand the cold at Dartmoor and died from amputation of severely frostbitten extremities. Any prisoner was offered release if he would "take the King's shilling" and join the Royal Navy. Surprisingly, few took the offer. This does not speak well for life aboard His Majesty's men-of-war.

Officers were sent into the towns on parole and housed at their own expense in local homes. Parole meant that an oath was taken by the officer to remain in the local area, stay on roads, and not venture out at night. Financial arrangements were made with maritime agents. They were experienced in prize money and credit arrangements for naval officers and were often found in port cities like Plymouth and Portsmouth, England. Some officers even married local girls.[16]

1811: Arrogance of the Royal Navy

In spite of all the missions, diplomatic communiqués, best of intentions, and years of restrictions, it all fell apart on May 1, 1811. HMS *Guerriere*, one of His Majesty's frigates, became known for the first time, but not the last time, to Americans. In those times, ships and their distinctive names were known by every newspaper reader in the country. The only source of mass media in 1811, newspapers were read religiously in every corner of the new republic. The *Guerriere* kicked the golden door at the mouth of New York harbor. While just off of Sandy Hook, New Jersey, a stone's throw from where the Verrazano Bridge stands today, she attacked and boarded the American brig *Spitfire*, taking off American citizen John Deguyo. Within days, she also impressed Gideon Caprian and Joshua Leeds, both Americans from a second ship. It was widely reported in newspapers as yet another flagrant assault on American sovereignty. Deguyo and Caprian would be repatriated, but Leeds was not. The secretary of war, James Monroe, ordered American warships to sea, to "protect the coast and commerce of the United States."[17] Captain John Rodgers, a former commander of USS *Constitution*, was in command of USS *President*, the best sailing frigate of the fleet. Eleven days later she put to sea from Annapolis, Maryland, in a hunt for HMS *Guerriere*.

A passing vessel in open water outside the entrance to the Chesapeake Bay told Rodgers that she had seen the quarry to the north. The captain prepared the ship for combat and plowed toward New Jersey. Soon the Royal Navy ship-rigged sloop *Little-Belt* was sighted heading south. She was carrying dispatches for the *Guerriere*'s captain from Bermuda Station. Mistakenly thinking that the frigate on the horizon at midday could be her own, she approached the *President* and hoisted the encrypted signal of the day, a three-digit number. The *President* was flying her American colors, but Captain Arthur Bingham was not put off because ships often disguised themselves with false flags. When the *President* did not respond to the code, the *Little-Belt* turned away and continued on her course. She did not expect to be attacked since the two countries were not at war.

The American closed in and signaled that the captain wanted to speak. By early evening, before dark, Captain Bingham slowed his progress and allowed the *President* to approach. The Royal Navy vessel readied her guns just in case.

Seeing the crew at their guns in furious activity, the *President* passed by and soon found herself in a raking position. This dance continued as each vessel maneuvered close in, while shouts from both went unheard and therefore unacknowledged by either. A gun was fired accidentally; it is not known who fired the first shot. A general melee ensued. Within a half hour, it was over; the British ship was incapable of defending herself. The British account in James says, "The greater part of her standing rigging and the whole of her running rigging were cut to pieces. Not a brace or a bowline was left. Her masts and yards were all badly wounded, and her gaff were shot away. Her upper works were completely riddled, and her hull in general were much struck: several shots were sticking in her side, and some had entered between wind and water."[18] Eleven were killed and twenty-one wounded on board the Royal Navy sloop. The *President*'s damage was slight, mostly to the sails and rigging. The ships separated for the night to repair themselves. By morning the *Little-Belt*'s suffering was very apparent to Captain Rodgers, and he drew up and sent a Lieutenant across with his apologies when he realized how inferior his opponent had been. The *Little-Belt* limped to Halifax Station and the *President* continued to search for the *Guerriere*. It was the *Little-Belt*, a courier intended for the *Guerriere*, that reaped the aftermath of the attack on the *Spitfire*. America expressed its regret over the incident and England raged.

The newspapers inflamed the American public; the *Guerriere* had earned a reputation, which within the next year would be revenged, much to their delight. Ships began to take on personalities of their own. Everyone knew the names of the American frigates and scanned the papers daily for accounts to share with their neighbors as the war began. It had become obvious to all that Great Britain took little notice of her former colony and that incidents of impressment and blatant disregard for the United States as a nation would continue, keeping America in her place. By the time James Madison took office in 1809, Thomas Jefferson's attitude toward England was shared by the legislators in the Congress.

War in 1812

Nearly thirty years after the Treaty of Paris, in the spring of 1812, the sovereign nation of the United States of America declared war on Great Britain because of intolerable grievances. The young officers culled from the British militia to man the Continental army were now in their mid- to late fifties. They had left the army and gone about their business. The Massachusetts minutemen had also gone back to their farms and shops; their fighting days were over. The United States would have to depend on their sons if the need to defend liberty ever occurred again. Defense was not on the minds of the people building the new nation ruled in the absence of royalty. If they were to be free, John Adams said, they must be educated. Turning away from defense, the citizens who would rule themselves began to establish a model for the world to emulate. The Continental army was not totally disbanded, but it might as well have been. Now numbering a few thousand, it was a shadow of its former self. The militias, some of which garnered federal support, became social drinking clubs closely connected to political machines. The militiamen did not look like soldiers; few had uniforms. Other than mustering on the village green and marching to the tavern, they had little training. The Continental navy did not survive the transition, and her last ship of war was sold before the Quasi War with France in 1797. The navy Madison could call upon, though very small, was, however, fresh from the Barbary Coast conflict.

The parsimony of Jefferson's regime should have tempered the war talk. An examination of military preparedness when stacked up against the adversary should have spurred expenditures to the War Department in time to stand up a creditable opposition. All of the blustering since 1806 and the trade restrictions, which were largely an ineffective muddle, should have been coupled with military appropriations. But it appears that no one was really spoiling for a fight on the scale of the first real war to engulf the nation. The idea seems to have come on the leadership suddenly, as if there were no other alternative. Jefferson led President Madison to believe that it was an opportunity not to be missed. Perhaps he misjudged England's ability to take on still one more adversary in light of the times. Neither leader seems to have understood the enormous strength and overwhelming sea power possessed by Great Britain in 1812. What consideration they offered for uniformed forces was skewed by their witness of the Revolutionary War. Both believed in the minutemen's invincibility. There was no need for a professional military in the New World. Jefferson had General Henry Dearborn, his secretary of war, now commander of a tiny army, prepare for a ground invasion of Canada. President Madison was made aware of a plan written in the spring of 1812 for a multipronged border crossing of the Canadian frontier. In November of 1811 President Madison convinced Congress to bring the army up to strength. Ten new regiments of infantry, two of artillery, and one light dragoon regiment were authorized.[19] Authorized does not equate to recruited nor trained and provisioned.

It was left to the American navy to meet the might of Great Britain's maritime machine. Yet the navy was a remnant of the Barbary action, much of it in ordinary. Neglected by Jefferson, it was not equipped to mount a campaign against the world's most experienced navy. In defense of the Republican government, which had turned toward commerce, it did not understand the military use of sea power and had not invested.

In President Madison's plea to Congress for war he described "intolerable grievances." In short they were:

1. Impressment of Americans into the Royal Navy
2. The violation by the Royal Navy of the sovereignty of the United States (highlighted by the *Chesapeake* and *Leopard* incident, as well as the *Guerriere's* attack on the *Spitfire*)
3. The intermittent naval blockading of American ports
4. Orders of Council, which restricted neutral ships from trading with European countries and favored British traders over American

On the streets these wrongs were marked by the slogan "Free Trade and Sailors' Rights." Not as catchy as "Don't Tread on Me" or, much later, "Remember the Maine," it did not survive in our history. Yet, at the time, it was heartfelt. The loss of a family man to impressed service in an oppressive and cruel Royal Navy must have been terrible. I am sure it stuck in the minds of America's impressed sailors, all ten thousand of whom were serving against their will in the Royal Navy during the Napoleonic Wars. A considerable number of the crew of HMS *Victory* at Trafalgar were not British, and many of those men were American.

Impressment

Congress, composed of men who had fought or at least lived through the American Revolution, saw the outrageous treatment of sailors aboard Royal Navy ships as intolerably brutal and the act of a sovereign who was an unscrupulous tyrant. King George III, the man Americans regarded as their nemesis, was still on the throne, and many believed he was intent on regaining his former colony or at least punishing it for disloyalty.

The English government did not understand what the fuss was all about. It had furnished its navy in wartime with crewmen through impressment since its inception. The average Englishman regarded it as an outrage as well. The writer Jonathan Swift, author of *Gulliver's Travels*, wrote that in his most fervent imagination, he could not conceive of a more barbaric practice. To the Admiralty, it was like a modern-day draft for national service. The government did not see it as the ruthless theft of a person and loss to his family with no notice or concern for the human being. The Admiralty believed it was a legitimate exercise in recruitment.

The new French government regarded impressment as an act of reckless desperation that was not in character with the culture of England. However, Britain claimed the right to search neutral ships for British subjects in an effort to supply its navy with experienced sailors.

Veterans from Marblehead, Massachusetts, who saved USS Constitution from Confederate seizure during the Civil War campaign to save the ship from the breaker's yard in 1906. (U.S. Naval Academy Museum)

Massachusetts Civil War veterans send Congress a petition, rolled out in the chamber of the House of Representatives, demanding the restoration of USS Constitution, January 18, 1906. (U.S. Naval Academy Museum)

Schoolchild's letter, one of thousands, presenting the funds collected in her classroom for the restoration of USS Constitution. (National Archives)

Crowds come by boat to see USS Constitution *in Gloucester, Massachusetts, harbor in the summer of 1931. (U.S. Naval Academy Museum scrapbook)*

Painting by Marshal Johnson of USS Constitution. *Prints were sold to raise money for restoration. (U.S. Naval Academy Museum)*

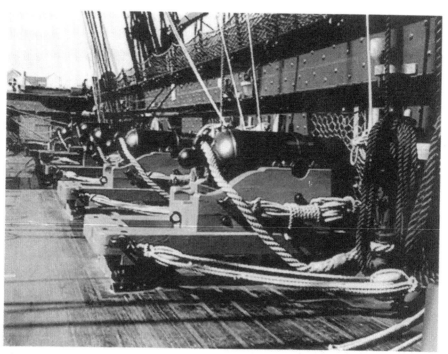

Thirty-two-pound carronades all in a row along the port side of the quarterdeck, October 2003. (Author's photograph)

USS Constitution *today, docked in Charlestown, Massachusetts, next to the dry dock where she was restored. (Courtesy of the author)*

Lieutenant William Marks, USN, first lieutenant of USS Constitution, *in period dress, during the turnaround voyage, October 2003. (Courtesy of the author)*

USS Constitution *today, docked in Charlestown, Massachusetts, next to the dry dock where she was restored. (Courtesy of the author)*

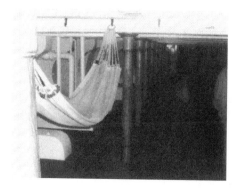

One of the hammocks on the crew deck strung between timbers with the ship's knees visible in the background. (Courtesy of the author)

Twelve-pound cannon from USS Constitution, used during the war with the Barbary pirates in the siege of Tripoli, North Africa, 1803. Rescued in 1880 by Abram Hewitt, gunmetal manufacturer, and placed in front of his home at Ringwood Manor, New Jersey. (Courtesy of the author)

HMS Trincomalee, Royal Navy frigate of the Napoleonic era, restored at the Historic Quay in Hartlepool, England. The plans for the construction of the ship were on board HMS Java when she was sunk by USS Constitution in 1812. As a result, she was not ready for sea duty until after the War of 1812 was over. She is a 38-gun frigate of the pattern engaged by Old Ironsides. (Photo courtesy of the HMS Trincomalee Trust)

USS Constitution *enters the dry dock at the Charlestown Navy Yard in 1931. (U.S. Naval Academy Museum)*

Model of the French class of frigates to which HMS Java *belonged. (U.S. Naval Academy model collection)*

Model of the French class of frigates to which HMS Guerriere belonged. (U.S. Naval Academy model collection)

Old Ironsides at the Charlestown dock in Boston in 1927, before her restoration. (U.S. Naval Academy Museum)

Headquarters of the fund-raising campaign in Philadelphia in 1927. These offices were replicated in most major and many minor cities across the country just before the Great Depression began. (U.S. Naval Academy Museum)

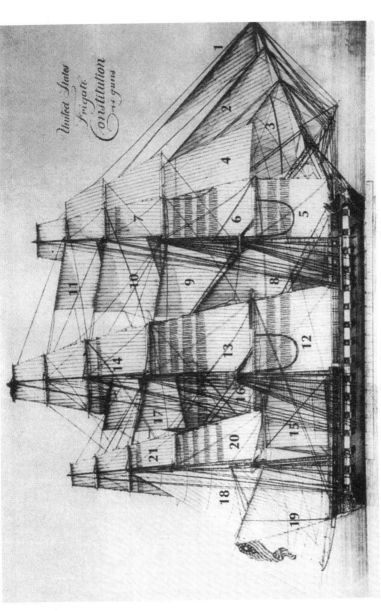

The original sail plan of 1796 for the USS *Constitution*, provided by the National Archives, Washington D.C. 1. Flying Jib. 2. Jib. 3. Fore topmast staysail. 4. Fore staysail. 5. Foresail, or course. 6. Fore topsail. 7. Fore topgallant. 8. Main staysail. 9. Maintopmast staysail. 10. Middle staysail. 11. Main topgallant staysail. 12. Mainsail, or course. 13. Maintopsail. 14. Main topgallant. 15. Mizzen staysail. 16. Mizzen topmast staysail. 17. Mizzen topgallant staysail. 18. Mizzen sail. 19. Spanker. 20. Mizzen topsail. 21. Mizzen topgallant. Note: sails above the topgallants are the royals.

Sailors from USS Constitution at the wheel in uniforms of the War of 1812, during the turnaround voyage of October 2003.

Author in civilian clothes
First row left, ET-2 Edwind Dillaby
First row right, BM-2 Terry Kinney
Back row left, SN Jason Gualenes
Back row right, BM-2 Ronnie Leavell

Captain Joshua Barney, privateer during the War of 1812. (U.S. Naval Academy, Beverley R. Robinson Collection)

Commodore James Barron, captain of USS Chesapeake when attacked by HMS Leopard in 1807 on the way to relieve USS Constitution in the Mediterranean. Fought a duel with Steven Decatur in 1820, which resulted in the death of Decatur. (U.S. Naval Academy, Beverley R. Robinson Collection)

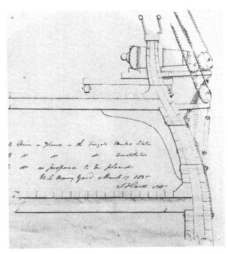

Plan showing placement of channels and the mounting of carronades. (U.S. Naval Historical Center)

Captain James Dacres, Royal Navy, commander of HMS Guerriere, defeated in the first single-ship action with the big American frigate Constitution. (Public Records Office, Kew, England)

In her first action of the War of 1812, USS Constitution, nearly becalmed with studding sail out, is rowed out of danger at sea, pursued by a Royal Navy flotilla, July 1812 off the coast of New England. (U.S. Naval Historical Center, by Anton Otto Fisher)

Commodore John Rodgers commanded USS Constitution *twice, first in 1804 against the Barbary pirates. In 1809 he was given command again but did not care for the handling characteristics and traded her for USS* President, *"a better sailer." (U.S. Naval Academy, Beverley R. Robinson Collection)*

Deck of USS Constitution, *showing seamen cheering at the commencement of the action with HMS* Guerriere. *(U.S. Naval Historical Center)*

HMS Cyane, *USS* Constitution, *and HMS* Levant *battle off the coast of Africa in February 1815, the last naval engagement of the War of 1812. Both Royal Navy ships were defeated and captured. The* Cyane *was converted to an American warship, while the* Levant *was recaptured by the Royal Navy. (U.S. Naval Academy, Beverley R. Robinson Collection)*

HMS Guerriere, *defeated by USS* Constitution *off the coast of New England in August of 1812. The first defeat of a Royal Naval frigate in single combat with an American shocked the people of England, who had become confident that their ships and crews were invulnerable. (U.S. Naval Academy, Beverley R. Robinson Collection)*

Captain Isaac Hull, commander of USS Constitution at the start of the War of 1812, narrowly escaped capture by a Royal Navy flotilla. A month later the Constitution attacked and destroyed HMS Guerriere, the first of several defeats suffered by the Royal Navy in the first six months of the war. (U.S. Naval Academy, Beverley R. Robinson Collection)

HMS Java attacked USS Constitution off the coast of Brazil in December 1812, believing her to be USS Essex, a much smaller opponent. Totally defeated, the crew was taken off the wreck, which was burned. (U.S. Naval Academy, Beverley R. Robinson Collection)

HMS Java and USS Constitution (U.S. Naval Academy, Beverley Robinson Collection)

Marine Corps officer "Captain Carmick Joins the Constitution." (Provided through the courtesy of the artist, Colonel Charles Waterhouse, U.S. Marine Corps, retired)

Marines swarm aboard a French privateer sandwich during the Quasi War at Puerto Plata, Hispaniola, in the Caribbean. Titled "Cutting out the Sandwich," it shows the heroic action of the Marines from the sloop Sally. Research indicates that the Marines of the day may not have had musket slings nor worn belts. (Provided through the courtesy of the artist, Colonel Charles Waterhouse, U.S. Marine Corps, retired)

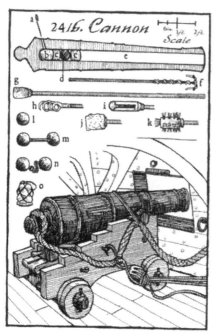

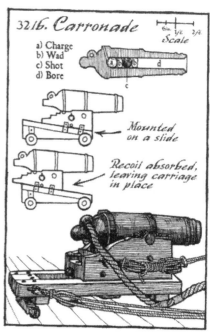

Naval cannon, twenty-four pounds, found on board the American's big frigates during the War of 1812, with an effective range of more than a mile. (Illustration by Andrew Brozyna)

Naval carronade, know as the "smasher," fired a thirty-two-pound projectile, with an effective range of five hundred yards. (Illustration by Andrew Brozyna)

a) Charge
b) Wad
c) Shot
d) Bore

Mounted on a slide

Recoil absorbed, leaving carriage in place

Ready for relaunch at the Portsmouth Navy Yard, New Hampshire, May 27, 1858, after being reconstructed. (U.S. Naval Historical Center)

Heroic naval officers of the United States Navy, during the age of sail.

(top left) William Bainbridge, defeated HMS Java

(bottom left) James Lawrence, commander of USS Hornet and Chesapeake

(center) Stephen Decatur, captured HMS Macedonian

(top right) David Porter, captain of USS Essex, ventured into the Pacific

(bottom right) Thomas Macdonough, victor of Lake Champlain (U.S. Naval Academy, Beverley R. Robinson Collection)

Commodore Edward Preble, captain of USS Constitution during the siege of Tripoli, North Africa, in 1803. After the burning of the captured USS Philadelphia, he attempted to rescue the interned crew through negotiations combined with cannon fire. Many of the future American naval heroes were "Preble's Boys." (U.S. Naval Academy, Beverley R. Robinson Collection)

Repair at Old Navy Yard, Philadelphia, 1873. The strakes have been removed, showing the close framing, only four-inch gaps, which is much smaller than English construction, adding to the strength and resistance to cannonballs. No wonder she was known as Old Ironsides. (U.S. Navy Historical Center)

USS Constitution *before a storm, sailing under reduced canvas off of Malta, in the Mediterranean Sea. (U.S. Naval Academy, Beverley Robinson Collection)*

Captain Charles Stewart, commander of USS Constitution *in the winter of 1815, defeated both HMS Cyane and HMS Levant off the coast of west Africa after the Treaty of Ghent had been signed but not ratified. (U.S. Naval Academy, Beverley R. Robinson Collection)*

The public that saved the ship with its personal interest and intervention throngs, as one hundred thousand a day visit in New York City, 1931. (National Archives, Washington D.C.)

To determine who was English and who was not was up to the presiding officer. In the USS *Chesapeake* incident, the English boarding party had the names of former crew members from HMS *Halifax*. Men who spoke with a distinct British accent were very common. The distinctive American speech patterns were evolving but had not yet become diverse. We were a people divided by a common language. Often the look of an experienced leading seaman was obvious to the inspector, and if he needed the man, he took him. When the war moved on and the need increased, even landsmen were vulnerable.

While Great Britain did not seek war with the United States, when it occurred there were many in the leadership of the Admiralty who saw a chance for rich prizes. Royal Navy captains were eager to win prizes. The increasing numbers of American merchantmen cluttering the sea-lanes were a tempting target and easy pickings since there was no effective American navy to protect them. Their handsome ships and desirable cargoes, when offered up in this new war, were highly sought after.

It is true that Napoleon's government encouraged President Madison and indicated that it was in support of expanding the war against England. But much more importantly, Jefferson drove the government into conflict, hinting of French interest once again. Former president Thomas Jefferson, though perhaps the most brilliant framer of the Constitution and the Revolution, could not help himself when it came to intriguing against England. Seeing Great Britain decisively engaged with Napoleon and the continental system, he saw a chance to revenge her excesses and refusal to acknowledge the United States as a sovereign nation. He would ensure that Great Britain lost Canada. "The taking of Canada this year is a mere matter of marching" is the never-to-be-forgotten overstatement that puts Jefferson in a very bad light. It plunged the unprepared and utterly incompetently led American army into two years of fighting, which accomplished little but the killing and maiming of untrained and ill-equipped young men.

England versus America

When war was declared in June of 1812, England published "Orders of Council" in the *London Times* newspaper. They instructed all Royal Navy ship commanders to bring into port all ships belonging to the United States of America. At the same time, the British government recognized the need to protect its merchant fleet from the attacks by marauding American navy ships and privateers. It reinstated the Convoy Act, which required British merchantmen involved in Caribbean and North American trade to travel within the confines of protected convoys. In a way, Jefferson's attempt to penalize and interfere with English trade, which he had tried to impose through his policies while in office, was accomplished when Madison asked for a declaration of war. The Royal

Navy was now burdened with convoy duty, which it did not seek. It preferred to sweep the seas of privateers, prizes, and American navy ships in offensive actions. The defensive posture of acting as nursemaids for lumbering merchant vessels took valuable elements from the fleet. The traders were even more put out by the order. They would be delayed as they waited for rendezvous and be restricted by the speed of the slowest ship in the convoy. To them, time was money.

In 1812 the Royal Navy had 191 ships of the line and 245 frigates in addition to hundreds of armed men-of-war of lesser size. It boasted the largest ship-building capacity in the world, which extended all the way to India. There was a man serving in the fleet for every two hundred men, women, and children in Britain's population.[20] In addition to the cost to the Royal Navy, England had a great deal at stake in the War of 1812. Jefferson was correct: Britain did not want more war; it had had its fill. By fall, the British government requested talks to settle the conflict and had repealed some of the restrictions imposed on trade. But Mr. Madison had his war and was not interested in calling it off. There were a mere 3,500 English regulars in Canada, and sending more was out of the question. Adding the American navy to Great Britain's list of enemies was significant in that more warships would have to be built and crews impressed. It was very much akin to the nearly intolerable drain the wars of the twentieth century put on the British economy.

Perhaps Jefferson was correct, and he could extract Canada from the colonial grip of Great Britain. He was not aware of future events but had to rest his judgment on his own time. He had been a vital part of the defeat of England during the American Revolution. Since Great Britain had lost before against a colonial uprising, she could do so again. The majority of the population in Upper Canada was French. He could have expected that they had been nursing a desire for self-determination since their loss on the Plains of Abraham in 1760. It was well established that the French Canadians were not overly enamored with English rule. Projecting world affairs beyond the first twelve years of the century, he could have been very wise to think that England had had her day, that she was overcommitted and unable to reinforce her last remaining colony in North America. Earlier, as ambassador to France, he had seen the "people's France" emerge from the Revolution and witnessed its rise to prominence. As the years passed by quickly, he applauded France's success when he was president. He was a Francophile, steeped in her culture and learning. Jefferson knew men in the French government. The former president corresponded with the Marquis de Lafayette. Napoleon was tremendously successful in his continental wars. Between 1796 and the summer of 1812, he had rolled over all opposition. When he was in command in Spain, he had routed the British army. He had seriously threatened an invasion of the British Isles. The Great Ogre could do so again. It was no stretch of the imagination to believe that the emperor would rule for many years to come and continue to drain England of her wealth and power. Jefferson, Madison, and the Congress did not foresee Napoleon's disastrous Russian campaign and that he would be stuck in the winter snow that very year of 1812. Who would have predicted that by the spring of 1814 Napoleon would be gone, leaving England victorious? Jefferson did not have the advantage of our hindsight.

Napoleon's invasion only sent Russia deeper into the arms of Great Britain, and with her came Sweden. This opened up vital trade, particularly for the shipbuilding industry in England. Hemp for rope and timber for masts and hulls flowed into English shipyards. The loss of the American forests would not curtail the royal dockyards. Wellington's successful campaign in Spain made the Spanish ulcer bleed more profusely than ever. American merchant-ship owners ignored restrictions and continued to supply the British Army through Lisbon. Indeed, the British Army in Canada, which could not sustain itself, relied on American beef and shipbuilding materials along the border of Quebec and Ontario. The American smugglers preferred English gold coin to the U.S. dollar. The provisioning had been going on, unabated by the customs service, since Jefferson imposed the trade restrictions in 1807.

The primary markets of the farmers and foresters of the northern border states of New York and Vermont were across the Saint Lawrence River in Upper Canada. Roads to the south were nonexistent. The water route down Lake Champlain, with portages to Lake George and portage again to the headwaters of the Hudson River, was not attractive. Three hundred dreadfully slow miles could not compete with the lure of the near neighbors of Montreal. President Jefferson's dispute at the federal level meant little to hard-pressed northern American merchants in the harsh land halfway to the North Pole.

American Privateering, or Just Plain Pirates?

The one thing that the English government did fear in a war with the United States was the specter of more privateers. Commercial raiding was profitable to America because it gave employment to so many in the maritime community and mercantile industry.

The *Statesman*, a London newspaper, complained within a week of the start of the American War of 1812, "America cannot certainly wage war with us, She has no navy. But America has nearly 100,000 as good seaman as any nation in the world, all of whom would be actively employed against our trade in every part of the ocean in their fast sailing ships of war. . . . They will be found sweeping the West Indian Seas and even carrying desolation into the chop of the channel."[21]

A Chilling Account of American Activity

What follows is the personal account of First Lieutenant George Little on board the privateer *George Washington*.

> The 120 ton schooner was barely armed with one 12 and two long 9 pounders. We were after little vessels that had no real impact on England's merchant industry. Yet we wrapped ourselves in the "star-spangled-banner" and went plundering. I feared injury but prison even more but it did not deter me from the adventure and quest for wealth. We sailed from Norfolk, Virginia in July of 1812, only a month after the declaration of war.
>
> The crew was scraped together from the lowest dens of wretchedness and vice and only wanted a leader to induce them to any act of daring and desperation. We cruised on the Spanish Main and between the islands of the Caribbean. We joined with the *Black Joke*, a privateer sloop out of Albany, New York.[22]

The glory of fighting the old foe, the British, and the memory of flags waving in the streets of Boston, Baltimore, and Norfolk soon left the young officer when he witnessed his first engagement. After combat he writes,

> This affair very much disgusted me with privateering, especially when I saw so much loss of life, and beheld a band of ruthless desperadoes, for such I must call our crew, robbing and plundering a few defenceless beings who were pursuing both a lawful and peaceable calling. It induced me to form a resolve that I would relinquish what, to my mind, appeared to be an unjustifiable and outrageous pursuit, for I could not help believing that no conscientious man could be engaged in privateering, and certainly there is no honour to be gained by it.[23]

It was true, there were one hundred thousand qualified seamen in the United States prior to the war who could be lured into privateering by the hope of cash rewards. Americans today don't think of themselves as a maritime nation, as deep-water sailors, but just prior to the War of 1812, America was tied to the sea. An immediate upward reaction in the London insurance rates caused great consternation and called for the Admiralty to "do something."

CHAPTER SIX

~

The War of 1812 Begins

Now lads, we have got something to do that will shave the rust from our jackets. War is declared. We shall have another dash at our old enemies. It is the very thing you have long wanted. The rascals have been bullying over us these ten years, and I am glad the time has come when we can have satisfaction.

—Captain John Rodgers, USS *President*

The face of the War of 1812 can be most discouraging when one considers the opponent's capability. The U.S. Navy in 1812 had 8 frigates and 12 sloops of war in commission, total of all accounts—20 warships in various states of disrepair. The Royal Navy had 584 men-of-war. Yet the American naval officer corps welcomed the engagement. The incredible euphoria among the leadership of the American navy can be attributed to their experience in the Barbary conflict, where they gained a confidence in Joshua Humphreys's design of the big frigate. Though they had not taken on a Royal Navy rater, they could see that they fit into a niche, as Humphreys had predicted. While undergunned to take on a 64-gun or above ship of the line, they could outrun one. Anything smaller, to include all of His Majesty's frigates, was well within their fighting profile.

Call in the Expert

At this point it may be important to establish USS *Constitution*'s credentials. I went to see Captain Kenneth Johnson, USN (ret), an authority on the ship, at the Naval Historical Center in Washington, D.C. The question I put to him was, "What was the gun configuration at the start of the War of 1812?" He assured me that the baseline of armament at the start of the war was thirty 24-pounders on the gun deck, twenty-four 32-pound carronades, and one 18-pound cannon on the quarterdeck which was a trade for two 24s. Between 1810 and 1813, the big 44-gun frigate carried 51 total guns. In response to further inquiries, Johnson added, "The attitude of the ship was bow up so that under sail the nose of the ship would not be pushed down by the press of the sail and she would be level." Further, the navy began to identify its vessels by class, while the Royal Navy rated theirs. The big 44s were first class, and the smaller ones in the 30s became second class. Sloops of war and brigs were third and fourth class. As the navy began to build larger ships, after that war, ships moved within classes into the age of steam. To relieve my confusion over names, which seem to me to be tossed around in nautical circles, a brig has two masts and is ship rigged (square sails), while a sloop of war has three masts and is ship rigged but, unlike a frigate, has only one deck.

Sailors Become Uniform

The skills and duties of the ordinary and able seamen were well defined by June of 1812. However, there were no prescribed uniforms; the men wore "slops," or simple loose clothing of their own. When it became necessary to replace them, the purser provided a stock, which he sold at cost plus a small commission. Since the crew was paid off at the end of each voyage and a new crew recruited, it seemed to work. However, it was difficult to build a service with a "pickup team." Therefore, Secretary Hamilton issued the following instructions:

Purser Samuel Hambleton
St Michael. E Shore Md
15 June, 1812

I have received Your letter, of the 8. Inst. The Navy agent at N York has made a contract, with Mr. Macy of Hudson, for a considerable supply, of blue cloth, for navy use; I wish such cloth use in preference to any other.

On your arrival at N York You will make a requisition on the Navy agent for such supply of Slop Clothing, as may be necessary who will accordingly furnish such supply.

The following are considered articles of the first neccessity., & what is generally understood, by the term, Slop Clothing, viz.

Common Hatts.
Com. Shoes
Pea Jacketts
Stockings
Cloth Jacketts
Blankets
Duck Jacketts Cloth.

Mattresses
Cloth. & Duck Trowsers
Duck frocks
Guernsey ditto
Check Shirts

In order to enable You safely to keep these articles, you will be allowed, at the public expense, a suitable room; & You will also be allowed a room, in which to keep Your accounts.

Each of the gunboats will be allowed a steward, & You will be allowed one extra Steward.

Upon the articles of Slop Clothing to be issued out by You, to the Crews of the Gunboats stationed at New Port, You may charge to the men to who You may issue them, a commission of 12½ P/Cent.

The Navy agent at N York, will advance You such sums, not exceeding $2,000 as may be required, to enable You, to Provide a supply of Small Stores.

Signed P. Hamilton[1]

While this is a far cry from "uniform regulations," it appears to be an early attempt to address the problem.

A New Captain Takes the *Constitution* to War

Isaac Hull took the *Constitution* from John Rodgers in an exchange of ships in June of 1810 for no apparent reason except that Rodgers found the *President* to be "more responsive." He did so even after his redistribution of the *Constitution*'s ballast, which he said improved her performance. Isaac Hull was one of the most experienced maritime officers at thirty-seven; his character was calm and collected no matter what the situation. Early in his tenure, he experienced the same sluggishness in the *Constitution* reported by Rodgers and investigated the underside to discover that it was encrusted with sea life. It clung to the copper bottom. The solution was to seek out the freshwater of the Delaware River to kill the crustaceans and scrape them off. With the streamlining improved, Hull took to the patrolling of the eastern seaboard.

Boredom Bred Bad Behavior

Peacetime in home waters changes the focus of the young. Rather than enjoying the breather and training for the future, the young midshipmen became entangled in affairs of the heart. Such dealings were a dangerous practice in the early part of that century, brought on by hurt, inexcusable insults, or challenges of honor. In the most immediate cases, all three played their theatrical part. It may be hard to understand today, when a person's word means little. At that time a reputation was to be maintained unsullied at all cost. So it was that a ruse was hatched allowing two hotheads to go ashore with their seconds and a brace of single-shot pistols. The duel was not of the magnitude of Hamilton versus Burr or, later, the tragic demise of Decatur in yet another senseless encounter. Messrs. Rodgers and Morgan managed to kill the former and seriously wound the latter, while seconded by Midshipman Archibald Hamilton, son of the secretary of the navy.

"The following day—during the funeral a sailor fell from the mast head and was killed. Fifteen minutes later another fell from the same place and later died. While moving him to the cockpit, a sailor fell backwards into the hold and broke his leg. Two days later, while under sail, a midshipman fell overboard and drown. While attempting to rescue him three men fell out of a boat and nearly drown."[2] The *Constitution* was beginning to acquire the reputation of a "hard-luck ship." In the days of highly superstitious seafarers, that was not of assistance when recruiting a new crew.

During this period, her crew extensively refurbished the *Constitution*. Captain Hull could see that war was coming on at lightning speed. The caboose, or galley stove, had the flat stones replaced underneath. The only open fire permitted, it rested on rock rather than a wooden deck, which would surely catch fire. The stove was installed on the gun deck under the forecastle, and the smoke was vented out through the "Charley Noble," or stovepipe, to the deck above. During cold nights the cabins and crew deck were warmed with "heat pots" that were filled with coals from the cook fire. Even cannonballs were heated and put in the suspended pots. The cast-iron containers were fifteen inches high and the size of a five-gallon bucket. They could be safely rested on the deck for a few brief minutes due to the curled iron feet that held them three inches off the deck. (Today they hang in the officers' cabins of USS *Constitution*, moored on the Charles River in Boston.)

A change in the ship's silhouette made her recognizable to all navies. Hull installed a split dolphin striker to her bow. This was a short perpendicular spar under the cap of the bowsprit used for holding down or guying the jibboom by means of a martingale. It was a necessary spar to support the rigging needed to counteract the upward pull on the jibboom from the fore topgallant stays. The name, of course, comes from the position of the spar, which pointed vertically down toward the sea just beyond the bow of the vessel. It was said it would strike a dolphin if one were to leap out of the water just beneath it.[3]

War Was About to Inject Reality

On the eve of war, two years later, Hull was captain of the *Constitution*, preparing to meet Commodore John Rodgers, USS *President*, off the coast of New York. He received the following message from the secretary of the navy as war began.

June 18th, 1812
Sir:

    This day war has been declared between the "United Empire of Great Britain & Ireland" and their dependencies and the United States of America and their territories and you are with the force under your command entitled to every belligerent right to attack and capture and to defend—You will use the utmost dispatch to reach New York after you have made up your complement of men & c[argo] at Annapolis. In your way from thence, you will not fail to notice the british flag, should it present itself—I am informed that the Belvidera is on our coast, but you are not to understand me as impelling you to battle, previously to your having confidence in your crew unless attacked, or with a reasonable prospect of success, of which you are to be at your discretion to Judge. You are to reply to this and inform me of your progress.

Respectfully yrs.

Paul Hamilton[4]

    The next day, one day following the beginning of the hostilities, Commodore Rodgers sent the secretary his assessment of the enemy situation (he was not yet aware that war had been declared):

U.S. Frigate President
New York 19th June 1812

    . . . British naval force at present on this side the Atlantic consists of one sixty four—seven frigates—seven sloops of war—seven Brigs, & two or three schooners—Hallifax & Bermuda are their ports of rendezvous; & permit me to observe, Sir, that should war be declared, & our vessels get to sea, in squadron, before the British are apprised of it, I think it not impossible that we may be able to cripple & reduce their force in detail; to such an extent as to place our own upon a footing until their loss could be supplied by a reinforcement from England.

    The President & Hornet are ready for sea & the Essex will I hope be ready in ten days from this date.

    It is this moment reported that the frigates U States & Congress are off the Bar. The British frigate Belvidera & sloop of War Tartarus were seen off Sandy Hook yesterday morning—The schooner Macherel with Mr. Ruff (English messenger) sailed last evening for Hallifax,

    With the greatest respect

Jn Rodgers.[5]

Some of the First "Few Good Men": The United States Marine Corps

As might be expected, fighting infantry was a primary concern to Secretary of War Eustis. The rapid expansion of the army was not going well. An incentive of sixteen dollars, part paid on sign-up and the rest when the new soldier mustered, was augmented by the promise of a severance pay of three months' salary and 160 acres. The land was in Ohio, Indiana, and Illinois, part of a plan to move the frontier westward. A death benefit was also to be included if the soldier did not survive. The Marine Corps, in a sense naval infantry, could not compete without some stimulus. None was forthcoming from Congress.

The secretary of the navy took it upon himself to assist the recruiters.

To: Lieutenant Colonel Commandant Franklin Wharton, U.S.M.C.
19 June, 1812
Sir,

After having performed your business in N York you will proceed to Hudson.

Congress having offered extraordinary inducements to Soldiers to enter the army, it becomes proper that some additional inducement should be offered to persons to enter the Marine Corps. You will therefore consider yourself at liberty to allow to each man who shall enter the Corps—Twenty dollars bounty—of which 10$ are to be paid at the time of signing the articles—& 10$ on their being first mustered

I am Sir etc
Paul Hamilton,
Secretary of the Navy.[6]

In September of 1776 the uniform coat of green with white facings and a leather stock was prescribed for the Continental marines. It was green because that was all that was available. Their recruiting drum sported a coiled American rattlesnake and the words, "Don't tread on me." The four-inch leather detached collar was ostensibly to protect the neck from saber cuts but in reality was, as in the British Army, meant to keep the head up on parade and improve the stature of the marine. Of course, like the British "Tommies," the men hated them and seemed to lose them at every opportunity. However, the name "leatherneck" stuck. At Christmas 1776, as a part of Washington's crossing of the Delaware River, they took part in the action against the British garrison at Trenton, New Jersey. Later, aboard the *Ranger* with John Paul Jones, they raided the English coast in 1778.

Samuel Sewall's bill to establish a marine force rather than placing a quota on newly commissioned ships for a marine contingent authorized the creation of a Corps of Marines. With central authority, the corps would provide recruitment, training, equipping, and managing of the force, as an arm of the U.S. Navy. Thus, July 11, 1798, became the true birthday of the Marine Corps. The old blue coats with red facings, left behind by Anthony Wayne's Continental legion and stored at West Point were issued to the new Marine Corps in place of the green. Round, black broad-brim hats, edged in yellow with the left side pinned up, were the most impractical for wear on the windy sea, in the tops. The hats were not unlike the Royal Marines' hats with the turned-up brim piped in white. The domed crown of the hat was a little lower in the American version.[7]

Going to Sea

The secretary had his hands full during preparations to send the American fleet out against the Royal Navy. Initially he deployed two squadrons. Commodore Rodgers took the *President* and the *United States*, both 44s; the *Congress*, 36; the *Hornet*, 18; and the *Argus*, 16, and assumed a station east of New York harbor. They extended far out to intercept English Caribbean prizes. Commodore Decatur's squadron, which consisted of the frigates *United States*, 44, and *Congress*, 36, took the southern approaches and waited outside Norfolk for the English convoys from the Caribbean. The *Constitution* under Isaac Hull struggled out of the Chesapeake Bay, after hosting a visit by Secretary Hamilton at Annapolis, and sailed north to join Rodgers. Soon, Hamilton had second thoughts and sent orders that restricted Rodgers's operation closer to the Atlantic coast so he could accomplish two things at once. Not only could he pick up British vessels that Decatur missed, but he could also protect American shipping near New England ports. Hamilton feared the Halifax Royal Navy squadron to the north. But his afterthought was too late; Rodgers was moving east, now out of reach, that summer of 1812. Hull also missed his rendezvous and was left alone off of Massachusetts.

Secretary Hamilton's instructions to the commanders at sea were in accord with those of all politicians of all time. He directed the vigorous pursuit, capture, and destruction of the enemy, "unless he is too powerful and might endanger the command." Such warnings appear over and over again in orders throughout military history. At the end there is always the caveat not to lose the battle. Implied is the politician's tail-covering warning to protect him from public wrath. If there were a tragedy, the political leader could always clear his own name by saying, "I warned him of the danger, which went unheeded." But that is part of the game and the risk associated with command. The reward of victory is as high as the consequences of defeat are low.

Very Nearly First Blood

Rodgers, secure in the center of his clustered squadron, was called to the quarterdeck when the lookout in the tops spotted the sail of a square-rigged ship that could not be American. It was a gift. The frigate, HMS *Belvidera*, which Rodgers had reported to be off New York harbor, was making tracks north.

Almost immediately Rodgers's big 44-gun frigate *President* outpaced the squadron in pursuit of the smaller English frigate. Winds were light and the sea was nearly calm one hundred miles off the New York coast. The studding sails (pronounced "stun" sails) were hauled up and spread like billowing white wings. Water was sprayed and dumped on them to improve performance, but little to no gain was achieved. The chase turned into a slow dance, hour after hour. Rodgers's account is telling:

> I gave orders to commence a fire with the bow chase guns, at his spars and rigging, in the hope of crippling one or the other, so far as to enable us to get alongside: the fire from our bow chase guns he instantly returned with those from his Stern, which was now kept up by both Ships without intermission until 50 minutes past four when one of the Presidents chase guns burst and killed and wounded sixteen persons among the latter myself. This was not however the most serious injury, as by the bursting of the Gun, and the explosion of the passing box, from which it was served with powder, both the Main and Forecastle decks (near the gun) was so much shattered as to prevent the use the Chase Gun, on that side, for some time: Our main deck guns being single shotted I now gave orders to put our helm to Starboard and fire the starboard broadside, in the expectation of disabling some of his Spars, but did not succeed, altho I could discover that his rigging had sustained considerable damage, and that he had received some injury in the Stern.

Rodgers repeated this maneuver several times, yawing the *President* to one side or the other to fire a broadside rather than the single bow chase that was left in action. Each time he did so, the *President* lost what little of the closure he had worked so hard to gain.

The English ship was unaware that the American government had declared war. The report of the *Belvidera's* captain, Richard Byron, confirms the American account, but he does not comment on the amount of destruction caused by the *Constitution's* fire and is unaware of the burst gun:

> At 4:20 he opened his fire from his foremost Guns I had given the most positive orders to my Lieutenants to prick the Cartridges but not to prime the Guns. Although ignorant of the War, we were of course prepared, and about five Minutes afterwards opened ours with two Carronades 32 Pounders and two long Eighteens from the Stern. In light Winds the President sail better than the Belvidera, and as his second, a very heavy Frigate, sail'd as well. I acknowledge I was much surprised at the nearest Ship, yawing repeatedly and giving starboard and larbard Broadsides, when it was fully in his power to have run up alongside the Belvidera. I thought it my duty to make a firm retreat from three Frigates of the largest Class accompanied by a small Frigate or sloop and a brig of War two of which bore broad Pendants.

The *Belvidera* also deployed studding sails to increase her speed. What Byron fails to mention is that he jettisoned a considerable amount of weight in the end to outdistance the American pursuit. The use of the carronades by the British ship indicates that the two ships were indeed close, not more than five hundred yards apart at times.

The Mirror Image

Within three weeks, Captain Isaac Hull took on the role of Captain Richard Byron. It was England's squadron, hunting American combatants, that saw a square-rigged ship that could not be Royal Navy, several hundred miles north of the *Belvidera*'s encounter. The one common thread in the first two engagements of the naval war of 1812 was Byron's ship, the *Belvidera*. The Royal Navy squadron out of Halifax station contained a rater with which the Americans could not contend. She was the *Africa*, a ship of the line rated at 64 guns. Not alone, she was in company with the *Belvidera*, 36; the *Shannon*, 38; the *Guerriere*, 38; the *Acolus*, 32; and a schooner. But the *Africa* was slow, too slow. Off the coast of Cape Cod, at first the winds were fresh from the south, but soon they dropped off. The air seemed to hang on a hook and steering could not be maintained. Through the night, nothing changed. By sunrise, conditions were stark still, and the bow of the *Constitution* swung lazily around to face the enemy squadron, becalmed at sea five miles away.

Captain Hull's after-action report to the secretary of the navy was penned on July 21, chronicling the previous days' extraordinary slow-motion chase.

> The Boats were instantly hoisted out and sent ahead to tow the Ship's head round and to endeavor to get her farther from the Enemy. . . . The boats of the Enemy were got out and sent ahead to tow which with the light air that remained with them, they came up very fast. Finding the Enemy coming fast up and but little chance of escaping from them, I ordered two of the Guns on the Gun Deck, run out at the Cabbin windows for Stern Guns on the gun deck and hoisted one of the 24 pounders off the Gun Deck, and run that with the Fore Castle Gun, an Eighteen pounder, out at the Ports on the Quarter deck, and cleared the ship for Action, being determined they should not get her, without resistance on our part. Notwithstanding their force, and the situation we were placed in. At about 7 in the Morning the ship nearest us approaching with Gun Shot, and directing astern, I ordered one of the Stern Guns fired to see if we could reach her, to endeavor to disable her masts, found the shot fell a little Short, would not fire any more.
>
> At 8 four of the Enemy's ships nearly within Gun Shot, some of them having six or eight boats ahead towing, with all their oars, and sweep out to row them up with us, which they were fast doing. It soon appeared that we must be taken, and that our Escape was impossible four heavy ships nearly within Gunshot, and

coming up fast, and not the least hope of a breeze, to give us a chance of getting off by out sailing them.

Hull said to his first lieutenant, Morris, "Lets lay broadsides to them Mr. Morris, and fight the whole. If they sink us, we'll go down like men."[8] Words, I am sure, that reflect the heat of the moment. Isaac Hull's character was under siege; he wanted to fight, not run.

In this Situation finding ourselves in only twenty four fathoms of water [suggestion of that valuable officer Lieutenant Charles Morris] I determined to try and warp the ship ahead, by carrying out anchors and warp her up to them. Three or four hundred fathoms [1,800 to 2,400 feet] of rope was instantly got up, and two anchors got ready and sent ahead, by which means we began to gain ahead of the Enemy. They however soon saw our Boats carrying out the anchors, and adopted the same plan, under very advantageous circumstances, as all the Boats, from the Ship furthermost off were sent to Tow and Warp up those nearest to us, by which means they again came up. So that at 9 the Ship nearest us began firing her bow guns. Which were instantly returned by our Stern guns in the cabbin, and on the Quarter Deck. All the shots from the Enemy fell short, but we have reason to believe that some of ours went on board her, as we could not see them strike the water.

Soon after 9 a Second Frigate passed under our lee, and opened her broadside but finding her shot fall short, discontinued her fire, but continued as did all the rest of them, to make every possible exertion to get up with us. From 9 to 12 all hands were employed in warping the ship ahead, and in starting some of the water in the main hold to lighten her, which with the help of a light air, we rather gained of the Enemy or at least hold our own. About 2 in the afternoon, all the Boats from the line of Battle Ship [Africa] and some of the Frigates, were sent to the Frigate nearest to us to endeavor to tow her up, but a light breeze sprung up, which enabled us to hold way with her notwithstanding they had Eight or Ten Boats'ahead, and all her sails furled to tow her to windward. The wind continued light until 11 at night, and the Boats were kept ahead towing, and warping to keep out of the reach of the Enemy. Three of their Frigates being very near us. At 11 we got a light breeze from the Southward, the boats came along side, and we hoisted up, the ship having too much way to keep them ahead. The Enemy still in chase, and very near.

19th. At day light passed within gunshot of one of the Frigates but she did not fire on us, perhaps for fear of becalming her as the wind was light. Soon after passing us, she tacked, and stood after us, at this time Six Sail were in Sight under all sail after us.

At 9 in the morning saw a Strange sail on our Weather Beam, supposed to be an American merchant ship the instant the Frigate nearest us saw her she hoisted American colours, as did all the Squadron in hopes to decoy her down. I immediately hoisted English colours that she might not be deceived, she soon halted her wind, and it is to be hoped made her escape. All this day the Wind increased gradually and we gained on the Enemy, in the course of the day Six or Eight miles, they however continued chasing us all night under a press of Sail.

20th. At day light in the Morning only three of them could be seen from the Mast head, the nearest of which, was about 12 miles off directly astern. All hands were set at work wetting the Sails, from the Royals down, with the Engine, and fire buckets and we soon found that we left the Enemy very fast. At ½ past 8 the Enemy finding that they were dropped astern gave up the chase.

Signed

Isaac Hull

At sea,

USS Constitution

The sight of a cluster of warships knotted together with wet towlines in a slow dance across a calm, motionless blue sea is difficult to believe, if not seen. It was an incredible feat of endurance and tenacity on both sides. It was also an exceptional feat of leadership, a wonder that the officers could maintain the crew's energy. The men must have been exhausted after the first day of rowing. To continue to warp and haul all the next day and into the third must have been grueling work. While the two bower and single-sheet anchors weighed near to 5,000 pounds, the two kedge anchors used were 700 and 400 pounds. The double capstans, one on each deck on the same axle, were normally used to raise the main anchors. But rather than pulling up an anchor, the capstan could be employed as a winch. Often in port, in order to move the ship a short distance or to turn it around at the dock, the light kedge anchor would be rowed out and dropped. Once it took a bite on the bottom, the line could be wound around the capstan, which was rotated by a party of men pushing on the bars, until the ship was brought directly over the anchor. The action taken by the *Constitution*, while extremely rare in combat, was also used to get a ship out of the "doldrums" in shallow water. Some small frigates had oarlocks fitted to the hull to row the ship if necessary.

There were several types of boats available on the ships. The wherry was a small boat for the use of the officers and captain. The pinnace was a large boat for on-shore replenishment. But likely the boats used in the chase were quarter boats, sometimes called whaleboats. They were twenty-eight feet long, which was ideal since they could handle both the anchor and the crew necessary to propel the ship.

The American sailors were no doubt motivated by the threat of capture and prison in England. The press had been filled with horror stories of sailors languishing in pestilent holes, abandoned and forgotten. The thought of captivity must have provided the necessary adrenaline. The British crews wanted that first victory of the American War of 1812 (the name given in England to the conflict) and the prize money that would come to them all for a big frigate. She would be worth a fortune and could provide a life of ease in old age and a good deal to drink.

Captain Richard Byron, of HMS *Belvidera*, recorded the account of the chase in a letter to Herbert Sawyer, Esq., vice admiral of the blue at Halifax Station.

At 3 PM on the 16th a strange sail was seen in the winds eye, which afterward proved to be the Constitution of 56 guns, on her way from Chesapeake Bay to NY. A general chase insued, and was continued during the night. At day light on the 17th it being then calm, the enemy's ship and her pursuers hoisted out their boats to tow, and at 7:30 the former began warping herself ahead in 24 fathoms of water. She then bore from the Belvidera S.W. By S. distant four miles at 9 o'clock. A light air sprang up from the S.S.E., and the Belvidera trimed sail on the larbored tack. At 10:30 the breeze freshened, but in a few minutes died away to calm; when Capt. Byron, observing the benefit that the Constitution had derived from warping, immediately commenced the same operation, bending all his hawsers to one another, and working two kedge anchors at the sametime, by paying the warp through on house-hole as it was run in through another opposite. The effect of this was soon visible, and at noon the American, whose *boomes* had just before been throuwn overboard, was with gunshot of Belvidera. At 2PM the enemy opened fire from his stern-chasers, which was returned occasionally by Captain Byron's bow guns. At 3, a light breeze enabled the Constitution to gain ground, and firing ceased; but the chase continued till day-light on the 18th, by which time she was four miles ahead, and being a clean ship she ultimately effected her escape.[9]

(Note that the calendars appear to differ in the two accounts.)

Know Your Enemy

Looking back a bit, as the year 1800 loomed and Napoleon grew in power and influence in central Europe and the Baltic, England saw a need for more warships to maintain its interests, which were the most expansive in the Western world. While the great rated ships of 64 and above were impressive and brought adversaries to think twice before marauding the trading lanes, there was a need to build more every day. The cost was prohibitive and so England sought to follow the lead of the French and Americans, who were developing bigger frigates that were fast, resilient, well armed, and cheap, to maintain control of the seven seas. When faced with an enemy frigate, the Admiralty earnestly believed that the quality of its ship-handling captains and their well-schooled gun crews would lead to victory over equal vessels manipulated by lesser men. HMS *Shannon*, built in 1801 at the Brindley, Finsbury, England, launched in September 1803, and fitted out at the Chatham Royal dockyard, was grounded and destroyed on December 11, 1807. A new frigate was built and named *Shannon*; like the phoenix, she rose again in the War of 1812. Redesigned along French lines, sleek and fast, she would prove a threat.[10]

The "on again, off again" war with Napoleon in 1804 jump-started the Royal Navy, which had neglected the building program, and it laid down the keels of eleven new frigates and three major 120-gun ships. A year later, the epic battle of Trafalgar reminded the nation, government, and military men of England of the importance of sea supremacy. The first sea lord, Lord Barham, known for his comptrollership, naturally took advantage of the latest design, which combined speed, armament, and combat experience. There was conflict at the highest level, however. The dominant Lord St. Vincent looked at ships merely as steady gun platforms. Sweeping away the French and Spanish fleet in one stroke, Admiral Lord Nelson overshadowed the single-meeting engagement. After the 1805 victory at Trafalgar, the Admiralty turned its attention to smaller, faster, and more numerous warships to control what had been gained by the big fleet. Domination of the seas could mean control of the ports by blockade, which defined the offense, while convoy support became the defense. England showed her colors with station fleets. Several fast frigates accompanied the first-, second-, and third-raters, the 120- to 74-gun ships. Brigs and cutters, fast fliers, scouted, ran errands, and managed resupply. Their enemies had little choice since they could no longer afford tactics based on huge behemoths. They turned to hit-and-run navies and provided "letters of marque" to privateers to take what they could from the British merchant fleet and decoy away Royal Navy blockade ships. The American navy's prime warships rated well down the scale to between fourth and fifth.

England's Forty Thieves

While French designs of frigate hulls were fast and strong, they had the disadvantage of a severe tumble home (the topmost deck was smaller than the deck below), which caused some instability.

The captains complained that English design established the lower gun decks too near the waterline, so that in heavy or even moderate seas, the bigger guns on the lower deck could not be brought into action for fear of shipping too much water. The new second surveyor, the designer of ships, Henry Peake, a bit of an old-school man, believed that would be solved by reducing the sheer of the gun deck, thereby raising the height of the gun ports.[11] The frigates, while sleek, could not carry a great supply of food and water and needed constant replenishment compared to the higher raters. The English in 1806 laid down the keels of twenty-one frigates. Their hulls were primarily of French design. A boon came in 1806 when they captured eighteen frigates from engagements with the French and Danes. This allowed the Royal Navy to increase the number of third-rate 74s. These warships, then turned against their makers, were to be known as the "forty thieves."

The Difference in Design

In general, British frigates were small compared to American ones. They were built in numerous small yards spread around England, and the builders were thought to be operating on such a small scale that they were not capable of larger forms. The major naval yards, both government and commercial, were overbooked because of the cutback in construction prior to the resolution of the war with France. The yards were committed as well to the restoration of serving warships, which was very demanding. The cost of materials and labor in commercial shipyards continued to escalate, forcing the Royal Naval Board to go back to the government yards, which could reduce the cost by 5 percent.[12] There is an old saying among the military-industrial complex that applies here: "One can never afford the price of the new weapon technology of the day, but one must have it."

By 1808, the Royal Navy was able to increase production with the help of its dockyards in Bombay, India. The designs they produced were French in origin. English naval officers, perhaps the best in the world, praised the handling and speed of the captured French frigates. There were two basic patterns taken from the French frigates, which became England's Lively and Leda classes. The Leda hull was more shallow and required the forward magazine to be hung just abaft of the foremast. In spite of their good ship characteristics, Leda frigates were small compared to the throw weight of the American 44s. Though the British ships were quick, the big American frigates were just as fast or faster. A great deal depended upon the captain and crew to get the best out of each design.

The Captain Was Fixing for a Fight

Having outsailed, or, to put it bluntly, outrowed the enemy, Captain Hull and his crew were looking for a fight. It was humiliating to have had to run, even though the odds were so against them that it would have been foolish to risk the valuable ship at the start of the war to certain defeat and internment. The commander chafed as the days went by in Boston during a week of replenishment. Captain Hull wasn't looking for Rodgers's squadron when he returned to patrolling off Nantucket Island. USS *Constitution* was going to go it alone. The noted author Henry Adams believed that Captain Hull expected to be relieved of command by Captain Bainbridge, who had been busy refitting the *Constellation*, and put to sea without orders before losing his command. The citizens of Boston watched the *Constitution*'s proud stern pass by Castle Island Fort and turn north toward Halifax. She was going hunting.

However, historian William S. Dudley points to two letters that Captain Hull wrote to his boss, Secretary Hamilton, just before departure, on July 28 and August 2. In them, he regrets that no orders were waiting for him and provides an analysis of what he believes the secretary would expect of him under the circumstances. He explains the need to get out of the harbor before a blockade is thrown up.

As they sailed north, the weather was clear and the wind solid. Chains were put around the mast to secure the spars at the parrels, still allowing the yards to be braced. It prevented the heavy yards from plunging to the deck from enemy cannon fire. Tons of loglike spars, strung with yards of smothering canvas, were not going to clutter and entangle the fighting men when they met the British. The *Constitution* was led further north by an American privateer of fourteen guns from Salem, the brig *Decatur*, which reported having sighted a British frigate the day before.[13] Hull hastened on. At 2 p.m. on August 19, a month after his encounter with Sir Philip Bowes Vere Broke's Royal Navy squadron, he found a lone enemy ship on the horizon coming his way. She was a frigate not of American design.

A Meeting Engagement: The *Constitution* versus the *Guerriere*

The English vessel was the infamous frigate *Guerriere*, which in the spring of 1811 had mauled the American brig *Spitfire* outside New York harbor and impressed several men. Days later, Captain Rodgers on the *President* had attacked HMS *Little-Belt* (same as *Lilli Belt*) by mistake while searching for the *Guerriere*. HMS *Guerriere* had also been one of the frigates chasing the *Constitution* earlier, a part of Broke's squadron. The crew of the *Constitution* wanted to settle the score with the *Guerriere*.

Captain Dacres would have said, "That goes double for us as well." James Richard Dacres, Esq., was the son of Vice Admiral J. R. Dacres of Cambridge, England. Only three days before, Captain Dacres had entered on the log of a merchantman a challenge to any American frigate to meet him off Sandy Hook. Not only had the *Guerriere* for a long time been extremely offensive to every seafaring American, but the mistake that had caused the *Little-Belt* to suffer so seriously for the misfortune of being taken for the *Guerriere* had caused a corresponding feeling of anger in the officers of the British frigate. The meeting of August 19 had the character of a preconceived duel.[14] Painted on her mainsail was the name of the ship, *Guerriere*, while on her foresail the words "Not the Little Belt" issued the challenge. She had hoped to introduce herself as the avenger to Commodore Rodgers on the *President*.[15]

There was no running before the wind in this engagement; they were going to go at it. Like two giant winged animals they circled, backed, and wore, feeling each other out. Both wanted the weather gauge; neither was looking to the lee to escape. The *Constitution*'s first lieutenant sent men aloft to reef up the fore and main courses, which were tied off by anxious hands. The men aloft kept an eye over their shoulder, expecting the enemy to send a broadside of cannonballs at

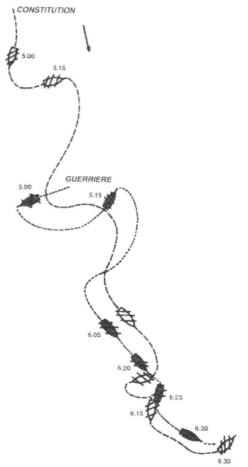

HMS Guerriere *versus USS* Constitution, *August 1812, off the New England coast.*

any moment to test the range and heat up the barrels. Top men took to the rat-lines of the fore- and mainmast to secure the royals. They were counting on getting back down from two hundred feet up before the first shot. They tangled with the marines climbing into the tops, as they struggled through the soldier's hole with their five-foot-long muskets slung over their shoulders, which became snagged on the underside. Some of the sailors avoided the tangle by seizing running rigging and coming down hand over hand, landing with a thud on their bare feet on the planked deck. The gallants and topgallants, along with the jib and mizzen sails, were quite enough to maintain way and provide maneuver speed.

The guns were double shotted and run out. The black iron chunks stuck out along the stripe, which was painted a gleaming white in 1812. The officers, in dark blue coats piped in gold, drew their swords, blades shining with a light coat of oil, and used them to point out directions to the gun crews and reinforce their shouts as the men scampered to their stations. The men did not speak, or, if they did, it was in very low whispers. There were those leaders who were allowed voice on the gun deck who guarded their prerogative jealously. With more than four hundred men in a space that was 170 feet long and 40 feet wide, communications were prescribed to a minimum of voices. The marine drummer stood behind the captain on the quarterdeck, beating out the calls. At each of the twenty-five guns on the port side, the crews were over strength. They hoped it would remain so. The cabin boys shot down below to the magazines, one forward and one aft. These 12-by-12-foot rooms, nearly suspended at the orlop deck, were lined with copper, a soft metal, to prevent sparks. The big boxes, for that is what they looked like, had one door and no light. A lamp behind a glass illuminated the space. As they gathered up the flannel bags of powder, the boys' shadows blocked the dim light. Some groped in the wooden stanchions, which looked like an oversized wine rack. The gray bags were cylinder shaped, a foot long. Sewn shut by the sailmaker, some leaked blacker-than-black granules that coated the hands with stains that were not likely to come out. The floor was gritty, good for traction, and the grit was ground into soles and left footprints on the deck and ladders as the boys scampered back up past the berth deck to the gun deck. Some had to go up one more deck to the carronades on the quarterdeck. There, under the gaze of the captain, they put the bags in wooden boxes and closed the lids to keep the powder dry.

The blue-coated marines in the swaying tops secured themselves to the mast with lines, more to steady themselves for better aim than to preserve their perch. The marines had practiced loading. They began by biting off the ball from the paper cartridge and holding the lead ball in their mouths. Each musket was hoisted up on a hip, the pan opened, and a sprinkle of black powder shaken into the primer slot. The remainder was poured down the musket, which was now standing on its butt. The ball was spit into the hole of the hexagonal barrel, and a bit of paper stuck to the tongue. The taste of sulfur and charcoal remained in the mouth, while the lips were covered with black lipstick. The last bit of paper was shoved down the barrel with the four-foot slim steel ramrod, which was then replaced in its holder under the rifle. During the battle, there would be no time to use the rammer, and the rifleman would bang the butt of the rifle on the boards under his feet, setting the ball in place, he hoped. A string secured the awkward hat, which would surely not survive the battle in place. The ship lurched one way and then the other as the master steered to get position on the enemy frigate.

Now, before the battle, the crews stood by their guns on both sides, straining to follow the action of the agile men-of-war. All the guns were loaded by the numbers as they had practiced. Crisp orders had been passed, echoed, from the quarterdeck to the lieutenants in charge of a section. Each lieutenant was in his best dark blue coat and white pants with a gold epaulet board on one shoulder. These were not as bright in the sun as one would expect; the younger officers often soaked them in salty seawater to take off the shine to appear seasoned, thus disguising their youth in grade. They all aspired to have two, one on each shoulder, the distinctive identification of a captain. Even so, they contrasted with the slops worn by the crowd of crewmen that stood between the lieutenants and the rail. Standing twenty inches above the rail were nets, which had been stuffed with the hammocks of the crew. There for the airing, this day they would provide a little extra protection from flying lead and debris when the enemy closed within rifle range.

Less classy were the midshipmen, who, one step below the lieutenants, directed the action of the individual gun. The men were dwarfed by the massive big end of the gun as it rested on the squat wooden body of the carriage. The thick, chunky wooden wheels appeared too flimsy. With a black iron barrel no man could get his arms around, they were expected to provide the trundling recoil across the rough deck planks.

Idlers No Longer Idle

While the decks were cleared for action, the idlers were just as committed. The surgeon and his mate were below in the cockpit at a table, setting out the dreadful-looking saws and knives. Their tools appeared to be on loan from the carpenter, just a little shinier. The doctor knew that the primary tactic of the day was surely not to sink the ship. The enemy guns and attendant Royal Marines would attempt to disable the ship's running gear and kill the crew. Then they woulds take her as a prize. No matter what the outcome, there would be numerous bloody casualties. Damaged limbs would be sawed off close to the trunk and the wounds cauterized to stop the bleeding. If the operation was successful, the man would live, forever an invalid. If the wound was to the trunk, there was little that could be done, and if the man did not bleed to death, infection would surely kill him. Head wounds, a graze, could be treated. A splinter, though painful, would be removed. Anesthetic took the form of alcohol, which, if spilled into the wound, might also cleanse it. Leather buckets of seawater and fresh drinking water were slouching about against the bulkhead. The chaplain was there as well, preparing to give hope to the hopeless.

The carpenter and his assistant were down in the orlop deck crawling around the catwalk against the double hull. They were responsible for the integrity of the wooden walls against the sea. They carried skeins of caulking hanging from their belts and dragged several wooden shot plugs. The round flat plates were just the size of the enemy's cannonballs. Often a cannonball would make a neat hole that could be plugged with the shot plugs, like a stopper in a bottle, and caulked shut. The sailmaker stood by on the orlop deck as well, below the waterline, dragging out spare sails, which could be called up at any moment to replace ones torn to bits by cannonballs. The cook put out his precious fire in case the caboose was upset and spilled its hot coals on the wooden deck. He went below and broke out dried food that could be distributed as the day wore on. Hard ship's biscuits and salt-dried meat were not appetizing but would suffice along with plenty of drinking water.

The order was given to light the slow matches, an alternative to the flintlocks on the guns. The officers checked their pistols to ensure that the priming powder had not leaked out. Cutlasses were brought out of the arms locker in the wardroom by the marines and distributed at each gun position. A marine contingent was set on the forecastle and quarterdeck in a tight formation, ready to respond once the enemy was within rifle range. All the time the ship responded to the rough handling, as the deck crew braced the yards in response to command. The waisters were up and down the ladders bringing up cannonballs and stacking them within reach of the gun crews. A few cannonballs got loose and rolled around the deck like lethal bowing balls, crushing feet and banging shins as the ship rolled, pitched, and yawed into position.

It was reported to Captain Hull that the ship was ready to make history.

The Royal Navy Perspective

If naval history was to be made in 1812, the Royal Navy would make it. A major British historian writes,

> It is a remarkable fact, that no one act of the little navy of the United States had been at all calculated to gain the respect of the British. First, was seen the *Chesapeake* allowing herself to be beaten, with impunity, by a British ship only nominally superior to her. Then the huge frigate *President* attacks, and fights for upwards of half an hour, the British sloop *Little-Belt*. And, even since the war, the same *President*, at the head of a squadron, makes a bungling business of chasing the *Belvidera*. While, therefore, a feeling towards America, bordering on contempt, had unhappily possessed the mind of the British naval officer, rendering him more than usually careless and opinative, the American naval officer, having been taught to regard his new foe with a portion of dread, sailed forth to meet him, with whole of his energies roused. A moment's reflection, taught him, that the honour of his country was now in his hands; and what, in the breast of man, could be a stronger incitement to extraordinary exertions?[16]

Captain Dacres had seen the *Constitution* weeks before and was not impressed with anything other than the ability of her crew to row. Yes, she was a little bigger. C. S. Forester, the American author and historian, observed,

But Dacres did not expect defeat; even the recent encounter had not convinced him of the quality of the American Navy. Nor could he have run away in any case without facing the gravest risk, the positive certainty, of a court-martial. At that moment the captain of any British 38-gun frigate who refused battle with the *Constitution* would have been promptly condemned, not merely by legal process, but by the whole of the professional opinion of the Royal Navy.[17]

England Expects

As at Trafalgar in 1805, Captain Dacres was expecting that each man would do his duty. Until then the *Guerriere* had not fought another frigate. The Royal Navy had a long history, and it was prepared to write one more glorious chapter that day. Dacres's crew was composed of long-serving professionals. His marines were smart, dressed all in red with dark blue collars and cuffs, crossed with wide white belts. They took to the tops just as the American marines had done and clung to the driving masts as the British man-of-war maneuvered in arcs. The two vessels, alone on the blue sea, churned up the water, leaving white, bubbled corkscrew wakes in the foaming water. Each ship prepared alike; they looked like twins, not adversaries. It was striking, however, to both parties how much larger the United States ship *Constitution* was, so close now to His Majesty's ship *Guerriere*. Her masts were taller, her beam was wider, and her hull was a little longer. The British had painted their ships black to make them look small and vulnerable. It was intended to invite attack. The *Guerriere* was about to get her wish.

Close With and Kill

William James, the recognized authority, gives us the English account of the start of the engagement: "*Guerriere* . . . opened her starboard broadside at the *Constitution*. The Guerriere then filled, wore and on coming round on the larboard tack, fired her larboard guns, 'her shot,' says Captain Hull, 'falling short,' a proof, either that the Guerriere's people knew not the range of their guns, or that the powder they were using was of an inferior quality: both causes, indeed, might have co-operated in producing the discreditable result."[18]

Black powder is a mixture of charcoal, saltpeter, and sulphur, which when ignited in a closed space creates gas pressure that propels the shot out of the open end of the barrel as the gas tries to escape, taking the path of least resistance.

The effectiveness of the powder depends upon:

1. The quality of the ingredients
2. The proportions within the mixture

3. The size of the powder particles
4. The efficiency of firing, that is, the rate of combustion within the chamber
5. The gun quality: bore accuracy, tightness of the charge, ergo the degree of "windage," and the seal provided by the wadding
6. The weight of the charge in proportion to shot weight and barrel length[19]

It was known that powder, after prolonged storage, could be contaminated and lose its punch. Therefore, it was tested on a regular basis.

Forester's account says,

> The *Constitution* came rushing down on him, he did his best to cut her up during the important minutes of the approach. But he was opposed to a man whose judgement of time and distance was superior to his. Dacres awaited his coming with his ship hove-to, fired a broadside when he judged the ships were within range, and then put his ship before the wind on roughly the same course as the *Constitution*'s, in order to prolong as far as possible the period of the approach, and he yawed first to port and then to starboard so as to present his broadside to the advancing enemy and rake him as he came down. Dacres's eye was not keen enough, or excitement may have clouded his judgment, or his gunners were not well enough trained, or the gunnery control—there was an elementary system practiced at the time in all ships—was ineffective.[20]

The Words of the American Commander

The after-action letter to the secretary of the navy tells the tale of the victor:

> Sir,
>   . . . after all was clear the Ship was ordered to be kept away from the Enemy, on hearing of which the Gallant crew gave three cheers, and requested to be laid close alongside the chace. As we bore up she hoisted an English Ensign at the Mizen Gaff, another in the Main Shrouds, and a Jack at the Fore, and Mizentop-Gallant mast heads. At 5 minutes past 5 PM as we were running down on her weather quarter She fired a Broadside, but without effect the Shot all falling short, she then wore and gave us a broadside from Larboard Guns, two of which Shot Struck us but without doing any injury. At this time finding we were within gun-shot, I ordered the Ensign hoisted at the Mizen Peak, and a Jack at the Fore and MizentopGallant mast head, and a Jack bent ready for hoisting at the Main, the Enemy continued wearing, and maneuvering for about ¼ of an hour, to get the wind of us. At length finding that she could not, she bore up to bring the wind, on the quarter, and run under her Topsails, and Gib, finding that we came up very slow, and were receiving her shot without being able to return them with effect, I ordered the MaintopGallant sail set, to run up alongside of her.

At 5 minutes past 6 PM being alongside and within less than Pistol Shot [twenty-five yards] we commenced a very heavy fire from all of our Guns, loaded with round and grape, with some great Execution, so much so that in less than fifteen minutes from the time, we got alongside, his Mizen Mast went by the board, and his Main Yard in the Slings, and the Hull, and Sails very much injured, which made it very difficult for them to manage her. At this time the Constitution had received but little damage, and having more sail set than the Enemy she shot ahead, on seeing this I determined to put the Helm to Port, and oblige him to do the same, or suffer himself to be raked, by our getting across his bows, on our Helm being put to Port the ship came too, and gave us an opportunity of pouring in upon his Larboard Bow several Broadsides, which made great havock amongst his men on the forecastle and did great injury to his fore rigging, and sails. The Enemy put his helm to Port, at the time we did, but his Mizen Mast being over the Quarter, prevented her coming too, which brought us across his Bows, with his Bowsprit over our Stern [they collided]. At this moment I determined to board him, . . . [21]

At that moment the lieutenant of the American marines, Lieutenant William Bush, at the head of his boarding party, yelled to Captain Hull, near him on the quarterdeck, "Shall I board her, Sir?" and was shot dead.[22]

. . . but the instant the Boarders were called, for that purpose, his Foremast, and Mainmast went by the board, and took with them the Gib-boom, and every other spar except the Bowsprit. On seeing the Enemy totally disabled and the Constitution received but little injury I ordered the Sails filled, to haul off, and repair our damages and return again to renew the action, not knowing whither the Enemy had struck or not, we stood off for about half an hour, to repair our Braces, and such other rigging, as had been shot away, and wore around to return to the Enemy, it being now dark, we could not see whether she had any colours, flying or not, but could discover that she had raised a small flag Staff or Jurymast forward. I ordered a Boat hoisted out and sent Lieutenant Reed on board as a flag to see whether she had surrendered or not, and if she had to see what assistance she wanted, as I believed she was sinking. Lieutenant Reed returned in about twenty minutes, and brought with him, James Richard Dacres Esqr. Commander of his britanic Majesty's Frigate the Guerriere, which ship had surrendered, to the United States Frigate Constitution, our Boats were immediately hoisted out and sent for the Prisoners, and were kept at work bringing them and their Baggage on board, all night. At daylight we found the Enemy's Ship a perfect Wreck, having many shot holes between wind, and water, and above Six feet of the Plank below the Bends taken out by our round Shot, and her upper works so shattered on pieces, that I determined to take out the sick and wounded as fast as possible, and set her on fire, as it would be impossible to get her into Port.[23]

The remainder of the report tells of the heroic conduct of Hull's officers and men and provides a list of casualties. There is little bravado in the victory report; that would come later when the press elevated Isaac Hull to sainthood. I believe that a professional naval officer of the day had little hatred for defeated men and did not relish the destruction of a beautiful man-of-war like the *Guerriere*. I do not doubt that looking into the eyes of the surrendered Captain Dacres, Hull saw the despair that was to follow him all of his life and knew that the positions could have been reversed.

The captive Royal Navy captain watched as his men were evacuated from his former command. In a sinking condition, she was set on fire by the American sailors and sunk. Captain Dacres wrote his report to his commander from the deck of the enemy's ship.

Captain James R. Dacres R.N. to
Vice Admiral Herbert Sawyer, R.N.
Sir,
    I am sorry to inform you of the Capture of His Majesty's late ship Guerriere by the American Frigate Constitution after a severe action on the 19th of August . . . At 2 PM being by the Wind on the starboard Tack, we saw a Sail on our Weather Beam, bearing down on us. At 3 made her out to be a Man of War, beat to Quarters and prepar'd for Action. At 4. She closing fast wore to prevent her taking us. At 4:10 hoisted our Colours and fir'd several shot at her. At 4:20 She hoisted her Colours and return'd our fire, Wore several times, to avoid being raked, Exchanging broadsides. At 5 She clos'd on our Starboard Beam, both keeping up a heavy fire and steering free, his intention being evidently to cross our bow. At 5:20, our Mizen Mast went over the starboard quarter and brought the Ship up in the Wind. The enemy then plac'd himself on our larboard Bow raking us, a few only of our bow Guns bearing and his Grape and Riflemen sweeping our Deck. At 5:40 the Ship not answering the helm, he attempted to lay up on board at this time. [They collide.] Mr. Grant who commanded the Forecastle was carried below badly wounded. I immediately order'd the Marines and Boarders from the Main Deck: Master was at this time shot thro the knee, and I receiv'd a severe wound in the back. Lieutenant Kent was leading on the Boarders, when the Ship coming too, we brought some of our bow guns to bear on her and had got clear of our opponent when at 6:20 our Fore and Main Masts went over the side, leaving the Ship a perfect unmanageable Wreck. The Enemy shooting ahead, It was hope to clear the Wreck and get the Ship under Command to renew the Action but just as we had clear'd the Wreck our Spritsail yard went and the Enemy having rove new Braces & c[anvas], wore round within Pistol Shot to rake Us. The Ship laying in the trough of the Sea and rolling her main Deck Guns under Water and all attempts to get her before the Wind being fruitless, when calling my few remaining officers together, they were all of opinion that any further resistance would be a needless waste of lives, I order'd though reluctantly, the Colours to be struck.[24]

Later in the letter he alludes to the early misses from his broadside: "On coming into action, the Enemy had such an advantage from his Marines and Riflemen, when close and his superior sailing enabled him to choose his distance."[25] It is true that once the ships were within "pistol range," the accurate rifle fire was devastating to the *Guerriere*. The captain could swear to that since an American marine had shot him from the tops.

Once released, Captain Dacres appeared before a court-martial at Halifax on the second of October. He was charged with improper conduct in surrendering his ship, but the court acquitted him of the charge. The *Naval Chronicle*, official medium of the day, published not only the verdict but also the court's absolution. The court-martial was assembled and held aboard His Majesty's ship *Africa* in Halifax Harbor on October 20, 1812.

Present
Vice Admiral Herbert Sawyer—President
Captains
Sir Beresford-Philip Bowes Vere Broke
James Sanders
Charles Gill
John Bastard

Captain Sanders having received orders to sail his presence was dispensed with.

The Court in persuance of an order from the Rt. Honorable Admiral Sir J. B. Warren, Bart KB dated the first Instant proceeded to try Captain Dacres, the officers and company of His Majesty's late ship Guerriere who were on board when she struck to the United States Frigate Constitution; and the Court having heard the Evidence produced and having maturely and deliberately weighed and considered the whole arc of opinion that the surrender of the Guerriere was proper in order to preserve the lives of her valuable remaining crew and that her being in that lamentable situation was from the accident of her masts going, which was occasioned more by their defective state than from the fire of the enemy, though so greatly superior in guns and men; The Court do therefore unanimously and honorably acquit the said Captain Dacres, his officers and the Company of his majesty's late ship Guerriere, and they are hereby unanimously and honorably acquitted accordingly.

The Court at the same time feel themselves called upon to express the high sense they entertain of the exemplary conduct of the ship's company in general when Prisoners, but more particularly of those who, withstood the attempts made to shake their loyalty by offering them high bribes to enter into the land and sea service of the enemy and the Court will represent their merit to the commander in chief.
Signed
H. Sawyer
I. P. Beresford
P. B. V. Broke
John Bastard
Charles Gill
William Ayre, Officiating Judge Advocate.[26]

The English believed strongly that the offer of asylum in the United States extended to British prisoners of war was not "cricket." Yet England continued to impress innocent Americans into Royal Navy service until the conclusion of the war, Christmas eve of 1814.

To his father, Vice Admiral J. R. Dacres, Captain Dacres wrote:

> Sir—the loss of the ship is to be ascribed to the early fall of the mizenmast, which enabled our opponent to close his position I am sorry to say we suffered severely in killed and wounded and mostly whilst she was on our bow, from her grape and musketery; in all, 15 killed, and 63 wounded, many severely. None of the officers quited the deck till the firing ceased.
>
> The Guerriere was so cut up, that all attempts to get her in would have been useless.
>
> I hope, in considering the circumstances, you will think the ship entrusted to my charge was properly defended. [unreadable] his superior sailing enabled him to choose his distance.[27]

Other English Opinions, So to Speak

Royal Navy lieutenant Burden recorded his thoughts when he left American custody:

> It was extremely fortunate that the American returned to us after we were dismasted, as I have no doubt that the Guerriere would have gone down before we got her in here, So many shot struck her between wind and water, that her hull was nearly shattered to pieces. . . . We were carried to Boston, where I remained about ten days, and was then sent here [Halifax]. God knows what the people of England will think of the captain of Guerriere, but they certainly cannot expect more than to fight her until she was sunk. No one that has seen the Constitution would believe there should be such a ship for a frigate, the nearest ship to the British navy, as to her dimensions and tonage is the Orian of 74 guns. She was laid down for a 74 gun ship, is 180 ft. long as her upper deck 45 ft. 10 inches breath of beam. She has no gangways, but two complete decks, the same as a line-of-battle ship and is 1630 tons.[28]

The lieutenant was enlarging his enemy, no doubt to justify the loss. Perhaps that is where William James, the English historian, got the idea that she was a 74-gun ship in disguise.

Royal Navy officers Commander Robinson and John Leyland were more blunt when it came to excuses for the loss of the first Royal Navy frigate to an American.

> The British Tar in fact and fiction, attribute the loss of Guerriere and the Royal Naval frigates not to the superior throwing weight of the US frigates which is menial

(684 US to 556 British). After Trafalgar, the Royal Navy stood at the height of its splendor, and its officers felt the fullest confidence in their prowess. They had despised their foes, and when they encountered the young American Navy they despised their new foes also. They had begun to pay less attention to gunnery and the failure in this matter, rested partly upon too much pride and self-confidence, prepared the way for many discomfitures.[29]

Americans had their opinions as well. In 1856 New York historian George Coggeshall, who was a clerk in the district court of the United States, wrote

Guerriere had fifteen killed, Missing 24, Wounded 62 for a total of 101.
Constitution, 7 killed, 7 wounded
Captain Dacres, son of an admiral made three mistakes
1 holding his enemy too cheap
2 Boasting before the battle
3 Firing to soon. . . . he threw away two good broadsides. This last mistake envined a great want of cool, deliberate judgement. It matters not how large the shot may be, if it is badly directed and thrown into the water, at very close range the 18 to 24 lbs. shot had not made that big a difference.

From the commencement to the end of the War, the same practice and determination were carried out with all our ships of war. The old fashioned way of playing at long balls for several hours with their enemy does not suit the nature or the heart of the Americans. They make up their minds on a subject, and then, to use a familiar phrase, "go Ahead" regardless of consequences.[30]

The great battle that opened the naval war of 1812 was the first of several single-ship victories. There is plenty more action to come. But there is one more item to bring to your attention that has stuck in the memory of Americans through to today. It is as important as Francis Scott Key's poem that became the American national anthem.

It was said not by an American but by an English sailor on board *Guerriere*, when within "pistol range." He saw the British cannonballs bounce off the hull of USS *Constitution*: "HUZZA, her sides are made of iron."

She became, from that day to this, the United States ship *Constitution*, "Old Ironsides."

~

CHAPTER SEVEN

England's Worst Nightmare

The American sailor was handy at all kinds of work. There is in the handling of those transatlantic ships a nucleus of trouble for the Navy of Great Britain.

—Admiral Lord Nelson, 1805

In England the accolade "Ironsides" did not go down half as well. It was hurtful that an Englishman had granted the title, which implied superiority and invincibility of the big American frigate. The defeated Captain Dacres's last public statement was taken out of his court-martial and printed in the newspapers. "Notwithstanding the unlucky issue of this affair, such confidence have I in the exertions of the officers and men who belonged to the *Guerriere*, and I am so well aware that the success of my opponent was owing to fortune, that it is my earnest wish, and would be the happiest period of my life, to be once more opposed to the *Constitution*, with them under my command, in a frigate of similar force to the *Guerriere*."[1] Fellow captain Brenton of the *Spartan*, who was in the same waters at the time, echoed his statement.

Thus far the two ships had fought with an equal chance of success, when the day was decided by one of those accidents to which ships of war are ever liable, and which can be rarely guarded against. The inference is erroneous (that our navy was declining and our officers and men deficient in their duty), founded on a supposition, that, if two ships happen to be allied frigates, the lesser one, being manned and commanded by Englishmen, ought to take the greater, though a ship very nearly double her force in guns, and men: we need scarcely enter into any argument to prove the fallacy of such an expectation.[2]

Captain Brenton exaggerated the *Constitution's* physical prowess. The phrase "double her force" does not compute. The battle occurred at a time when it was not understandable to the London press or its readers that such a loss could occur without blame. The *London Times* said it quite plainly, however, so there was no mistake.

> It is not merely that an English frigate has been taken, after, what we are free to confess may be called a brave resistance, but that it has been taken by a new enemy, an enemy unaccustomed to such triumphs, and likely to be rendered insolent and confident by them. He must be a weak politician who does not see how important the first triumph is in giving a tone and character to the war. Never before in the history of the world did an English frigate strike to an American.[3]

William James, in his history of the Royal Navy, written years later, laments the condition of the *Guerriere* prior to the battle. "*Guerriere* had nearly expended, not only her water and provisions, but her boatswains and carpenters stores—that her gunners stores were also deficient that what remained of her powder, from damp and long keeping, was greatly reduced in strength—that her bowsprit was badly sprung, her mainmast from having been struck by lightning, in a tottering state and her hull from age and length of service, scarcely seaworthy."[4] He, however, does not fault the admiral at Halifax, who sent her to join Captain Broke in August. She is not described during the chase of the *Constitution* as lagging behind or inoperative. A month later, she was still at sea when she chose to take on the *Constitution*. In later correspondence, it was said that the *Guerriere* was on her way to Halifax for repair. Surely, she could have made it to port before the *Constitution* found her a month later, still hundreds of miles off the coast. It was only after her defeat that it was discovered that she was not only incapable of defending herself but also "not seaworthy." Because she was not taken as a prize but left a burned wreck at the bottom of the Atlantic, it was not possible to determine the validity of the claims.

While the *Constitution* went home in victory, the admiral at Halifax Station had more to worry about than the U.S. Navy. Notwithstanding the loss of the *Guerriere*, the most serious British losses were caused by the influx of American privateers, which brought unprecedented grief to the mercantile interests of British North America. Sixty-five of the privately owned commerce raiders were at sea by mid-July, a large number of which were operating in the sea-lanes of the Maritime Provinces. These craft would cause the Royal Navy to turn to defense and forestall the blockading of American ports.[5]

A Great Day for the Navy but Not the Army

The victory of an American frigate over its counterpart proved not only the triumph of the design but also the value of American naval officers, crews, and marines. The Royal Navy was thought to be unchallengeable in a fair fight. On entering the waters of Boston Harbor, it was fitting that Captain Hull landed his prisoners at Castle Island, where the great guns had come from. The citizens of Boston regarded the battle as a personal victory. They had constructed the ship for their protection. At nearly the same moment, out west at Detroit, the Jefferson plan, expressed in his boast, "The taking of Canada this year is a mere matter of marching," would suffer its first in a two-year-long series of defeats. General Dearborn had opened his grand campaign with the invasion of Canada at what is today Windsor. Within a matter of days, with little fighting, Governor William Hull, in command of the left wing of the army, surrendered to British Major General Brock. The loss was of particular sorrow to Captain Isaac Hull in the face of his triumph over the Royal Navy frigate. He was the nephew of the defeated general.

The army's loss way out west was overshadowed by the navy's triumph on the eastern seaboard. Captain Hull was wined and dined in Boston while Congress voted him a gold medal. The officers were granted silver medallions. Prize money was also awarded to the crew even though they were unable to bring the *Guerriere* to port where she could be sold by the government. As with Decatur, Hull's portrait was painted and copies adorned trinkets and souvenirs. However, the big winner in the hearts of the people was the great frigate, the *Constitution*. They took "Ironsides" to their hearts and never forgot her.

Ironsides, the One and Only

Cannons were the queen of the naval battle. As in a chess game, the method of employment of heavy artillery was paramount to the outcome. All cannons were to be feared, no matter what their size. The smallest, rail guns, which shot a pound or so of solid shot, could punch a hole in the bottom of a boarding party and send the craft to the bottom, leaving the marauders swimming like rats rather than slashing and killing. The truly destructive, serious cannons ranged from 6 to 32 pounds in 1812. That was all the weight the ship and the men could handle. While the biggest could put a solid shot skipping across the water at a mile and a half, its effective range, where it could be expected to hit what it was aimed at, was three-quarters of a mile. The big, nearly 3-ton 32-pounders were confined to ships of the line and land fortifications. Frigates could not withstand the weight of these guns nor their recoil. The 24s and 18s were standard, along with the big carronades. In reality, there was not much difference in shot size between the 18 and 24, and with a casual glance one could not tell them apart. Both were between five and six inches in diameter, half the size of a bowling ball. Although the 18 sounds much too small when up against 24s, it could destroy a thickness of 30 inches of oak within 100 yards. The 24s were slightly more lethal, throwing out showers of splinters as they broke through the side of the ship's rail or gunwale.

Double shotting, a practice common on the first broadside in close, provided an interesting effect. The first ball would often penetrate and go completely through the ship and out the other side.[6] The second would drop like a sinker thrown by a baseball pitcher. It made a hole near the waterline and let the sea in. With a double shot, the crew often increased the six-pound gunpowder charge considerably. The result could burst a flawed gun barrel and kill the crew, while setting off other charges nearby.

While I was watching a demonstration at Chatham Royal Dockyard conducted by Captain Adrian Caruana, RA, the ball from a cannon struck the barrel of a carronade set in a mock-up of a ship's hull. The projectile hit the tube end with such force that it tore off the base plate, which was cast as part of the barrel, and sent it flying to the rear. The *Guerriere's* cannonballs should not have bounced off the hull of the *Constitution*. It may be the best evidence yet that the Englishman's powder was deteriorated. On the other hand, the hull of the *Constitution* was more dense than the English ships'. There were only four inches between ribs, futtocks, and sisters.

Captain William Bainbridge Assumes Command

Within two weeks of returning a hero, Isaac Hull relinquished command to William Bainbridge. Hull would remain in service as the commandant of the Charlestown Navy Yard. There he got down to the repairs the *Constitution* needed to wipe away the battle damage and corrosion of the sea. She was taken down to her main masts. Both running and static rigging was reworked, masts and spars were disassembled, inspected, and replaced, and paint was renewed. Meanwhile, the new captain planned how he was going to wipe out the two major black marks on his career. During the Quasi War, he had surrendered his command to a French attack. During the war against the Barbary pirates, he had run the frigate *Philadelphia* aground in Tripoli harbor. While the daring destruction of that ship had made others, Preble, Decatur, and Macdonough, heroes, it followed him to every encounter on land like a bad dream. It certainly did not improve his temperament as he aged. Even in his portrait, done much later, the haunting of the Barbary pirates and their prison camp is in his eyes.

The loyalty of the crew was with the departing captain, which is not surprising. Like all new commanders, Bainbridge would have to earn their respect. He was not a warm human being, and the crew knew it from the first moment he was piped on board. Not only would he command the ship, but he was also the appointed commodore, and his second vessel, the *Hornet*, joined him off Castle Island on October 16, 1812, as they looked for favorable winds to carry them out into the Atlantic. His orders were vague. He was to protect American commerce any way and anywhere he saw fit. The navy secretary perhaps had learned that it did no good to pass out detailed instructions since none of his captains seemed to follow them. By the end of the month, Bainbridge was edging his way down the eastern seaboard looking for trouble in the sea-lanes that carried British commercial prizes. He expected to find a convoy escorted by a Royal Navy frigate and produce a victory comparable to his predecessor's. It was important that he clear his name. The further south he went, the less he found. Perhaps it was getting too late in the year. The sailing season would soon be deteriorating into hurricanes and winter storms.

Black Sky and White Water

The weather was certainly more challenging than any enemy. It came at Bainbridge from the south, a bad omen that time of year. The most prominent danger in storm conditions was the fear of being run up on the rocks near shore as the storm surged. But the *Constitution* was several hundred miles off Norfolk, Virginia, and the Outer Banks, free of the fingers of land that would reach out and run the captain aground once again. As the sea came up, the ship was altered for storm running. Hours were going to be long and wet. The fire was put out in the caboose, and just when they needed a hot meal most, it would not be available. Before the coals were shoveled into heating buckets where at least their warming heat could provide some comfort, soup heated by the red-hot cast-iron range provided a last hot meal before it cooled.

While sails were shortened, the rudder came in for serious alterations. Four helmsmen manned the double steering wheel in a storm. It called for brute force to maintain course into the southerly gale by tacking into its face. A square-rigged ship cannot steer into the wind. Its forward motion is best served from winds on the beam or the aft. In fact, 33¼ degrees on the compass either to port or starboard of the direction of the wind are unsailable. In other terms, that is 6 points on either side of a wind in the face of the ship (a point is just a shade over 11 degrees).[7] Tacking back and forth across the wind, Bainbridge was able to maintain a heading. It called on the crew to be standing by to brace the yards around, which swung the bow sharply in front of the wind, installing a distinct zig-zag into forward progress.

As the force of the southerly wind rose and the sea swelled, further modification to the rudder was begun. On the orlop deck the manual tiller was reinforced with added lines and blocks. A compass was set up with an encased light near the wheel when the binnacle was damaged and steering had to be altered below. Exterior rudder tackle was rigged from the rails over the side to the rudder in case it broke free. If it was allowed to flop or slam against the buttock, the heavy panel would damage the hull where it beat itself to death.

Guns were an enormous danger. Weighing over two tons and mounted on wheeled carriages, they could not be allowed to careen around the deck like mad bumper cars, crashing into the masts and rail or running down the crew. The most effective method was to lash the muzzle tightly to the rail in a nose-up condition while the carriage was trussed to eye and ring bolts in the deck. The bower anchor was next to be secured. A painter, or additional small rope, was applied to the cat lines that held it to the outside of the rail. It was wrapped around both the flukes and the shank ring at the top.

Messengers

At a glance, the amount of blue on the globe or any world map never fails to impress the viewer. We know from land travel the great distances from coast to coast in North America and can appreciate the tales of the Trans-Siberian Railway, which takes nearly two weeks to get to Vladivostok. Yet the oceans are even more vast. Yet, like terrestrial superhighways, the sea-lanes can be crowded. So it was in the days of sail when ships were the only option. A man-of-war scanned the horizons from first light to inky darkness, ready to challenge all sails. In our view today, it was like watching grass grow, when ten miles per hour was good speed. After all, on land a horse did twelve miles per hour and later any bicycle rider could top that with ease. To the sailors, anything over twelve miles per hour was gossamer reserved for the angels. Once a strange ship was seen, the chase began. Even a friendly merchantman was reluctant to slow for the opportunity of speaking to a friendly man-of-war. He was aware that the navy vessel was fast and could catch up with him if it were necessary. The commercial ship knew that time was money and kept to his course unless fired upon.

Signals at Sea

With embargoes in effect and wars under way, nearly every vessel sighted had to be "spoken." That is to say that the warship would come up for identification. Ships were hailed by voice, shouted through a speaking trumpet, and ships' names, ports of origin, and destinations, along with the mix of cargo, were the first priority. Since nearly everybody flew false flags, a suspicious engagement meant that a boarding party would have to be sent. Intimidated by a row of loaded cannons at "pistol-shot range" (25 yards), few refused to brace around their sails in opposite directions, which very nearly brought a halt to their progress. The warship could have been on station for several months and was always interested in the news or perhaps needed to put a sick sailor or prisoner aboard to be delivered on land.

Codebooks

Warship encounters were quite different. Many combatants were known by their silhouette or the news that a particular enemy ship was in the area. True national colors were furled until the last moment. A series of signals could save time. A coded signal book was issued by the nation's naval headquarters and distributed to outgoing vessels. Small, long, and narrow, the books would fit in the tailcoat pocket of the officer's uniform. I was handed an original one from HMS *Victory* in the Admiralty Library. As a Signal Corps officer for thirty years, I felt as if I were holding the Holy Grail. I was surprised how modern it was. Perhaps I should say I was surprised at how little things have changed. It was strikingly similar to the Signal Operating Instruction (SOI) I issued monthly to the 173rd Airborne Infantry Brigade in Vietnam. There was even a note telling the holder to attach a weight to the book to ensure that if lost in battle it would sink and prevent the enemy from compromising the code. In 1965 I attached a similar note telling the user to tie a bootlace through all pages to ensure that it did not blow out of the helicopter's open sides.

On stiff paper, it consisted of about fifty pages. In contained the names of Royal Navy ships with a number assigned to each. It assigned letters and numbers to small, colored, graphic square pennants. There was also a section on commonly used phrases, such as "will depart," "acknowledge," "You shall," "I am intending," and so forth. The names of ports of call and nations were assigned numbers, as were prominent personages and offices. One of the junior lieutenants was assigned the duty of reading and making up strings of signal flags as directed. When a message was confirmed, it was strung up on running rigging line from the mast.

Most prominent was the identification, or "private," signal. An annex to the common book, it was issued by a command and changed more often. It looked like a matrix; the challenge would be taken from one column, and the other party would read across the field of random numbers to provide the proper response. The signal would be spelled out in a series of flags, which were hoisted upon encountering a ship of war. That signal should have prompted a counter-response. Today it is known as "identification, friend or foe," or IFF, and is done electronically, and it is not always as successful as the old method. At that point, the enemy would raise his true national colors instead and fire upon the inquirer. Or perhaps, if he were to lee, he would run away as fast as possible. Like the SOI of 1965, the last page of the codebook told the user to notify the originator if it was lost so that a new set of codes could be issued as soon as possible to prevent the enemy's use. (Nothing changes in warfare, except technology.)

Any ship flew common messages. The most important proclaimed the health of the crew. Ships liable to quarantine were supposed to fly a large yellow flag of six breadths of bunting from the main-topmasthead if free of disease but a similar yellow flag with a black circular mark or ball equal to two breadths of bunting in the middle if there was illness on board.[8] Outside of harbors there was a quarantine station or buoy where incoming vessels would lie for fifteen days before being allowed to discharge cargo.

When visibility was poor or nonexistent in fog, which was common along the northeastern coast of North America, sound signals were employed. Particularly in convoy, these were important to prevent collisions or to change the course of the entire body. They were done with the assistance of drums or cannons. There was a set of instructions contained in the signal books for that process. Two guns followed a minute later by one more would turn everyone to starboard. A different series would instruct the ships to slow down by changing sails. If a signal was heard, there was a response, as well as the obligation to pass the signal along to vessels further out. This method was not always effective but a little better than nothing. If nothing else, it alerted one to the proximity of another ship. To see a man-of-war loom up out of the blue-gray sea fog, prow up and bowsprit poised like a battering ram, must have been frightening.

Here is the most famous flag signal in sail history, provided by Dudley Pope in his great book *Life in Nelson's Navy*: 253, 269, 863, 261, 471, 958, 220, 370, 4, 21, 19, 24. Or, "England expects every man to do his duty." The last four numbers are the spelling out of the word *duty*. All the other words were a single flag in the book. There were many flags in different colors and configurations; these were contained in a long cabinet on the quarterdeck, which was divided into pigeonholes for ease of construction.

Gale

Now the twins of wind and water were the culprits that must be fought. The gale whipped up the water into swells. The *Constitution* and the *Hornet* kept a respectable distance between them for fear of being driven into one another. The storm rose higher, forcing them to alter course and scud before the wind. Scudding, or running with the wind, meant abandoning the southerly course for the duration of the blow. Sails were brought down and courses furled, leaving near-bare poles. The jib and two stays were allowed up to help with the steering. To scud with the wind could be very dangerous since the ship could be pooped. Pooping occurs when a heavy sea breaks over the stern. It usually comes about when the speed of the ship is approximately the same as the speed of the following sea, so that the rudder has little or no grip on the sea. In such cases, a sea that poops a ship is very apt to swing her off course until she is broadside on the sea, with the danger of rolling over.[9] Even if a fat prize was sighted, there was no chance either vessel could fight under those sea conditions. Both would be at the mercy of Neptune, the sea god.

Sea Conditions

Today there is a scale from 0, the doldrums, where the air is still, to 12, where winds exceed sixty-four knots and wave height is more than fifty-two feet. At force 12 the sea and the sky are both white. At force 8, when the winds are in excess of thirty-five knots and wave height is around twenty feet, a sailing ship would have to give in and rig for heavy weather. I have crossed the English Channel in a force 10 gale on board a modern three-hundred-foot warship and found it extremely tough going. The crossing from France took four hours rather than one and a half. The pitching and rolling called for one firm handhold at all times.

Weather is a function of the heat of the sun and the rotation of the earth. The atmosphere, which is composed of gases, water vapor, and particles, is in a layer about 36,000 feet thick above sea level. It becomes less dense at higher altitudes. Within that level of air, weather occurs. The winds created revolve around the earth in generally predictable patterns. They are particularly dangerous in the winter to sailing ships above 45 degrees latitude, where sea spray collects in the form of ice on exposed surfaces like masts, yards, sails, rails, hulls, and decks at temperatures below freezing. The accumulating ice will significantly change the balance of a tall ship.[10] When the exposed portion of the ship becomes heavier than the hull under the water, the ship will capsize. In the time of sail, few ventured north or attempted to swing around the tip of South America. Small amounts of ice can be chipped away by deckhands with metal chisels. It is a bone-chilling task.

To prevent water from gushing down the open waist of the frigate, canvas was stretched and blocked in place, cutting out the light to the decks below. Lifelines crisscrossed the open quarter and forecastle. The helmsmen were secured with rope in position. Tarpaulin weather cloths were taken to the fighting tops to protect the lookouts, who crouched behind them and waited out the storm. A sea anchor made up of metal rods in a circle with sail cloth attached in the form of a parachute was hooked to a length of line and tossed off the stern. The drogue, filled with water and acting like a drag, produced more control for the helmsmen.

Naturally, all hatches were battened down, and the waisters were sent to the pumps. The roar of the sea deafened the sailor. Commands could not be heard, especially in the tops. Runners were sent with messages of command at critical times, ensuring the safety of ship operations. If the helmsmen could keep the ship turned slightly to the lee, it could reduce the rolling.[11] Ships floundered far more often than they were taken by pirates or men-of-war. The sea was the real danger. The skill of the captain and crew, based largely on experience, both good and bad, coupled with the physical condition of the ship, was pitted against nature. In the case of the *Constitution*, all became well as they resumed their sail south through the Caribbean and to the trading lanes favored by the British merchantmen.

Two More Victories for the American Navy

Captain Jacob Jones, master of the sloop of war *Wasp*, literally tangled with HMS *Frolic* while transiting 600 miles off the Delaware coast. He was heading for Commodore Rodgers's squadron at the time and was challenged by the Royal Navy sloop, which was escorting an English merchant convoy. The two combatants were nearly equal in all respects. However, the American gunnery ripped the British crew apart. In one of the closest encounters of the period, the vessels locked together so tightly that the ram handles protruding from the muzzles of the American cannons pierced the side of the *Frolic*. When the Englishman was boarded, the fight was nearly concluded. Only a handful of the crew were able to resist. Unfortunately for Jacob Jones, an English rater, the 74-gun *Poictiers* arrived shortly after the melee and took charge. The *Wasp* and her crew were captured and taken to Bermuda. Soon it was reported as a single-ship victory, and the American newspapers had another hero.

A week later, on October 25, 1812, Captain Stephen Decatur, commander of the frigate *United States*, alone off the Azores was making more history. It was going to be a rematch of a Royal Navy 38-gun frigate against an American 44. This time, no one could call foul since HMS *Macedonian* was a "crack ship." Lieutenant David Hope, Royal Navy, said that "the state of discipline on board was excellent, in no British ship was more attention paid to gunnery. Before this cruise, the ship had been engaged almost every day with the enemy; and in time of peace the crew were constantly exercised at the great guns."[12] She was originally French and of the same class as the *Guerriere*, which had been lost to the *Constitution* in a single-ship encounter the month before. The English naval historian William James admits that the "*United States*' broadsides were delivered with almost twice the rapidity of those of the Englishman." British captain John S. Carden submitted the following after-action report.

Captain John S. Carden, R.N. to
Secretary of the Admiralty John W. Croker

On board American Ship
United States
At sea. 28 Oct, 1812

Sir.

It is with the deepest regret I have to acquaint you for the information of my Lords Commissioners of the Admiralty that His Majesty's late ship Macedonian was Captured on the 25th Instant by the United States Ship, United States. . . . at 9 O'Clock I closed with her and she commenced the Action, which we returned, but the Enemy keeping two points off the Wind, I was not enabled to get as close to her as I could have wished. After an hours Action the Enemy back'd and came to the wind, and I was then enabled to bring her to close Battle, in this situation I soon found the Enemys force too superior to expect success, unless some very fortunate chance occur'd in our favor, and with this hope I continued the Battle to two hours and ten minutes, when having the mizen mast shot away by the board, Topmasts shot away by the caps, Main Yard shot in pieces, lower Masts badly wounded, lower Rigging all cut to pieces, a small proportion only of the Foresail left to the Fore Yard, all the Guns on the Quarter Deck and Forecastle disabled but two, and filled with wreck, two also on the Main Deck disabled, and several shot between wind and water, a very great proportion of the Crew Killed and wounded, and the Enemy comparatively in good order, who had now shot ahead, and was about to place himself in a raking position without our being enabled to return the fire, being a perfect wreck and unmanageable Log.

I deemed it prudent th'o extremely painful to surrender.[13]

The *Java* versus the *Constitution*

Commodore Bainbridge was unaware of the victories while he watched and waited for Captain Porter and the frigate *Essex* to join him on patrol off the coast of Brazil. He was also unaware that the independent captain of the *Essex* had sailed on by to hunt the British where it would hurt them most, in the East Indies. There, much later, while causing havoc, he would be trapped and destroyed in Valparaíso.

Christmas passed in the sunny waters of the South Atlantic, while the *Constitution* and the *Hornet* maintained their station. Captain James Lawrence took the *Hornet* into San Salvador to acquire supplies for both vessels. There, he was told by the American naval agent that His Britannic Majesty's frigate *Bonne Citoyenne*, loaded with gold for England, was about to depart. Lawrence challenged the commander, by letter, to meet him at sea and fight it out. The commander declined, and rightly so; his mission did not include endangering the English Treasury. Bainbridge ordered Lawrence to remain near the port and engage the prize ship when she attempted to go to sea.

Leaving Lawrence in place, the *Constitution*, now resupplied, continued to patrol the coastline. On December 29, Commodore Bainbridge came face to face with his destiny. HMS *Java*, heavily embarked with a hundred extra men and a high-ranking diplomatic party destined for India, fell into his hands. English-built along the pattern of the famous French frigate *Renommee*, she was transiting to Saint Helena with dispatches.[14] The *Java* was a 38-gunner that carried 49 cannons and carronades. James disagrees and says she carried 46. A

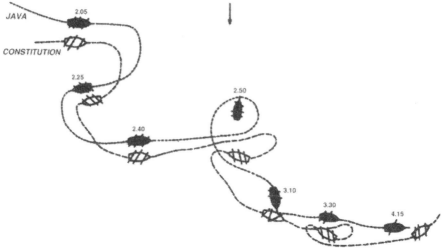

HMS Java *versus USS* Constitution, *December 1812, off the coast of Brazil.*

little smaller in tonnage, nonetheless, she was capable of defending herself. She had taken an American merchant ship, the *William*, as a prize, which she sent off at the sight of the big American. Her captain was H. Lambert, whose career had been as spotted as Bainbridge's. He had lost a ship and been a captive. If the captain had any trepidation when confronted by the *Constitution*, he did not show it and went straight into the attack.

Royal Navy Account

Letters of which the following are copies and extract, have been transmitted to this office, by rear admiral Dixon, addressed to John Wilson Croker, Esq. by Lieut. Chads, late first Lieut., his majesty's ship Java;

United States Frigate Constitution, off San. Salvador, December 31, 1812. Sir:

It is with deep regret that I write you, for the information of the Lords Commissioners of the Admiralty, that his Majasty's ship Java is no more, after sustaining an action on the 29 instant for several hours with the American Frigate Constitution, which resulted in the capture and ultimate destruction of his Majesty's ship. Captain Lambert, being dangerously wounded in the height of the action, the melancholy task of writing the detail devolves on me. . . . We soon found we had the advantage of her in sailing, and came up with her fast. . . . Both ships now maneuvered to obtain advantageous positions, our opponent evidently avoiding close action, and firing high to disable our masts, in which he succeeded too well. Having shot away the head of our bow sprit with the jib-boom, and our running rigging so much cut as too prevent our preserving the weather gauge.

At five minutes past three, finding the enemy's raking fire extremely heavy, Captain Lambert ordered the ship to be laid on board [the intention was to board USS *Constitution* at that instant] in which we should have succeeded, had not our fore-mast been shot away at this moment, the remains of our bowsprit, passing over his taffrail [the railing at the stern of the American quarter-deck] shortly after this the main top-mast went, leaving the ship totally unmanageable, with most of our starboard guns rendered useless from the wreck lying over them.

At half passed three our gallant Captain received a dangerous wound in the breast and was carried below; from this time we could not fire more than two or three guns until a quarter past four when our mizzen mast was shot away; the ship then fell off a little, and brought many of our starboard guns to bear; the enemy's rigging was so much cut that he could not now avoid shooting ahead which brought us barely broadside. Our main-yard now went in the slings both ships engaged in this manner till 35 minutes past four, we were frequently on fire in consequence of the wreck lying on the side engaged. Our opponent now made sail ahead out of gun shot where he remained an hour repairing his damages, leaving us an unmanageable wreck, with only the main-mast left, and that tottering. Every exertion was made by us during this interval to place the ship in a state to renew the action. We succeeded in clearing the wreck of our masts from our guns, as sail was set on the stump of the fore-mast and bow sprit, the weather half of main-yard remaining aloft, the main-tack was got forward in the hope of getting the ship before the wind, our helm still being perfect; the effort unfortunately proved ineffectual from the main-mast falling over the side, from heavy rolling of the ship, which covered the whole of our starboard guns. We still waited the attack of the enemy, he now standing towards for that purpose. On his coming nearly within bail of us, and from his maneuver perceiving he intended a position ahead, where he could rake us without a possibility of us returning a shot, I then consulted the officers, who agreed with myself that our having a great part of our crew killed and wounded, our bow-sprit and three masts gone, several guns useless we should not be justified in wasting the lives of more of those remaining, who I hope their Lordships and the country will think have bravely defended his Majesty's ship.[15]

The news of the loss of another Royal Navy vessel in single combat reached England by the end of January. The capture of the *Guerriere*, the *Macedonian*, and now the *Java* was a terrific blow that could not be covered with thin alibis. It was the last straw as far as the British people were concerned. They demanded to know what had happened to their great navy. The news that Napoleon had lost mightily in the Russian winter campaign was of far more importance in the war with France, which they had been fighting for twenty years. However, the newspapers were consumed with England's own naval losses against a former colony. The following account taken from Commodore Bainbridge's journal was published in England nearly four months later, as if the event had happened the day before.

London Times, April 15, 1813

Below is an extract from Commodore Bainbridge's journal, kept on board the U.S. frigate *Constitution*, as printed in the *London Times*:

Tuesday, Dec. 29, [1812] at nine AM, discovered two strange sail on the weather-bow. At 10, discovered the strange sail to be ships. One of them stood in for the land, and other stood off shore, in a direction forwards us. At 10:45 AM we took ship to the northward and westward, and stood for the sail standing towards us. At 11 AM tacked to the southward and eastward, hauled up the mail-sail and tack in the royals. At 11:30 made the private signal for the day, which was not answered; and then set the main sail and royals, to draw the strange sail off from the neutral coast, and separate her from the sail in company.

Wednesday Dec 30 [nautical time]. In latitude 13.6 longitude 33.W. ten leagues from the coast of Brazil, commences with clear weather and moderate breezes from East, N.E. hoisted our ensign and pendant. At 15 minutes past meridian, the ship hoisted her colors, an English Ensign having a signal flying at her main.

At 1:26 PM being sufficiently from the land and finding the ship to be an English frigate, took in the main sail and royals, tacked ship, and stood for the enemy. At 1:50 the enemy bore down with an intention of raking us, which we avoided by wearing.

At 2 PM the enemy being within half a mile of us, and to windward, and having hauled down his colors, except the Union Jack at the mizen-mast head, induced me to give orders to the officer of the Sd division to fire a gun ahead of the enemy, to make him show his colors, which being done brought on a fire from us of the whole broadside. On which the enemy hoisted his colors, and immediately returned our fire. A general action with round and grape then commenced, the enemy keeping at a much greater distance than I wished; but could not bring him to a closer action, without exposing ourselves to several rakes. Considerable maneuvers were made by both vessels, to rake and avoid being rak'd. The following minutes were taken during the action;

At 2:10 PM commenced the action at good grape and canister distance, the enemy to windwind, (but much farther than I wished).

2:30, our wheel was shot entirely away, at 2:40, determined to close with the enemy, not withstanding his raking; set the fore and main sail, and luffed up close to him. [The intention of the American was to board the Englishman. The captain of the *Java* had the same plan at that time. Cannonade fire was directed into the helpless *Java*, whose nose was hung up, three-quarters of the way down the hull of the *Constitution*. The 32-pound solid shot, fired from the forecastle and quarterdeck, shattered the rails and chopped down masts on the *Java*. A hail of splinters, stripped from oak planks, saturated the air. Boarding parties were formed of marines and sailors armed with bayoneted rifles, pikes, and cutlasses on both vessels. Firearms were of little use after the first shot. Long rifles could not be reloaded in the middle of a melee. The parties huddled in two groups, while marines on both ships fired their rifles down into the cluttered decks below. Smoke rose in acrid clouds and obsured the accuracy of the men in the tops. The captain of the *Java* was fatally wounded by an American marine in the tops.]

At 2:50, the enemy's jib-boom got foul of our mizzen-rigging.

At 3 pm the head of the enemy's bowsprit and jib-boom shot away by us.

At 3:05 shot away the enemy's fore-mast by the board.

At 3:15, shot away his main-top mast just above the cap.

At 3:40 shot away the gaff and spanker boom.

At 3:55, shot away his mizzen-mast nearly by the board.

At 4:05, having silenced the fire of the enemy completely and his colors in main rigging down, supposed he had struck, and then hauled down the course to shot ahead to repair our rigging, which was extremely cut, leaving the enemy a complete wreck; soon after discovered that the enemy's flag was still flying, hove-to to repair some of our damage.

At 20 minutes past 4, the enemy's main mast went nearly by the board. At 50 minutes past four, wore ship, and stood for the enemy. At 25 minutes past five, got very close to the enemy, in a very effectual raking position, athwart his bows, and was at the very instant of raking him, when he most prudently struck his flag; for had he suffered the broadside to have raked him, his additional loss must have been extremely great, as he lay an unmanageable wreck upon the water.

After the enemy had struck, wore ship and reefed the top sails, then hoisted out one of two only remaining boats we had left out of eight, and sent Lieut. Parker, first of the Constitution, to take possession of the enemy, which proved to be his Britannic Majesty's Frigate Java, 38 but carried 49 guns, and manned with upward of 400 men, commanded by Captain Lambert, a very distinguished officer, who was mortally wounded.

The action continued from commencement to the end of the fire, one hour and 55 minutes. The Constitution had 9 killed, and 25 wounded. The enemy had 60, killed and 101 certainly wounded: but by a letter written on board the Constitution, by one of the officers of the Java, and accidentally found, it is evident the enemy's wounded have been considerably greater than stated above, and who must have died of their wounds previously to being removed. The letter states 60 killed, and 170 wounded.

The Java had her own complement of men complete and upwards of 100 su-pernumeraries, going to join the British ships of war in the East Indies, also several officer passengers going out on promotion.

The force of the enemy in the number of men, at the commencement of the action, was no doubt was considerably greater than we have been able to ascertain, which is upward of 400 men.

The officers were extremely cautious in discovering the number. By her quarter bill, she had one more man stationed to each gun than we had.

The Constitution was very much cut in her sail, rigging, and many of her spars injured.

At seven PM the boat returned with Lieut. Chads the first Lieutenant of the enemy's frigate, and Lieut. General Hislop [appointed governor of Bombay], Major Walker, and Captain Wood.

Captain Lambert was too dangerously wounded to be removed immediately. The cutter returned onboard the prize for the prisoners, and brought Captain Marshall, master and commander in the British Navy, who was passenger on board, also several other naval officers.

The Java was an important ship fitted out in the completest manor, to carry Lieut. General Hislop and staff to Bombay.[16]

Lieutenant Henry Ducie Chads, the son of a naval captain, at his court-martial in May of 1813 at Spithead said that "the crew was exceptionally bad, a large portion had never been to sea and drafted from prison. Crew drill was neglected since the ship was overcrowded."[17] By June, Chads had been promoted to captain and was serving as commander of the sloop *Columbia*.[18]

Defeated Captain's Last Request

The wounded were all transferred at sea by boat, along with the officers' baggage, to the *Constitution*. The account by the *Java*'s surgeon, Thomas Cooke Jones, of the captain's treatment on the sinking ship is most descriptive. He reports,

> Captain Lambert was wounded about the middle of the action with a musket ball fired from the tops of Constitution. I saw him almost immediately afterward and found that the ball had entered the left side under the clavicle fracturing the first rib, splintering of which had severely lasorated the lungs. I put my finger in the wound, detected and extracted several pieces of bone, the hemorrhage was particularly trifling, his pulse became very quick and weak, the respiratory organs did not appear much affected, he said he felt no agony from the wound in his breast, but complained of pain extending the whole length of the spine. In a short time, he became very restless, his pulse hardly perceptible and his countenance assumed a most piteous appearance of anxious solicitude; from this state of irritability he became exhausted and generally fell into a partial one of asphyxia from which I hardly expected him to recover.[19]

The *Java* was abandoned; Captain Lambert was the last to leave. Carefully secured in a boat, he was taken to the *Constitution*, to the captain's cabin. Dying, Captain Lambert was asked if there was anything he wanted. He requested that the Bible his mother had given him, which had always been a great comfort to him, be salvaged from the *Java*. An American officer retrieved it from the wreck, and he was the last man to be on board the Royal Navy frigate. The wounded Captain lived for two more days on the American ship. On the morning of January 2, 1813, he, along with the crew, was landed at San Salvador, Brazil. Surgeon Cooke Jones continues, "There he talked incoherently during the greater part of the day. At 10 o'clock his pulse grew faint and he died."

Royal Navy Captain Lambert could not defend himself. The *London Times* could, and on March 23, 1813, it printed the following:

We find it stated in an American paper, that when the Java fell in with the Constitution she mistook her for the Essex, which is a frigate of less force, carrying carronades (42 32-pounders and 4 long guns), and, therefore kept at a long range of shot, (farther than he supposed the carronades would carry): and that it was til the Java's top-mast were shot away and she was otherwise disabled; that the mistake was discovered. Captain Lambert had heard a few days before, that the Essex had been into Porto Braya, which led him to believe that the frigate he was chasing as he had not heard of any other being upon the coast, was her: It was the Constitution, when commanded by Commodore Hull, which captured the Guerriere.

Three days earlier, the newspaper had exposed the public to the following account.

London Times, March 20, 1813

The public will learn with sentiments, which we shall not presume to anticipate, that a third British frigate has struck to an American. On 29th of December, his Majesty's frigate Java captain H. Lambert, was captured by the United States Frigate Constitution, Commodore Bainbridge, after a desperate action, of an hour and fifty five minutes, in which the Java lost 60 killed, and 101 (other accounts say 170) wounded. Among the latter, we lament to say, was the gallant commander of the Java, and it is added, mortally.

This is an occurrence that calls for serious reflection—this, and the fact stated in our paper yesterday, that Lloyd's contains notices of upward of five hundred British vessels captured, in seven months, by the Americans. Five hundred merchantmen, and three frigates! Can these statements be true; and can the English people hear them unmoved? Anyone, who had predicted such a result of an American war, this time last year, would have been treated as a mad man, or traitor. He would have been told, if his opponents had condescended to argue with him, that long ere seven months had elapsed, the American flag would be swept from the seas, the contemptible navy of the United States annihilated, and their maritime arsenals rendered a heap of ruins. Yet down to this moment, not a single American frigate has struck her flag. They insult and laugh at our want of our enterprize and vigor. They leave their ports when they please and return to them when its suits their conveyance; they transverse the Atlantic; they beset the West India Islands; they advance to the very chops of the Channel; they parade along the coast of South America; nothing chases, nothing intercepts, nothing engages them but to yield triumph. The friends of Ministers allow that it "does seem extraordinary" that the Americans should have such "good fortune." We say it is still more extraordinary that strict enquiry has not yet been made into the causes to which that good fortune is owing. We say that such enquiry must terminate in over whelming managers of the war with utmost disgrace. We may be accused of feeling too strongly on such a subject; but at least we are sure that it is not a party feeling that we indulge. It is an earnest and sincere feeling for the honour and interest of our country. Let it be seriously considered, that the very years of such a warfare would annihilate our mercantile marine, and render our vaunted navy the laughing-stock of the universe. Let it be considered, that these extraordinary losses have befallen us, not in a contest with a superior or equal maritime enemy, but with one whom, to name as a naval power, would, a short while since, have been deemed impossible. We have often stated the root of the evil. We repeat it. The whole results from a weak timid policy, native and endued into the element of those minds by which it is administered, a policy, which, under the shallow pretence of not irritating the enemy, engenders in him feelings of contempt and haughtiness toward ourselves, nurses up his power and creates for him a reputation and a spirit directly tending to our destruction. This policy has been adopted in spite of the most distinct warnings, and in defense of the plainest lessons of experience and common sense. In proof of this, we have only to quote the following passage from a deservedly popular writer, whose work was published, and very generally read, in 1810: "if we should be forced," says he, "into a war, contrary to our interest, by an unreasonable or unjust demands of the Government of America; as the contest, by preventing us from acting with so much energy and vigor in Europe, upon which our safety depends, will be highly pernicious to us; we ought to consider the United States as the wanton and bitter enemies of our existence, and threat them according."

In order to make them weary of the war, we should use our naval force, not only to destroy their shipping, but to harass and alarm them by frequent descents, so as to keep their troops employed on the defensive, along their vast extent of sea-coast, and thus prevent them from overpowering us with superior numbers, our own possessions. In short, we ought not to make war against them by halves; but to do them all the mischief possible. Here let us carefully guard ourselves against misinterpretation. We speak, and the author before us speaks, not of the conduct of a single department (for instants of the Admiralty), but of the whole scheme and character of our warfare. It is idle Ministers in detail and without reference to their common principles of action. What would the nation gain by removing perhaps a laborious and skillful individual from a particular office whilst the views of the Cabinet remain unchanged. Ever since the death of Mr. Perceval, a uniform littleness have marked every feature of our public transactions. Nothing great has been done or attempted. Palliation, excuse, and apology, have been the continued topics of those, whose hard lot it has been to support the cause of Ministers. Such a course of things can not continue long. It will waste away the strength of the country; and what is worse, it will break down the national spirit so that gallant enterprise and far-sighted undertakings will become foreign to our very nature, and the English character will dwindle into effetainacy and decrepitude.

Recurring with most painful feelings to the loss of the Java, we have to state, that this melancholy event receives a melancholy alleviation, if such it can be called, in contemplating the individual bravery displayed on the occasion. The British flag was not struck until the Java was made a complete wreck, having her bow sprit and every mast and spar blown out of her; so that it was found necessary two days afterward to destroy her at sea. She was a fine French built ship seven or eight years old and was captured after a gallant action, from the French in the East Indies, about two years and a half ago. She mounted 28 18 pounders, 16 32 pound carronade and two long 9 pounders, in all, 46 guns [perhaps 49]; where as the Constitution carries 56 guns [the *Constitution* had 51] and the difference of the weight of metal in favor of the latter is still more considerable, being as 15 20 to 10 34. This circumstance, together with the vast superiority of built in the American frigate, she being of the very largest class sufficiently exempts every individual on board the Java from censure, and leaves us only to regret the unavailing exertion of so much bravery in so unequal a contest. But though we agree that "no personal honour of our officers and men has been forfeited," we can not say the same of "the national glory." That is alike tarnished naval losses whether they arise from the fault of one class of persons or another. "The enterprise of the Americans in pushing out on such distant and unexpected attempts," is so far from forming an excuse for the supineness and folly of our Government, that it constitutes the very ground of our complaint. You do not expect your enemy to be on the alert; you leave it in his power to push out. Then you are culpably ignorant of the nature of hostility, and grossly inattentive to your most obvious duties. That any one of the three large American frigates should ever have had an opportunity of leaving port, that they were not watched by squadrons of observation before the war, and closely blockaded ever since, are alone sufficient proof incompetency, in those who took upon themselves the high responsibility of supporting the national interest and honour.

Instead of being the blockaders, our ships are actually blockaded.

It is perhaps easy to understand the frustration of the public and the Royal Navy when reviewing the statistic. During the twenty years of the Napoleonic wars the British lost 17 frigates—sunk or captured—while taking 229 frigates from enemies all over the world. Until the Americans came along in the last five months of 1812, the astounding record was attributed to superior ship handling of the officers and warrents of the Royal Navy. Little credit was given to the crewmen. They were often "pick up" crews comprised of multinational sailors not serving in a voluntary capacity. In spite of language and discipline problems the success was awarded to the officer class.

American Frigate Victories Altered the Royal Navy

Here the newspaper is condemning the Parliament for its lack of resolve in fighting the war with the Americans, who should not have been allowed to tweak the nose of the royal lion. The victories of the *Constitution* over the *Guerriere* and the *Java*, coupled with that of the *United States* over the *Macedonian*, fired up the British population. They did not believe that the American ships and crews were superior to the Royal Navy, which was perpetually victorious. The word *frigate* meant equal, and the statistics of 44 guns to 38, along with a much higher throw weight favoring the Americans, who were in larger ships, had no impact on the public. The public was well aware that the number attached to a ship was not an accurate description of her power. An English frigate was simply superior to any other. In fact, both the *Guerriere* and the *Macedonian* were not of English make, and the English crews were roughly 30 percent alien. Of course, that was also true of Nelson's flagship, which was served by many a foreign hand, including Americans.

The Admiralty responded by clamping down the blockade of American ports and increasing convoy escorts, which altered the importance of the American War of 1812. At the start, six months before, it had been regarded as a mere distraction, even a boon to some speculators.

In the past, the Royal Navy had put down as few as eight new frigates a year. Public opinion, concerning the conduct of the American war, insisted that England make a serious effort to counter the American navy. In 1813 the Admiralty planned to build thirty-five frigates. The hubbub forced even yellow-pine ships to be laid down. The soft wood was not nearly as resilient as red pine, which lasted as little as four years. Yet the service of these new ships was expected to help shorten the conflict, and thus they would pay for themselves. Jefferson's prediction had proved correct: the American intervention into the Napoleonic Wars was becoming a severe pain, a thorn in the paw of the English lion. The threat of the American navy, though very slight, was having a much bigger impact than anyone had expected. The cost of keeping the enemy ships bottled up in home ports was becoming disproportionate to its threat.

Avoid Contact

By November of 1812, the Admiralty was treating frigate building as a war emergency, even before the loss of the *Java*. But the red-pine modified 38s and yellow-pine 36s were still gunned with 18-pounders. An order was put out to all Royal Navy frigates to avoid single-ship combat with the American frigates. However, on December 26, 1812, the superiority of the American design was acknowledged with the order for a 40-gun Royal Navy frigate, which was to be armed with 24-pounders. The standard English frigate, which carried thirty-six or thirty-eight 18-pounders, was no match for the large American frigates in single combat. The Royal Navy reached all the way back to the design of the French *Endymion* in 1797. Built along the same lines as USS *Constitution*, the new English frigates would be of the same vintage. The Admiralty had taken the heat for those 18-pounders that had become famous when a British sailor coined the title "Old Ironsides." There would be no more ricocheting shot from the new line of ships. One reason Ironsides became famous was that all of England saw those 18-pound cannonballs bouncing across the front page of the *London Times*.

As a result of the American victories in single combat and the need to supply convoy escort due to French and American privateers that spring of 1813, twenty-five new frigates were readied for outfitting. However, some new ships went directly into ordinary. Crews could not be provided, and impressment, the cause of the war with America in the first place, was increased.

The Turning of the Tide of War

The order to suspend attacks on single American frigates by Royal Navy frigates, which were armed with 18-pounders, proves that it was not just USS *Constitution* that had iron sides. Additionally, the new British frigates were made of pine and were far more susceptible to damage from the heavy guns of the big American frigates. During the close contact at the conclusion of a fight, the 32-pound American carronades could shatter England's pine frigates like glass.

By the spring of 1813, many things were happening within English shipbuilding. Thirty-three new pine frigates were built, and thirteen other old ships were converted—cut down—to frigates. The yellow pine, supplied from Canada, had a short life span and thus was not thought to be cost effective by Parliament, which pointed out to the Royal Navy that a pine ship was just as expensive as a hardwood. By not using hardwood for frigates though, the navy made the ever-dwindling supply of oak, much of which now came from the Nordic countries and Canada, available for the massive rated ships.[20] There were other problems with pine, including the need for inner-hull strength. Oak, a hardwood with coarse grain knotted within the curves, was ideal for knees, which formed the skeleton of the hull, and withstood the twisting of wave action. Straight pine has no such strength and could not be used for either hanging or lodging knees. Iron trusses were applied to reinforce the pine knees, which was not nearly as strong. The experiment with softwood was found to be a bad idea and was abandoned by the Admiralty soon thereafter.

New Idea: French Razors

The English turned ship construction to the razee, or razor, which was a cutdown 64, and integrated into the Royal Navy a copy of the French modification. The Royal Navy saw razors as a solution to single-ship combat with the big American frigates. They were very stiff and rolled so much that they endangered their masts and yards in just a little weather. Moving and reducing the ballast to improve the trim did little to alleviate the problem, much to the discomfort of the crew. There was not a lot of latitude when it came to shifting ballast on a frigate. Cannons, powder, and ammunition accounted for 20 percent of the on-board weight, which was set in place for battle. The remaining 80 percent, which included the rigging, sail, yards, and consumable supplies, couldn't go far. There was not a great deal that could be done to retrim a vessel of that kind, unlike a cargo ship. Razors were powerful men-of-war carrying 24s and carronades. By May of 1813 the first, HMS *Endymion*, a 44-gun frigate, went to join the fleet blockading American ports.[21]

The razors were also deceptive since they looked like light frigates but carried 24s and were well built to withstand combat. In addition to their ability to carry more guns than the 38s, they also carried more sail and thus were good in pursuit. Built similarly to the French-designed *Pomone*, HMS *Endymion* raced up and down the coast of the United States of America like a prowling cat.

Later, Decatur would fight HMS *Majestic* from USS *President*, but that is another story. One benefit of that contact was that the original architectural drawings of the *President* were captured as well and survive in the Greenwich Maritime Museum, in England. In 1997 they were key to making Ironsides seaworthy once again. Humphreys's original plans for the *Constitution* were no longer available.

~

CHAPTER EIGHT

The Battle That Never Was: USS *Constitution* versus HMS *Trincomalee*

If I were to die this moment, 'want of frigates' would be stamped on my heart.

—Admiral Lord Nelson

USS *Constitution* was constructed in 1797. The technology of the time moved at the speed of the ship, slowly. Therefore, the English frigates that were vexed by the big American were little altered both before and after the War of 1812. The sweep of the hull underwent various but slight modifications, while the rigging of sails added and subtracted, changed shape, and changed back again. The great windjammers were still a decade and more away. My wife and research assistant, Carol, and I concentrated our research at the usual places. While in England, we scoured museums, libraries, and private collections in London, south to Greenwich, and beyond to Chatham Royal Dockyard. I did not pass up a visit to Portsmouth. In fact, in order to get a better appreciation for the scene, we took a ferry from Dinard, France, which passed along the edge of the Cherbourg Peninsula and out across the English Channel to Portsmouth harbor. It took eight hours at twenty knots, which gave me an appreciation for the breadth of the busiest waterway in the world. I had crossed half a dozen times a year when stationed in Belgium, but that was in the north, from the Pas-de-Calais. When I was stationed in East Anglia, England, in the late 1970s, we took the overnight ferry from Felixstowe to Zeebrugge across the wide North Sea entrance to the English Channel. All we ever saw were chunky modern metal monsters, which barely resemble those sleek sailing ships. Now, I put my best imagination forward as we vibrated with the engine, passing by the round stone forts a mile out in the channel, closing slowly into Portsmouth. There the king's men watched for Napoleon's raiders flying false flags. Tourists waved from the variegated battlement as we approached the primary fortification on the point. The white masts of HMS *Victory* came into sight, high above the museum roofs, crossed with yards and strung with ropes.

The museum that surrounds Admiral Lord Nelson's flagship, of the decisive battle of Trafalgar in 1805, alone is worth the excursion. By train one can easily reach the Royal Dockyard from London. One gets off at the last stop, at the very edge of the harbor, and there is a choice between the ferryboat to the Isle of Wight or a hundred steps to the original gate of the Royal Dockyard. I was stopped in my tracks by the sight of HMS *Warrior*, the black snake of the channel. The most modern ship of her day, she dominated the navies of the world at the height of Queen Victoria's reign. But the *Warrior* is another story. I was captured by the shipyard museum as I walked toward the masts of HMS *Victory*. Housed in the original setting, room after room portrays the twenty-six trades it took to make a sailing ship. The new Nelson museum is just across the tracks. It rivals and then surpasses the one at Monmouth, Wales, though it does not have the charm. HMS *Victory* must be seen, for it cannot be described. The sight and smell of the huge wooden sailing man-of-war brought me a shudder of delight, while gangs of tourists clomped above and below during the tour. Built thirty-seven years before the *Constitution* at Chatham, she stands in a dry dock today. The keel was never meant to take the weight out of the buoyancy of the water. Therefore, all but one of her 110 guns are plastic. High and dry, she shows off her true size both above and below the waterline. It was at the moment of seeing her that I grasped the true capacity of a sailing ship. Fifty yards away stands the hall housing the remains of the *Mary Rose*, King Henry VIII's ship of war. A bit worse for wear, she is behind glass in a spacious humidified chamber, with water trickling down her blackened sides and timbers, day and night. Her treasure has been preserved nearby and is truly astonishing.

Trincomalee

I must not waste time and should get on with our most remarkable experience. Lionel Leaventhal, publisher of Greenhill Books, introduced me to a gentleman at the International Napoleonic Fair in London. Mr. Allen Gilham, a restoration architect, wanted to tell me about a project to preserve HMS *Unicorn*, which is docked near Dundee, Scotland. "Of course you know *Trincomalee*," he said, rather offhandedly. Of course I did not. "What's a trincomalee?" I interrupted.

A few days later Carol and I were on our way north to Hartlepool, to see HMS *Trincomalee*. When we lived in England I was familiar with Hartlepool, since they had a soccer team and were in the list of winners and losers on BBC radio every weekend. It was a fishing village on the northeast coast below Newcastle, according to my map. We went to London's King's Cross railway station and I tried to purchase tickets. "The train does not go there, dear. You will have to go to Darlington and get something from there," I was politely assured by the gray-haired lady behind two inches of bulletproof glass. I did not like the sound of "something," but I thought, well, she has never been there and is just unaware of the local trains. Hartlepool is a big place, I thought; they have a football team.

The train was a joy, high speed—it was like an airliner inside. I enjoyed watching the greener than green, rather wet countryside whiz by. I knew Darlington too, from BBC 3. It was a horse-racing mecca, and since we had lived near Newmarket, the home of the national stud, I was sure there would be a train from there to Hartlepool; after all, they had a football team. At Darlington, "Information" confirmed that the advice was correct and we would have to walk a quarter mile to the bus station. It was March and rather wet. The bus lady, behind the desk with a raincoat on, said that they did not have a bus to Hartlepool. We bought two tickets return and caught a local bus to Sedgefield only a few minutes later across the street. When the driver heard we were going to Hartlepool, he indicated that we should sit across from him and he would get us on another bus, once we got to the town high street. One hour later, twenty miles down the back roads, we popped out onto the high street, in a very remote little picturesque damp rural town. The bus to Hartlepool was crowded, and I knew why. There was no other way to get there. The bus was also the local school bus, and groups got on and groups got off. Another hour later, twenty miles down the road, after going through numerous housing estates, we careened down a long hill into the fishing village of Hartlepool. I was looking for the football ground. I had begun to doubt my memory.

The driver was curious, and at a stop in the town center he was surprised that we did not get off. I told him that we wanted to see the sailing ship. "You mean the Historic Quay, right you are, just stay on and I'll get you there," he proclaimed with a smile. It was not a scheduled stop. "I did not think you two were from around here, come from London did you?" It was my turn now: "No, Lake Placid, New York."

HMS *Trincomalee* was set in a dock surrounded by quaint buildings of the time. These were a museum of the trades and times of the Napoleonic Wars that formed a horseshoe around three sides. As we walked across the huge empty cobblestone parking lot, I could plainly see the triple-whitewashed masts of a tall ship.

India

When the *Java* left England from Chatham, she was carrying far more than just a hundred extra men and the new governor general of Bombay, Lieutenant Hislop. Bombay was the center of the shipbuilding industry established by the East

India Company. The Indian yard was needed because the capacity of the commercial and government dockyards in Great Britain was fully committed in 1812. In India the new frigates were being built out of teak rather than oak. This was a native hardwood, yet it was expensive to harvest, and the Indian frigates were just as costly as those built in England. It takes more than wood to build a ship. The metal hardware was coming from England, crammed into the dank hold of HMS *Java*. Copper fittings in particular were among the cargo lost when the English frigate was defeated and wrecked off of the Brazilian coast in December of 1812. Little copper was used since teak provides a natural resin that retards ferrous metal from corroding. Indiamen could be hammered together with iron nails. Most importantly, though, the *Java* was carrying the plans for a new fast frigate that would challenge the big Americans. She was to be christened HMS *Trincomalee*, named for a port city in Ceylon. Built ultimately during 1816, after the end of the War of 1812, she was a Leda class frigate not unlike the *Belvidera*, the *Guerriere*, and the *Java*. When commissioned, she would carry twenty-eight 18-pound cannons, sixteen 32-pound carronades, and a pair of 9-pound cannons on the forecastle—an actual count of forty-six guns on that "38-gun frigate." That damp, cold, windy day at the water's edge on the North Sea, I had the great good luck to be standing on her deck listening to a gale buzz her rigging.

Ships Made in India

Teak has some advantages over oak. It is more durable, stronger, and highly resilient, unappetizing to the infestations of marine critters. It is extremely dense and therefore hard to drill, shave, chip, and bend. Rather than chopping teak trees down, foresters cut a notch ring low completely around the base. That interrupts the osmosis of the sap, which no longer supports life, and the tree dies. Sometime later the foresters come back and take it down. Since it no longer has any sap, it is light and will float down to market.

Ready for service in 1817, the *Trincomalee* had one experience that touched the Napoleonic Wars. In January of 1819 she delivered supplies to Saint Helena Island for the complement guarding the deposed emperor, who was imprisoned there. Laid up in ordinary during the long peace, she did not see service again until 1847. The *Trincomalee* sailed in the West Indies, a part of the effort to destroy the slave trade, which had been outlawed in England in 1832.[1] There she joined the *Constitution*, who had the same mission. During the American Civil War she plied the Pacific and called at San Francisco. But the day came when she went to school. As a training ship and barracks for the new kind of career sailor, she served out her country's investment. A wealthy ship enthusiast loved her lines and the soundness of her teak hull. In 1897 he restored the hulk she had become and put her once more into service for coastal excursions. Her benefactor died in 1931. Looked after by the leaders of Trinity House, she trained young sea scouts for many years. Bombed at anchor by the Germans in 1940, the *Trincomalee* continued to serve as a training vessel to modern times. In 1987, with the contributions from donors of all classes, she was moved to Hartlepool for restoration. The hard job of fund-raising and restoration was completed in 2001.

On Board the Indiaman

We were taken in hand by the director of the restoration, whom I had called days before. He was as anxious to show her off as we were to see her. There was very little conversation. Standing amidships on the dark teak deck, I felt as if I were inside a great wooden machine. Throwing my head back, I could see that the high masts and yards were complete with both standing and running rigging. Much higher than I expected, the ship's masthead would have been visible above a twelve-story building. The yards were imposing, massive telephone poles tapered at the ends, caught there by a spider's web of lines. The tops were much bigger than I had envisioned from reading, broad enough for four royal marines to stand on one side and fire down. I was introduced to the only other person on board, who was painting the inside of the taffrail a red lead. He was a volunteer, like all those I would meet on shore. Schoolchildren were expected, and he wanted to finish before they upset his bucket.

While my first thought was of war, the second was of the sea. I have crossed the Pacific twice, and I tried to imagine doing it once again on this little ship. She was 150 feet long at the gun deck and 39 feet wide. She only drew 13 feet of water, according to the plan I saw on the bulkhead in the wardroom. Yet, I thought, many a man served on far smaller vessels, brigs, sloops, and schooners, some half that size, that tended the *Trincomalee* on all seven seas. They must have felt like our astronauts who looked into space through thick glass portholes and wondered at the same stars, "What am I doing here? Will I ever get back?" Once safely home again from a sailing voyage, which could easily take a year or two, sailors shipped over and signed up to do it all over again. I crawled around the orlop deck and peered into the magazine. Thin copper sheeting was attached to not only the walls of the little cabin but the floors and ceiling as well. Kneeling outside the hatch, caught in the glow of the flame cast by the oil lamp, I wondered, "What was I missing?" In another time, this would have been the most advanced machine man had ever built. Those who served were on the cutting edge of the future. They would have told friends in the waterside pub that there could never be anything to come that would rival a frigate. "Aye mate, you should come aboard." Next time we go to England, and I am sure it will be soon, I will return to the "Indiaman," but this time I am hiring a car.

British Blockade America, 1813

Englishmen, steeped in the lore of the Royal Navy, were exasperated with the conduct of the American war. The newspaper editors knew that England was capable of squashing the American navy like a bug. They said so in the *London Times* on January 6, 1813:

> Whatever insensibility the friends of ministers affect, with regard to the triumphs of the American navy, they are abundantly anxious to retort upon them, in the way of rumor and reports, not a day passes, without some asserted capture by our cruisers, to which, though we lend a most [illegible] ear, we hitherto unfortunately found no sufficient reason to attach entire credit. Yesterday [illegible] more than usually prolific of these air-drawn victorious morning papers gratified us with assurances of the [illegible] of the United States, recapture of the Macedonian; but an evening paper went still farther, and noticed the reported surrender of Commodore Rodgers and his whole squadron [numerous erroneous rumors taken by reporters from drunken sailors in pubs were being printed in error]. Most happy should we have been to find either of these reports correct. It is high time, something should be done, to recall to the memory of our brave tars the sentiments which were once universal among our countrymen, and which inspired the patriotic hymn of "Britannia rule the waves." Not withstanding all, which that has been done to depress the courage and deaden the spirit of that body of men, our naval heroes, by representing the striking of the British flag as a very natural occurrence a mere accident, by analysing the constitution of a British crew, and proving it far inferior to an American one, by exaggerating the size and strength of the enemy's ships and diminishing those of our own, by attempting to save the Ministers from blame at the expense of the naval officer; not withstanding all these and thousand other weak and despicable attitudes, which have been exercised by the defenders of a weak and despicable policy, we still think that our navy, if it has but fair play given to it, will soon annihilate the bostrial spirit of Americans, and sweep from the seas the whole of that contemptible force which has been too long suffered to struggle for the scepter of the ocean.
>
> We have said, and we say again, that our censure is not directed against a partial misconduct, in the particular department which has the immediate disposal of our naval force. It directed against the feebleness and timidity of that policy, which overrides the exertions of every department. Political cowardice alone, as we conceive, prevented Ministers from commencing the war against America in a style, which the Americans themselves expected. It prevented them from having a plan matured and ready, for falling upon the sea-coast of America, blocking up her ports, hindering her privateers from sailing, and capturing or destroying every frigate she might dare to send to sea. These would have been vigorous measures but not more vigorous than the Ministers had ample means at that time to

effect. They had, say their defenders, 85 sail to oppose to 14; then, say we, they had enough, and more than enough to have done all that we have described as necessary. If it was not done, the failure was not for want of means, but for want of plans; and the plan, we have no doubt, would have been readily enough furnished by the proper department, if the Cabinet had thought fit to call for it: but, in the words of an almost inspired Statesman, "littleness in object, and in means to them appears soundness and sobriety." They, therefore, begin, on all occasions, too low. They bring out the impatient "dogs of war" muzzled and clogged. What is the consequence? The enemy is animated. He obtains advantages. His forces increases. The war drags on heavily: the expense augments daily. If we had 85 ships at first, we soon find it necessary to have 100. If we hesitated to send a cruising squadron on his coasts in the summer, we are obliged to place two stationary squadrons there in the winter. If we thought frigates but two-thirds manned were strong enough, we presently discover that we must cut down our 74's, and increase the complement of our ships of all classes. In short, the exertions and expense from which we timidly shrunk in the outset, must in the progress of the contest be more than doubled.[2]

The government and the Admiralty, under the unrelenting anger of the public and press, were going to have to change tactics and stop treating the American war as a sideshow.

The Turning Point

In America the early naval successes of the first six months of the war were fading all too soon. The long winter of the War of 1812 was beginning for the United States as it had done for the emperor Napoleon. It was not that the English were learning or adapting. They did not need to change that rapidly for they had the big ships and the years of experience to use them.

Napoleon was significantly weaker in 1813 after losing hundreds of thousands of troops in the freezing cold of Russia. He wanted to sue for peace, but the allies would have none of it. Along all frontiers, he began to retreat as he was squeezed slowly back into the French homeland. Great Britain also pressed on French ports with an ever-improving naval blockade. The French blue-water navy was no longer a threat. Now England could afford to look away from Europe and concentrate much of her sea power on her former colony in North America in an effort to sustain British Canada.

The young Theodore Roosevelt sums up the period: "Our victorious seafights while they did not inflict any material damage upon the colossal sea-might of England, had the most important results in the feelings they produced at home and even abroad."[3]

The Heavy Press of Blockade

The feeling produced in France may have been favorable, but in England things had turned nasty. In an article titled "American Treachery," a blockade ship off the Connecticut coast complains:

> Captain Sir Thomas Hardy, of the Ramillies, was off New London in June 1813, when his boats captured a schooner, making for that harbour; the crew had left her. The vessel was brought close to the Ramillies, Sir Thomas Hardy ordered her to be placed alongside of another prize. Lt. Geddes, and 13 men were in execution of this order, when about ½ past 2, the vessel blew up and the Lt. and 10 of his men perished; three men only escaped, but were dreadfully scorched. Such was the effect of wicked and cruel artiface planned by American merchants of New York and sanctioned by the government. It had been reported that the Ramillies was short of provisions, they had therefore placed some articles of this description in the hatchway, in hopes the vessel might have been taken alongside. In the hold were several barrels of gunpowder; trains were laid to explode at a given time by means of clock work. A quantity of arsenic among the food would have been so compatible that it is a wonder it was not resorted to. Should actions like these receive the sanction of governments, the science of war, and the law of nations will degenerate into the barbarity of the Algerines; and murder and pillage will take place of kindness and humanity to our enemies. Every honorable mind in America must blush for his country when he reads this account and detest the authors of such diabolical treachery.[4]

The feeling of imprisonment brought by sea stories of the fleets of enemy ships skirting the coast and seizing American cargoes not only dampened the economy, but it also infuriated the people. The king of England was grasping at his old colonies, bent on undoing the Revolution, which was still in the heart of every citizen. The English correspondents in Washington monitoring the American government kept the British public apprised of the "hysteria" the blockade was causing. It must be remembered that the vast majority of the people in the United States had close relatives in Great Britain. Many were anxious over the plight of their kin and wanted that war to end with as little loss of life and property as possible. English business investment in the United States was high, and the city of London's financial institutions were not happy with the increases in marine insurance and the possibility of the war getting completely out of hand. After all, a great deal of investment money from England was resting in the new nation with the hopes of bringing a new bonanza.

The following article appeared in the *London Times* on Saturday, March 27, 1813.

> By farther arrival in American papers yesterday, it appears that several different bills have been brought before Congress, for the more active, and in some respects

vindictive prosecution of the war. Of the latter description is a bill submitted by a Mr. Campbell, under an impression that the British government had in contemplation to execute such natives of Ireland or Great Britain as should be found in arms against their native country, although naturalized as American citizens. The bill in question; proposes, that life shall answer for life; with the distinction, it is said, that the first description of persons to be seized and executed in retaliation shall be traitors; the next are Tories and refugees; and lastly, British of any description. This extravagant proposal we take to be rather the sketch of some violent party news writer, than the serious statement of a grave legislator. The Americans admit the right of every state to allegiance of its native borne subject; and there can be no doubt, that that right justifies the infliction of capital punishment on the unnatural traitors who turn their arms against the sacred bosom of their country. It has been an ancient practice, at the commencement of any war, to notify all who may be seduced into the enemy's service that "they will thereby become liable to suffer the pains of death, and all other pains and penalties of high treason and piracy." Such was the form of the proclamation of 1798, at the breaking out of the French war and such we conceive to be the customary and justifiable conduct of all states, when circumstances demand the infliction of such severity. In the present instants, humanity would induce us to make much allowance to individuals; and the intervention of the ceremony of naturalization, though perfectly destitute of legal effect in this respect, might afford great excuse to the ignorant class of men whose conduct would be likely to come in question. It is probable, therefore, that few, if any capital punishments will ever be applied to cases of this description: but if they should, to talk of retaliation in the manner above stated would be an utter perversion, not only of justice, but of common sense. Retaliation can only apply where the parties are similarly situated; and, therefore, in the instants here supposed, it could only justify the punishment of a native borne American citizen, taken fighting on our side against his country. A Mr. Beadley also, has brought a bill, which seems perfectly unnecessary in as much as it goes only to authorize the destruction of British ships in American ports. It contains, indeed, a vague reference to some sort of catamaran scheme by which this object is to be effected: but we do not see how the mode of operations can be made more or less justifiable by an American Act Of Congress. The preceding bills indicate little more, than the alarm which seems to have been excited by the arrival of blockading squadrons, and by the report of their having on board Congreve Rockets, and other means of annoyance to the sea port towns [which would be fired on Baltimore on September 13, 1814]. The other bills however, have passed the House of Representatives which contain more reasonable provisions for the prosecution of the war, the one by appointing an additional number of officers to the land forces; the other, by the increase of the navy. Our ministers, who, to due them justice, are far from incorrigible in their errors, it is seen at last to have opened their eyes to the necessity of meeting these measures by corresponding energy on their part. We understand they have at last resolved to put the whole American coast, except Boston and Rhode Island, under a strict blockade.[5]

Interestingly, after the surprise attack on New York City, similar calls for the death penalty came forward in 2002 when it was discovered that Americans were fighting on the side of the Taliban in Afghanistan.

Englishmen Turn Their Attention to America

The *London Times* for Tuesday, March 23, 1813, shows the interest and intelligence capabilities setting the stage, as the war went on.

> By the Detterell, which arrived on Friday, Portsmouth, from Bermuda, we learn, that Sir J. B. Warren had returned to that island with the St. Domingo and Dragun, from blockading the American ports, during which he captured thirty five merchantmen, and drove the Constellation on shore on the bar of the Delaware; but she was afterwards got off and refitted. The only ships of the American Squadron now at sea, are the Chesapeake, Essex, and Hornet. The two latter are cruising on the coast of Brazil, and blockading the Bonne Citoyenne, Bahia. The Chesapeake had sent into port four merchantmen, valued at New York at 600,000; the President, Constitution, and Constellation, were lying at Boston; they had taken eight months provisions on board. The United States, and Macedonian were nearly ready for sea, at New York. The American ships go to sea without any restrictive orders, but cruise according as they may obtain information.

With new Royal Navy men-of-war arriving daily at both Halifax and Bermuda, the blockade widened and deepened. English squadrons, headed by principal ships, accompanied by frigates and sloops, maintained station outside of Boston, Philadelphia, and New York. The Chesapeake Bay was closed off as well, which slowly strangled commerce all along the eastern seaboard. The prize American frigates for the most part were trapped in the ports of Boston and New York. In the Chesapeake Bay, British raiding parties sacked Hampton, Virginia, and many other waterside communities with little naval response. USS *Constellation*, one of the lighter frigates, often confused with the *Constitution* because of the similar name, became bottled up for the duration of the war on a backwater near Norfolk, Virginia.

Some of the smaller American sloops and brigs had passing engagements with similarly classed enemy vessels. Captain James Lawrence continued to distinguish himself as commander of the *Hornet*, cruising north toward home. Commodore Rodgers slipped out with his command and scouted the North Sea and Irish Channel in an effort to bring the American War of 1812 a little closer to home for the British. He could not take on the English squadrons along his own coastline, so he attempted to take the pressure off with an incursion into John Bull's home waters, as John Paul Jones had done in *Bon Homme Richard* during the Revolutionary War in the previous century. Stephen Decatur with the *United States* and the reflagged *Macedonian* was confined for the war at New London, Connecticut.

HMS *Shannon* versus USS *Chesapeake*

American captain James Lawrence gave up the *Hornet* for the frigate *Chesapeake*, 38 guns, which was replenishing in Boston. Famous in both England and America because of the incident at Hampton Roads in 1807, which nearly started a war, she had not distinguished herself. Armed with 18–pounders, she looked more British than American. The Royal Navy captains had been cautioned to abstain from single combat with the big American frigates. But not all of the Americans were that big. It was June of 1813 when Captain Phillip Bowes Vere Broke sailed the *Shannon* to America. He was known as a tough trainer, exercising his crew with drills at every opportunity. He believed that the three previous Royal Navy losses were due to unprepared ships and unskilled labor. He trained his men daily on gun drill, and twice a week they fired the big guns at floating barrels. Prizes were given out for marksmanship for both rifle and cannon. A member of the blockading force from Halifax, the *Shannon*, 38, lurked in the waters just outside Boston Harbor.

The final gun count of the two ships was nearly equal, at fifty for the American and fifty-two for the Englishman. This time it was Lawrence who was challenged to come out and fight; it was the reverse of when he had sent a note in Brazil to the captain of HMS *Bonne Citoyenne*.

On one of the longest days of the year, June 1, 1813, the two ships met on the horizon east of Boston lighthouse. It was still bright at the dinner hour when the two warriors closed on each other. Both captains were known for their sailing skill. They maneuvered one against the other, tacking and sparring, both looking to take the windward. The *Chesapeake* won position on the windward side and made a run at the *Shannon*. It was just before six o'clock when the *Shannon*'s guns, which had held fire, bore on the quarterdeck of the American, only yards away. "Broke the *Shannon*'s captain was afraid that Lawrence would pass under his stern, rake her, and engage her on the quarter; but either overlooking or waiving this advantage, the American captain luffed up within 50 yards upon the *Shannon*'s starboard quarter, and squared his main-yard."[6] Not taking the best advantage of passing astern and raking the enemy ship, Lawrence leveled the field and opted to stand side by side and trade broadsides. That was a fatal mistake. At 5:50 the *Shannon* fired the first broadside of twenty-six guns.

The *Chesapeake* replied with her whole compliment of guns. Three minutes later, finding he was forging ahead, hauled up a little. The *Chesapeake*'s broadsides were doing great damage, but she herself was suffering even more than her foe; the men in the *Shannon's* tops could hardly see the deck for the American frigate through the cloud of splinters, hammocks, and other wreckage that was flying across it. Man after man was killed at the wheel, the fourth Lieutenant, the master and the boatswain were slain, and at 5:56 having had her jib sheer and foretop-sail tie shot away and her spanker brails loosened so that the sail blew out, the *Chesapeake* came up into the wind somewhat, so as to expose her quarter to her antagonist's broadside, which beat in her stern-ports and swept the men from the after guns. One of the arms chests on the quarter-deck was blown up by a hand-grenade thrown from the *Shannon*.[7]

The two ships were twenty yards apart. The *Chesapeake* was no longer under control; the helmsmen died when the wheel was shot away. Both vessels suffered the loss of so much sail and running rigging that the captains could no longer control direction. The two impacted together and stuck fast. It was up to the crew now, in hand-to-hand fighting. Lieutenant Law of the Royal Marines fired his pistol at Captain Lawrence as he mounted the rail of the American frigate. Shot, James Lawrence was carried below, imploring as he went, "Keep the guns going and fight the ship til she sinks. Don't give up the ship, blow her up."[8] But it was all over. Only the fifth lieutenant was left to take command of the *Chesapeake*; he was the lone officer left standing. The battle had lasted about twelve minutes. The American frigate was captured and taken to Halifax. Captain Lawrence and his crew did not give up the ship; it was taken away from them in a fair fight. England was back on top and likely to stay there.

Land Campaign in North America

The land campaign waged by the commanding general of the American army, Major General Henry Dearborn, had not enjoyed a period of early success, as had the navy. After the surrender by General Hull at Detroit within weeks of the start of the war, the next foray was a bigger mess. Major General Stephen Van Rensselaer was everything except a military man. A militia commander, appointed by political party affiliation, he was expected to establish, equip, and train an expeditionary force to invade Upper Canada at Queenston on the Niagara River. Once accomplished, this would isolate western Canada from the capital at Montreal. England attempted to arbitrate a way out of the war in the late summer of 1812, but President Madison would not hear of it. It gave the beleaguered Van Rensselaer time to cobble together a force of militia and borrowed regulars. Among them was Lieutenant Colonel Winfield Scott. With about four thousand troops he attempted a river crossing and invasion; this would have been a very ambitious operation for the best of professional soldiers. It was October, and at the same time, the U.S. Navy was riding high. Swift water, a lack of boats, and skittish militiamen doomed the expedition at its midpoint. The field commander, Lieutenant Colonel Soloman Van Rensselaer, was killed in the town fighting and Scott had to take command. In spite of spirited fighting by heroes like Captain John Wool, the entire American army that managed to get across the river, about one thousand, was captured. Their battle flags hang high above the heads of the red-coated pensioners today in the dining hall at Chelsea Royal Hospital in London, England, along with the captured eagles of Napoleon.

Major General Dearborn persisted with his plan even though the first two phases had failed and the winter was closing in. In late November, not the time of year to campaign in Canada, Dearborn led six thousand soldiers from Plattsburgh to the border at Champlain, New York. There, a force of Canadians confronted him, one-fifth the size of his own formation. He dithered and then changed his mind and retreated. So ended the first year of the land war.

In 1813 there were more serious attacks on Canada, which are characterized by Colonel John Elting in his *Amateurs to Arms* as mud, marching, and misery. William Henry Harrison enjoyed the successes in the west, while attacks along the Niagara were in fits and starts. Political affiliations dominated the choice of militia officers, who lost their stomachs for war soon after meeting the enemy. The regular army had a corps of officers who were not much better than the militia. Many were party hacks from Washington, D.C., like the Virginia lawyer Alexander Smyth, a personal friend of Jefferson, who found himself in command of the rifle regiment in the Niagara. Made a brigadier general at the start of the war, before the year was out he had given up the military life to return to practice. Battles were fought at Chrysler's Farm, the Raisin River, Chippewa, and other locales with the loss of life on both sides and nothing else. The gain of territory achieved when the French Canadians came over to the United States side, which had been prophesied by Thomas Jefferson, was worse than a myth. In March of 1814, Major General James Wilkinson, a veteran of Saratoga in 1777, attacked Canada for the last time. With 4,000 troops he waded across the stream at La Colle Mill, six miles into Canada, where he faced deep snow and a garrison of 180 men. He sent his men in with these words: "Return victorious or not at all." Fearing that the enemy might be reinforced, Wilkinson, firmly in the show, got cold feet and called a retreat. When relieved of command, he told the newspapers, "Artifices . . . deprived me of my sword in the dawn of the campaign."[9]

On the Lakes

When General Hull was given the task of taking Canada at Detroit in June of 1812, he asked for naval transport to cross the river. He was told to capture it from the enemy. That was the level of American naval support on Lakes Erie and Ontario. As things got going, a naval base was established, along with an army barracks at Sacketts Harbor, New York, near the beginning of the Saint Lawrence River, the border between English Canada and the United States.

There naval commodore Isaac Chauncey began to establish a presence to deny the freedom of Lakes Ontario and Erie with a small fleet of gunboats, sloops of war, and armed brigs constructed at a makeshift dockyard. The peculiar aspect of naval warfare on the inland Great Lakes was that they were not sailable from late October to March. The road network on both the Canadian and United States sides was poor to nonexistent. Therefore, transport of large military formations laden with artillery, ammunition, and supplies was slow to stop. The extreme cold and snow, combined with bugs, impenetrable forest, disease, and hostile Indians who were notoriously tyrannical, made recruitment more than disappointing. It was a land and naval war in miniature, yet filled with all the horror and suffering of the biggest battles of the Napoleonic age.

Oliver Hazard Perry

At Put-in-Bay in the southwest corner of Lake Erie, below Detroit, Master Commandant Perry was without men or vessels. If he was going to be the commodore, he needed lots of help, and Isaac Chauncey was interested in feathering his nest at Sacketts Harbor, where he was building a fleet. With the able assistance of Lieutenant John Brooks, U.S. Marine Corps, Perry found the men in Pennsylvania to crew his brigs, the *Lawrence* and the *Niagara*, which he had built at the edge of the lake. Provisional marine commodore Robert H. Barclay led an enemy flotilla of small armed craft and challenged Perry for control of the lake. Perry amassed a passel of nine light sailing craft. The *Tigress* and the *Trippe* had one gun, while the *Lawrence* and the *Niagara* each had eighteen 32-pound carronades. Barclay's flagship, the *Detroit*, had nineteen guns of varied sizes and was assisted by five other craft.

In September 1813, Commodore Perry was out there in the west all alone. What contact he had with his boss, hundreds of miles east, was of no assistance. He might as well have been Captain Porter in the Pacific Ocean on the other side of the world. Yet he prepared to defend the lake in a single battle that would be decisive.

The young American commodore flew a square dark-blue flag, with the last words of his friend James Lawrence emblazoned in white, "Don't Give Up the Ship." The two fleets met at close quarters late on the morning of September 10, 1813. Gerard Altoff, in his book *Oliver Hazard Perry and the Battle of Lake Erie*, relates the experience of seaman David Bunnell, taken from Bunnell's writing in *Travels and Adventures*:

> British round shot and grapeshot gouged saw-toothed holes through the *Lawrence*'s bulwarks with distressing frequency, launching showers of deadly wood splinters. The iron projectiles and wood splinters decimated the flagship's

crowded gundeck. A British shot mashed the head of a gunner standing near Seaman David Bunnell. The man's brains were sprayed so thickly in his face that Bunnell was temporarily blinded. Once the horrified Bunnell was assured that the brains were not his own he continued to serve his carronade.[10]

Perry's action at this naval battle, very near the international border on Lake Erie, was unique among his contemporaries. The *Lawrence* became heavily damaged in the fighting; cannon fire from the British fleet smashed her sides and wrested her rigging. Unable to get support from the *Niagara*, which had fallen behind, the animated Perry left his ship and under fire was rowed to the *Niagara*. There he took command and continued the fight. The battle lasted the day and left both sides extremely exhausted. In the end, Commodore Barclay surrendered his shattered ships and complement.

Perry wrote the following letter to General William Henry Harrison.

Dear General:
    We have met the enemy and they are ours:
    Two Ships, two Brigs,
    one Schooner & one Sloop.
        Yours with great respect and esteem
            O. H. Perry[11]

A hero for all services, Perry was more like an army commander; having his horse shot out from under him, he remounted and continued to fight and win. Those in Boston reported that some of Perry's men were former crewmen from the *Constitution*, which was laid up in Charlestown.

Captain Charles Stewart, Commanding

Captain Bainbridge had brought the victorious ship home in February of 1813 for refitting. It was not until June that command of the *Constitution* was changed. Charles Stewart was a veteran of the Barbary campaigns and former merchant captain. In June he had given up command of USS *Constellation*, which was blockaded in Norfolk. The repairs to Ironsides took a considerable time. It seemed that everything was rotted through, particularly the masts and yards. Some deck beams had to be replaced and the ship completely provisioned. In spite of the great victories she had achieved, it was difficult to maintain the crew once in port. The United States Navy was not yet a standing regular service. Soon the crew was paid off. The ship would remain idle from February to December 1813 while being refitted, as the war raged around her. Once it was determined that she was to voyage once again, a call was put out for able and ordinary seamen. Some of the warrants remained during refitting.

It was most difficult to recruit after the defeat of the *Chesapeake*, which took place just outside Boston Harbor. The British blockade was intended to deny, divert, disrupt, disorient, destroy, and demoralize the United States, her commerce, and her navy. It was having a devastating effect.

It was not until the first day of January 1814 that the *Constitution* was completely clear of the blockading Royal Navy fleet that crisscrossed the trading lane leading to the Atlantic. Nearly an entire year had gone by since she had acquired her title, "Ironsides."

The Exciting Start of Spring of 1814

The *Constitution's* winter and early spring patrol into the Caribbean was not a notable success. Captain Stewart realized that his mainmast was severely cracked and decided to go home to Boston for the repair. A passing ship told him that the *President* was blockaded in New York harbor. As the *Constitution* came up on Marblehead from the south, he was not surprised to find two Royal Navy frigates in chase. HMS *Junon* and *Tenedos* were nearly in range and closing fast. With a mast that could snap at any time, Stewart was not prepared to fight, nor was he about to make Ironsides a prisoner. Turning for the shelter of the American harbor, he was nearly becalmed. Thoughts of kedging his way to safety crossed his mind as he lightened ship. The two enemy frigates gained on him and he jettisoned water and spars while adding "stun sails," reaching for both a slight breeze and the estuary at the same time. His skill, coupled with the *Constitution's* ability to sail, brought him past Halfway Rock, where the pursuers dared not risk their keels. It was not a glorious victory, but Charles Stewart had saved his crippled ship, the one mandate all captains shared.

Meanwhile, England's Ordeal Was Ended

It was even more exciting in France that spring. The emperor Napoleon's retrograde action to save his army, nation, and throne came to an end at the Palace of Fontainebleau, in Paris. He said farewell to his "children" and was escorted into exile as the ruler of a small island, Elba, in the Mediterranean. The Ogre was not dead but he was defeated. The allied governments returned a Bourbon king to France who was nearly as inadequate as the one guillotined during the revolution. At the Congress of Vienna, the Duke of Wellington, Arthur Wellesley, ambassador to Paris, was having a hard time getting the respect of the czar of Russia, king of Prussia, and emperor of Austria. They said that he never had fought Napoleon in person, which was true. That the British Army was not nearly as large as their armies. He began to realize that the Russians and Prussians were about to form a military coalition and threaten the central European states and principalities that had been left alone with the departure of Napoleon.

He informed his friend Lord Bathhurst, the colonial secretary in London, of the plight that could arise if he were correct. It would mean that in the spring of 1815 England might have to fight to prevent such a takeover. If that were true, he would need the splendid British Army that was about to be demobilized. To keep that army at strength, it could be employed in the meantime to settle the conflict with the United States, now that war was over in Europe. As a result, a secret military order was issued. It was called "Reinforcements Allotted for North America and the Operations Contemplated for the Employment of Them," dated June 3, 1814. A very detailed plan, it called for an invasion of New York State from Montreal, Canada, where a major army and Royal Naval force would attack to the south. It was similar to the Burgoyne campaign of 1777. The plan allowed for diversionary attacks along the New England coast and inland shore of the Chesapeake Bay, in addition to the successful blockade of the American navy. With an occupying land force in the United States along the Lake Champlain–Hudson River corridor, peace talks would be initiated at Ghent, Belgium. The matter of the American War of 1812 could be successfully concluded in England's favor in time to return the troops to Wellington on the Continent. The command of the punitive expedition was offered to the great duke, but he turned it down.

By June of 1814 the governor general of Canada, Lieutenant General Sir George Prevost, was told to prepare to receive ten thousand additional troops and to go on the offensive for the first time in two years.

In the meantime, the *Constitution* was able to slip out of the Salem waters and into her berth at Charlestown. There she went into the repair facility once more to renew her sprung mainmast.

Lake Champlain, the Largest and Most Decisive Battle of the War

In August the British swung into action. An attack on Washington, D.C., was met with little resistance at Bladensburg, Maryland. More than a thousand redcoats burned the public buildings in the capital, retribution, they said, for the attack on York, Canada, by General Zebulon Pike the previous year. It was, however, a diversion for what General Sir George Prevost had prepared in Montreal. His force of British and Canadian soldiers, combined with a Royal Navy flotilla, would number fifteen thousand as it crossed the northern border at Plattsburgh on Lake Champlain, intent on destroying both the small American army and navy huddled there in defense. Then he would continue to move south before winter closed down the campaign season. (It was September 11, 1814, exactly 187 years to the hour before the attack on New York City and Washington, D.C., in 2001.)

America Saved from Invasion on 9/11/1814

Thomas Macdonough, the thirty-year-old naval lieutenant and master commandant of Lake Champlain, sat at anchor in Cumberland Bay, guarding the
regular army's right flank, which was dug in at Plattsburgh, New York. There
were 1,500 regulars and 2,500 untried militia facing the finest army and navy in
the world, outnumbered four to one. Unlike Perry, who enjoyed a superior force,
Macdonough could not go into open water since the English guns outranged his
carronades by three to one. He hoped that in the confined bay he could take
advantage of the winds, which were variable, and not allow the Royal Navy to
remain for long outside of the 500-yard circle of death that surrounded his little fleet. But that is another story.

Two days later a second major diversion landed at Baltimore. This time the
people of the tidewater knew it was coming. The English fleet of warships had
been gathering for several days prior to landing. The fleet bombarded the city's
inner harbor while fewer than four thousand British soldiers, royal marines, and
sailors scurried ashore. The men of the American Fort McHenry fought through
the night and into the morning as Congreve rockets, which were also used at
Plattsburgh on the eleventh, rained down on Baltimore on the thirteenth. The
American lawyer Francis Scott Key of Frederick, Maryland, went on board an
English man-of-war to negotiate prisoner exchange and was caught up in the
scene. From his observation post in the outer bay he penned the words to the
poem that would become the American national anthem.

The British commissioners at the peace talks in Ghent, Belgium, later ad-
mitted that if Plattsburgh could have been taken, they could have succeeded
in accomplishing all of their demands. England would have lopped off a major
portion of the northern United States extending clear across the bottom of the
Great Lakes. How different United States history would have been with such
a loss.

Peace Treaty of Ghent

The peace treaty of Ghent was signed by both parties on Christmas eve, 1814.
However, the hostilities would not end officially until it was ratified by both
governments. Because of the plodding movement of ships in those days of sail,
the Senate would not ratify the terms until February 17, 1815. Therefore, the
momentum of the war continued, even though there were many rumors of
peace. The third diversionary force was committed to an attack on New Or-
leans, Louisiana, which began the last week of December 1814. There, General
Andrew Jackson stood strong behind his cotton bales when a British force of
fewer than seven thousand attacked without success.

USS *Constitution*'s previous crew had lasted only three months and had little to show for the effort. Secretary of the Navy William Jones questioned Stewart's lack of aggression. The court headed by Captain Bainbridge exonerated the captain on all counts. It made no mention of the condition of the ship since Bainbridge was responsible for her fitness before the voyage.

Blockade Runner

By the fall of 1814 the Royal Navy was looking for a place to put the new fir frigates that were equal to the Americans'. Combining them with 74-gun ships of the line, freed up in the Mediterranean Sea, the famous admiral Thomas Hardy, former captain of Nelson's *Victory* at Trafalgar, was leading the blockade of the United States. All that summer and on into fall, when sailing conditions worsened, the Royal Navy put the hammer down and no American man-of-war was at sea to contest the grip that supported the land campaign the Duke of Wellington had set in motion. The victories on the Great Lakes and Lake Champlain kept the hopes of seafarers alive. After six months in port, Charles Stewart's vigil was rewarded when he seized a temporary letup on December 18, 1814. Painted with an ocher gun-hatch stripe rather than the black and white checkerboard, the *Constitution* looked the part of a blockader and not a runner. USS *Constitution* was free. The only warship to break the blockade in six months, she went hunting across the Atlantic.

As the ship sailed south and then east against the trade winds, progress was slow and tiring. Supplies were consumed at a high rate. By Christmas everything was in short supply and yet the *Constitution* was well out at sea. Providence smiled on this lucky ship. A Royal Navy supply ship, the *Lord Nelson*, was delivered into the crew's outstretched hands on the New Year. Acting chaplain Humphreys, who was also the ship's clerk, wrote, "There were lots of corn beef in rounds, smoked salmon, dried beef and codfish, tongues and rounds, fine apple cheeses & barrels of loaf sugar of the most superior kinds, pipes of best brandy, gin and port wine, chests of imperial and gunpowder tea, barrels of flour, hams inferior not even to Smithfield Virginia, etc."[12]

As she neared the west African coast and began to mingle with the commercial vessels, contacts came frequently. They were mostly neutral and not fair game for the crew that wanted prize money. The winds were blowing with great strength in the Bay of Biscay off the Spanish coast in January, the worst month of the year in those waters.

Acting chaplain Humphreys regales all the readers of his diary with the tale of a terrier dog named Guerriere. It was owned by the second lieutenant, Beekman Hoffman. Beloved by the deckhands, he joined in on the ends of lines, lending his pulling ability, which was always welcome. By February, the wind blew fiercely in the face of the lookout on the tops. On deck, Chaplain Humphreys and First Lieutenant Henry E. Ballard passed the quarterdeck in the late afternoon. Guerriere kept pace, the "watchdog," so to speak.

> Guerriere who was playing about the heels of Lieut. Ballard appeared uncommonly frisky and was rather troublesome at length becoming an incumbrance he attracted the particular attention of the Lieut, perceiving which he jumped upon the stowed hammocks on the rail and stretching his head to windward began to bark most vehemently,—upon looking to discover what attracted his notice lo and behold! There was a large frigate standing down before the wind under a press of sail, which the gentlemen at the mast head had not yet discovered.[13]

The dog was rewarded with food, and the lookouts had twelve strokes of the whip laid on by the boatswain's mate. The ship was the *Amazona*, a Portuguese frigate going into Lisbon. Such a dereliction could have cost the sailors and the ship their lives.

HMS *Cyane* and *Levant* versus USS *Constitution*

At home in Washington, the Congress was about to end the war with the acceptance of the status quo of June 1812. Far out at sea, the captain had been apprised of the likelihood of a treaty by passing vessels. He knew that soon hostilities could end, yet he was under orders. The rumors of settlement had been going on since the inception of the war. The first attempt had come from the British within months of the start. The czar of Russia, Alexander I, had formalized the talks in Saint Petersburg in 1813, but nothing was settled after a year of negotiations. The talks had resumed in August in Ghent, Belgium, but the captain had not received any instruction or changes to his standing war orders.

While the food was holding out, the cold off of Cape Finisterre chilled the men; soaked through on the windy deck, they were bone cold. Belowdecks the heating pots, black iron buckets hung on chain from the hammock hooks, were filled with embers and coals from the caboose, providing some radiant heat. The shot furnace installed by Captain Stewart in Charlestown provided an extra source to keep the pots warm. The shot furnace was just another edge the *Constitution* might use in an emergency. It could turn black iron solid shot to glowing red. The sailors did not like the idea; the heated shot was hard to handle. Fired by the carronades, it was expected to lodge in the hull of the enemy and set fire to the ship. If nothing else, it took fighting men and many a bucket of water to keep a fire from starting. The French used heated shot but set several of their own ships alight during the loading operation. Heated cannonballs were against the Royal Navy regulations because they were so dangerous. The swinging hot buckets were welcome. They supplemented the body heat of the four-hundred-man crew and made the

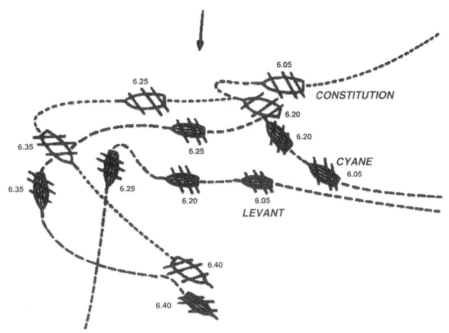

HMS Cyane *and HMS* Levant *versus USS* Constitution, *February 1815, off the coast of west Africa.*

environment just tolerable. Music was played on pipes and jigs were danced while the men sang to distract themselves from the tedium of the fruitless voyage.

Just after the noon meal, excitement rose as a pair of what appeared to be British warships appeared on the horizon. They were going away with the wind. Captain Stewart did not hesitate. He gave chase, only pausing to repair the top of the mainmast at midafternoon. The speed of the *Constitution* soon brought her up within chase-gun range at a little after five o'clock, as the sun was setting. By then the crew had been held at battle stations for four hours. The long-boats were strung out like link sausages. They were considered insurance for picking up casualties, which also kept them from being destroyed on deck, where they were stowed in the open. Loaded pistols and cutlasses were resting in wooden tubs on the centerline of the deck, ready for the boarding parties to arm themselves. The surgeon and his mate were in the wardroom surrounded by buckets of water and piles of lint. His awful instruments were wiped clean and lined up. Vials of laudanum and bottles of spirits were broken out. The captain's furniture was stowed away, along with the bulkhead that separated him from the crew. All the niceties, crockery, crystal goblets, silver flatware, and brass candlesticks, were taken down to the orlop deck and placed in lockers.

The carpenter and his mates were on the crew deck prepared to set stoppers, shot plugs wrapped in flaxen blankets, in the double-thick hull at the waterline. They were hoping to be going to windward, which should keep her hull down in the water and expose the underside of the enemy as he rolled to lee.

Two against One

The Royal Navy ships were not running. They knew who the American frigate was, but the warning had been not to take her on alone. These British sailors were game. As the ships traveled west, the wind was on beam and the *Levant* was in the lead of the *Cyane*, 24 guns, as the *Constitution* closed on their starboard side. The *Levant* was a single-decked corvette of 20 guns and was ship rigged with all nine yards. Some called her a sloop. The American account adds one 12-pound cannon, which was shifted about as a chaser.

The *Cyane* followed close behind. There was never any doubt that the enemy was at hand, in spite of the ocher gun stripe used earlier to conceal the *Constitution*'s identity. The light was fading, but it was quite enough to identify the stars and stripes that topped the mast. It was a classic engagement, as all three ships opened up with broadsides at nearly the same moment. The *Cyane*'s shot screamed through the rigging, snapping lines and punching holes in the yellowed flaxen topgallants. Wooden spars, the size of telephone poles, came crashing down. They were momentarily slowed by the crisscross of cables strung above the quarterdeck to protect Major Archibald Henderson's marines, who stood ready to repel boarders. Fortunately for the Americans, the shorter-range 32-pound carronades on the *Levant* were at their limit, while the *Constitution*'s long 24s sizzled through the Englishman's rails and hull. Both Royal Navy vessels turned toward the path of the *Constitution* to close the gap.

Captain George Douglas, commander of HMS *Levant* and the senior officer, describes in the third person the hailed instructions he passed to Captain Gordon Thomas Falcon, commander of HMS *Cyane*: "*Cyane* arrived and Douglas hailed and indicated to Falcon to attack *Constitution*. They were attempting to protect two convoys from Gilbraltar in their company. Superior sailing ability of *Constitution* prevented maneuver. Captain Falcon returned fire but his shot fell short while the enemy's long 24's were producing their full effect."[14] The captain of the *Levant* attempted to cross in front of the *Constitution* and rake her as he went. Douglas's two 9-pound cannons, which could reach, did little damage to the great ship but played around the heads on the forecastle. The American captain saw it coming and slowed. "In 15 minutes the *Constitution* ranged ahead and became engaged in the same manner with the *Levant*. The *Cyane* now luffed up for the larboard quarter of the *Constitution* where upon the latter, backing astern, was enabled to pour into *Cyane* her whole broadside."[15]

The *Cyane* did not enjoy iron sides, and the 24-pound solid shot crashed through the hull and embedded itself in the opposite side. Soon, water gushed in, breaking loose barrels of food and water, which became buoyant. Floating debris prevented the powder monkeys from ready access to the magazine. Water lapped around the ankles of the surgeon and his mate as they treated the first of a flood of bleeding and broken shipmates. The keelson was covered with water, which was rising at an alarming rate. The carpenter was commandeering men to help plug the holes in the hull. The noise of the American cannonballs thudding on the bulwarks sounded like the muffled drums of death, there in the dark, belowdecks. The moon was bright, but the smoke hung in the air and obscured the vision of the American captain.

Meanwhile the *Levant* had bore up, to wear round and assist her consort. The *Constitution* thereupon filled, shot ahead, and gave *Levant* two stern rakes. Seeing this the *Cyane*, although without a brace or bowline except the larboard fore brace, wore, and gallantly stood between the *Levant* and *Constitution*. The latter then promptly wore, and raked the *Cyane* astern. The *Cyane* immediately luffed up as well as she could, and fired her larboard broadside at the starboard bow of the *Constitution*. The latter soon afterwards ranged up on the larboard quarter of the *Cyane*, within hail, and was about to pour in her starboard broadside, when at 6h 50m p.m. having had most of her standing and running rigging cut to pieces, her main and mizenmasts left in tottering state and other principal spars wounded, several shots in the hull, nine or ten between wind and water, five carronades disabled, chiefly by the drawing of the bolts and starting of the shocks, and the *Levant* being two miles to leeward still bearing away to repair her heavy damage, the *Cyane* fired a lee gun and hoisted a light as a signal of submission.[16]

While the larger of the two Royal Navy ships had capitulated, HMS *Levant* had slipped away into the darkness. Captain Stewart's blood was up as he looked at his own shattered decks and the piles of debris that littered the quarterdeck. Below, the gun deck had little damage and the men serving the cannons were looking past the muzzles of their run-out 24s, peering into the darkness for the *Levant*.

The *Levant*'s captain, the Honorable George Douglas, the son of Lord Douglas of Lancaster, though outgunned, had cleared away the busted yards and tangled lines and was coming on. He made a large sweeping turn to the wind and came back at Ironsides once again with blood in his eye. He bore straight at the *Constitution*, and they came together head-on and passed at twenty-five yards on their larboard sides.

More than two hours had passed since the engagement began. The sailors on all the ships would not have noticed. They were overwhelmed with tasks. Shift the wounded, stack the dead, clear the broken rails, and reposition the guns. The tangled sheared-off spars were cobbled together by shredded lines that were hung with broken blocks. The decks were slick with blood pumped out by the last thumps of the stout hearts of men who had bled to death. The discipline of silence was maintained in those who were unharmed. Others, wrapped in pain as they slipped into shock at the sight of their ghastly wounds, dark red and black, could not keep their tongues quiet.

> At 8h 15m which was as soon as the *Levant* had rove new braces, the gallant little ship again hauled her wind, as well to ascertain the fate of her companion, as to renew the desperate contest. On approaching the *Constitution* and *Cyane*, the *Levant* with a boldness bordering on rashness, ranged close alongside the *Constitution* to leeward, being unable to weather her, and at 8h 30m these two ships while passing on opposite tacks, exchanged broadsides. The *Constitution* immediately wore under the *Levant's* stern and raked her with a second broadside. At 9h 30m finding that the *Cyane* had undoubtedly surrendered, Captain Douglas again put before the wind, but in the act of doing so, the *Levant* received several raking broadsides, had her wheel shot away and her lower masts badly wounded. . . . Seeing the *Constituiton* ranging up on her larboard quarter, the *Levant*, at 10h 30m p.m. struck her colours.[17]

The casualties among the Royal Navy, according to their count of 300 on both ships, suffered 19 killed and 44 severely wounded. The American navy had 6 killed and 6 wounded. In a way, this is exactly how a naval battle should come to pass. The actions were not designed to either sink the ships or wipe out the crew. The battle was expected to bring honorable surrender. The wooden ships were fragile when struck by heavy iron projectiles. Their masts, yards, and ropes would disintegrate in spectacular displays, blown to smithereens and scattered in all directions. Once the running gear was destroyed, the ship was immobilized and defeat was a matter of course, left in the hands of boarding parties. The mental and physical exhaustion must have been all consuming. It was then that the iron men of wooden ships succumbed.

While the British account does not mention that it was two vessels against one, Captain Charles Stewart does in his after-action report. "Considering the advantages derived by the enemy, from a divided and more active force, as also their superiority in the weight and number of guns, I deem the speedy and decisive results of this action the strongest assurance which can be given the government that all under my command did their duty and gallantly supported the reputation of American seamen."

The battle became moot since it occurred after the war was concluded, and it was only of interest to the respective navies, who still argue over its implication. To my surprise, the newspapers in London were absolutely silent. It quickly passed into history, and, as we all know, "History is an unending argument."

~

CHAPTER NINE

The Last Act of the War of 1812

> I would never consent to have our ships perish, and transform our navy into
> a fleet of sea monsters.
>
> —Secretary of the Navy James K. Paulding,
> during the transition to steam

In December of 1814, HMS *Newcastle*, 50 guns, was a part of the squadron blockading Boston Harbor when the *Constitution* escaped. The Englishman followed her across the central Atlantic but had no luck in pursuit. By stopping passing vessels, the captain learned that he was always a day or two behind. The Royal Navy ship of the line, accompanied by two frigates, searched hungrily in the Azores, calling at Madeira. On March 11, 1815, she found the *Constitution*, along with the *Cyane* and the *Levant*, repairing at anchor in the Cape Verde Islands. Within ten minutes, all three were off, with American prize crews sailing the former Royal Navy warships. The *Newcastle* fired on the *Constitution*, but her shot fell short as the latter pressed for the open sea. The British ships then attacked the *Cyane*, thinking that she was a smaller American frigate. The diversion allowed the *Constitution* to escape and remain undefeated. The vision that Joshua Humphreys had incorporated in his design, a fast, well-armed big frigate, represented a gap in the Royal Naval force that the British did not fill until they resurrected the French Razor late in the War of 1812. The *Cyane*, with only enough men aboard to sail her, surprisingly succeeded in evading her former masters and escaped into the open ocean. Once free, she scurried to her new home and was converted to an American warship. The *Levant's* prize crew, finding that she was not yet capable of going to sea, returned to the anchorage, where she was recaptured by the British.[1]

Arguing among Themselves

The *Mariner's Mirror* of London published a rebuttal to an Englishman's assessment of the U.S. Navy's performance during the War of 1812, as if it had ended the day before.

Dear Sir,

May I point out what appear to me mistaken inferences in Berry Lohnes's article in your August 1973 number, "British Naval Problems at Halifax during the War of 1812": these fall into two categories, one arising from a failure to put the American War into perspective as an unwonted incident in Great Britain's life or death struggle with Napoleon's "Continental System," the other arising from a failure to analyse the force and sailing power of the ships on the two sides. This is epitomized in the statement, "the nascent American Navy, though miniscule in comparison to the British Navy in British North America, won more ship battles than it lost . . ." But of course the American possessed three ships, Constitution, United States and President, which could not be caught by the only heavier British ship on the station, the ancient 64-gun Africa, and which outmatched the heaviest British frigates in sailing power in all weathers—by 3:2. These ships were evidently the capital units in the area until the British Admiralty most reluctantly sent out a 74 or two. Barry Lohnes's failure to realize that those great American frigates bore much the same relation to normal European frigates as Sturdee's battle-cruisers bore to von Spee's cruisers at the Falkland Islands leads him to totally misrepresent the Constitution-Guerriere, Constitution-Java and United States-Macedonian duels in the usual American manner! On the first of these engagements may I quote from my own *Broke and the Shannon* [out of print].

The Constitution had an advantage over the Guerriere of 17' in length, nearly 5' in beam, some 5" in thickness of topside planking, 7" in diameter of mainmast. Below the maindeck gunport sills her sides had the scantlings of a British 74 gun ship. Her fifteen long guns each were 24-pounders, the Guerriere's fourteen were 18-pounders, above this main battery the Constitution had twelve carronades 32-pounder each side against the Guerriere's eight—a total advantage in weight of shot of nearly 3:2. She had a similar advantage in tonnage, 1,500 against 1,100 and carried nearly double the men, 463 against 244 at quarters in the Guerriere.

Not only was the British force in North America actually inferior to capital units in the early stages of the war, but was inadequate to deal with the length of coastline involved, so it is not much use concluding that the British side of the war was poorly prosecuted considering the force at Halifax was formidable in comparison to the United States Navy.

However, the basic mistaken emphasis in the article, it seems to me, is the failure to place the British naval difficulties at Halifax and the often feeble prosecution of the war in the context of Britain's desperate struggle against Napoleon's "Continental System." The British government never wanted this additional local difficulty and went about it half-heartedly both because they could ill spare the ships and men and because they hoped that the dispute might be resolved peacefully. When Admiral Warren was sent out to relieve Sawyer at Halifax he was empowered to make peace, either with the central government or with separate States' governments whose trading communities disapproved of the War, not to prosecute the war so vigorously that peace-making would be impossible.

It is not generally known that the Royal Navy commander on station was interested in splitting the New England States, if possible, from the remainder of the country. Earlier in 1809, the Governor General in Montreal, Sir James Henry Craig, had attempted profit from the sentiment against Jefferson's trade restrictions, believing that he could bring some States back into the Kingdom.

Finally, the problems of the Halifax Station could be called the problems of the Royal Navy during the second decade of its remorseless struggle against France. When the Shannon commissioned at Sheerness long before the American War, out of a ship's company of 250 odd only 70 had been trained to the sea, and among these many were Portuguese, Italians, Hamburgers, West Indians, North Americans, and even a Frenchman. . . . Please do not think me anti-American, where should we all be without the U.S. Navy? But it really is time that the events of the 1812 War were put into proper perspective.[2]

In addition to the comparisons of one ship to another, he leaves out some decisive points about the American frigates. The American live and white oak was more dense than the English oak. Additionally, when Captain Rodgers's *Constitution* was being refitted, he insisted that the planks be oak and not pine, as was common at that time. The futtock (rib) clusters were closer together, and the sister frames were cross bolted as well. The Royal Navy ships used less framing, concentrating it only at the gun ports. When examining the Constitution's framing, notice that there are only four inches between sisters, presenting a denser, therefore more resilient, target to the careening 18-pound English cannonballs. It is no wonder that the shot ricocheted off her iron sides.[3]

Peace and the United States Navy

For the Royal Navy, the Treaty of Ghent, which ended hostilities and marched time backward to June of 1812, meant no change to borders and an end to the blockade of the seaboard of the United States. The officers and crews of the Royal Navy dreaded blockade duty. The tedium of endless circles plowed in unfriendly waters was the pits. However, it called out of reserve officers who needed employment and boosted the shipbuilding industry, which was poten-tially the largest single source of jobs in England. It was hard on the men and ever harder on the ships, which by the end of the war overwhelmed the dock-yard repair facilities. With the wars over, England reaped the bonanza of world trade, which would sustain it into the Victorian era, the highest point in the history of the island empire. Her maritime industry surged as never before.

In America the end of the war was hailed by merchants, who were at last free of arbitrary restrictions and political interference. Congress acknowledged the danger waiting to pounce on America's unprotected merchant ships. That rein-forced the need for a strong and stable United States Navy. While the regular army turned to the protection of the western expansion, the navy was the big winner in the War of 1812. It went into the conflict a weak and unknown ele-ment of national power. It emerged as the nation's flag bearer, thanks to news-paper accounts filled with exploits that created the first national heroes, whose portraits hung in homes topped with wreaths of laurel. Towns in the expanding West echoed the interest. Perry, Bainbridge, Preble, and Macdonough would all be so honored. Cities gave banquets, presented swords, dedicated parks, and raised statues to the naval officers whose adventures fit the national character. The navy was considered to be an honorable career.

Captain Isaac Hull, now the commandant of the Charlestown Navy Yard in Boston, Massachusetts, was directed to prepare to refurbish USS *Constitution* in April of 1820. Dismasted and unrigged, sitting motionless with only a caretaker looking after her, Ironsides was not expected to rejoin active service. Congress had appropriated eight million dollars to build a proper navy led by ships of the line, great 74s. Hull got down to the heavy work. An inspection proved that she was indeed seaworthy after a good number of planks were replaced, partic-ularly below the waterline. The knees and futtocks were sound, as was her keel. Minor replacement was done to exposed strakes and decks. Her guns were re-stored and the masts and rigging established. The sails were taken out of the loft and some new configurations were added to improve her ability to sail closer to the wind. A new copper bottom was applied and a crew recruited. It took ten months before Captain Hull reported her ready for duty.

Back to the Mediterranean

The new commander, Jacob Jones, arrived to witness his ship's humiliation be-fore the citizens of Boston. Old Ironsides had been rigged with broad wooden paddle wheels, which were slung over her side at midships, destroying her grace-ful lines. Sailing Master Brisco Doxey had invented a set of paddle wheels that could propel the ship at three knots. Even though Robert Fulton had invented the steam-powered ship in the early 1800s, little had come of it. He had offered it to everyone, including Napoleon, and all had turned him down. There were three major problems. The steam plant was unreliable, prone to breakdown during operations. Commodore Thomas Macdonough, in dire need of fighting vessels to contend with the Royal Navy on Lake Champlain, in 1814 had converted a steam vessel to sail for just that reason. His conversion, the *Ticonderoga*, would make naval history. The second shortcoming was the amount of fuel the steam plant required and the procurement of fuel in foreign ports. Third, the plant was vulnerable to enemy action, and it took very little to knock it out of commission.

Side-Wheeler

However, Doxey's side-wheel paddles, powered by the ship's company, were free of such criticism. The broad wheels were slung over both sides on axles stuck through a pair of gun ports, amidships. A line in the form of a solid loop extended from the capstan to a pulley far forward. The crew would rotate the capstan and the rope would in turn spin the shafts of the paddle wheels. The wheels would provide locomotion if the ship was becalmed. The only good thing about the invention was that it was portable and was soon stored below.[4] Hull was unimpressed. Equally unimpressed was the new captain, Jacob Jones, fifty-two, who had commanded the *Argus* and the *Wasp* and assisted in the capture of the *Macedonian*. He had been a junior lieutenant on the *Philadelphia* when she was captured and had spent months as a prisoner of war. His intentions were to land the entire mechanism as soon as possible, meanwhile keeping it packed below. He took Ironsides out to sea on May 13, 1821. The duty in the Mediterranean was not a repeat of the Barbary pirates, which had gone out of style. For the next three years she circled around the edges, showing the flag as Europe recovered from twenty years of war with Napoleon, who was dying on Saint Helena Island in the South Atlantic. The only noteworthy incident during the cruise was her relief. In April of 1824, her place was taken by USS *Cyane*, the former Royal Navy frigate captured by the *Constitution* in 1815.

The Hero of Lake Champlain

In June of 1824, Captain Thomas Macdonough, the commodore who prevented the British invasion of the United States on September 11, 1814, was put in command. He sailed in October once more for the Mediterranean Sea. Diplomatic excursions crowned by port visits and the showing of the flag took the place of war. It was all very dull stuff for the officers and crew confined for months on the big frigate that got smaller every day. The American squadron under Rodgers ringed round the ports of the Ottoman Empire, establishing good relations to ensure safe transit for American merchants. By fall of 1825 Captain Macdonough received word that his wife was terminally ill. He was suffering from tuberculosis and gave up command in October to return home to Delaware. In attendance on board the American merchantman *Edwin* was his surgeon and his midshipman son, Thomas. The victorious commander of Lake Champlain died within sight of his home state. It is said that he weighed seventy-five pounds. As a fallen hero of the War of 1812, he followed Decatur, who had been killed in a duel several years before.

Suffering from her age, the *Constitution* had spent much of her last cruise at dockside in Minorca, through 1826. It was not until the Fourth of July, 1828, that Ironsides came home to Boston and was placed in ordinary. The navy was coming of age. After the War of 1812, a Board of Naval Commissioners made up of experienced officers and headed by three senior captains assisted the secretary of the navy. The new, bigger 74s were essentially the same hull that Humphreys had laid down in 1797. The navy expansion mirrored that of the American merchant fleet, which could be found in every major port on the oceans and seas. America was becoming a world marine power, and the navy was scrambling to keep up. Fortunately, that period was free of major wars as the colonial powers of Europe expanded their empires on other continents. America tagged along, providing ships and expanding trade exponentially each year.

The navy was expecting to spend more money in the near future. Not only did it need to build ships, but it was also required to support them around the world. Naval agents and funds for the replenishment abroad had to be in place, and the annual naval budget was growing at an alarming rate for the young country that had not yet seen itself as a potential global power. The nation's interest was torn between maritime adventures and western expansion into Indian country on the other side of the Mississippi and beyond to the lands of the Louisiana Purchase. Steam power was beginning to get a great deal of press, and it was clear that the navy was going to change. A look at the cost of keeping the older ships of the line in service naturally exposed the *Constitution*, which was covered over with a wooden frame and roof in an attempt to keep her timbers from rotting. The ship was twice surveyed, and the cost continued to climb, until in 1830 news spread that Old Ironsides, undefeated in battle, would lose for the first time to economic cuts. A Boston newspaper would not stand for it and said so. The navy did not realize that the ship did not belong to them but to the inhabitants of the town that built her. As far as the people were concerned, Ironsides was on loan to the United States Navy.

Boston: "That Is Our Ship"

The storm broke over the navy on Tuesday, September 14, 1830, when the *Boston Daily Advertiser* attacked. "Such a national object of interest so endeared to our national pride as Old Ironsides is, should never by any act of our government cease to belong to the Navy, so long as our country is to be found upon the map of nations." The banner, to the surprise of the navy, was picked up by the New York Journal of Commerce.

Old Ironsides.—It has been affirmed upon good authority that the Secretary of the Navy has recommended to the Board of Navy Commissioners to dispose of the frigate Constitution. Since it has been understood that such a step was in contemplation we have heard but one opinion expressed, and that in decided disapprobation of the measure. Such a national object of interest, so endeared to our national pride as Old Ironsides is, should never by any act of our government cease to belong to the Navy, so long as our country is to be found upon the map of nations. In England it was lately determined by the Admiralty to cut the Victory, a one hundred gun ship (which it will be recollected bore the flag of Lord Nelson at the battle of Trafalgar), down to a seventy four, but so loud were the lamentations of the people upon the proposed measure that the intention was abandoned. We confidently anticipate that the Secretary of the Navy will in like manner consult the general wish in regard to the Constitution, and either let her remain in ordinary or rebuild her whenever the public service may require.

But it took a twenty-two-year-old law student in Boston, the yet unknown Oliver Wendell Holmes, to put the hat on it. His poem, published first in the Daily Advertiser and then around the country in all sorts of publications, reads:

Old Ironsides
By Oliver Wendell Holmes
September 16, 1830

Ay, tear her tattered ensign down!
Long has it waved on high,
And many an eye has danced to see
That banner in the sky;
Beneath it rung the battle shout,
And burst the cannon's roar;—
The meteor of the ocean air
Shall sweep the clouds no more.

Her deck, once red with heroes' blood,
Where knelt the vanquished foe,
When winds were hurrying o'er the flood,
And waves were white below,
No more shall feel the victor's tread,
Or know the conquered knee;—
The harpies of the shore shall pluck
The eagle of the sea!

> Oh, better that her shattered bulk
> Should sink beneath the wave;
> Her thunders shook the mighty deep,
> And there should be her grave;
> Nail to the mast her holy flag,
> Set every threadbare sail,
> And give her to the god of storms,
> The lightning and the gale!

The part that got me was the last phrase of the second stanza, "eagle of the sea." For me, that summed it up, as it did for an entire nation. Her fate was taken out of the hands of bureaucrats and bean counters, and we all have known and come to love her.

A Further Survey

In Washington the navy brass were stunned by the reactions and actions of the population. The response was not confined to New England but played into the western states. Hate mail flooded the secretary of the navy's correspondence. No longer was the department unknown, dealing with Congress and the maritime interest that camped on its doorstep. The ordinary citizen had found out what it was and did not like it. Congressmen were besieged as well, and they told the navy so in no uncertain terms. Backpedaling, as the defense establishment often does in the face of criticism, the navy mended its ways. Soon the naval officials were denying that they had intended to scrap Ironsides. They accepted another survey, which put a price on the extensive repairs that was "just fine."

The Navy Surrenders to the People

In 1820 the diagonals had been taken out of the inner hull and cast-iron water tanks had been installed. This appears to have contributed to the hogging. With less support, the stern and bow of the ship sagged on the ends about fourteen inches. This was not so alarming; most ships hog. It is a common problem today with large metal tankers as well. However, the replacement of the water casks with the stout iron tanks changed the trim of the ship because they were higher up in the structure.[5] With a new dry dock under construction in the Charlestown dockyard, it was decided to delay the restoration until the best possible facility could be provided for the effort. By then even President Andrew Jackson was watching to ensure that promises were being kept.

In June of 1833, Captain Hull supervised the floating of the *Constitution* into the new dry dock as a crowd of dignitaries from Washington watched as the water was pumped out, exposing the encrusted bottom of the great lady, now in her dotage. The naval commissioners adorned their offices and the offices of politically sympathetic officials in Washington with memorabilia. Wall plaques, card boxes, hat racks, bookends, and walking sticks were passed out, made from wood harvested from the discarded yet venerable timbers.

The yard master ordered a figurehead carved in the standing image of the president, Andrew Jackson. To lumber the great ship with the image of a serving president was not the intention of the navy commissioners in Washington who were providing the funds and charged with oversight. The idea had come from the commandant of the Charlestown dockyard, Captain Jesse Elliott, soon to be her new captain, who had had more than one run-in with his bosses. The people of Boston were particularly distraught over the image. It looked a great deal like a cigar-store wooden Indian, very stiff and most unflattering. On a bet, Sam Dewey waited until the *Constitution* had been refloated and was tethered to another ship in dock. On a dark night in early July, a year after the ship was put into dry dock, Dewey rowed a small boat up under the figurehead and climbed up level with the head of the wooden president. He sawed it off just above the neck, leaving the decapitated head of state stuck up on the prow for all to see the next morning. Dewey won the bet, and the head appeared in bars all over Boston and later made its way to Washington. No one should have been surprised that such a desecration should take place in Boston. The citizens were not supporters of the president, who was most unpopular. The incident was not unlike their response to tax on tea in an earlier age, but instead of dumping the image into the bay, the people of Boston proudly promenaded before the headless figurehead. It was a reenactment of the "Boston Tea Party," which came quite naturally to people with such a defiant past. In Washington, it was a further notice not to fool with their ship.

Diplomatic Transportation

In 1834 France was concerned with the repayment of debt between the United States and France, begun during the Revolutionary War and extended to money owed to the United States, which amounted to over twenty million dollars. The French government had delayed negotiations over the exact amount and the payment, and President Jackson sent Edward Livingston to France on board the refurbished *Constitution* to settle the affair. With the assistance of the English government, the affair was settled and the *Constitution* returned safely. Dispatched to the Mediterranean yet again, the ship was stationed at Port Mahon, Minorca, in 1835. There, duties were mundane, making discipline difficult. Captain Elliott was not a pleasant man, rather eccentric and erratic, but the time put little demands on him and his crew. On return to Norfolk, Virginia, in

1838 it all bubbled over at Hampton, where many years before the son of the captain had died and was buried. This time the crew got drunk and became mutinous. It blotted the reputation of the ship and within months she was put in ordinary.

In March 1839, Captain Daniel Turner was given command and the mission to take the *Constitution* on the longest voyage of her career. He was ordered to join the U.S. Navy Pacific fleet in the protection of American commerce along the coast of South America. In addition to the New England whalers, pioneers were settling the Far West. Business was spreading, and the land route across the continent was not for the faint of heart. Voyages around the horn were beginning to take an increasing number of passengers. Many would regret the decision at the extreme southern tip of South America.

Around the Horn

At the southernmost tip of South America the two great oceans come together in the most turbulent waters in the world. The westerly winds are extreme, even at the best of times. Good weather is rarely seen, and many ships foundered or turned around in the face of violent storms. The passage could take two months and no one opted to take it a second time. Once one had experienced it, it was easy to see why the dream of a canal across the Isthmus of Panama was thought of as a good moneymaking idea long before it became a reality.

On September 29, 1839, bucking the winds, the *Constitution* "was laboring under almost bare poles against the tempestuous elements."[6] Only the foregallant was strung up to provide way and steerage. The royals, topgallants, spanker, and courses were gotten down, along with their rigging. The studding and stay sails were taken below. All the unnecessary rigging was taken down, while the remaining parrels were doubled to prevent damage. Lines, or halters, were passed over the remaining sail to protect it from being blown out. The spanker boom was brought down to the deck and secured to keep it from beating itself to death. The lower masts were reinforced with side tackle, which was hooked to them and taken somewhat forward of the foot of the mast. The process, which was not taken unless absolutely necessary since it was so much work, nearly unrigged the ship. Lifelines were strung for the crew to prevent loss overboard on the deck that had gone mad.

The ship pitched and rolled to the extreme limit of forty-six degrees and wallowed in between giant waves at the bottom of watery caverns. Worse, the next moment it was climbing up a wall of water while being chased by a larger wave just behind. Heavy wooden triple blocks swung like wrecking balls, breaking loose, hunting for bobbing heads as the sailors tried to snare them. The running rigging still in use was whipped and stretched. Mats, or "roundings," were fished around points of chafe to prevent the ropes from sawing their way through. Yet some play had to be left in the standing rigging to allow the masts to bend and not snap under the pressure of the howling wind. It was a delicate balance. Commands could not be heard over the bellowing roar of the sea. According to John Harland, "The ship should not be allowed to tear herself to pieces for want of more sail to steady her, which is the practice of keeping the ship under low sail in a high sea. The result of which may prematurely require re-caulking. In this connection, in a stiff, hard sailing ship, the jerky nature of the oscillation might be aggravated by diminishing the weight aloft."[7] A sailor aboard reported, "The gale continued without interruption for sixteen or seventeen days buffeting in which Old Ironsides proved herself the sturdy and efficient seaboat she was always celebrated for. No ship was ever more comfortably secured against the bitter blasts and drenching billows than was ours on this occasion."[8]

On Station on the Peaceful Pacific

The threat of intervention into American maritime affairs along the long coast-line of South America did not materialize. By the summer of 1840 the *Constitution* was on her way home once again. No action was required. In the winter of 1842 the home squadron was formed, giving Commodore Stewart command of all the naval vessels from Maine to Mexico, including those in the harbors and estuaries of the great rivers.

Transition Is Never Easy

The navy, as a whole, was in transition. Steam-powered ships were literally on the horizon. The navy budget, which was never enough, was partitioned by a divided community. There were navy steam-powered vessels, but they had been confined to harbor duty. A new mission, direct support of the army expedition to Mexico, caught the navy unprepared. In the past it had configured itself for ship-to-ship conflict and the occasional bombardment of fixed fortifications. The transport of troops, amphibious operations, and the handling of draft animals and heavy equipment were new skills that had to be mastered. Replenishment by sea in support of a field army required management dexterity as well as watercraft. The employment of sea power was becoming complicated. In 1843 Matthew Perry, of Japan-expedition fame some ten years later, lobbied for steam-augmented ships, leading the reformers. USS *Princeton*, launched that year, was the first operational stern-propeller-driven American warship. It epitomized the future. It made those interested in preserving Old Ironsides nervous. As expected, though, there was always someone in power to raise the cry of "nonsense." In 1841 that man of the hour was the secretary of the navy, James K. Paulding, who said he "would never consent to have our ships perish, and transform our navy into a fleet of sea monsters."[9] The "steamers" were divided, causing a serious delay in the progress of the technology. The side-wheel, which was somewhat efficient in calm river waters and harbors, was not so in heavy seas. Yet fifteen years were lost following the wrong piper.[10]

New Era and the Naval Academy

During this turbulent time it was recognized that the old midshipman system for providing a professional officer corps was unstable. The top brass had suffered from the patronage system, which had brought them to power. Witnessing the benefit the army derived from the academy at West Point and taking a page from both the French and British, they founded the United States Naval Academy at Annapolis, Maryland, in 1845. There were internal rumblings after the Mexican War over states' rights and slavery, and the graduates would be matured in service for the catastrophic events to come.

Secretary of the Navy Abel Upshur selected the venerable ship *Constitution* for a special expedition, a "round-the-world voyage." Some repair was done to bring her up to challenge. Captain Percival, sixty-five, supervised the reconditioning at Norfolk, Virginia, where she had lain for more than a year. The *Constitution* was back in commission in April of 1844 under a man twenty years older than the ship. He was not thinking of steam or other newfangled ways. Instead he outfitted Old Ironsides for a very arduous journey of the old school. His mission was to protect American maritime, chart the waters, establish coaling-station connections, and make it known that the United States was a sea power with friendly intentions.

It all began in New York City at the end of May 1844. The first leg took the new American ambassador to his post in Brazil. The trade winds demanded the prudent sailor to make a crossing eastward and then south to the Canary Islands. A little further south, the equator was crossed off the east coast of Africa, and then the ship was blown directly to Brazil. It was July before the ambassador and his family gave up the captain's quarters and landed in Rio. It took sixty-eight days, with stops in the Canary Islands and Azores to show the flag and replenish supplies. By then the ambassador and, more particularly, his wife and four children were longing for solid land. While in port the ship was painted white with a red gun stripe, to reduce the heat absorption of the southern ocean.[11]

It took until early October to round the Cape of Good Hope, the southern end of the continent of Africa, and sail into the Indian Ocean. While the passage was rough, it was nothing like the rounding of South America. They called at Madagascar and Zanzibar, and creeping up the eastern coast of Africa, they turned toward Indonesian islands and stopped at Sumatra, but off the Malay Peninsula they spoke to a number of American merchant ships trading peacefully. On the way to Singapore they must have angered the gods, for they were caught up in one of the notorious storms that frequent the area in January. Like many who visit the faraway lands and partake of the food, the crew came down with "island revenge," which delayed the trip. Zigzagging, they called at Borneo and Brunei. They paused at Da Nang, Vietnam, to replenish and repaint the ship to black with the white checkerboard gun stripe. The captain visited Hong Kong and the related area on the rivers in fulfillment of his mission to bring American interest to the attention of the constituted governments. In mid-August he had turned for home and passed through the Philippine archipelago, pointed for the Americas. It took nearly two months to reach Hawaii. There the ship was repaired.

Royal Visit

King Kamehameha signed the visitor's log, proof that the captain was accomplishing his mission. On to California, where he glanced off the edge of Monterey Bay and turned south to Mexico, which was involved in another sovereignty dispute at the time. The Mexican War was at a crucial point in the spring of 1846 and the *Constitution* joined the blockading naval force at Mazatlán for the next three months. Nothing happened to involve the ship, and in April she slipped away toward Valparaíso, Chile. At last she was free to go home. On the Fourth of July she exited a passage around the horn. The spirits were high and the weather was blowing them in the correct direction, home. She completed her 52,000-mile voyage around the world on September 17, 1846, at Boston. It was one month short of forty-nine years since she had been launched there at Charlestown. What a story she had to tell.

Mediterranean

Captain John Gwinn took the regunned *Constitution* out in December of 1848 to join the American fleet in the Mediterranean. There a death knell was sounded when USS *Princeton* joined the squadron. Smoke poured from the extendable funnel just ahead of the mainmast. Onlookers believed that she was on fire. They had never seen a steam-powered ship before, and when they were told, they did not believe it. The spring and summer was spent watching from a safe distance as the Austrians fought the Italians in a ground war. Europe was again in turmoil, but the United States had stayed out of the arguments. The American base was La Spezia, on the western coast of Italy.

Pope On Board

In July of 1850 Captain Gwinn informed his new boss, Commodore Charles Morgan, that the number two man at the American Embassy in Rome had informed him that Pope Pius IX and King Ferdinand II were expected to visit the American man-of-war. The pope had been forced out of Rome by the fighting and was sheltering with the king by Naples. Morgan ordered a stop to the plan since it smacked of taking sides, which was contrary to his instructions, which were to protect American interests in the area only. Gwinn was a naval commander who took little counsel upon his own quarterdeck. The two men were heads of state and he believed that if the American ambassador, a representative of the president of the United States, well above his commodore in rank, wished them to visit, they would be welcome. Five days later, in opposition to his orders to sail off in support of American interests, he took the State Department's John Rowan to Gaeta, Italy, a seaside resort, to meet the guests. The dignitaries came on to a twenty-one gun salute and remained several hours, speaking with the crew and inspecting the spaces. It was a very cordial event and unique to have the head of the Roman Catholic Church, recognized as a head of state, standing on an American ship, officially a part of the nation. Captain Gwinn's commander was livid and asked that he be censured, but Gwinn was dead within a month from a stomach complaint. He was buried in Italy.[12] Ordered home, the *Constitution* completed her duty to the country on January 10, 1851, and was sent into ordinary in Boston along with her sister, the *United States*.

Slave Trade

In the 1850s the navy concentrated on modernizing the power plants and trying various combinations of steam and sail. The identification of fuel sources around the world's ports and the placement of agents and money was an ongoing expedition.

In March 1853 the *Constitution* sailed out as the flagship of Commodore Isaac Mayo. Captained by Commander John Rudd, she was destined to interrupt the slave trade off the west coast of Africa. There the fleet landed a party of two hundred to settle a tribal dispute between two native tribes, which was successfully completed with the aid of a 12-pound cannon. The *Constitution*'s last capture was of an American crewed slave vessel, which had no human cargo at the time. She returned to Portsmouth, New Hampshire, on June 2, 1855, and was decommissioned.

Civil War Duty at the Academy

The United States Naval Academy had been expanding ever since its inception in 1845. It was obviously a great idea whose time had come. The "on-the-job training" of prospective officers, a true school of hard knocks, wasted more than it produced. Established on the water's edge of the Severn River, the academy was protected from the open Chesapeake Bay but provided easy access to big water and ultimately the Atlantic Ocean. Rather than build an elaborate mock-up for sailors to use to "learn the ropes," the cheapest solution was to bring in a man-of-war that had outlived its operational usefulness. USS *Constitution* was called back into service and made seaworthy. She was modified at Portsmouth, where her gun complement was reduced to a little over a dozen and her inside converted for student use. She was then recommissioned and sailed to the academy, where she took up residence on October 18, 1860.

President Lincoln's Navy

By the spring of 1861, civil war was inevitable. Maryland was split between sympathy for both sides. When it came time to take a vote as to Maryland's succession from the Union, the governor was aware that it would be close. He suspended the session. Within days, the assembly was moved from Annapolis to Frederick, forty miles west. Then only those members in favor of staying with the Union were informed of the location. The vote was taken in special session, which went for President Lincoln. At Annapolis, copperheads (Southern sympathizers), threatened to seize Old Ironsides and take her south. The frigate *United States* had been burned at Norfolk to prevent her from serving the Confederacy. Copperheads knew that those who sailed into the arms of the Confederacy with Old Ironsides would be heroes.

A Narrow Escape

The academy commandant, Captain George Baker, moved four of the *Constitution's* 32-pounders to the stern in an attempt to defend the moored vessel. His command included a small cadre of instructors and several hundred midshipmen. He was not capable of moving the big frigate to a more advantageous position. The Severn River and the mouth to Annapolis Bay were replete with shoals and mud bars, which had caused problems when the ship was brought to the academy. He knew that they would prevent the ship from being captured and sailed out, which was some consolation. His orders were to destroy her if necessary.

Traffic in the bay alerted the ship to beat to quarters before dawn on April 22, 1861. A steamboat approached and moored at the academy. A warning that they were about to be fired upon brought the comforting response that the vessel was transporting Colonel Ben Butler's regiment of volunteers from Massachusetts. They were headed for Washington to protect the national capital. They had stumbled on Old Ironsides instead. It was as if the cavalry had come to the rescue.

Fortune Smiles Once Again

Butler's men were soldiers, but many of them were professional seamen from the Boston area. The novice midshipmen were put in defense of the school grounds while the soldiers crewed the frigate and turned her toward open water by kedging her out into the channel and over the obstacles. Now she was in a position to defend herself. News was received that the copperheads were planing to disrupt any attempt to put Old Ironsides back into the fleet. Captain Baker put together a crew composed of his own cadre, midshipmen, United States Marines, and a large number of soldiers from Boston in an attempt to follow his new orders to get the *Constitution* safely to Newport, Rhode Island. It would require the ship to travel down the Chesapeake Bay while rebel contingents snapped at his heels. There was no time to seek favorable winds, and he sought a tow from the steam-powered gunboat *RR Cuyler*. With the morning tide, they made a dash for Fortress Monroe and the safety of her giant Rodman guns. The *Constitution* broke out of the bay on April 27 and was towed north to a final mooring at the new Naval Academy in Rhode Island. There she remained during the Civil War training midshipmen for the navy, which was not only engaged in war but in transition to ironclads.

Iron Ships and Iron Men

Not all Massachusetts men were fond of a standing navy. John Quincy Adams was quoted as saying that not only did we not need steamships for the navy, but why did we need a navy at all? Now, years later, the need for a navy could not be disputed. There was a danger that England or France could ally itself with the Confederate States of America (CSA) because of the cotton, which was needed at the Lancastershire mills, and the South's tobacco, which was clamored for in Europe. England had fifty-three steam-powered warships of the line, while America had none. France was nearly as modern as England. Stephen Mallory, secretary of the Confederate navy, was planning on building steam-powered ironclad vessels as early as 1860, before the war. A man of foresight, he knew that the Union navy was made of wood and sail. An early conversion to armored-sided steam-powered war vessels could eliminate his enemy, while his steam-driven commercial raiders could paralyze the North and bring England or France to his direct assistance. With little money, he did his best to mount a credible force. By 1862 Mallory had four operational ironclad warships; CSA *Virginia*—ex-*Merrimack*—was the most notable.

After the Confederacy sank two Union wooden men-of-war at Hampton Roads, USS *Monitor* arrived in the nick of time and saved the remainder of the fleet moored outside Fortress Monroe. The *Monitor* was the first of a fleet of similar ironclads that revolutionized the Union navy, much to the heartburn of the brass. But neither of the navies produced an oceangoing version comparable to the Europeans'. The technology was hostage to a great struggle that called heavily on the resources of both sides. CSA *H. L. Hunley*, the first operational submarine, successfully sank the sloop of war *Housatonic* at Charleston but sank soon after. While many strides were made in guns, ammunition, and small arms, little could be spared outside for craft on inland waterways and harbor navies.[13]

Civil War Ends

Before the end of 1865, the *Constitution* was back at Annapolis for the resumption of academy class work. There she continued to serve the postwar students until the summer of 1871, when she was sent into ordinary at the navy yard in Philadelphia. In 1873 the navy recognized that the venerable ship, which was being allowed to slowly rot, could make one last contribution. She was to be restored for the centennial of the nation in 1876. High and dry in the shipyard, she was stripped of everything down to her ribs. The eight-inch-thick strakes that surrounded the hull were pried off. All the other modifications, with the exception of the replacement of her diagonal braces, accomplished, she was put back as near as possible to her 1797 birth. While the old Philadelphia navy yard was being decommissioned, in January 1876 USS *Constitution* was floated free once more. The closure of the yard meant the renovation had to be completed by a commercial firm at Camden, New Jersey. There, the ornamentation was restored, the masts erected, and the rigging installed. From January to December 1877, she was docked to provide a school for teenage boys. They were trained to become ordinary seamen for the enlisted ranks of the active navy.

The Second Hundred Years of the United States

The Paris Exhibition of 1878 put the *Constitution* back on the front pages. In Washington, plans to send the American contribution turned to the big frigate to make a splash in France. She had been born during the Quasi War, fought at Napoleon's side, and cruised the Mediterranean for much of her life. In the peace of March 1878, only a pair of salute guns were left in her battery, allowing space for the cargo that was rather overwhelming.

Even though she was revered in naval history, Neptune did not offer her a free passage. Caught as they entered the channel from the south, the ship and her crew fought valiantly for France but had to settle in the end for England. It had happened to many a ship in the past, yet it became a close-run thing.

> An easterly gale struck the ship as she was nearing the western end of the English Channel. For several days, she tacked back and forth on long reaches trying to make headway in the adverse wind and steep seas. It seemed almost as if she couldn't gain an inch. With everyone approaching exhaustion from the continuous sail handling and pumping, it was decided to take a chance and try sailing as close to the wind as possible without being beaten to pieces, driven on a lee shore. It was in many respects a gamble . . . a cliff-hanger. And once again she made it, her stout bows smashing through the swells, driven by more canvas than many would have dared to sheet home in those conditions. The sheltered peace of Carrick Bay at Falmouth allowed everyone a solid night's rest so sorely needed.[14]

The sea god then rewarded their efforts the following day by allowing them safely into Le Havre, France, with honors. Repairs were made after her offloading while she waited for the return voyage. After the New Year, the elements of the display, packed and crated, were stowed and they were once again under way.

The sailing conditions in January were not ideal, so the captain moved her well out into the middle of the channel before turning south. In the early morning darkness the "Old Lady" surprised the master and navigator when she grounded on the English shore. They had miscalculated the frigate's ability to sail and were high and dry below the famous white cliffs. Towed into Portsmouth Royal Navy Yard, the great American frigate passed by HMS *Victory*. There the masts of two of the most notable warships of the age of sail graced the same harbor. What a sight. Within days the *Constitution* bid farewell to the *Victory* as she resumed the passage home.

Medals of Honor

Early America believed that a system of honors and medals was a throwback to the Old World, which it did not intend to emulate. General Washington understood the value of recognizing the brave and decorated heroes with the Purple Heart. It was his personal honor and was not incorporated into the military services of the United States. When the servicemen of the War of 1812 performed acts of valor and achievement, Congress recognized them with medals struck for the occasion. During the Civil War the Union forces adopted the

Medal of Honor as the only decoration given nationally. Many of these were awarded years after the event and often smacked of political expediency.

However, on the return voyage of the *Constitution*, the ship was in serious danger due to storm damage inflicted in the Bay of Biscay. The rudder broke loose from its controls and began to beat wildly against the stern, threatening to seriously damage the ship in the worst possible seas. The usual attempts to pass a chain around it and block it with timbers were unsuccessful as conditions worsened. Carpenter's mate Henry Williams and able seamen Joseph Matthews and James Horton risked their lives to save the ship. Going over the stern, tethered to the ship's taffrail, they secured the giant rudder, which was thirty feet high and six feet wide at the keel. This enormous three-story-high, two-foot-thick swinging "barn door" was at the mercy of the storm and smashed so hard into the hull that it could be heard and felt throughout the entire ship. The citation awarded to the three men read, "for gallant conduct." Within a month, another medal was granted to U.S. Marine James Thayer for life saving. Today that act of life saving could receive the Navy and Marine Corps Medal, the same granted to Lieutenant John F. Kennedy, commander of *PT 109* during World War II.

New Role

Once in port, the *Constitution* joined an apprentice-training scheme and sailed with young aspiring crewmen down to the Caribbean and up to Canada. The cadets called at all ports showing the flag. She witnessed the reenactment of the British attack on New London, Connecticut, in August of 1881. It was her last appearance. In 1882 she was turned into a receiving ship and later a barracks with a barn built over her deck in place of the magnificent masts crossed with yards like telephone poles. There at the Portsmouth, New Hampshire, navy yard she languished; her days were numbered.

A Good Citizen Steps Forward

Abram S. Hewitt is not a familiar name to me from American history, but it should be. He was a gunmetal maker. His family had settled on the far northern border of New Jersey and begun the Ringwood Foundry, fed by the rich iron deposits contained in the surrounding hills. One of his forefathers, Peter Cooper, had founded the Cooper Union in New York City. Situated in Cooper Square, it still provides free education to deserving students. Hewitt was reported to be the sixth-richest man in the country. During the golden age, his firm had made gunmetal that was used for the chain across the Hudson at West Point and cannons for the Revolutionary War, the War of 1812, and the Civil War. Hewitt lived in the city but had a country home of thirty-five rooms at Ringwood Manor, New Jersey. In front of the grand house there is a section of the West Point chain and a mammoth black-iron mortar from the Civil War. On a visit to the Philadelphia Navy Yard in 1880, Hewitt witnessed the melting of old iron cannons. He inquired about the history of the guns that were being destroyed. When he was told that the pair of 12-pounders in front of him on the ground were from USS *Constitution*, he bought one.[15] It was transported by the Pennsylvania Railroad, and the bill of lading contains a note on the back. It warns the train crew to be careful of the trunnions, since Hewitt was told that they were weak.

Boston Men Save the Ship

By 1896 the water was seeping in as the navy budget was also leaking badly. There was no money to bring the *Constitution* back to life this time. Congressman John F. Fitzgerald went to see the secretary of the navy and former governor of Massachusetts, John D. Long. The two patriots found enough money to keep Old Ironsides afloat. But the money was limited. There was only enough to refurbish the hull and tow her back to Boston. It would be up to the people to do the rest.

CHAPTER TEN

~

America's Treasure

The ship, never has she failed us, let her not sink and decay into oblivion.

—Captain William Bainbridge

The *Constitution*'s Happiest Birthday

The hard scraping done for money in Washington's long, cluttered hallways by Congressman Fitzgerald and Secretary of the Navy Long resulted in the following letter.

To. Hon. J. D. Long   Sept 23, 1897

Sir; Will you kindly inform me if the frigate "Constitution," just arrived in Boston from Portsmouth is to be restored to her original shape as nearly possible, and to remain here!

I understand that Congress has made appropriation for such a purpose, but as that report has been questioned, I venture to apply to you for the truth.

I am Sir, Respectfully yours,

Walter Rouland
Allston, Massachusetts[1]

Mr. Rouland, the marine contractor, was wise to not go forward before settling the question as to where the cash was and when it would arrive. Even though the money only covered the funds required to allow her hull to be made sound for a safe journey under tow, the ship had been saved. The very tired and much scarred *Constitution*, altered by previous service and now nearly unrecognizable, was moored in Charlestown. She had come home at last and seemed to be leaning against the dock were she was begun, resting comfortably after one hundred years of good and faithful service. A century had gone by under her proud prow. To think that though she had been finished in September of 1797, she had refused to go into the water, preferring to be launched in October. The Boston newspapers ran the headline, "Old Ironsides Home."

A ship, any ship, is just a vehicle of the sea and, like land vehicles, can expect to be recycled or destroyed when it is no longer economically viable. This has happened daily since man built conveyances. There is, however, a sentiment attached to great things, and they demand to live on. The Eiffel Tower, the Tower of London, HMS Victory and Old Ironsides all stood in the center of events that highlighted a story of past people not to be forgotten. We all enjoy retelling great stories. They conjure up sights of long ago, and as sagas of dire circumstances and despair that gave rise, through toil and strife, to triumph, they provide us hope in our own times. Worn sayings, such as, "It is always darkest before the dawn," accompany these tales to ensure that the audience gets the point. No time, especially ours, is ever easy. There are things that must be believed in if adversity is to be overcome. No population ever revels in hopelessness. So we look for symbols of former glory and personal achievement and borrow a little piece for ourselves.

The legend of a navy ship of the age of sail, made of wood and crewed by men of iron, that was tossed by the tempest storm and hammered by enemies yet was never defeated by either was a natural for the people to cling to. Yet neither the federal government nor the Department of the Navy was aware of such interest until they allowed the ship to deteriorate and begin to sink on its own accord. Time was moving and the technology had pushed the Constitution into the backwater. While her sister and sailing mates slowly dissolved from history, the people had something to say about Old Ironsides.

The Age of Reconstruction and Restoration

Others had tried to arouse a momentum for recovery of the great ship.

In Washington on May 1, 1895, at the Annual National Congress of the Sons of the American Revolution, the following resolution was passed. "RESOLVED; that it is the sense of the National Society of the Sons of the American Revolution, that the Historical battleship 'Constitution' should be rebuilt, and forever preserved as an illustration of the type of warship which has immortalized the United States Navy, and that she be located at the National Capital, Washington, to be used as a National Naval Museum." The minutes of the meeting note the support of Mr. Herbert, the secretary of the navy, and his assistant, Mr. McAdoo, as expected. However, members of the society found little support for the resolution during a probe before the meeting. The public, when questioned, was in favor of the proposed saving of the ship as long as the government paid for it. In fact, the public was "lethargic," so they turned to the press, which did not react. The leaders of the society "felt that the restoration of the ship by private contributions would lack the dignity and the power which would characterize the reconstruction by Act of Congress, of the ship which was great only because it was American and belonged to the American Navy."

The probe included a letter to the editor, a copy of which is preserved in the minutes of the meeting. "Our dependence is then upon the American Navy, which has always been animated by the noblest devotion and keenest intelligence. Let the Nation show its appreciation by rebuilding 'Old Ironsides,' its noblest ship, establishing her at Washington as the National Naval Museum in which to forever preserve the trophies and records of the best of navies and bravest of men." However, it did not produce a result and was abandoned.

The Women of Massachusetts Pick Up the Banner

However, other groups persisted. A year later, the Massachusetts State Society of the Daughters of 1812 appealed to Congress, not finding it undignified at all to seek the subscription of the people. Secretary Long responded as follows.

Navy Department   October 25, 1899
Dear Madam:
    I have your letter and I see no objection to your starting a fund for the restoration of the old frigate CONSTITUTION, which I understand your society would like to do by popular subscription rather than by application to Congress for appropriations. If, when Congress meets, you shall write me a formal letter, asking me to call the attention of Congress to the matter, and to suggest to Congress the propriety of an act authorizing your society to carry out this work under the supervision of the Navy Department, I shall be very happy to commend it to the favorable consideration of that body,

                                    Very truly yours.
                                    John D. Long
                                    Secretary of the Navy

In the very next session Congress, in the spring of 1900, provided the authority for organizations to publicly solicit funds to pay for the cost of restoration.

The same act of Congress authorized the sale of souvenir items. The theme of the campaign taken up across the nation was, "Old Ironsides saved the nation. Now let us save her." Led first by the historical societies, associations, and foundations, it soon grew out of its shoes. The primary reason was the tangible merchandise, which put a piece of the great ship in homes from landlocked North Dakota to Oklahoma and beyond.

The ads read, "Things you can buy to save Old Ironsides."

1. Plaque of original timber with bronze tablet & Medallion—$5
2. Gavel & Block of original live oak keel timber attractively labeled in bronze—$25
3. Knees of original live oak—length 72", breadth 24", width at throat 19"—$100
4. Souvenir cannon—$35
5. Timber with bronze plaque denoting origin—$3
6. Iron bolts, copper nails, cordage, small pieces of timber & copper sheathing—25 cents
7. Book ends—per set—$5[2]

The direct approach touched the heart of the consumer nation. In 1902 *Colliers*, a story and photo magazine that reached nearly everyone in the country, through the ubiquitous barbershops, hair salons, and doctor's and dentist's offices, featured the movement of the ship to Boston. In Boston the Veterans of the 8th Regiment of Massachusetts's infantry picked up the standard and took it to Washington. Members of the Grand Army of the Republic from Marblehead signed a petition in the town hall for the preservation of the famous American frigate. The hall was fittingly known as "cradle of liberty of Marblehead." A number of the signers were credited with the saving of Old Ironsides from Confederate raiders at the start of the Civil War. The petition, over a hundred feet long, was displayed in the Old State House in Boston before presentation to the United States Congress. Photos of the scroll across the desks of the representatives graced the front page of every newspaper in the nation on January 18, 1906.

Progress was slow. The old barn roof and cabin debris were demolished and the *Constitution* took on the lines of a man-of-war once more. But the years were telling. The strakes of oak were shattered in places; her sides scarred by the years at sea. The wood had soaked up a great deal of water. Due to the shortage of funds, only minor maintenance was in evidence by 1907. Moored as an unofficial museum, she put up with the occasional dress parade. Casual visitors brought out-of-town relatives to walk her upper decks and enlisted the caretakers to tell of her days of glory. The money raised was only sufficient to barely keep her afloat. On the eve of the First World War, in 1916, a survey demanded extensive repair or dissolution. She lingered on through the war but by 1924 it was obvious that she was dying. A survey called for nearly half a million dollars to restore her to good health.

Secretary of the Navy Curtis Wilbur favored the people's contribution over the government expenditure. This time, fund-raising effort called for a partnership of government, business, and the public, which committed the public's best and brightest to leading an organized national campaign. Recalling Oliver Wendell Holmes's poem of 1830, which had inspired the nation once before, leaders turned to enlist the power of the printed word. An early move was the personal involvement of the sitting president. In order to raise awareness across the land, they enlisted him in picking out the school writing themes for the campaign, which promised prizes. The president's response follows.

The White House   24 August, 1925
                                             White Court
                                             Swampscott. Mass

My dear Mr. Secretary:

I have your letter of August 21st, requesting me to select subjects for essays by young people dealing with the historic frigate, the U.S.S. CONSTITUTION.

I select the following topics:

For Colleges—The contribution of the U.S.S. CONSTITUTION to human liberty and to national progress.

For High Schools—Why did the victories of the U.S.S. CONSTITUTION contribute so largely to our success in the war of 1812?

For Elementary Schools—why will the preservation of the U.S.S. CONSTITUTION promote patriotism?

The active service of "Old Ironsides," extending as it did over the 84 years from 1790 to 1882, covers the greater part of our history, and a study of her record will turn the thought of our young people to many of the most important events in the development of our nation. I therefore trust there will be widespread competition for the Old Ironsides medals, because an understanding of the fundamentals of our history is most helpful to discharging the duties of citizenship.

                                        Very truly yours,
                                        Calvin Coolidge

The president's letter was published widely, and both political parties hosted the efforts in every district as the momentum that was so vital began to build. But they hit the jackpot when Hollywood produced a motion picture, *Old Ironsides*, for the Christmas holiday film-going audience. In 1926 it was the only show in town, and the people were given a moving black-and-white image to put with the story of the *Constitution*. Numerous prints of the ship, by a number of superb artists, received enormous interest. Calendars for 1927, sporting her sails billowing, were featured in most kitchens in the country. Personally taking up the cause, teachers found it a welcome supplement to American and world history, which could be boring. All that interest generated money, enough to start the process of restoration.

1927: Restoration Work Begins

The call went out to Ohio and West Virginia for white oak, Delaware cut white-oak knees, and Washington State sent Douglas fir for the deck planking. In "Commodore's Pond" at Pensacola, Florida, 1,500 tons of live oak was found still curing from the cutting in 1850.[3] By April 1927 the craftsmen had stripped away sodden planks, which disintegrated in their hands, leaving her ribs showing. The sight of the great lady down to her corset was shocking. But there was no other way; it had to be done. There were serious problems with the skeleton. Laid down 130 years before, the keel was hogging again to fourteen inches below the center, on either end. Some marine historians, such as Alexander Magoun, believed that the hogging could have been caused by the mishap of launch in 1797. However, that is an extreme position.

A ship is built to rest in the water, not on dry land. In the water, the tremendous tonnage the *Constitution* was built to carry was dispersed over the entire area of the hull. As she sat high and dry in the dock, all that weight would come to rest on the injured keel and could break her backbone. Much of the weight was jettisoned. The rigging, sails, and masts, along with her guns and ammunition, were landed.

Once the ship began to dry out, she was bound to change shape, which was not desirable. The solution was to brace her inside and out with heavy timbers. Caged, the hull could be taken to pieces and replaced in stages. By the spring of 1928, the work was slow. It must have been like building a watch from the inside out. There were no standard pieces; everything was a little different. Even a sister rib on the other side of the hull, which was originally part of a pair, was skewed a little one way or the other. It was becoming obvious that the bills would rise beyond a million dollars before she was finished. It was a cost overrun caused by the price of specialized material, transportation, and long hours requiring extraordinary skill. The national committee had done a terrific job raising over $600,000. It came from souvenirs, prints, and gifts. The donations of schoolchildren alone totaled $135,000.

Quakertown, Pennsylvania   26, Oct, 1925

Hon. C. D. Wilbur
Sec. Of Navy
Washington, D.C.

Dear Sir:

Am enclosing check for $2, which amount was donated, by the children of Stover's School, Bucks Co., Penna. We hope it will help to "save" Old Ironsides.

Very respectfully,
Mrs. Florence Fluck
Teacher

The collection amounted to pennies in a glass jar, which sat at the corner of the teacher's desk. What is so remarkable about the collection of such a large fund from all corners of the country was that it was still going on during the Great Depression. It was difficult to be a philanthropist after the fall of the markets in 1929. The grind of the Depression stopped the flow of funds. There was no doubt that the fund needed a boost. Congress, in the spring of 1930, appropriated the remaining $300,000 to finish the process.

Even though there were fewer coins jingling loose in the pockets of the people, the letters kept coming.

Honorable Herbert Hoover,
President of the United States, 5, April, 1930
Washington, D.C.
Dear Mr. President:

I am writing you in behalf of the student body of the South Pasadena Junior High School, of South Pasadena, California.

It is rumored that the historic vessel, Old Ironsides, is to be put out of commission as a part of the economy program of the United States Navy.

This ship is pointed out to the school children of the nation as a landmark of our history—a symbol of American patriotism and independence; and holds a place of deepest love and reverence in the heart of each of us. This admiration was manifested several years ago when we subscribed money with which to restore this venerated vessel. In view of this fact, we feel sure that you will understand and appreciate our interest in the matter.

If the above mentioned rumor proves to be correct, we trust you will utilize every power of your high office to preserve historic Old Ironsides intact, that it may remain an object of inspiration and reverence to all Americans.

Most respectfully yours,
Kathleen Hughes, Secretary

The students wanted to remind the president that they, the people, built her, crewed her, sailed her, and paid again and again to keep her. If he was going to break faith with them, he must be sure to tell them in time. In a way, it was a warning that was not exclusive to Kathleen and her classmates.

Dear Sir

Allow me, as one of the fifth generation of the family of Commodore Edward Preble, to express my gratification at your recent announcement that his, Old Ironsides, is to be kept afloat. With economy the fashion, it is a relief to know that the sentiment for our country's early naval achievements is strong enough to preserve the good old Constitution.

Faithfully yours,
Blanchard M. Preble

Everyone was getting involved in the worst of times to ensure that nothing else was going to be lost to the Depression.

The Jackson Figurehead Reappears

The very enterprising rear admiral, who was the commander of the First Naval District, in April of 1928 wrote to the secretary of the navy about a discovery he had made. A friend in Boston had called to tell him that he had missed the purchase of the Andrew Jackson figurehead at auction. He had offered $35, and it had sold for $40 to a Brick Row shop. A Mr. Leeds had bought it for his home in Long Island. The rear admiral implied that the navy should make an attempt to get the new owner to donate it to the *Constitution* for display.

The next day a second letter was sent to the secretary with an entirely different tone. The rear admiral had suddenly found that it was Mrs. Payne Whitney, a very prominent socialite, who had bought the figurehead. In the letter, he backtracks, hoping to put a quick end to the matter and still save face. "I don't think really it makes any difference to us who bought it or what becomes of it. If we had it, it could not be put back on the ship, and as a matter of fact it wasn't a part of the original Constitution anyway. . . . the only thing that could be done with it is to put it in the museum."

History Repeated

It was decided that the ship, which had changed her inner and outer appearance many times over her long life span, should take on the trappings of the War of 1812. After all, it was then that the nation had been in peril. It would mean that the heavy guns and large carronades that were put on in 1809 would be the big frigate's battery once again.

The *Constitution* had always been a lucky ship and it was so once more. With the Hoover administration came the appointment of a man of Boston as secretary of the navy. He was Charles F. Adams, who had a personal interest in the ship. It would be up to him to decide what was to be done with the restored national monument.

What to Do with a Movable Monument?

Before she was finished, letters were pouring into the Department of the Navy. They all got the same consideration and the poignant reply note stating that the ship was not going anywhere until operational funds were provided.

Dear Sir:

Replying to your letter of July 27th requesting information as to when OLD IRONSIDES will be anchored at Seattle, Washington, I regret to inform you that no decision has been made in regard to the future movements of the CONSTI-TUTION (OLD IRONSIDES) upon completion of reconditioning, about July 1, 1931. Unless appropriations are made by Congress for placing her in full commission, she will no doubt be preserved as a naval relic at some Navy Yard and, therefore, will make no cruise.

> Very truly yours,
> W. S. DeLany
> Lieut. Cmdr., U.S. Navy
> Office of Ship Movements

The navy knew that the first step was to put her back in the fleet if there was to be any hope of sending her back to sea.

The order came, at last.

Navy Department Office of the Naval Operations, 2 July, 1931
From: Chief of Naval Operations,
To: Bureaus and offices, and Divisions of Office of Naval Operations,
Subject: USS CONSTITUTION—commissioning of
1, The CONSTITUTION was placed in commission at the Navy yard Boston on 1 July 1931.

> H. E. Kimmel
> By direction

Admiral Kimmel, who would become better known for the defense of Pearl Harbor, advises his keynote speaker on the ceremony in the following cable of June 20, 1931:

NAVY DEPARTMENT

JUDGE CURTIS G. WILBUR CONSTITUTION TO BE COMMISSIONED TWO THIRTY AFTERNOON JULY FIRST COMMA LENGTH OF SPEECH TWENTY TO TWENTY FIVE MINUTES COMMA HOPE TO HAVE PROGRAM BROADCASTED COMMA APPROPRIATE DRESS CUTAWAY COAT AND HIGH COLLAR COMMA STRAW OR PANAMA HAT COMMA THIS BEING THE DRESS GENERALLY WORN IN THIS COMMUNITY ON SIMILAR OCCASIONS PERIOD

The process that took place at the Department of the Navy with the new secretary was not recorded. There is a spark provided by the following. Received at the Navy Department on April 13, 1931, it sums up what would come to pass.

The handwritten note was sent initially to the chairman of the Military Affairs Committee, U.S. Senate, accompanied by five world charts requested by the Senate. The note reads,

> With special attention to Pres. Hoover.
> Secretary of War & Navy
> . . . I hereby respectfully request that the Old Constitution be refitted for active service and to make a *Good Will Trip* around the world on the great circle, under her own power in 100 days or less, escorted by the picked Battle Wagons, first Class Cruisers and Scouting Fleet.
> *OBJECTIVE*
> To hook up the Northern & Southern Hemisphere East & West, to promote real international reciprocity & to provide *permanent prosperity in peace or war.*
> Respectfully yours
John S McAvoy

Mr. McAvoy's direct approach caught someone's attention. McAvoy was not aware that an around-the-world trip was impossible, but a series of voyages to show the nation what it had accomplished on behalf of the United States Navy was just the ticket. As soon as the rumors began to spread, the department was overwhelmed with requests. One, from a port city that the ship could not reach, must have been a nightmare for the action officer, one Commander John Adams, USN.

It began in spring with the certain expectation that Old Ironsides was to visit cities that were clamoring for her presence. The request of the president of the New Jersey State Board of Education seems to be the most memorable. Since Bordentown was the home of Captain Charles Stewart and, in addition, the town was celebrating its 250th anniversary, he requested that the navy arrange for the ship to dock there as the center of attractions. The navy secretary sent the request, along with many others, to a staff officer tasked with the schedule. Commander Adams checked the route to Bordentown and discovered that the depth of the river prevented the ship from making the passage. He informed the New Jersey officials of the problem and denied the request. However, that did not faze the requester. He wrote to Adams the following:

> I am in receipt of your letter of February, which seems quite evasive. You do not tell me the depth of water needed for the CONSTITUTION, and I suppose you already know that they are dredging the river from Trenton to Philadelphia now, and have been doing it for sometime allowing ocean going vessels to come to Trenton.
>
> The City of Bordentown is awaiting advices as to when they would set their date for their anniversary in October.

The staff officer wrote and explained the issue to the New Jersey inquirer, but it did not make any difference. The next letter came from New Jersey's senator. In March, the senator received the following information, which had been supplied to the authority in Bordentown.

It was found that there is a dredging project underway which is to carry only twenty feet of water to Bordentown in a two hundred foot channel. This project is expected to be completed in September of this year, but covers only the removal of soft material and does not provide for the removal of boulders and other hard material, which may be in this channel. The Commandant of the First Naval District at Boston has informed the Department that the draft of the CONSTITUTION will be in excess of twenty feet.

The Senator passed it on, but it made no impression on the Garden State's representatives. The secretary of the navy received the following telegram in July.

HON HAROLD WELLS ON BEHALF OF COMMITTEE IN CHARGE 250TH ANNIVERSARY CELEBRATIONS BORDENTOWN NJ HAS WRITTEN YOU ASKING THAT ARRANGEMENTS BE MADE TO HAVE OLD IRONSIDES PUT IN AT BORDENTOWN FOR ONE DAY DURING CELEBRATION FROM HISTORICAL VIEWPOINT NO PLACE IS MORE ENTITLED TO RECEIVE OLD IRONSIDE THAN THE HOME OF ITS FORMER COMMANDER IN CHIEF CAPTAIN STEWART I THEREFORE HOPE THAT IT MAY BE POSSIBLE FOR YOU TO ARRANGE FOR A VISIT OF OLD IRONSIDES TO BORDENTOWN.

Having served on the Army General Staff in Washington, I can just imagine what transpired at navy headquarters down at the staff action level. With much discussion, the telegram passed down the staff through six or seven levels, and every staff member attached another piece of paper to the file. By the time it got back to Adams, it had become a major "flap." He was called up to personally review his action at least three levels above, which produced the following telegram to New Jersey. "REPLYING YOUR TELEGRAM FOURTEEN JULY BEG ADVISE THAT THERE IS ONLY A TWENTY FOOT CHANNEL TO BORDENTOWN WHEREAS CONSTITUTION WILL DRAW TWENTY-THREE FEET PERIOD FOR THAT REASON REGRET IMPOSSIBLE BRING SHIP THAT CITY." Frankly, it did not matter. The letters continued to flood into navy headquarters three more times in spite of Commander Adams's reasoned replies, up until October, when they finally stopped. New Jersey's Education Department was never convinced that considerations other than the fact that the ship could not travel on land should have prevented the visit of the ship.[4]

Under Way, July 2, 1931

No time was lost the day following commissioning as the *Constitution* passed Castle Island and was turned north by her constant companion, the faithful tug *Grebe*, a wooden-hulled minesweeper. She carried a new complement of sails, which were a gift from an admirer. She could still turn heads at the age of 134. On the Fourth of July, Independence Day, she was back at Portsmouth, New Hampshire. Old Ironsides was welcomed by a flotilla of private and government craft. She had left there in 1897, and the people had never expected to see her again. The *Constitution* was familiar with the city; she had cruised from it during the War of 1812. The captain and crew looked upon the port city as their second home, which was why it was chosen for the first outing. Between July 1931 and April 1932, Old Ironsides called at thirty port celebrations from Portland, Maine, to Baton Rouge, Louisiana. More than two million visitors scuffed the wooden planks of her historic decks and spread the story of the experience. It made the headline of every family letter, for USS *Constitution* was, after all, their ship.

Christmas of 1932 was not a happy one for most as the people of the West Coast awaited the promised visit of the great frigate. She stopped briefly at the naval station in Cuba and then plunged into the narrow Panama Canal. If the waterway had not been opened, the *Constitution* could never have negotiated the treacherous waters off the tip of South America. But the generous donors of the West were not to be forgotten. In January 1933, the tall masts of Old Ironsides were seen again in San Diego, as they had been during her 'round-the-world voyage in the 1840s. The West Coast did not have the natural deep harbors of the East. Ironsides was only able to get into Los Angeles, San Francisco, and Seattle. Hundreds of thousands of people flocked to stand on the hallowed decks and listen to her story. The gentleman who had written to the Department of the Navy in the spring of 1931 witnessed his answer in July of 1933. Old Ironsides thrilled half a million who came to tour—I am sure he was one of them, but he never made himself known. I wish there were a second letter telling the navy what he thought of her. What could have passed through his mind when his letter was answered?

Some expected the ship to return to Washington, D.C., which was the talk that surrounded her during the years of collecting and reconstruction. Since the secretary of the navy, Charles Adams, was from Boston, we shouldn't wonder. In May 1934 the *Constitution*, while still in service, was decommissioned at Charlestown Navy Yard.

The Philadelphia Inquirer
Editorial Room
                                                    October 17, 1935

United States Navy Dept.
Gentlemen:
    I shall appreciate it if you will tell me where the Frigate Constitution now is
and what are the plans for her in the future. Our last news item indicates she was
in the Charleston, Boston, Navy Yard but that was in 1934. We have received this
query in Everybody's Column.
                                            Very truly yours.
                                            Mary Missett, editor

The question had been asked by an ordinary citizen who could not believe
that the great ship had passed out of sight once again. The answer lay in a curt
military notification not shared with the public.

NAVAL MESSAGE
Received at Navy department
1934 JUN 4 AM 1030

From: COMONE
Action: OPNAV
0004 OPNAV 3802 1035 FRIDAY EIGHT JUNE RECOMMENDED DATE
FOR DECOMMISSIONING CONSTITUITION 0850

Franklin Delano Roosevelt

It was great to have a close friend as the secretary of the navy, but it did not
compare to the outcome of the visit by the president, in May 1940. A great
friend to the navy, Mr. Roosevelt did the expected and placed USS *Constitution*
back in commission. During the worst of the Depression, however, the president
was given a chance to appropriate for Ironsides upkeep. The following was received at the Department of the Navy.

Bureau of the Budget   May 19, 1936
[to Secretary of the Navy]
My dear Mr. Secretary:
    Referring to your letter of January 15, 1936, and subsequent correspondence
concerning H.J. Res. 372 "for the permanent preservation of the United States
Frigate Constitution and other vessels having historical tradition," there are enclosed herewith copies of correspondence relative to this matter for your information and guidance, not hereto-fore made available to you.

From the enclosed copies of the letters of the Acting Executive Director, National Emergency Council, of January 23 and April 15, 1936, and the notations made thereon by the President, it would appear that the legislation proposed by H.J. Res. 372 would not at this time be in accord with the financial program of the President.

. . . with respect to the possibility of obtaining an allotment from relief funds with which to accomplish preliminary work on this project.

Very truly yours.
Signed D. W. Bill
Acting Director

World War II at the Boston Navy Yard was hectic. The yardmen repaired the fleet that fought the battle of the Atlantic and protected the East Coast from marauding Nazi submarines. There, tied to the dock in the 1950s, the *Constitution* slowly deteriorated; her sails rotted and her masts cracked.

President Eisenhower

Ike, as he was known in the army, ordered in 1954 that the *Constitution* was to be restored and that her permanent home would be Boston, Massachusetts. It was a little surprising for a man from Kansas. But it emphasized that while Boston had first claim, if she did not take up that option, many places, large and small, would provide the *Constitution* with the home she deserved. After all, they moved the London Bridge to Arizona.

A worthiness survey was done in 1970. These inspections were taking longer and getting harder since few experts could be found with the experience to truly evaluate her. But science was taking over in modern times. Analysis of wood fiber was completed at universities, and new tools were available to evaluate stress, torsion, and tension. Wave tanks at the U.S. Naval Academy and commercial interests were brought into the process as her 200th birthday neared. At the highest levels, it became apparent that the *Constitution* would sail free once again.

She was given one year in dry dock and emerged in 1974. Ironically, Ironsides' luck was only applicable to herself. For the second time, a navy yard was being closed out from under her, as had happened in Philadelphia during the repair of 1876. The Boston Navy Yard was being closed, while work hurried forward. By the Fourth of July, 1976, the Eagle of the Sea, so named by Oliver Wendell Holmes, who had become as famous as the ship during his long and distinguished life, was operational. Moving out with an attendant tug, she greeted HMS *Britannia* with a twenty-one-gun salute for the sovereign who was aboard. One cannot help but think back. If it had been 1812, those twenty-one

24-pounders would have made short work of any British blockader trying to molest the citizens of Boston. But old enemies become friends in later generations, as the people of the United Kingdom have become allies with the United States in so many wars.

1992: Only Five Years to Her 200th Birthday

The hogging of earlier years had returned. The assemblage of nautical men sent to the Maritime Museum, in Greenwich, England, for the original plans of USS *President*, which had survived her capture by the British. Her sister ship showed the position of the diagonal riders, which were a prime feature of the original design drawn by Fox. They had been taken out when the iron water tanks were installed in the 1860s. Computer analysis discovered that the riders provided added stability necessary to support the keel. They were replaced, along with many ribs, sisters, and knees from oak, which grew on protected land in Indiana. By the summer of 1996 she was venturing out, as authorities contemplated a sailing voyage from nearby Marblehead back home into Boston Harbor.

They Said It Couldn't Be Done

One hundred and sixteen years after the *Constitution* had been under sail, the skeptics agreed that she could not be allowed to sail free. They said the hull could not take it or that it would cost too much for such a stunt. The risk was too high: her seams would split, water would deluge the pumps, and she would be lost. Better she should stay tied to the dock, an immovable monument like the one behind her on Bunker Hill.

Charlie Deans, leader of the Naval Center detachment, did not agree and pushed, along with her captains, to see her once again as she was, the Eagle of the Sea. The restoration took four years and twelve million dollars to prepare her once again to lead the navy to the sea. The sails had to be constructed at a cost of $150,000. Captain Robert Gillen turned down the money offered by a single donor and began a fund-raising project that would replicate earlier campaigns. He wanted the schoolchildren, those who would have to look out for her in the future, to start young. He organized a national program, which collected pennies in glass jars on teachers' desks, just as before. He knew that he needn't fear. The children of America filled those containers with fifteen million copper coins, which purchased six sails. They are known as the battle sails, those put up during close combat.

Battle Sails

The largest was the main topsail, which was as large as a basketball court. The weight of the original flaxen canvas was cut in half with a new waterproof material used by sailmakers in Maine and Charlestown. In the old sail loft, adjacent to the USS Constitution Museum, months were spent on monster sewing machines as the sailmakers cobbled the narrow sheets of material together with strong stitching. The fore and mizzen topsails, along with the jib and flying jib, were finished, leaving the spanker for last. Although these six sails were less than half of the sail complement that the frigate was capable of carrying, they were sufficient to drive her forward in July of 1997.

The crew had certainly been surprised two years before when Commander Michael Beck, USN, captain of USS *Constitution*, had told the crew that they were all going to school. He was turning back the clock to 1812, and instead of acting as tour guides, the members of the crew were going to sail the ship at sea. It all came together on a bright day that summer. The architects declared the ship sound. (Note the foreword to this book, ably written by Howard Chatterton, naval architect, who was pivotal to her bicentennial cruise.)

While the sails provided the power to move the vessel, it was the sailors who spent themselves positioning those sails. The hoisting, rigging, unfurling, and bracing round consumed all the energy of the young men and women who had learned to climb and tend that historic power plant.

The test began with a shakedown cruise twenty miles north to Marblehead, Massachusetts, at noon on July 20, 1997, her two hundredth year in service. Saved during her construction by George Washington, the *Constitution* was put into commission during his time in office. Two hundred years later, the tugs brought her out into the Charles River and turned her out to sea once they were free of the islands that guard the harbor. While she was still tethered to one remaining tug, the crew jumped eagerly onto the ratlines, climbed to the yards, and loosed the sails. The ship took the light wind and turned north at six knots.

The sight of her rounding Marblehead took the spectators' breath away. Those both on board and in the throng, which numbered in the hundreds of thousands lining the harbor banks and afloat, gulped back emotions and squeezed hands. This was their past; one-third of the crew in 1812 had been their forefathers. On that clear day, one of the top men said he could see the towers of Boston over the land from his perch, 220 feet above the water. This tall ship would not have been able to clear the Cape Bridge, whose deck was eighty feet lower than Old Ironsides. Charlie Deans assured reporters that the hull could withstand the pressure of the sail. They had replaced the diagonal riders, which acted like a ribcage and added new strength to the old hull. In his opinion, the frigate would be strong three generations from that day.

In the morning, the weather held and, in fact, was a little too calm. As the ship was towed out of the channel, past Halfway Rock, by the towline, the captain and crew could feel that she wanted to be free, she wanted to sail. The tether was ordered off by Captain Beck standing on the starboard rail, six feet above the quarterdeck. With one hand to secure himself, gripping a line, he motioned with the other to the deck captain to loose the main topsail. The crew on that historic day was nowhere near the original four-hundred-man strength of her fighting days. The senior enlisted chief had only sixty able seamen and women to tend the sail. It took time to climb to the yards and untie the shrouds. A smaller group tended to the jib and flying jib. On deck, they waited for the command to brace the sails into the wind. With the deployment of the spanker, which aided in steering, all six sails were waiting for the wind. The captain skillfully turned her to the north, and the light easterly filled the sails. Everyone felt the bow dip and the ship pick up speed.

Free at Last

And so it was that there off the Massachusetts coast, where she was so familiar, USS *Constitution*, "Old Ironsides," heeled over and took the wind. The sea was nearly calm, but a rolling swell caused her to pitch just enough for a reporter to become seasick and go below for the remainder of that long summer day. "Four knots" was shouted to the captain at the rail in his long, tailed dark-blue coat piped in gold, his eyes fixed on the canvas above, which was filled with the welcome sea breeze. Old Ironsides' bow plunged in, spray wetted the deck, and she flew free, once again the Eagle of the Sea.

A Most Fortunate Call

By the fall of 2003, before traveling to see USS *Constitution* at her home in Boston, I had been researching her life story for eighteen months. I knew how complicated a sailing ship was just by looking at photos, staring at models, and watching films and documentaries. Because the *Constitution* is a public exhibit, I could not expect to examine her in isolation. Nor could I ask unending and uninformed questions of the crew. Therefore I examined records, viewed institutional microfilm, and questioned experts unmercifully to educate myself so that the little time spent on the ship would be most rewarding.

I was ready in September of that year to tread the decks and put a picture with the mental images summoned in my mind's eye. The navy Internet site told me that there was a lottery offered to citizens from the New England states to go on board during the turnaround voyage in October. That left me out since

I live in Lake Placid, New York. I sent an e-mail to the commanding officer, Commander Lewin Welch, to come up with a date that I might visit when it was not too busy. I waited until the grammar schools were back in session, hoping that the summer crowds would be gone. In the note I enclosed my biography and acquainted him with the book I was writing. Within hours I received a phone call inviting my wife Carol and me to join him on the turnaround voyage. As a result of the call, it was clear to me that the navy considered USS *Constitution* to be the property of the people and thought of itself as the careful custodian who were there to ensure that she was accessible.

Driving in Boston is never a treat. We picked a hotel a ride away on the municipal transit system, the T. At the North Street Station stop at 8 AM we picked up doughnuts to take along—the three-hour voyage was not catered. A twenty-minute walk across the bridge into Charlestown and along the channel was interesting since we could catch glimpses of the masts. Originally over two hundred feet tall in the old days, they were shorter on that gray morning. The first sight of the *Constitution* at the water's edge was warming. "By God, there she is," was all I could manage to say. She was big and shiny black, picked out with a white streak, and the masts drew the eye up the ropes to the imposing yards. She was moored across from a gray metal World War II destroyer escort, USS *Cason*. There was no resemblance between the two men-of-war, designed to do exactly the same job. The more modern swift, narrow, low-silhouetted rake resembled a knife on edge in the water. Just across the puddled pier scratched with railroad tracks, the majestic sailing ship rested.

We were very early because I wanted to get some pictures before the other guests arrived. First Lieutenant William Marks, in uniform of the navy of 1812, took us on board and turned me loose. Stepping off the boarding ramp after saluting the ensign and requesting permission to come on board, I was immediately struck by what had impressed men of her day. She was huge, a truly big frigate. I, like them, could compare since I had been on HMS *Trincomalee* earlier that spring. Stepping amidships, just ahead of the mainmast, I turned to see the row of 32-pound carronades tied down with grayed restraining hawsers as thick as my arm. Massive fat, black, stubby barrels sat chest high, clamped down on painted slides. I could see from the size of the cannonballs, stacked neatly in a pyramid, how they earned their name, "smashers." The bleached deck was as smooth as a bowling ally, leading to the double ship's wheel, worn down by endless traffic. I counted the rope turns around the barrel and made a note to look at the tiller below. When the *Java* shot away her wheel, the American marines went below and steered the ship. The binnacles that had the iron nails replaced by the ship's clerk on her maiden voyage were there, one on each side of the wheel, low down on the deck where the steersman could look down through the glass and read the card. It was all too real and in Technicolor. So many of the references I had pored over were in black and white. We carefully picked our way down the aft ladder. The gun deck was cluttered with huge cannons that made the carronades on the quarterdeck appear underpowered. These were mounted on carriages, which rode on chunky wooden wheels, allowing the great guns to recoil a dozen feet before being caught and restrained for reloading. The scene was peaceful, but I tried to imagine the noise of the discharge as they ripple fired and came careening toward the center of that low deck. The gun portholes were larger than I expected. The crew could have easily witnessed the strike of the ball on the hull of the enemy, if the smoke did not linger.

The berth or crew deck was very large, hung with flat black metal heating buckets and canvas hammocks. After being on board HMS *Victory*, I found the frigate most accommodating. The officers' cabins were little more than boxes, too low to allow standing.

On deck I was struck by the lack of visibility. The rails of the forecastle and quarterdeck were above six feet. We stood on the wooden grate over the waist in order to watch the impressive skyline of Boston slide by as the tug turned us up the Charles River. In order to see forward, the captain stood on the rail, clinging to a rope, dressed in period regalia. The entire crew was in 1812 dress, and a contingent of reenactment marines educated the guests on their heroic history aboard the big frigate.

George Washington Saw This Ship

After passing the Castle Island stone fort, we were turned around. I saw our escorting fireboat for the first time, with all pumps going, as it passed on the port side. Circling, a cluster of several sizes of coast guard protection craft secured the voyage. It was a reminder that freedom is not free. Dozens of pleasure craft and excursion boats made up the outer circle. As we neared the fort once again on the return, Old Ironsides fired a gun salute witnessed by the enthusiasts on the battlements. It was a three-hour experience I recommend. To stand on the decks of a moving monument that was crewed for over two hundred years by exceptional men and captained by professionals, there adjacent to Bunker Hill, is a must for every American family. As president, Washington, who was instrumental in the completion of the big frigates, saw in her billowing sails the embodiment of the document he had defended. It was in my final thoughts as we docked. We walked past the trunk of a white oak tree lying on its side near the dock, ready to be cut up for future repairs. I have seen the Eagle of the Sea. She will sail again, I am sure, sometime during her next hundred years afloat in the twenty-first century.

This great ship reminds me of the ravens of the Tower of London, who had their flight feathers clipped so that they would remain on the grounds and thus preserve the throne. Old Ironsides, America's treasure, is tethered to her dock, carefully cared for at the place of her birth. As long as she and her sister ships of the United States Navy are afloat, our nation need not fear.

~

Appendix One:
United States Navy

Dimensions of the USS *Constitution*

Length overall	204 feet
Beam	44 feet 8 inches
Draft	22 feet 6 inches
Speed	13½ knots
Displacement	2,200 tons
Armor	21½ inches oak[1]
Complement	475[2]

Complement and Pay Scale (in Dollars) for a First-Class Frigate, Excepting Ordinary and Able Seamen

1 captain	3,500
5 lieutenants	7,500
1 master	1,000
1 surgeon	2,314
1 purser	3,000
1 purser's assistant	1,500
2 assistant surgeons	2,150
8 midshipmen	6,900
1 boatswain	700
1 gunner	700
1 carpenter	700
1 sailmaker	700

1 captain's clerk	500
1 purser's clerk	500
1 yeoman	420
1 armorer	240
1 ship's steward	288
1 master at arms	228
4 boatswain's mates	912
2 gunner's mates	456
2 carpenter's mates	456
1 sailmaker's mate	180
1 ship's cook	216
8 quartermasters	1,728
12 quarter gunners	2,160
4 captains of forecastle	864
6 captains of tops	1,080
2 captains of afterguard	350
2 captains of hold	360
1 cooper	180
1 painter	180
1 surgeon's steward	216
2 ship's corporals	360
1 master of band	216
1 cabin steward	216
1 cabin cook	180
1 wardroom steward	216
1 wardroom cook	180
88 total	43,376[3]

Diet Fixed by Congress for Each Man

Sunday: 1½ pounds beef, 14 ounces bread, ½ pound flour, ½ pound suet, ½ pint spirits

Monday: 1 pound pork, 14 ounces bread, ½ pint peas, ½ pint spirits

Tuesday: 1 pound beef, 14 ounces bread, 2 ounces cheese, ½ pint spirits

Wednesday: 1 pound pork, 14 ounces bread, ½ pint rice, ½ pint spirits

Thursday: 1½ pounds beef, 14 ounces bread, ½ lb flour, ½ lb suet, ½ pint spirits

Friday: 14 ounces bread, ½ pint rice, 4 ounces cheese, 2 ounces butter, ½ pint molasses, ½ pint spirits

Saturday: 1 pound pork, 14 ounces bread, ½ pint peas, ½ pint vinegar, ½ pint spirits[4]

Bread was usually stale. Spirits were always good.

A Crew Complement for USS *Constitution*

Captain	1
Lieutenants	4
Lieutenants of marines	2
Sailing master	2
Sailing master's mates	2
Midshipmen	7
Purser	1
Surgeon	1
Surgeon's mates	2
Clerk	1
Carpenter	1
Carpenter's mates	2
Boatswain	1
Boatswain's mates	2
Yeoman of the gunroom	1
Gunner	1
Quarter gunners	11
Coxswain	1
Sailmaker	1
Cooper	1
Steward	1
Armorer	1
Master at arms	1
Cook	1
Chaplin	1
Able seamen	120
Ordinary seamen	150
Boys	30
Marines	50
Total	400[5]

How to Measure the Displacement

The *Constitution*'s displacement is 2,250 tons in water. "Measure from the forepart of the main stern to the after part of the sternpost above the upper deck; take the breadth thereof at the broadest part above the main wales, one-half of which shall be counted in depth; deduct from the length ⅗s of such breadth, multiplying the remainder by the breadth and the product by the depth; divided by 95 established the tonnage."[6]

List of Supplies Loaded Aboard USS *Constitution* in June of 1799 in Boston Harbor, Kings Road, Near Castle Island

Foodstuffs came in containers of various sizes and shapes—leaguers, butts, gang casks, firkins, puncheons, tierces, pipes, chaldrons, hogsheads, and half hogsheads. There were 18 tons of salt beef, light quantity of pork, 37,500 gallons of water, 5,880 pounds of flour, 3,000 gallons of rum, 2,800 gallons of vinegar, 250 gallons of molasses, and 20 tons of coal for the caboose. There were also quantities of bread, rice, beans, raisins, peas, candles, potatoes, oil, butter, and cheese, and a barrel of suet.[7]

U.S. Navy Frigates of the Period

Constitution, 44 guns, 1,576 tons, out of Boston
President, 44, 1,576 tons, out of New York City
United States, 44, 1,576 tons, out of Philadelphia
Constellation, 38, 1,265 tons, out of Baltimore
Chesapeake, 36, 1,244 tons, out of Norfolk
Congress, 36, 1,286 tons, out of Portsmouth, New Hampshire
Essex, 32
Adams, 28
John Adams, 28
Philadelphia, 38
New York, 36
General Green, 28

Other American Vessels

Sloops
Wasp, 18
Siren, 16
Argus, 16
Scourge, 14
Vixen, 12
Nautilus, 12
Enterprise, 12
Hornet, 12

Supply Ship
Franklin

Striking of the Ship's Bell

The following description of the keeping of time on ships is by E. H. Gartley, acting superintendent, Library and Naval War Records, National Archives.

September 12, 1912
Ref: Old Sea Wings, Ways and Words

About 1720 an instructor in Navigation, Joshum Kelly, of London, England, published "the Compleat Modern Navigator" in it he gives directions for preparing a very perfect and true-running sand-glass, which may precisely run twenty-four hours without error, to be set exactly at noon on leaving land. [There was a watch on board some ships used for navigation, but the glass, kept at the helmsman's side, was a quick reference for him.]

Time on shipboard was then estimated by the glass. Less than 50 years ago a sand glass of half an hour, or an hour, was the only check by which sea time was kept on shipboard. The chimes of this clock were the ship's bell, struck by the man at the wheel or quartermaster, who eight times in each watch turned his half hour glass marking at the same time, by strokes upon a small bell near him, the number of half hours that had passed since he took charge of the helm: these strokes being repeated by the larger bell in the belfry over the ship's great bell was a richly decorated little structure, apparently capable of being easily removed if necessary. The bell itself was usually a fixture and was struck by a lanyard attached to the clapper.

The book from which the above notes have been made was written by Robert C. Leslie, and was published in London in 1890.

~

Appendix Two:
Great Britain's Royal Navy

In England the *Constitution* was considered a fifth-rate vessel. The hulls of the big U.S. frigates were as long as that of a British third-rater. First-, second-, and third-raters had gun decks and a weather deck with carronades (100 to 120 guns). Carronades were not always a part of the count of the "guns" on ships of the line. First-raters were 190 to 200 feet long and weighed 2,000 tons. There were ten in Royal Navy service in 1805. The *Victory* was one. Second-raters had 80 to 100 guns, and there were thirty-seven in 1805. Third-raters had two decks and fewer than 80 guns; most had 74. There were ninety-four in 1805. Forty-one of those were 64s. Fourth-raters had 50 to 60 guns and two decks. The Royal Navy had nineteen in 1805. Fifth-raters had one deck and 50 or fewer guns. There were sixty-three in service in 1805.

At the beginning of the trouble, with Jefferson in office, the Royal Navy had 170 men-of-war as large as or larger than U.S. frigates.[1]

Royal Navy Vessels

Ship of the Line
  Africa, 64 guns

Frigates
  Acolus, 32
  Belvidera, 36
  Cyane, 34
  Guerriere, 38

Jason, 32
Java, 38
Levant, 21
Little-Belt, 20
Macedonian, 38
Newcastle, 50
Shannon, 38

A Royal Navy commander wore one epaulet on the left. A captain wore one epaulet on right. A post captain wore two epaulets after three years of service.

Complement for HMS *Java*

The National Archives in Washington, D.C., provide the following information concerning the capture of HMS *Java*.

List of H.B.M. Military and Naval Officers paroled at El Salvador, Brazil, by Commodore Bainbridge, January 3, 1813.
Military Officers (British Army)

1	Lieutenant General
1	Major
1	Captain

Naval Officers

1	Post Captain
1	Master & Commander
5	Lieutenants
3	Lieutenants of Marines
1	Surgeon
2	Aprentic's
1	Purser
15	Midshipman
1	Gunner
1	Boatswain
1	Master
1	Carpenter
2	Capt'ns Clerks
38	Officers

323 Petty Officers, Seaman, Marines & Boys in exclusive of 9 Portuguese seaman liberated and given up to the Governor of El Salvador, and three passengers private Charters whom the Commodore did not consider Prisoners of War and permitted them to land without any restraint.

London Times, April 20, 1813

On Sunday evening arrived at Spithead two cartels, the *Mercury* and the *Albuquerque,* from St. Salvador, Brazil, with the surviving officers and ships company of his Majesty's late frigate *Java,* captured by the American ship *Constitution.* The following is a list of the officers who have arrived: Lieuts. Chadds, Hirlingham, and Buchanan, R.N.; Lieuts. Mercer and Davis, R.M.; Mrssrs. Robinson, Master; Pattinger, Purser; Jones, Surgeon; Armstrong, Gunner; Humble, Boatswain (with the loss of an arm); Cormick, Burke, Reel, Brigstock, Darsole, Oliver, Brown, and Lawrence, Midshipman; Captain Marshall, Royal Navy; Gen. Hislop; Major Walker, Captain Wood, his aid-de-Camp.

Among the killed were Captain Lambert; Mercers. Hammond, Jones, Gascoigne, Master Surates; Krel and Salmon, Midshipmen. When in lat. 36 long. 40 they fell in with the French frigate L'Arethuse, which chased them three days and on coming up sent on board her, first Lieut., who informed them that she had lately fallen in with his Majesty's ship Amelia, and in a dreadful engagement with her had upwards of 100 of her crew killed and wounded. She was commanded by Commodore Bouvet with a captain under him and upwards of 400 men: she was making the best of her way for the first French port she could reach. Captain Lambert on board was wounded early in the action, after which the ship was fought by Lieut. Cribbs in the most gallant manor for an hour and twenty minutes: Captain L survived three days. Our loss was 60 killed 100 wounded, many of the latter dangerously: that of the Americans, ten killed, her commander, Bainbridge, five lieut., and 46 men wounded, of whom four afterwards died.

British Pronunciation of the word Lieutenant

In answer to the question, "why we the British pronounce the word *lieutenant* as 'leftenant,'" the *London Times* of January 2002 gave the following confusing answer:

The Americans say; "lootenant" which is surely correct, given the French root?

Although frequently averred, the theory that the British pronunciation of "leftenant" is based upon a misreading of "v" for "u" in medieval manuscripts has to be rejected in face of the evidence. The forms "luftenant" and "leeftenant" are attested as early as 1375 and 1387 respectively.

"Lieutenant" derives from the Latin "locum tenens" that is one who temporarily holds the place of a superior. In passing to its present French form, this seems to have gone through a stage where the case ending of Latin was dropped (along the lines of "loc' tenens"), with the "c" here representing a guttural, throaty noise something like the "ch" of Scottish "loch."

In later French, this became a "labial glide" ieu. In English, the guttural sound came to be pronounced as "f" (as it also was in "cough") though the spelling eventually came to follow the French.

This is so confusing that it explains to me why they call a Royal Navy first lieutenant "number one."

Gunpowder

The following is taken from the Chatham Royal Dockyard Historical Society's journal *Chips*.[2]

Gunpowder was probably invented by the Chinese and was used by them a long time before it was known in Europe during the late 1200's and early 1300's. Roger Becon (1219–1294), an English philosopher/scientist, is credited with the European discovery. Because of the danger of fire on ships it was carefully stored in the "magazine," or powder-room; where it also had to be kept dry before being weighed out in cloth "cartridges," and carried to the guns in wood tubs or canvas bags by boy sailers—known as "powder monkeys"—to suit the shot e.g. about ½ or ⅓ the weight in powder of the shot to be fired.

Canvas and paper for making cartridges were recorded in the Ordnance office since 1559, and the general size of the cartridges was "a little less than the diameter of the bore and about 4 diameters long." The paper tubes were made on wooden formers, given glued seams and smeared with tallow to prevent sticking. In later years flannel was preferred to paper as it burnt away more fully when fired. Powder was made in large factories.

~

Appendix Three:
Sayings and Sea Lore

"Don't give up the ship. Sink her or blow her up," was said by American captain James Lawrence, on board USS *Chesapeake* during a battle with HMS *Shannon*, commanded by Captain Broke, in June of 1813. Lawrence was shot by Royal Marine lieutenant Law and died. Captain Oliver Hazard Perry named his flagship *Lawrence* for his lost friend and flew a flag from the mast with the words "Don't give up the ship" in white on a blue background.

When Perry defeated the British flotilla on Lake Erie, his victory message was, "We have met the enemy and they are ours."

"Shall I board her, Sir?" was asked by American marine lieutenant William Bush of Captain Isaac Hull on board the *Constitution* against HMS *Guerriere* in August 1812.

Commonly Used Phrases in Current Language
That Have Their Origin in the Age of Sail

To "sail under false colors" meant that a ship did not fly its own national flag but disguised itself using another country's flag.

To "belay" was to secure a line or stop action.

"The whole nine yards" refers to a ship that is fully rigged and ready to go.

"Show a leg" was shouted by the boatswain's mates as they entered the crew sleeping area. Women were often on board in the hammocks (on English ships in particular it was common for a number of woman to accompany the men). At the call, the ladies stuck out a naked leg to show that there were no men left behind at the call of "all hands on deck."

"Three sheets to the wind" meant that the ship was in peril since several sails had been blown out.

"A loose cannon" was a gun that had broken free of restraints and was careening around the deck, indiscriminately smashing everything in its path.

"To know the ropes" was the first duty of a seaman. Each rope had a specific role and none was tagged for identification.

The "caboose" was the galley stove or range used for cooking. Today it is the last car on a freight train where the observer rides and cooks his meals on a small coal stove.

"A fair-weather friend" came from the desired sea conditions for good and profitable sailing.

"He showed his true colors" refers to the tendency of sailing men-of-war to conceal their identities by flying false flags in order to close with the enemy or take a merchant ship by surprise. Ships would show their true colors just before attacking.

"To eat three square meals" comes from the shape of the wooden dinner plates used by sailors. They were used for three meals each day.

"Son of a gun" referred to a child born on a man-of-war. Each seaman's mess was oriented around a cannon. Wives often sailed with the crew in the 1800s and gave birth in the space between the cannons where they lived.

"High and dry": the worst thing a captain can do is to run aground so that the ship is high up on the shoal with her keel exposed.

"On an even keel": if the keel is warped in any way, it will no longer be perfectly even and will therefore cause the water passing under to cavitate and slow the progress of the ship through the water.

In the heyday of sailing ships, all warships and many freighters carried iron cannons. Those cannons fired round iron cannonballs. It was necessary to keep a good supply near the cannon, but the crew had to find a way to prevent them from rolling around the deck. The best storage method devised was a square-based pyramid with one ball on top, resting on four, resting on nine, which rested on sixteen. Thus, a supply of thirty cannonballs could be stacked in a small area right next to the cannon. There was only one problem: how to prevent the bottom layer from sliding or rolling from under the others. The solution was a metal plate called a monkey that had sixteen round indentations. However, if this plate were made of iron, the iron balls quickly would rust to it. The solution to the rusting problem was to make the monkeys out of brass. Few landlubbers realize that brass contracts much more and much faster than iron when chilled. Consequently, when the temperature dropped too far too fast, the brass indentations would shrink so much that the iron cannonballs would come right off the monkey. Thus, it was quite literally "cold enough to freeze the balls off a brass monkey." And all this time, you probably thought that was an improper expression, didn't you?[1]

~

Notes

Chapter 1

1. While Commander Ty Martin writes in errorless detail of Humphreys's childhood and education in America in his book *A Most Fortunate Ship*, noted English historian William James claims on page 2 of volume 6 of *The Naval History of Great Britain* that he was "English born."

2. Andrew Lambert, Trincomalee: *The Last of Nelson's Frigates* (London: Chatham Publishing, 2002), 16.

3. Robert Gardiner, *Frigates of the Napoleonic Wars* (London: Chatham Publishing, 2000), 49.

4. F. Alexander Magoun, *The Frigate* Constitution *and Other Historic Ships* (Salem, MA: Maritime Research Society, 1928), 64.

5. Magoun, *Frigate* Constitution, 85.

6. Peter Kemp, ed., *The Oxford Companion to Ships and the Sea* (Oxford: Oxford University Press, 1976), 443.

7. Brian Lavery, *Building the Wooden Walls: The Design and Construction of the 74 Gun Ship* Valiant (London: Conway Maritime Press, 1991), 35.

8. Kemp, *Oxford Companion*, 896.

9. Kemp, *Oxford Companion*, 212.

10. Kemp, *Oxford Companion*, 332.

11. Kemp, *Oxford Companion*, 838.

12. Kemp, *Oxford Companion*, 610.

13. Captain Kenneth Johnson, U.S. Navy, retired (USN, ret.), Naval Historical Center, Washington, D.C. Not to confuse "black smith" with "blacksmith." A blacksmith worked with iron, while a whitesmith worked with other metal.

14. Kemp, *Oxford Companion*, 379.

15. D. R. Frost, *The Ropery*, visitor guidebook, Chatham Historic Dockyard (Norwich, England: Chatham Dockyard and Jarrold Publishing, 1991), 7.

16. Frost, *Ropery*, 9.

17. Edwards Park, "Around the Mall and Beyond," *Smithsonian Magazine*, June 1988.

18. Adrian B. Caruana, *The Pocket Artillerist, or The Art of Coarse Gun Firing* (Rothefield, England: Jean Boudriot Publications, 1992), 9.

19. Tyrone G. Martin, *A Most Fortunate Ship: A Narrative History of Old Ironsides*, rev. ed. (Annapolis, MD: Naval Institute Press, 1997), 10.

20. Magoun, *Frigate* Constitution, 101.

21. Johnson, Naval Historical Center, Washington, D.C.

22. Lavery, *Building the Wooden Walls*, 75.

23. Lavery, *Building the Wooden Walls*, 97.

Chapter 2

1. USS Constitution Museum library, Charlestown, MA.

2. Peter Kemp, ed., *The Oxford Companion to Ships and the Sea* (Oxford: Oxford University Press, 1976), 300.

3. A parrel lashing is rope threaded with pulleys by which yards were held to the mast of a square-rigged vessel, giving them the freedom to be braced around.

4. F. Alexander Magoun, *The Frigate Constitution and Other Historic Ships* (Salem, MA: Maritime Research Society, 1928).

5. Magoun, *Frigate* Constitution, 67.

6. Kemp, *Oxford Companion*, 635, 822.

7. James Lees, *The Mastering and Rigging of English Ships of War, 1625–1860* (London: Conway Maritime Press, 1979), 135.

8. Kemp, *Oxford Companion*, 695.

9. John Harland, *Seamanship in the Age of Sail: An Account of the Shiphandling of the Sailing Man-of-War, 1600–1960; Based on Contemporary Sources* (London: Conway Maritime Press, 1984), 22.

10. Kemp, *Oxford Companion*, 428.

11. William M. James, *The Naval History of Great Britain: During the French Revolutionary and Napoleonic Wars*, vol. 6, 1811–1827 (1837; repr., London: Conway Maritime Press, 2002), 6.

12. Extract from the journal of James Pity, USS *Constitution*, August 1, 1798, courtesy of the National Archives.

13. Pity, September 9, 1798.

14. Pity, September 25, 1798.

15. Tyrone G. Martin, *A Most Fortunate Ship: A Narrative History of Old Ironsides*, rev. ed. (Annapolis, MD: Naval Institute Press, 1997), 37.

16. Magoun, *Frigate* Constitution, 105.

17. W. N. Glascock, *The Naval Officers Manual*, 2nd ed. (1848).

18. According to attorney Tom Ward, of Baltimore, MD, class of 1960, U.S. Coast Guard Academy, who served aboard USS *Eagle*, a square-rigged training ship.

19. Harland, *Seamanship in the Age of Sail*, 93.

Chapter 3

1. Alfred T. Mahan, *The Influence of Sea Power upon History, 1660–1783* (New York: Little, Brown, 1890; repr. Mineola, NY: Dover Publications, 1987), 29.

2. Mahan, *Sea Power*, 50.

3. Mahan, *Sea Power*, 54.

4. Mahan, *Sea Power*, 60.

5. Mahan, *Sea Power*, 70.

6. Mahan, *Sea Power*, 74.

Chapter 4

1. Captain Kenneth Johnson, U.S. Navy, retired, Naval Historical Center, Washington D.C.

2. Extract from the journal of Lieutenant Isaac Hull, USS *Constitution*, Captain Silas Talbot commanding, Wednesday, March 5, 1800, courtesy of the National Archives.

3. Edwin Howard Simmons, *The United States Marines: A History* (Annapolis, MD: Naval Institute Press, 1974), 21.

4. Note sent to the secretary on August 27, 1800, from USS *Constitution*, Naval Collection, courtesy of the National Archives, Washington D.C.

5. Virginia Mason Burdick, *Captain Thomas Macdonough, Delaware Born Hero of the Battle of Lake Champlain* (Wilmington, DE: Delaware Heritage Press, 1991), 20.

6. Burdick, *Captain Thomas Macdonough*, 21.

7. Peter Lamborn Wilson, *Pirate Utopias, Moorish Corsairs & European Renagadoes* (London: Conway Maritime Press, 2001), 26.

8. Robert Gardiner, ed., *The Naval War of 1812* (London: Chatham Publishing, 1998), 46.

9. C. S. Forester, *The Naval War of 1812* (London: Michael Joseph, 1957), 21.

10. Tyrone G. Martin, *A Most Fortunate Ship: A Narrative History of Old Ironsides*, rev. ed. (Annapolis, MD: Naval Institute Press, 1997), 103.

11. Martin, *Fortunate Ship*, 110.

12. Simmons, *United States Marines*, 23.

13. Paul H. Silverstone, *The Sailing Navy, 1775–1854* (Annapolis, MD: Naval Institute Press, 2001).

14. James Durand, *An Able Seaman of 1812*, ed. George Brooks (New Haven: Yale University Press, 1926), 32–38.

15. Durand, *Able Seaman*, 38.

16. Johnson, Naval Historical Center, Washington, D.C.

17. Peter Kemp, ed., *The Oxford Companion to Ships and the Sea* (Oxford: Oxford University Press, 1976), 763.

18. William Richard, *Life before the Mast: Sailors' Eyewitness Accounts from the Age of Fighting Ships*, ed. Jon E. Lewis (London: Constable & Robinson, 2001), 243.

19. Nathaniel Bowditch, *The American Practical Navigator: An Epitome of Navigation* (1802; repr., Bethesda, MD: National Imagery and Mapping Agency, 2002), 137.

20. Bowditch, *Practical Navigator*, 179.

21. Bowditch, *Practical Navigator*, 22.

22. Bowditch, *Practical Navigator*, 29.

23. Dava Sobel, *Longitude: The True Story of the Genius Who Solved the Greatest Scientific Problem of his Time* (New York: Walker Publishing Company, 1995), 2.

24. Sobel, *Longitude*, 1.

25. Sobel, *Longitude*, 57.

26. Bowditch, *Practical Navigator*, 4.

27. Commander William A. Murphy, U.S. Navy, VMI 65, Fordham University, MA, noted historian and experienced seafaring officer.

Chapter 5

1. Baron Jomini, *The Life of Napoleon*, trans. H. W. Halleck (New York: Van Nostrand, 1863), 118.

2. Napoleon Bonaparte, *Napoleon's Memoirs*, ed. Somerset de Chair (London: Faber and Faber, 1858), 270.

3. Bonaparte, *Napoleon's Memoirs*, 270.

4. Donald R. Hickey, *The War of 1812: A Forgotten Conflict* (Urbana: University of Illinois Press, 1989), 6.

5. Naval documents related to the Barbary Wars, *Naval Operations*, vol. 1, 1785–1801, published by the Department of the Navy, 294.

6. U.S. Navy Department documents, 1937. Sent to Samuel Brown, Esq., December 10, 1801, from Robert Smith.

7. Hickey, *The War of 1812*, 9.

8. James Towshend was the youngest son of George, First Marquis Towshend. He was born September 11, 1785, and had the rank of post captain on June 2, 1809.

9. Hickey, *War of 1812*.

10. William S. Dudley, ed., *The Naval War of 1812: A Documentary History* (Washington, D.C.: Naval Historical Center, Department of the Navy, 1985), 36.

11. Robert Gardiner, *Frigates of the Napoleonic Wars* (London: Chatham Publishing, 2000), 21.

12. Patrick Crowhurst, *The French War on Trade and Privateering, 1793–1815* (Aldershot, England: Grover Publishing Company, 1000), 11.

13. Crowhurst, *French War*, 31.

14. Crowhurst, *French War*, 181.

15. Crowhurst, *French War*, 190.

16. Crowhurst, *French War*, 191.

17. William M. James, *The Naval History of Great Britain: During the French Revolutionary and Napoleonic Wars*, vol. 6, 1811–1827 (1857; repr., London: Conway Maritime Press, 2002), 7.

18. James, *Naval History of Great Britain*, 11.

19. Colonel John Elting, *Amateurs to Arms: A Military History of the War of 1812* (Da Capo Press, 1995), 3.

20. C. S. Forester, *The Naval War of 1812* (London: Michael Joseph, 1957), 16.

21. G. J. Marcus, A Naval History of England, vol. 2, The Age of Nelson (London: George Allen & Unwin, 1971), 460.

22. George Little, Privateering, 1812–13, excerpted in The Mammoth Book of Life before the Mast: An Anthology of Eye-Witness Accounts from the Age of Fighting Sail, ed. Jon E. Lewis (London: Constable & Robinson, 2001), 395.

23. Little, Privateering, 402.

Chapter 6

1. William S. Dudley, ed., The Naval War of 1812: A Documentary History, vol. 1 (Washington D.C.: Naval Historical Center, Department of the Navy, 1985), 133.

2. The Royal Naval chronicle for 1812, vol. 28, courtesy of the Admiralty Library, Whitehall, London.

3. Peter Kemp, ed., The Oxford Companion to Ships and the Sea (Oxford: Oxford University Press, 1976), 258.

4. Dudley, Naval War, vol. 1, 136.

5. Dudley, Naval War, vol. 1, 138.

6. Dudley, Naval War, 139.

7. Edwin Howard Simmons, The United States Marines: A History (Annapolis, MD: Naval Institute Press, 1974), 21.

8. Lovette, Naval Customs, 196.

9. John Marshall, Marshall's Royal Naval Biography, or Memoirs of the Services of the Flag: Officers, Rear Admiral, Captains & Commanders, vol. 2, part II (London: Lungman, Hurst, Rees, Orme, Brown & Green, 1825), 625, courtesy of the Admiralty Library, Whitehall, London.

10. Robert Gardiner, Frigates of the Napoleonic Wars (London: Chatham Publishing, 2000), 11.

11. Gardiner, Napoleonic Wars, 22.

12. Gardiner, Napoleonic Wars, 24.

13. Dudley, Naval War, 232.

14. Henry Adams, The War of 1812 (New York: Scribner, 1889; New York: Cooper Square Press, 1999), 41.

15. Donald R. Hickey, The War of 1812: A Short History (Urbana: University of Illinois Press, 1995), 94.

16. William M. James, The Naval History of Great Britain: During the French Revolutionary and Napoleonic Wars, vol. 6, 1811–1827 (1857; repr., London: Conway Maritime Press, 2002), 98.

17. C. S. Forester, The Naval War of 1812 (London: Michael Joseph, 1957), 54.

18. James, Naval History, 98.

19. Marine Mirror, Society of Nautical Research, research paper no. 4, Chatham Royal Dockyard Historical Society, vol. 59 (November 1973): 453.

20. Forester, Naval War of 1812, 54.

21. Dudley, Naval War, 240.

22. Simmons, United States Marines, 24.

23. Dudley, Naval War, 238.

24. Dudley, *Naval War*, 243.

25. Dudley, *Naval War*, 243.

26. R. J. Stapleton, ed., *Naval and Military Chronicle*, vol. 3, courtesy of the Admiralty Library, Scotland Yard, London.

27. Marshall, *Royal Naval Biography*, 975.

28. *The Naval Chronicle for 1812, History of the Royal Navy*, vol. 28, July to December, 426.

29. Lovette, *Naval Customs*, 195.

30. George Coggeshall, *The History of the American Privateer* (New York: Edward G. Jenkins, 1856), 31–33.

Chapter 7

1. William M. James, *The Naval History of Great Britain: During the French Revolutionary and Napoleonic Wars*, vol. 6, 1811–1827 (1857; repr., London: Conway Maritime Press, 2002), 109.

2. James, *Naval History*, 109.

3. Tyrone G. Martin, *A Most Fortunate Ship: A Narrative History of Old Ironsides*, rev. ed. (Annapolis, MD: Naval Institute Press, 1997), 165.

4. James, *Naval History*.

5. Barry J. Loknes, *British Naval Problems at Halifax during the War of 1812* (New York: Da Capo Press, 199), 317.

6. Dudley Pope, *Life in Nelson's Navy* (Annapolis, MD: Naval Institute Press, 1981), 206.

7. Captain Kenneth Johnson, USN (ret.), Naval Historical Center, Washington, D.C.

8. Pope, *Life in Nelson's Navy*, 207.

9. Peter Kemp, ed., *The Oxford Companion to Ships and the Sea* (Oxford: Oxford University Press, 1976), 669.

10. Nathaniel Bowditch, *The American Practical Navigator* (1802; repr., National Imagery and Mapping Agency, 2002), 354.

11. John Harland, *Seamanship in the Age of Sail: An Account of the Shiphandling of the Sailing Man-of-War, 1600–1960; Based on Contemporary Sources* (London: Conway Maritime Press, 1984), 215.

12. Theodore Roosevelt, *The Naval War of 1812* (New York: Putnam, 1882; New York: Da Capo Press, 1999), 119.

13. William S. Dudley, *The Naval War of 1812: A Documentary History* (Washington, D.C.: Naval Historical Center, Department of the Navy, 1985), 649.

14. James, *Naval History*, 188.

15. Record of Court Martial, HMS *Java*, Lieutenant Henry Chads, May 15, 1813, Admiralty Library, Scotland Yard, Whitehall, London.

16. *London Times*, April 15, 1813, British Library Newspaper Library, London.

17. Record of Court Martial, HMS *Java*, Lieutenant Henry Chads, May 15, 1813, Admiralty Library, Scotland Yard, Whitehall, London.

18. *Dictionary of National Biography since 1900*, vol. 3 (London: Oxford University Press, Ely House, 1968).

19. Ira Hollis, *The Frigate* Constitution: *The Central Figure of the Navy under Sail* (New York: Houghton Mifflin Company, 1901), 258.

20. Robert Gardiner, *Frigates of the Napoleonic Wars* (London: Chatham Publishing, 2000), 38.

21. Gardiner, *Frigates*, 47.

Chapter 8

1. Andrew Lambert, Trincomalee: *The Last of Nelson's Frigates* (London: Chatham Publishing, 2002), 56.

2. *London Times*, January 6, 1813, British Library Newspaper Library, London.

3. Theodore Roosevelt, *The Naval War of 1812* (New York: Putnam, 1882; New York: Da Capo Press, 1999), 144.

4. R. J. Stapleton, ed., *Tales of the War: Naval and Military Chronicle*, vol. 3 (London), 200.

5. *London Times*, March 23, 1813.

6. Roosevelt, *Naval War*, 180.

7. Roosevelt, *Naval War*, 181.

8. Kenneth Poolman, *Guns of Cape Ann* (London: Rand-McNally Company, 1961), 120.

9. John Elting, *Amateurs to Arms: A Military History of the War of 1812* (New York: Da Capo Press, 1995), 177.

10. Gerard T. Altoff, *Oliver Hazard Perry and the Battle of Lake Erie* (Put-in-Bay, OH: Perry Group, 1999), 42.

11. Altoff, *Oliver Hazard Perry*, 54.

12. Tyrone G. Martin, ed., *The USS Constitution's Finest Fight, 1815: The Journal of Acting Chaplain Assheton Humphreys, US Navy* (Mount Pleasant, SC: Nautical & Aviation Publishing Company of America, 2000), 20.

13. Martin, *Finest Fight*, 20.

14. Marshall (admiralty), page 161, *Cyane*, Gordon Thomas Falcon, Esq., commissioned May 1800, description written April 28, 1815.

15. William M. James, *The Naval History of Great Britain: During the French Revolutionary and Napoleonic Wars*, vol. 6, 1811–1827 (repr., London: Conway Maritime Press, 2002), 372.

16. James, *Naval History*, 373.

17. James, *Naval History*, 373.

Chapter 9

1. Account taken from the "Naval Sons of William IV and Mr. Jordan." Midshipman Adolphus FitzClarence was on board the *Newcastle* during the chase.

2. *Mariner's Mirror*, vol. 59, no. 3 (St. Albans, England, Priory Press, August 1973): 376.

3. Information supplied by Captain Kenneth Johnson, USN (ret.), U.S. Naval Historical Center, Washington D.C., in reference to the question, "What contributed to the inability of the Royal Navy's cannons to cause significant damage to the hull of Old Ironsides?"

4. Johnson, U.S. Naval Historical Center, Washington D.C.

5. Johnson, U.S. Naval Historical Center, Washington D.C.

6. Tyrone G. Martin, *A Most Fortunate Ship: A Narrative History of Old Ironsides*, rev. ed. (Annapolis, MD: Naval Institute Press, 1997), 258.

7. John Harland, *Seamanship in the Age of Sail: An Account of the Shiphandling of the Sailing Man-of-War, 1600–1960; Based on Contemporary Sources* (London: Conway Maritime Press, 1984), 213.

8. Martin, *Most Fortunate Ship*, 258.

9. Donald L. Canney, *Lincoln's Navy: The Ships, Men and Organization, 1861–1865* (London: Conway Maritime Press, 1998), 13.

10. Canney, *Lincoln's Navy*, 13.

11. Martin, *Most Fortunate Ship*, 271.

12. Tyrone G. Martin, "The Pope's First American Visit," *Naval History*, December 2001.

13. Canney, *Lincoln's Navy*, 18.

14. Martin, *Most Fortunate Ship*, 326.

15. Erskine Hewitt, *The Forge and Manor of Ringwood: Guide to Some of the Outdoor Items of Interest and Relics* (1935), 9.

Chapter 10

1. This letter and the others in this chapter are from the Naval Section of the National Archives, Washington, D.C.

2. Edward J. Ludwig III of Philadelphia, collection of 1931, scrapbook, U.S. Naval Academy Museum.

3. Tyrone G. Martin, *A Most Fortunate Ship: A Narrative History of Old Ironsides*, rev. ed. (Annapolis, MD: Naval Institute Press, 1997), 345

4. Ten letters and correspondences were in the file of the administration of the secretary of the navy for October 24, 1931, National Archives, Washington, D.C.

Appendix 1

1. Measurements are from the National Archives, Washington, D.C., 1797.

2. F. Alexander Magoun, *The Frigate* Constitution *and Other Historic Ships* (Salem, MA: Maritime Research Society, 1928), 83.

3. Ira N. Holles, *The Frigate* Constitution (New York: Houghton Mifflin; Cambridge, MA: Riverside Press, 1900).

4. Holles, *Frigate* Constitution.

5. Magoun, *Frigate* Constitution, 57.

6. Magoun, *Frigate* Constitution, 86.

7. Tyrone G. Martin, *A Most Fortunate Ship: A Narrative History of Old Ironsides*, rev. ed. (Annapolis, MD: Naval Institute Press, 1997), 44.

Appendix 2

1. Thomas C. Gillmer, *Old Ironsides: The Rise, Decline and Resurrection of the USS Constitution* (Blue Ridge Summit, PA: TAB Books, International Marine, 1993).

2. Research Paper no. 4, Winter 1987.

Appendix 3

1. Story supplied by Mr. Gene Urban.

Glossary

1. Peter Kemp, ed., *The Oxford Companion to Ships and the Sea* (Oxford: Oxford University Press, 1976); Bowditch, *American Practical Navigator*.

2. Andrew Lambert, Trincomalee: *The Last of Nelson's Frigates* (London: Chatham Publishing, 2002), 17.

~

Glossary

Unless otherwise noted, all definitions are taken from *The Oxford Companion to Ships and the Sea*, *The American Practical Navigator*, or *Webster's Dictionary*, fourth edition.[1]

abeam The direction at a right angle to the fore-and-aft line of a ship.

aftersails The sails on the main- and mizzenmast.

amidship (or **midship**) A cross-section drawing showing the widest section of the hull. This was close to the geographic center of the ship but was not necessarily in the exact center of the vessel.

batten down The process of securing the openings in the deck and sides of a vessel when heavy weather is expected.

beakhead The very bow of the ship above the waterline that is directly under the bowsprit and shaped like a curved bird beak. Ornately gilded or painted, it supports the figurehead at the point of the hull above the waterline.

bearing The direction of one terrestrial point from another, expressed as angular distance from a reference direction.

Beelzebub One of the names sailors would use for the devil.

belay The operation of making a rope fast by taking turns around a cleat or belaying pin. It is also a general command to stop (as in, "Belay that").

bending (or **bent**) Attaching a sail to a yard or joining one rope to another. It is an archaic term still used by mariners.

bey A Turkish (Ottoman Empire) title of respect and former title of rank, also beyshaw and dey.

boltrope A line sewn around the edge of the sail for attachment to the yard and running or standing rigging.

brace To swing around the yards in order to present a more efficient sail surface to the direction of the wind. By bracing the yards at different angles to the fore-and-aft line of the ship, one can take the best advantage, of any wind that may be blowing. Thus, the yards are braced "aback" to bring the winds on the forward side of the sails to take the way (forward speed) off her and are braced "about" to bring the ship on the opposite tack when going about (changing tack).

brails Ropes that gather in sail close to the mast so that it is temporarily furled.

bread barge The tray of bread on the table in the officers' mess.

bulkhead A vertical partition dividing the hull into separate compartments.

buttock The shape of the bottom of the hull at the stern.

cable Four strands of cord twisted together. In the Royal Navy it was 200 yards long, or 600 feet, or two football fields. In the American navy, it was 720 feet in length.

caprice wind One that changed constantly and could not be depended upon in battle or to steer by.

capstan Crew-operated winch on the quarterdeck with a second position on the deck below. Primarily used to raise the anchor.

cardinal points of the compass North, east, south, and west.

carronade A gun that was lighter in weight than a cannon and cheaper to manufacture, required a much smaller crew, and fired a larger ball. All this was traded off for range of a cannon.

cathead A wooden arm that stuck out from the side of the bow and held the anchor high above the water until it was needed again.

chain-wales Large blocks of wood that terminated the standing rigging for the masts.

chandler A retailer of items used in the maritime: sails, hardware, instruments, etc.

channel-wales The added thickness of wood between the gun ports.

Charley Noble A chimney fitted to take the galley smoke above decks. The name was later extended to cover all portable chimneys fitted to the deck, including the chimney that conveyed the heat from the light by the magazine.

chart A map or conventional representation, usually on a plane surface, of all or part of the physical features of the earth's surface or any part of it.

chaser Gun fired directly forward or to the rear (as in bow or stern chaser).

cheeks (or **hounds**) Gripped the mast sections together and provided support for the trestle-tree.

cheese of wads A package of wads for the guns.

clewed up The state of the main- and foresails when the ship was ready for battle. The two lower corners were pulled up to the yard before the sail was furled.

coasters Small merchant craft with shallow draft allowing them to work in undeveloped ports and wharfs or on rivers. Found along most coastlines.

compass oak Oak that naturally twisted as it grew, usually for more than eighty years. Not found in planted oak forest, where the trees tended to grow straight.

coves An inexperienced junior officer.

crank When a ship heels over too far to the wind or when it cannot carry the needed sail without the danger of rolling over.

current The flowing of the sea in one direction. Currents may be periodic in relation to the tides, seasonal in relation to the prevailing wind, which blows only at certain times of the year, or permanent in relation to the main rotational or trade winds.

Davy Jones's locker Davy Jones was the devil. The locker was the sea floor, hell, where the bones of sailors rested forever, tormented, lost, and away from home and family.

dead reckoning The determination of position by advancing a known position for course and distances. A position so determined is called a dead reckoning position. The course steered and the speed through the water should be used, but the expression is also used to refer to the determination of position by use of the course and speed expected to be made good over the ground, thus making an estimated allowance for disturbing elements such as current and wind.

doldrums A belt of low pressure at the earth's surface near the equator. With minimal pressure gradient, wind speeds are light and directions are variable. There are often hot, sultry days with overcast skies and frequent showers.

dolphin striker A short perpendicular spar under the cap of the bowsprit used for holding down or guying the jibboom by means of a martingale. It was a necessay spar to support the rigging needed to counteract the upward pull on the jibboom of the fore topgallant stays. The name, of course, comes from the position of the spar, pointing vertically down toward the sea just beyond the bow of the vessel. It is said it would strike a dolphin if one were to leap out of the water just beneath it.

euphroe Fourteen inches long.

fid A square bar of wood with a wider shoulder at one end that takes the weight of a topmast when stepped on a lower mast. The topmast is hoisted up through a guide hole in the cap of the lower mast until a square hole in its heel is in line with a similar hole in the head of the lower mast. Then the fid is driven through both and hoisting tackles slacked away until the fid is bearing the weight. The two masts are then generally secured firmly together with a parrel lashing. This operation is done routinely in the yard.

figurehead A wooden appendage in the form of a character or person attached to the prow of a ship under the bowsprit. In the American navy the rule was changed to allow only ships of the line the privilege. Therefore the *Constitution* was not entitled to a figurehead by the time of the War of 1812.

fish A long piece of wood, concave on one side and convex on the other, used to strengthen a mast or a yard of a sailing vessel that has been sprung or otherwise damaged.

forecastle A small, short raised deck forward above the gun deck, directly over the galley.

forestay A standing rigging rope that provides support to the foremast.

futtock A separate piece of timber that forms a rib in a wooden ship.

gammon The wrapping of the sprung bowsprit with many twists of rope to secure it until it can be replaced.

gasket A rope, plaited cord, or strip of canvas permanently attached to the body of the sail in rows, used to gather in a portion of the sail and tie it to the yard, to reduce the area of the sail.

geographic mile The length of one minute at the equator, or about 6,087 feet.

goke The strand that is laid down the middle of a rope while other strands are twisted around—this core is not attached to the other strands.

gun numbering system Used to divide gun sections for supervison by midshipmen and officers. Each group of guns was then ordered to fire as the target bore into range. The left side forward division guns were numbered 1, 3, 5, and 7, and on the right side the guns were numbered 2, 4, 6, and 8, and so forth.

gunwales The extra reinforcing above the gun ports that formed a portion of the rail that ran along both sides.

Gut of Gibraltar The channel into the Mediterranean.

hawser A heavy rope with a circumference of five inches or more. It is three strands of cord twisted together.

heading The direction in which a vessel is pointed, expressed as angular distance from north, usually from 0 degrees at north, clockwise through 360 degrees. Heading should not be confused with course.

headsail A sail on the foremast.

heat buckets Buckets that were filled with coals from the fire or hot cannonballs. The cast-iron containers were fifteen inches high and the size of a five-gallon bucket. They could be safely rested on the deck for a few brief minutes due to the curled iron feet that held them three inches off the deck. (Today they hang in the officers' cabins of USS *Constitution*, moored in Boston Harbor.)

helm Another name for the tiller, which provides the steering of the vessel. The wheel is connected to the rudder so that the direction of turning is the same as the movement of the rudder. That is the reverse of the tiller.

HMS His Majesty's Ship. The designation is used before a vessel's name to indicate that it is a man-of-war, not a commercial vessel, in the Royal Navy of Great Britain.

hog A condition of a ship in which the bow and stern have dropped.

holed between wind and water Struck by a cannonball that penetrated the hull at the waterline.

hounds Wooden shoulders bolted to either side of the masthead to support the trestle-tree.

idlers Members of the ship's crew who did not stand watch. They were the specialists, carpenters, cooks, coopers, sailmakers, boatswains, surgeons, etc.

intercardinal points Northeast, southeast, southwest, and northwest.

jackass frigate A small frigate of only 28 guns built primarily by the British after 1815 to save money. The idea was to build a frigate the cheapest way possible.

jake Another term for the toilet; also privy or head.

jeer A heavy tackle with double or treble blocks used for hoisting the lower yards in an operation known as swaying up the yards.

kedging The movement of a ship by advancing a kedge anchor ahead of the ship in a small boat and dropping it. The ship would be winched up to the anchor by drawing in the attached line around the capstan. Used to move a vessel a short distance in port or when it was becalmed at sea in shallow water.

kite A light cloth sail flown in light winds; studding sails were kites.

knee A support fashioned at a right angle that supported the weight of the decks.

knighthead The two supporting timbers on either side of the bowsprit.

knot A unit of speed commonly used in navigation; a rate of one nautical mile per hour.

lascar An Indian sailor.

latitude The angular distance from the equator, measured northward or southward along a meridian from 0 degrees at the equator to 90 degrees at each pole.

leewardly and weatherly If a ship crabs sideways in the wind as it moves forward, it is said to be leewardly as a function of design. If it has too shallow a draft or carries too much on the top side, the wind will blow it to lee. It if maintains little leeway, it is said to be weatherly. Therefore, a leewardly ship could take a long time to tack and a weatherly ship could tack more efficiently and thus move faster even though the weatherly was a slower ship.[2]

levanter A wind that blew ships through the Gut of Gibraltar and toward the Levant.

liberty Free time away from the ship in a port of call.

longitude The arc of a parallel or the angle at the pole between the prime meridian and the meridian of a point on the earth, measured eastward or westward from the prime meridian through 180 degrees. It is designated east or west to indicate the direction of measurement.

midship *See* **amidship**.

mistral A northerly wind that travels down across France and into the Mediterranean as wind and rain.

nautical mile The international nautical mile is a hair over a standard mile, at 6,000 feet. A degree of longitude and latitude, therefore, is equal to 60 nautical miles.

nipperman Part of the anchor recovery team, which temporarily tied the anchor hawser to the messenger cable as it was pulled up out of the water by the men on the capstan.

oakum Tarred hemp made from condemned ropes that have been unpicked.

ordinary In reserve and afloat (as in, "lie in ordinary").

orlop The lowest deck of the ship, often in separate levels, for storage of supplies and access to the magazine.

painter A small rope used for added security.

parrel lashing Rope threaded with pulleys by which yards were held to the mast of a square-rigged vessel, giving them the freedom to be braced around.

partners A framework of short planks secured to the deck around the hole containing the mast.

pipe down A call on the boatswain's pipe made last thing at night on naval vessels, for all hands to turn in, for silence on the mess deck, and for the lights to be extinguished.

point-blank range A distance at which a gun could hit a target without elevating.

polarce A sailing sloop, not a ship (it may have three masts, but the sails are not rigged).

pooped Pooping occurs when a heavy sea breaks over the stern. It usually comes about when the speed of the ship is approximately the same as the speed of the following sea, so that the rudder has little or no grip on the sea.

In such cases, a sea that poops a ship is very apt to swing her off course until she is broadside on the sea, with the danger of rolling over.

port lids The hinged covers over the gun ports.

post captain [A] Royal Navy officer who has three years in grade and is on the seniority list, which will guarantee promotion to admiral sometime before he dies.

preventer stay Added lines put on temporarily in heavy weather and wind to support the masts.

prime meridian The meridian used as the origin for measurement of longitude; the position of the British Royal Observatory at Greenwich, England.

purchase A rope rove through one or more blocks by which the pull exerted on the hauling part of the rope is increased accordingly to the number of sheaves in the blocks over which it passes. On land it is often referred to as a double block and tackle.

quarterdeck Aft of the mainmast, above the gun deck, and the part of the ship from which she is commanded.

ratlines Thin, tar-coated cross rope steps tied every sixteen inches up the mast shrouds, which allowed the men to climb the masts to tend the yards and sails.

razeeing The cutting down of an old ship and refitting it with new armament. A battle ship could be cut down to a powerful frigate, and so on.

reef In a square-rigged ship, a reef is the amount of sail taken in by securing one set of reef points. It is the means of shortening sail to the amount appropriate to an increase in the strength of wind. On a square-rigger, sails up to the topsails normally carried two rows of reef points, enabling two reefs to be taken in; sails set above them usually had no reef points as they would normally be furled or sent down in a wind strong enough to require the sails to be reefed.

reef the sail To shorten the amount of canvas exposed to the wind by tying with gaskets. The main- and topsail are the only ones reefed.

rib Another name for the frame of timbers as they rise from the keel to form the shape of the hull.

sail parts The four sides of a square sail are the **head, foot,** and **leeches,** weather and lee. The two top corners are the **earring cringles,** and the bottom corners are the **clews,** or **clues;** again, they differ by weather and lee. The center portion of a square sail is cut with a full belly to catch the wind and is called the **bunt.** The sails are named, in ascending order, **course, topsail, topgallant,** and **royal.** If you add the mast name to the sail in question, you would get main topgallant for the third sail up the mast.

scantlings The dimensions of all parts that go into the construction of a ship hull.

scudding To scud in a sailing ship is to run before a gale with reduced canvas, or under bare poles in the case of a gale so strong that no sails could be left spread. It is very dangerous.

scuttlebutt A cask lashed near the most convenient spot, top of the ladder, that held drinking water. All water in the days of sail was limited and had to be used very sparingly to make it last until the next opportunity of landing and refilling the casks. In order to prevent too much water being used, a scuttle-butt had a square piece sawed out of its bilge, the wider part of its curved side, so that no more than half a butt was available daily. Since the crew congregated there for water, it was a natural place for gossip.

sheaves (or **shivers**) Rolling wheels in a block of a block and tackle or purchase. Can be wood or brass.

sheer Rise or platforming of the deck fore and aft on a frigate above the gun deck.

sheet anchor Also forward near the bow, the sheet anchor was an added security to reinforce the bower anchor.

shingle Iron ballast placed above the keel in the lowest part of the hull.

ship Must have three square-rigged masts, plus a bowsprit, rigged in lower, top, and topgallant.

shot rack Holds cannonballs near the guns and is filled just prior to use.

shrouds For lateral support the shrouds, in pairs, were attached to the hounds on the mast and the tops of the futtocks as they reached the rail. Crossed every two feet with ratlines, they looked like a spider's web as they reached to the top of the masts in ever-reducing numbers. They could be adjusted by pulling on the entwined deadeye pulleys near the rail.

sill The inside of the rail on the left side, where the guns were run up to.

sirocco The hot wind that blows off the desert of North Africa and out into the eastern Atlantic. It is the start of the trade wind to the Caribbean.

splinter nets Light rope net suspended above the heads of the crew on the exposed forecastle and quarterdeck to protect them from falling rigging and battle damage.

spring A long rope, fore and aft, to secure the ship from swinging. Often tied to a kedge anchor, it was used to move the ship a short distance.

standard (American) mile 5,280 feet.

standing rigging The fixed and permanent lines that were attached as soon as the masts were in place. They prevented the masts from falling forward or backward. Those lines were called stays, which could be adjusted when they became slack due to change in temperature or age.

staysails Sails that are trianglar in shape and have rings sewn into their edges called **brail cringles**, which are loops that ride on the standing rigging that supports the masts forward and aft.

strake A line of planking in a wooden vessel that runs the length of the hull.

stream anchor A smaller anchor that could be dropped upstream against the current to hold a vessel in a flowing river.

studding sails Pronounced "stun sails," studding sails are additional sails set only in fine weather, with light wind abaft the beam, outside the square sails of a ship. They are set by extending the yards with booms, which are run out through a ring at the yardarm, to which the studding sails are laced. These sails can more than double the amount of sail and appear to overwhelm the ship in white billowing cloth.

tack The path actually followed by a vessel, or the path of proposed travel across the wind in order to make headway.

taffrail The curved wooden top of the stern and railing at the stern of the ship on the quarterdeck above the windows of the gun deck.

tampions The caps put into the muzzles of the cannons to prevent water from filling the barrel.

tar A Royal Navy enlisted man.

teak A wood that is harder, stronger, and more durable than oak and that is insect repellent. The oil prevents rust of ferrous metal. It is hard to work and resists bending.

thick and dry for weighing Report given to the captain before he gives the order to **make sail**. This means that the anchor is free and being hauled in.

timbers Pieced ribs of the ship, which extended upward to form the frame.

trestle-tree Two short pieces of timber fitted to the top of each mast, fore and aft, to support a platform, sometimes known as the top or fighting tops. It is the perch for the lookouts (crow's nest).

trunnion The metal cylinders that stuck out of the side of a cannon barrel, just forward of the balance point, for attachment to the wooden gun carriage.

tumble home The amount by which the two sides of a ship are brought in toward the centerline after reaching their maximum beam.

up and down Command given as the ship begins to move and sail over its main anchor. Up with the anchor and down with the sail (topsail as a rule). This maneuver will loosen the anchor so the capstan, which has had the messenger cable nipped to the anchor line, can pull it free and bring it on board.

USS United States Ship. Designation that appears before the name of a vessel indicating that it is a man-of-war belonging to the United States of America.

wale An extra thickness of wood bolted to the side of a ship in positions where protection is needed.

ways A parallel platform of timber inclined gradually toward the water on each side of the keel of a ship being built, and down which the cradle on which she is held slides upon launch.

xebec Not a ship because it does not have a proper bowsprit.

yards Thick poles of pine that are tapered at both ends. These spars cross the masts of a ship horizontally or diagonally, and a sail is set from them. Yards were supported from the mastheads (top of each mast section) by rope slings and blocks, which were used to lift them into place. The yard was tied to the mast by rope parrels, which allowed the yards to be braced around to take advantage of the wind.

~

Selected Bibliography

Adams, Henry. *The War of 1812*. New York: Cooper Square Press, 1999.

Altoff, Gerard T. *Oliver Hazard Perry and the Battle of Lake Erie*. Put-in-Bay, OH: Perry Group, 1999.

Bellico, Russell P. *Chronicles of Lake Champlain: Journeys in War and Peace*. Fleischmanns, NY: Purple Mountain Press, 1999.

———. *Sails and Steam in the Mountains: A Maritime and Military History of Lake George and Lake Champlain*. Fleischmanns, NY: Purple Mountain Press, 1992.

Bowditch, Nathaniel. *The American Practical Navigator: An Epitome of Navigation*. (1802; repr., Bethesda, MD: National Imagery and Mapping Agency, 2002).

Burdick, Virginia Mason. *Captain Thomas Macdonough: Delaware Born Hero of the Battle of Lake Champlain*. Wilmington, DE: Delaware Heritage Press, 1991.

Canney, Donald L. *Lincoln's Navy: The Ships, Men and Organization, 1861–1865*. London: Conway Maritime Press, 1998.

Caruana, Adrian. *The Pocket Artillerist*. Rotherfield, England: Jean Boudroit Publications, 1992.

Chapelle, Howard I. *A History of the American Sailing Navy*. New York: Norton & Company, 1949.

Chatham Historic Trust. *The Historic Dockyard Chatham: Where the Legends Were Created*. Norwich, England: Jarrold Publishing, 1994.

Dudley, William S., ed. *The Naval War of 1812: A Documentary History*, vols. 1–3. Washington, D.C.: Naval Historical Center, 1985.

Forester, C. S. *The Age of Fighting Sail*. Sandwich, MD: Chapman Billies, 1956.

———. *The Naval War of 1812*. London: Michael Joseph, 1957.

Frost, D. R. *The Ropery*. Visitor guidebook, Chatham Historic Dockyard. Norwich, England: Chatham Dockyard and Jarrold Publishing, 1991.

Gardiner, Robert. *Frigates of the Napoleonic Wars*. London: Chatham Publishing, 2000.

263

———. *The Naval War of 1812*. London: Chatham Publishing, 1998.

———, ed. *The Heyday of Sail: The Merchant Sailing Ship, 1630–1830*. London: Conway Maritime Press, 1995.

Gillmer, Thomas C. *Old Ironsides: The Rise, Decline and Resurrection of the USS Constitution*. Blue Ridge Summit, PA: TAB Books, International Marine, 1993.

Goldsmith, Robert. *The Battles of the Constitution: Old Ironsides and the Freedom of the Seas*. London: Macmillan Co., 1961.

Goodwin, Peter. *Countdown to Victory: 101 Questions and Answers about HMS Victory*. Portsmouth, England: Manuscript Press, 2000.

Guttman, Jon. *Defiance at Sea: Stories of Dramatic Naval Warfare*. London: Arms and Armour Press, 1995.

Harland, John. *Seamanship in the Age of Sail: An Account of the Shiphandling of the Sailing Man-of-War, 1600–1960; Based on Contemporary Sources*. London: Conway Maritime Press, 1984.

Heyerdahl, Thor. *Early Man and the Ocean: A Search for the Beginnings of Navigation and Seaborne Civilization*. Garden City, NY: Doubleday, 1979.

Hickey, Donald R. *The War of 1812: A Short History*. Urbana: University of Illinois, 1995.

———. "The War of 1812: Still a Forgotten Conflict? Historiographical Essay." *War and Society: A Journal of the History of Warfare* (School of History, Australian Defense Force Academy, Canberra, Australia), August 8, 2001.

James, William M. *The Naval History of Great Britain: During the French Revolutionary and Napoleonic Wars*, vol. 6, 1811–1827. 1837. Reprinted, London: Conway Maritime Press, 2002.

Kemp, Peter, ed. *The Oxford Companion to Ships and the Sea*. Oxford: Oxford University Press, 1976.

Lambert, Andrew. *Trincomalee: The Last of Nelson's Frigates*. London: Chatham Publishing, 2002.

Lavery, Brian. *Building the Wooden Walls: The Design and Construction of the 74 Gun Ship Valiant*. London: Conway Maritime Press, 1991.

———. *Nelson's Navy: The Ships, Men and Organisation, 1793–1815*. London: Conway Maritime Press, 1989.

Lees, James. *The Masting and Rigging of English Ships of War, 1625–1860*. London: Conway Maritime Press, 1979

Lewis, Jon E., ed. *Life before the Mast: Sailors' Eyewitness Accounts from the Age of Fighting Ships*. London: Constable and Robinson, 2001.

Magoun, F. Alexander. *The Frigate Constitution and Other Historic Ships*. Salem, MA: Maritime Research Society, 1928.

Mahan, Alfred T. *The Influence of Sea Power upon History, 1660–1783*. New York: Little, Brown, 1890. Reprinted, Mineola, NY: Dover Publications, 1987.

Malcomson, Robert. *Warships of the Great Lakes, 1754–1834*. London: Chatham Publishing, 2001.

Maloney, Elbert S. *Dutton's Navigation and Piloting*, 13th ed. Annapolis, MD: Naval Institute Press, 1978.

Marshall, John. *Marshall's Royal Naval Biography*, vol. 2, part II. London: Longman, Hurst, Rees, Orme, Brown & Green, 1825.

Martin, Tyrone G. *A Most Fortunate Ship: A Narrative History of Old Ironsides*. Annapolis, MD: Naval Institute Press, 1997.

———, ed. *The USS Constitution's Finest Fight, 1815: The Journal of Acting Chaplain Assheton Humphreys, US Navy*. Mount Pleasant, SC: Nautical & Aviation Publishing Company of America, 2000.

Morris, Roger. *Guide to British Naval Papers in North America*. Compiled by National Maritime Museum, Greenwich, England. London: Mansell Publishing, 1994.

Munday, John. *Naval Cannon*. Buckinghamshire, England: Shire Publications, 1998.

O'Brian, Patrick. *Master and Commander*. London: W. W. Norton Co., 1971.

———. *Post Captain*. London: W. W. Norton Co., 1972.

Pope, Dudley. *Life in Nelson's Navy*. (Annapolis, MD: Naval Institute Press, Blue Jacket Books, 1981).

Roberts, William H. *USS New Ironsides*. Annapolis, MD: Naval Institute Press, 1999.

Roosevelt, Theodore. *The Naval War of 1812*. New York: Putnam, 1882; New York: Da Capo Press, 1999).

Sauer, Carl O. *Northern Mists*. Berkeley: University of California Press, 1968.

Silverstone, Paul H. *The Sailing Navy, 1775–1854*. Annapolis, MD: Naval Institute Press, 2001.

Simmons, Edwin H. *The United States Marines: A History*. Annapolis, MD: Naval Institute Press, 1974.

Snow, Elliot, and H. Allen Gosnell. *On the Decks of Old Ironsides*. New York: Macmillan Company, 1932.

Upham, N. E. *Anchors*. Buckinghamshire, England: Shire Publishing, 2001.

Waters, D. W. *The Planispheric Astrolabe*. National Maritime Museum. Greenwich, England: Crown Publishing, 1976.

Woodman, Richard. *The Victory of Seapower: Winning the Napoleonic War of 1806–1814*. London: Chatham Publishing, 1998.

Index

~

About the Author

Colonel David Fitz-Enz served as a regular army officer for thirty years. In Vietnam he was a combat photographer and paratrooper in the 173rd Airborne Infantry Brigade and, on his second tour, a signal officer in the 1st Squadron, 10th Cavalry, 4th Infantry Division. Among his decorations are the Soldier's Medal for Heroism, the nation's highest award for life saving, the Bronze Star for Valor with four oak leaf clusters, the Air Medal, and the Legion of Merit with three oak leaf clusters. He is a graduate of Command and General Staff College and the Army War College and the coproducer and writer of the PBS television program *The Final Invasion*. He is the author of *Why A Soldier?* his memoir of combat, and *The Final Invasion*, the story of the British invasion of Plattsburgh, New York, and Lake Champlain, which occurred on September 11 . . . 1814.

The Sovereign Order of the Temple of Jerusalem granted Colonel Fitz-Enz the Military Order of Saint Louis for contributions to military literature, and the U.S. Army Historical Foundation presented him with the book of the year prize for *The Final Invasion*. He is a guest lecturer at the British Army Museum in London and the National Archives in Washington. He has written for *Military Illustrated Magazine*, appeared on C-Span Book Television, and is in Who's Who in America.

He is married to Carol, his researcher. They have three grown sons, a daughter-in-law, and two grandchildren and reside near Lake Placid, New York, along with their two West Highland White terriers.

281